WASTE AND WANT

WASTE AND WANT

A SOCIAL HISTORY OF TRASH

SUSAN STRASSER

A Holt Paperback

Metropolitan Books | Henry Holt and Company | New York

Holt Paperbacks
Henry Holt and Company, LLC
Publishers since 1866
175 Fifth Avenue
New York, New York 10010
www.henryholt.com

A Holt Paperback® and ® ® are registered trademarks of
Henry Holt and Company, LLC.

Library of Congress Cataloging-in-Publication Data
Strasser, Susan, 1948–
Waste and want : a social history of trash / Susan Strasser.
p.   cm.
Includes bibliographical references.
ISBN-13: 978-0-8050-6512-1
ISBN-10: 0-8050-6512-1
1. Refuse and waste disposal—Social aspects.
2. Recycling (Waste, etc.)—Social aspects.   I. Title.
HD4482.S77 1999   99-17571
363.72'8—dc21   CIP

Henry Holt books are available for special promotions and
premiums. For details contact: Director, Special Markets.

Originally published in hardcover in 1999 by Metropolitan Books

First Holt Paperbacks Edition 2000

Designed by Michelle McMillian

Frontispiece: Ragpickers with their carts, New York City, 1896.
Photograph by Alice Austen. Romana Javitz Collection, Miriam and
Ira D. Wallach Division of Art, Prints and Photographs,
the New York Public Library, Astor, Lenox and Tilden Foundations.

Printed in the United States of America

D   20   19   18   17   16

For Bob,
and in memory of Susie Huston

Contents

WASTE AND WANT

Toward a History of
Trashmaking

"At first the new scavenger is filled with disgust and self-loathing,"
writes Lars Eighner, describing "Dumpster diving" in his 1993
memoir of American homelessness. "That stage passes with experience. The scavenger finds a pair of running shoes that fit and look and
smell brand-new. He finds a pocket calculator in perfect working order.
He finds pristine ice cream, still frozen, more than he can eat or keep.
He begins to understand: People throw away perfectly good stuff, a
lot of perfectly good stuff." To the Dumpster diver—as to the scavengers who live on the Mexico City dump, the ragpickers who fasci-
nated bohemian Paris, and the Chinese immigrants who foraged on
San Francisco streets at the end of the nineteenth century—what counts
as trash depends on who's counting.[1]

Daily experience suggests that trash is a dynamic category. Objects
move in and out of it in many ways besides Dumpster diving. The torn
sweater, consigned to the giveaway pile, is restored to service by a
friend who knits. The impossibly shabby cabinet, already repainted
twice, ends up on the curb; a neighbor takes it to his basement, where

it holds paint cans for twenty years until somebody strips the finish, rubs in some oil, and carries it up to the living room. The grotesque lamp, given away as the yard sale winds down, comes into fashion five years later; suddenly it's worth a mint.

What do we throw out? Like people in other cultures and at other times, we in contemporary developed societies rid our living spaces of corpses and bodily wastes. Like others, we consider rotting and rancid organic material impure—though the line between rancid and not, edible and spoiled, pure and impure is a matter for cultural and personal debate. So is the one between usable and worn-out, but every culture leaves some broken pottery and implements, which fill the trash dumps archaeologists study. People get rid of excess: We can eat only so many of the zucchini in the garden, we lack storage space for our grandmothers' crocheted bedspreads. Recognizing value in these things, we may give vegetables to the neighbors or hold an estate sale. Throughout the world, harvest and funerary customs include ways of dealing with excess that keeps it out of the trash.

We of the developed nations at the turn of the millennium have additional reasons for throwing things out—reasons that, while not entirely new, operate on an unprecedented scale. More often than people in less developed economies, we discard stuff simply because we do not want it. We buy things devised to be thrown out after brief use: packaging designed to move goods one way from factories to consumers, and "disposable" products, used one time to save the labor of washing or refilling. In addition, vast numbers of us declare clothes and household goods obsolete owing to changing tastes. Historians have described a consumer revolution that brought fashion to the wealthy in eighteenth-century Europe and America, but until the second half of the twentieth century, the great majority of people even in the most developed countries could not afford to discard clothes or household furnishings until they were worn out. Even then, many people made money from selling their rags and scraps. Similarly, people who could afford it have traded up for a sharper knife or a better timepiece throughout the history of technological innovation. Now watches, too, are styled for obsolescence, and the incessant proliferation of musical-reproduction formats and personal-computer technologies sometimes makes expensive equipment obsolete before it hits the market. These habits of disposing of out-of-style clothes and outmoded equipment promote a veneration of newness not widespread before the twentieth century, filling Dumpsters with "perfectly good stuff" that is simply not new anymore, stuff the owner is tired of.

If we focus on the categorizing process that defines trash, our attention will be drawn away from the rubbish heap and concentrated on human behavior. Trash is created by sorting. Everything that comes into the end-of-the-millennium home—every toaster, pair of trousers, and ounce of soda pop, and every box and bag and bottle they arrive in—eventually requires a decision: keep it or toss it. We use it up, we save it to use later, we give it away, or at some point we define it as rubbish, to be taken back out, removed beyond the borders of the household. As everyday life and ordinary housework have changed over time, so has this process of defining what is rubbish, as well as the rubbish itself, the contents of the trash.

Nothing is inherently trash. Anthropologist Mary Douglas resurrects and analyzes the common saying (sometimes attributed to Lord Chesterfield) that dirt is "matter out of place." Dirt is relative, she emphasizes. "Shoes are not dirty in themselves, but it is dirty to place them on the dining-table; food is not dirty in itself, but it is dirty to leave cooking utensils in the bedroom, or food bespattered on clothing; similarly, bathroom equipment in the drawing room; clothing lying on chairs; out-door things in-doors; upstairs things downstairs; under-clothing appearing where over-clothing should be, and so on." Sorting the dirty from the clean—removing the shoes from the table, putting the spattered clothing in the washing machine—involves systematic ordering and classifying. Eliminating dirt is thus a positive process.[2]

Sorting appears everywhere in the historical evidence about trash. "Attend to the following rules," Lydia Maria Child told readers of the

1835 edition of *The American Frugal Housewife,* explaining how to sort food waste. "Look frequently to the pails"—the slop pails, which held pig feed—"to see that nothing is thrown to the pigs which should have been in the grease-pot"—where fats were saved for cooking and soapmaking. "Look to the grease-pot, and see that nothing is there which might have served to nourish your own family, or a poorer one." An article about street children published in the *Atlantic* in 1869 describes groups of girls, "small Cinderellas," sifting ashes in search of unburned coal and the occasional silver spoon. An early-twentieth-century description of a factory that extracted useful products from bones declares that "the first operation is that of sorting . . . several women are constantly engaged separating the rags, iron, beefy matter, hoofs, horns, etc. As they are sorted the bones are pushed to the mouth of the crusher." And although he admits to occasional dysentery as a result, Lars Eighner provides instructions for sorting discarded food, useful to the aspiring Dumpster diver. "Eating safely from the Dumpsters involves three principles," he writes: "using the senses and common sense to evaluate the condition of the found materials, knowing the Dumpsters of a given area and checking them regularly, and seeking always to answer the question 'Why was this discarded?' "[3]

Sorting and classification have a spatial dimension: this goes here, that goes there. Nontrash belongs in the house; trash goes outside. Marginal categories get stored in marginal places (attics, basements, and outbuildings), eventually to be used, sold, or given away. Douglas calls special attention to boundaries and margins—especially the boundaries of the body and, by analogy, those of the household and the city—as locations for purifying activities. Indeed, disposal takes place in the intersection between the private and the public, the borderland where the household meets the city, the threshold between the male and female "spheres" of the nineteenth century. (This may explain why men have so often been delegated to take out the trash.) Reporters and fans insist that anything outside the walls of a celebrity's house is theirs to look at and keep, and the Supreme Court has ruled that to be so.* In public marginal spaces like the alley and the dump, household refuse becomes indisputably public matter, available for others to claim or reclaim; it also becomes *a* public matter, the topic of public debate, a problem to be solved by public means.[4]

Many examples demonstrate the importance of physical margins to a history of trashmaking and disposal. American cities and towns no longer operate swill yards or piggeries at the city limits, but they do maintain landfills and incinerators in places that are out of the way of all but the poorest citizens. The rural/urban cusp—the site for bales of recyclable paper awaiting a market and for abandoned cars squashed for scrap or organized in junkyards—has grown over time. Larger institutions and more complex technologies have enabled cities to move garbage and sewage farther from their points of origin, even to export toxic wastes to "underdeveloped" countries. Contemporary backyard composting and the burn pile at the corner of the rural yard echo long-standing practices of using the margins of personal property for disposal.[5]

Less familiar today are the nineteenth-century habits of using the borders of the house for disposal: throwing garbage out the door and emptying dishwater out the window, both practices frequently documented by archaeological discoveries of bones, bottle fragments, and pottery shards. The written record verifies these customs. Reformers

---

* This brand of enthusiasm became notorious in 1970, when the songwriter Bob Dylan physically assaulted A. J. Weberman, an obsessive scholar of Dylan's lyrics, for going through Dylan's Greenwich Village trash can. Nearly thirty years later, Weberman is still stalking Dylan, now in cyberspace, where he asserts that he can get into Dylan's computer (if he has one) and read the latest form of Dylan's trash, deleted files. In *California v. Greenwood* (1988), the Supreme Court declared that the borders of the household do not encompass the contents of trash cans, in a case that involved evidence found in a drug dealer's rubbish. The Court maintained that citizens may not reasonably expect their trash to be private and that law enforcement officers looking for evidence do not need a warrant to search the trash. (See H. Richard Uviller, "The Fourth Amendment: Does It Protect Your Garbage?" *Nation*, Oct. 10, 1988, pp. 302–04; "Search and Seizure—Garbage Searches," *Harvard Law Review*, 102 [Nov., 1988], pp. 191–201. Weberman may be found on the World Wide Web at weberman.com, dylanology.com, and garbology.com.)

urged the abandonment of slovenly routines. One speaker at an 1819 meeting of the Massachusetts Agricultural Society described doors "barricadoed by a mingled mass of chip and dirt," recommended receptacles "so that bones and broken utensils may occasionally be taken away and buried," and urged his listeners not to leave "the deposit of the sink to settle and stagnate under the windows." Many decades later, the granddaughter of a Connecticut governor described a near disaster in a letter to one of her children. Thinking she was through with her dishwashing, she wrote, she dumped her bowl "out of the north window when to my utter astonishment & chagrin I saw one of our 'spode' breakfast plates sailing out with the water." (The dish did not so much as crack.) Long after even rural houses had drains that emptied far from the house or into septic fields, women continued to use their dishwater to water their plants.[6]

Discussions of marginal places and marginal behaviors often merge with discussions about marginal people, who abound in the evidence about disposal practices: Lars Eighner and his fellow Dumpster divers, the ragpickers of Paris, or the "swill children" who once went from house to house in American cities collecting kitchen refuse to sell for fertilizer or hog food. Marginal people leave few records, and scholars who study them often find that the most accessible sources—the writings and records of elites *about* marginal groups—offer more enlightenment about the writers than dependable analysis of their subjects. Thus the swill children, for example, are described in a book about the "dangerous classes" of nineteenth-century New York.[7]

The sorting process that creates trash varies from person to person, it differs from place to place, and it changes over time. The categories of objects we use and throw out are fluid and socially defined, and objects move in and out of these classifications. Some individuals save things because they are particularly sentimental or especially frugal; many people speak with disparaging amusement of deceased relatives whose estates included (or might as well have included) a box marked "string too short to save." Some ethnic groups have probably valued saving and reusing things more than others, as the Scots have a reputation for doing, and groups develop distinctive cultural practices for using waste materials. Nomadic people, who must travel light, save less. Age matters, too. During the twentieth century, older people have been more likely to conserve. The young, for whom the new is normal, have more readily adopted the ideals of cleanliness and convenience that underlie "disposability."

But above all, sorting is an issue of class: trashmaking both underscores and creates social differences based on economic status. The poor patronize junk stores and charitable thrift stores, which depend on richer people to cast things off and even to subsidize their operations with cash or volunteer work. What is rubbish to some is useful or valuable to others, and the ones who perceive value are nearly always the ones with less money.

The wealthy can afford to be wasteful. In societies "where material shortage is the norm, discarding things is a notorious way of demonstrating power," writes urban planner Kevin Lynch, citing Thorstein Veblen's "conspicuous consumption," the Kwakiutl potlatch, the palaces of kings, and the equation in many cultures of obesity with wealth. Contemporary American practices suggest that, even in a culture of material abundance, wasting serves such power functions. From the start, "disposability" was promoted for its ability to make people feel rich: with throwaway products, they could obtain levels of cleanliness and convenience once available only to people with many servants.[8]

The poor generally waste less to begin with, and they scavenge for materials to use and to sell. Anthropologist Sidney Mintz stresses the creativity, originality, and talent with which people use waste materials outside developed economies, in "capital-scarce, labor-rich contexts," and the contribution these activities make to the effectiveness of so-called backward economies. "In the less developed world," he writes, "I have seen automobile bearings fashioned into portable vulcanizing kits; bits of toothbrush handles used as 'jewels' for rings, and ordinary tin cans turned into simple kerosene lamps."[9]

People in different social categories—rich and poor, old and young, women and men—sort trash differently in part because they have learned different skills. Fixing and finding uses for worn and broken articles entail a consciousness about materials and objects that is key to the process of making things to begin with. Repair ideas come more easily to people who make things. If you know how to knit or do carpentry, you also understand how to mend a torn sweater or repair a broken chair. You can appraise the materials and evaluate the labor of the original maker; you understand the principles of the object's construction; you can comprehend the significance of the tear or the wobble and how it might be mended; you know how to use needles or hammers; you can incorporate leftover scraps from your own previous projects or consign objects beyond repair to your scrap collections. Even at the end of the nineteenth century, when factory production was already well established, many Americans possessed the skills and consciousness required for repairing. Women, who continued to sew and to mend clothing, preserved the skills of handwork longer than most men. Now making and repairing things have become hobbies, perhaps not yet exceptional but no longer typical.

Indeed, mending and restoring objects often require even more creativity than original production. The preindustrial blacksmith made things to order for people in his immediate community; customizing the product, modifying or transforming it according to the user, was routine. Customers would bring things back if something went wrong; repair was thus an extension of fabrication. With industrialization and eventually with mass production, making things became the province of machine tenders with limited knowledge. But repair continued to require a larger grasp of design and materials, an understanding of the whole and a comprehension of the designer's intentions. "Manufacturers all work by machinery or by vast subdivision of labour and not, so to speak, by hand," an 1896 *Manual of Mending and Repairing* explained. "But all repairing *must* be done by hand. We can make every detail of a watch or of a gun by machinery, but the machine cannot mend it when broken, much less a clock or a pistol!"[10]

In the handwork necessary for repair, comprehension of the object is tied to an intimate, tactile understanding of materials. George Sturt, a British schoolteacher who went to work in his grandfather's wheelwright shop in 1884 and wrote a book about it forty years later, described skilled craftspeople's high standards for materials. Working on objects intended to last for years, unaffected by fashion or invention, they learned those standards, he asserts, from the work itself. "Under the plane (it is little used now) or under the axe (it is all but obsolete) timber disclosed qualities hardly to be found otherwise. My own eyes knew because my own hands have felt . . . the difference between ash that is 'tough as whipcord' and ash that is 'frow as a carrot,' or 'doaty,' or 'biscuity.'" This kinesthetic knowledge of materials guided handworkers—wheelwrights, seamstresses, knitters, and carpenters—when they brought tools and materials together. "A good smith knew how tight a two-and-a-half inch tyre should be made for a five-foot wheel and how tight for a four-foot, and so on," writes Sturt. "He felt it, in his bones."[11]

The handworker's mind, too, was constantly engaged, contemplating a collection of materials that accumulated throughout a lifetime of work. The anthropologist Claude Lévi-Strauss describes the French *bricoleur*, an odd-job man who works with his hands, employing the *bricoles*, the scraps or odds and ends. Unlike the engineer, Lévi-Strauss explains, the *bricoleur* does not carry out his tasks using "raw materials and tools conceived and procured for the purpose of the project. His universe of instruments is closed and the rules of his game are always to make do with 'whatever is at hand.'" He collects tools and materials because they might come in handy. Bricolage depends on a kind of functional arrogance, an assumption that the *bricoleur* knows what he is doing and is in the position to define his own success. His first step is always to consider new projects with respect to what he has on hand, "and finally and above all, to engage in a sort of dialogue" with the toolbox and the junk box, interrogating its heterogeneous contents to determine how he might put them to use.[12]

The dialogue with the toolbox and the junk box has had a feminine counterpart in women's relation to the sewing basket and the scrap bag. Well into the twentieth century, most American women were skilled in sewing and did a great deal of it. They continued to make clothes for themselves and their children long after men's clothing was customarily bought ready-made, and many sewed housedresses even if they bought their coats and their Sunday best. Women who sewed for hire or for their own families knew how to mend clothing as an extension of their skills at making it. Many went well beyond mending—remaking their own clothes to suit changing fashion or refashioning the legs of their husbands' trousers into new pants for their boys. When they finally gave old clothes up, they used them as raw material for rag rugs and quilts. The habits and skills of bricolage remained part of women's work in the home long after industrial production was the rule in most trades.

In cultures based on handwork, handmade things are valuable without being sanctified as art; they embody many hours of labor. People who have not sewed, or at least watched others sewing, value that labor less than those who have, and lack the skills and the scraps that enabled so many women to see old clothing as worthy of remaking. It is easier to discard a ready-made dress, cut and stitched in an unknown sweatshop (on the Lower East Side at the beginning of the twentieth century or in the Philippines at its end), than it is to throw away something you or your mother made.

Most Americans produced little trash before the twentieth century. Packaged goods were becoming popular as the century began, but merchants continued to sell most food, hardware, and cleaning products in bulk. Their customers practiced habits of reuse that had prevailed in agricultural communities here and abroad. Women boiled food scraps into soup or fed them to domestic animals; chickens, especially, would eat almost anything and return the favor with eggs. Durable items were passed on to people of other classes or generations, or stored in attics or basements for later use. Objects of no use to adults became playthings for children. Broken or worn-out things could be brought back to their makers, fixed by somebody handy, or taken to people who specialized in repairs. And items beyond repair might be dismantled, their parts reused or sold to junk men who sold them to manufacturers. Things that could not be used in any other way were burned; especially in the homes of the poor, trash heated rooms and cooked dinners.

All over the country, even middle-class people traded rags to peddlers in exchange for tea kettles or buttons; in cities, ragmen worked the streets, usually buying bones, paper, old iron, and bottles as well as rags. These small-time entrepreneurs sold the junk to dealers who marketed it in turn to manufacturers. The regional, national, and even international trade in rags was brisk because they were in high demand for papermaking and for "shoddy," cloth made in part from recycled fibers. Grease and gelatine could be extracted from bones; otherwise bones were made into knife handles, ground for fertilizer, or burned into charcoal for use in sugar refining. Bottles were generally refilled; the market for secondhand bottles grew throughout the nineteenth century, in part because mechanization was slow in the glassmaking industry.

This trade in used goods amounted to a system for reuse and recycling that provided crucial domestic sources of raw materials for early industrialism. Scavenging was essential to that system, a chore and a common pastime for poor children, who foraged for shreds of canvas or bits of metal on the docks, for coal on the railroad tracks, and for bottles and food on the streets and in the alleys. Food and coal went home to the children's families; they sold metal, rags, bones, and bottles to junk dealers.

The old systems of recycling began to pass into history during the decades around the turn of the twentieth century. Sanitary reformers and municipal trash collection did away with the swill children. New papermaking technologies substituted wood pulp for rags. Mechanization and, later, Prohibition destroyed the used-bottle business. Swift and Armour produced and sold enough bones to put an end to collections from scavengers. The giant modern meatpackers marketed byproducts to fertilizer companies and other firms that required massive amounts of skin, hair, and bones; they also produced their own fertilizer, glue, and other products that used animal wastes.

But mass production and mass distribution literally generated more stuff, and more trash. More people had more things, and less space for storage in tenements, apartment houses, and other city dwellings. New processes for making and filling cardboard cartons and tin cans, and new materials such as cellophane and aluminum foil, engendered a new class of household trash. Heinz, National Biscuit, Procter & Gamble, and other corporations producing household goods promoted not simply the contents of the container but a new kind of product that included the packaging, emblazoned with a brand that could be advertised. The advertising for the newly branded and packaged products in turn produced unprecedented quantities of paper trash. Magazines like the *Ladies' Home Journal, Country Gentleman,* and the *Saturday Evening Post* and the Hearst and Pulitzer newspapers set new standards for publications fat with advertising and circulations in the millions. Manufacturers themselves generated mountains of promotional booklets, trade cards, recipe pamphlets, coupons, and displays. Mail-order merchandisers, led by Sears and Montgomery Ward, blanketed the country with their wish books.[13]

As fewer people made their living doing handwork, their expert knowledge of materials became irrelevant; leftovers and scraps that they once might have valued became trash instead. This process of change over time was not even. Some habits and handcrafts typical in the nineteenth century were still commonplace among poor people in rural areas as late as the early 1950s. But their meanings had changed: now they were old-fashioned ways, fading as consumer culture developed.

To use an ecological analogy, households and cities have become open systems rather than closed ones over the course of the twentieth century. Just as the table scraps once fed the chickens and Dad's torn trousers provided the material for Junior's new ones, so cities, too, were once systems that incorporated ragpickers and scavengers to process the detritus of others. In this respect they resembled sustainable biological ecosystems, which are in general closed, or cyclical. Waste to one part of the system acts as resources to another; the dead body and excrement of one organism nourishes its neighbors.[14]

Industrialization broke the cycle. In an industrial system, the flow is one-way: materials and energy are extracted from the earth and converted by labor and capital into industrial products and byproducts, which are sold, and into waste, which is returned to the ecosystem but does not nourish it. Thus, the late-twentieth-century household procures goods from factories, mends little, bags the detritus in plastic, and places it at the curb to be conveyed to the transfer station or the incinerator. The late-twentieth-century city takes in most of what it uses by truck and train and airplane, and flushes its waste into landfills, sewage treatment plants, and toxic dumps.[15]

Of course, the ecological analogy idealizes: early-nineteenth-century industrialization created notorious air and water pollution. Indeed, no human system is perfectly cyclical; throughout history, urban households have taken in material produced by people outside the system, and they have excreted waste. Visitors to Pompeii can see the stepping-stones in the pavement that kept its citizens clean as they traversed the garbage-filled streets; tourists at Knossos and many other ancient sites can observe the material remains of drains and other disposal strategies. Even otherwise self-sufficient farmers have taken in materials from outside, buying or trading for salt and the wares of craftspeople, and created dumps on their property for broken pottery, glass, and other trash that would neither decompose nor serve as animal feed.

But the ecological analogy does offer a way to think about reuse and disposal as part of a process that also encompasses both extracting raw materials and manufacturing, distributing, purchasing, and using industrial products. The process was once generally cyclical, if not perfectly so: waste products were important to economic growth because they served as raw materials for other industrial processes. Toward the end of the nineteenth century, disposal became separate from production, and Americans' relationship to waste was fundamentally transformed.[16] Trash and trashmaking became integral to the economy in a wholly new way: the growth of markets for new products came to depend in part on the continuous disposal of old things.

Economic growth during the twentieth century has been fueled by waste—the trash created by packaging and disposables and the constant technological and stylistic change that has made "perfectly good" objects obsolete and created markets for replacements. On the eve of the Great Depression, Christine Frederick, a prominent domestic writer and advertising consultant, described "progressive obsolescence" as the source of America's economic achievement. Frederick declared that modern consumers should be open to new styles and technologies, that they should be willing to scrap their old possessions in order to buy new and better ones, and that they should willingly direct their incomes toward consumption rather than savings. "Buying plenty of new goods before the old wears out," Frederick wrote, "increases the general income. . . . Mrs. Consumer has billions to spend—the greatest surplus money value ever given to woman to spend in all history." Her words acquired a certain irony as the Depression deepened during the next few years, but the accelerating processes of a consumer culture that valued fashion, convenience, and the latest technology had already taken firm hold on American daily life. Neither the shortage of purchasing power during the 1930s nor the shortage of goods to purchase during World War II halted those processes.[17]

At the turn of the millennium, Americans know only a well-developed consumer culture, based on a continual influx of new products. Many of these are designed to be used briefly and then discarded; many are made of plastics and other materials not easily reused, repaired, or returned to nature. Discarding things is taken to be a kind of freedom; landfills and garbage disposers make disposal an arena for technical experts. American culture offers the world's most advanced example of the "throwaway society." An emerging global culture strives to establish flows of materials and energy that will not only satisfy current consumer demand but create new desires among the many people who make the products of developed economies but do not enjoy them. Economic development has created persistent assaults on the global ecosystem from air and water pollution and global warming, as well as from solid waste. These problems are urgent, and the solution will not come from going backward in time. Only by reflecting on how we got from there to here may we come to comprehend new solutions.

I bring to the topic of trash a stance derived from two previous books: *Never Done: A History of American Housework* and *Satisfaction Guaranteed: The Making of the American Mass Market*. Together, they explore complementary aspects of everyday experience. Both books focus on the intersection of the private and the public, viewing every-day events through an economic lens and asking how Americans have experienced economic and cultural change. *Never Done* juxtaposes the historical details of daily life—the tools and methods of sewing, cooking, laundry, and other tasks—with ideas about women's place in the home and with the broad scope of American industrial history; it describes how the traditional work of household production was replaced by the twentieth-century task of consumption. *Satisfaction Guaranteed* examines the business history of some of the same phenomena, the creation of consumer markets for household products. It concentrates on the early history of Ivory Soap, Quaker Oats, and the many other branded, packaged products that represented new kinds of relationships among consumers, manufacturers, merchants, and whole-saling firms. The two books share a focus on the substantial transition that took place in American cultural and economic life during the last decades of the nineteenth century and the first ones of the twentieth. It was then that the emblematic economic institutions of the early twenti-eth century—the manufacturing corporation, the department store, the urban newspaper—joined mass production and mass distribution into a national market. New products and new kinds of stores transformed the texture of daily life.

Waste and Want takes up another aspect of this transition. This time, I am inquiring about what has happened to homemade goods and industrial products at the end of their useful lives: how people have gone about reusing, recycling, and disposing of things they no longer wanted. Here, too, there is a history, a process of change over time. Here, too, the emergence of a mass consumer culture transformed the routines of private life and their meanings. Although people have always thrown things out, trash has not always been the same. During the forty or so years around the turn of the twentieth century, mass production and mass distribution created unprecedented quantities of trash that disturbed private citizens and plagued city administrations. Rubbish took on new meanings in an emerging consumer culture, as it became identified with the poor, people who stood outside that culture.

The history of trash, then—like the history of housework and that of marketing—offers fundamental insights about the history of industrial society and its consumer culture.

The topic of waste is central to our lives yet generally silenced or ignored. My initial research revealed both the silence and the centrality. There is much material about municipal solid waste, the rubbish in the alley and the various systems that cities have tried for collecting and disposing of refuse. But my essential questions were less about policy issues and public garbage than about how a throwaway culture replaced one grounded in reuse. In search of answers, I had to poke about for pieces of evidence that might be found nearly anywhere—in trade journals and popular magazines, government documents and novels—but that were often little more than shreds and scraps. Nor was there much theoretical help. Because conventional economics generally treats trash and other forms of pollution as "externalities," it ignores most of the topics for a social and cultural history of trash; ragmen, quilts, and garage sales have at best a minor place in the economics literature.[18]

My method was that of the ragpicker: I grazed for evidence in computer catalogs and periodical indexes, spearing bibliographic entries to put into my pack. Others have used the metaphor. The French poet Charles Baudelaire described the ragpicker as an archivist, a cataloger who sorted through "everything that the big city has cast off, everything it lost, everything it disdained, everything it broke." Commenting on Baudelaire, the German critic Walter Benjamin explained the ragpicker's fascination to bohemian Paris, and he employed the analogy to describe his own methods as a cultural historian. A contemporary scholar of Paris *chiffonniers* describes the historian "wandering the archives, sifting through a detritus from the past that has been used for other purposes and recycling the figurative and literal rags he turns up to give them new meaning."[19]

Like the ragpicker, I often found nothing more than scraps, even in the most promising sources. Household manuals, for example, are in general self-consciously thorough, explicitly addressed to women learning how to keep house far from the farms and villages of their birth, or cast adrift by the times because their mothers knew less about modern appliances and methods than they did. The manuals claim to be comprehensive, asserting that they encompass every household task. But they have little to say about trash. Although readers will find mentions of such books in the pages that follow, the references were gathered in a harvest whose leanness surprised me, despite many years of research in those sources. Public discourse about household trash has until very recently stopped at the borders of the household; not until toothpaste tubes and beef rib bones became municipal solid waste did they become civic concerns, and then they entered the province of technical experts.

This taboo, like many others, has been toppled during the last thirty years. Contemporary interest in trash as part of a global environmental crisis has made household waste-disposal practices into a topic for schoolchildren's lessons, television public service announcements, and utility bill inserts. Yet while this book addresses some of the issues of current solid-waste debates, it is not a book of contemporary data and social criticism but a history of trashmaking as a social process. An understanding of history rarely contributes in some straightforward way to the solutions to the problems of the present; indeed, the historical perspective often complicates the issues. I hope here, therefore, to suggest that important issues are always complicated and to show that matters deemed inconsequential are often significant indeed.

CHAPTER ONE

The Stewardship
of Objects

When a Virginia plantation called Flowerdew Hundred was excavated during the 1970s, a volunteer archaeologist noticed that
the newly unearthed fragments of a stoneware bottle neck, buried since
the 1620s, matched perfectly with the bottom of a large German jug
in the plantation's museum, though the two had been dug from different sites. One wit suggested that the bottle had exploded in midair, its
halves falling far from each other. Archaeologist James Deetz offers a
more likely explanation: the early colonists simply did not have many
things. For some time after the bottle broke in two, he hypothesizes, its
bottom served as a bowl, while the top was used as a funnel. Even the
more affluent Europeans used what we would now consider badly
damaged pottery, Deetz writes; he points to seventeenth-century Dutch
paintings that depict broken plates and bowls sitting on shelves along
with intact ones.[1]

During the nearly four hundred years since the "bowl" and "funnel" were discarded, the United States has overcome what Deetz calls
its colonial "scarcity of items." Most people had little by today's

standards until well into the twentieth century, but industrial production, economic growth, and the passage of time multiplied the nation's stock of utensils, serving pieces, and other household equipment. As more Americans worked for money wages and more factories produced more goods, people bought funnels and bowls instead of improvising with broken crockery.

The broken stoneware offers an image for "making do" in extremis. Except for people on the farthest reaches of the frontier, most Americans, for most of American history, have disposed of objects more casually than the residents of Flowerdew Hundred. Rich folks could always discard more than the poor; country people always depended on what they had at hand and on their own ingenuity more than those who lived near stores and markets. But the profligacy represented by home garbage disposers and throwaway cameras is new. Throughout most of our history, people of all classes and in all places have practiced an everyday regard for objects, the labor involved in creating them, and the materials from which they were made. Even as nineteenth- and early-twentieth-century Americans eagerly adapted to a consumer culture, they mended, reused, saved, and made do. They darned socks and fed food scraps to chickens and pigs. They dyed faded dresses and repaired rickety furniture. They handed things down to younger and poorer relatives or to servants; they turned old clothes and sewing scraps into rugs, quilts, and other home furnishings.

Everyone was a *bricoleur* in the preindustrial household of the American colonies and, later, on the frontier; saving and reusing scraps was a matter of course. Cloth, wood, and food could only be obtained by arduous spinning, weaving, chopping, sawing, digging, and hoeing, by bartering with other products of strenuous work, or by spending scarce cash. Whether things were purchased at stores or crafted on farms and plantations, the value of the time, labor, and money expended on materials and their potential value as useful scraps were evident to the people who worked with them. With the coming of the industrial revolution, the work of men and single women shifted to factories; most married women, however, continued to labor in the household, supervising themselves in routines that began when they woke up and ended when they went to sleep. Responsible for food, clothing, and household furnishings, they managed their household stores as *bricoleurs,* accumulating leftovers and castoffs to use in their work.

Without trash collectors or much cash for purchases, most nineteenth-century American women had to make do with whatever was at hand instead of solving problems with products. "Keep a bag for odd pieces of tape and strings," instructed Lydia Maria Child in *The American Frugal Housewife,* first published in 1829, "they will come in use. Keep a bag or box for old buttons, so that you may know where to go when you want one." Books of advice for farm women and urban housekeepers were full of ideas for using stored materials. Coal ashes could be mixed with well-rotted manure and used as fertilizer, scattered on slippery ice, or made into garden walks. ("If well laid down, no weeds or grass will grow, and by use they become as solid and more durable than bricks.") Corncobs could be dipped in tar and resin and dried for kindling; corn husks could be used as mattress fill. Soapsuds and ashes "are good manure for bushes and young plants." Used tea leaves would "brighten the looks of a carpet, and prevent dust. They should be scattered, and then rubbed about with a broom, and then swept off." They worked on hard floors, too: "Tea leaves are good to throw under a bed to collect the light flue which is apt to fly about, when sweeping." (Later in the century, when, after decades of scarcity, wastepaper began to pile up, *Good Housekeeping* suggested using dampened scraps of paper for the same purpose.)[2]

Reuse was easier in the country. Organic waste could be returned to nature; whether food scraps were dug into the ground or fed to animals, they would play their part in sustaining the family one way or the other. Country people had more room to accumulate waste products in sheds, attics, and basements or to simply leave them where they were until somebody found a use for them. One domestic writer noted that country housekeepers "are able to avoid waste in keeping things far better than city housekeepers can do. There is usually the spring-house with its running water; and with the freer air and the shade trees, closets and store-rooms can be kept cool and sweet."[3]

As the United States became an urban nation, country ways became old-fashioned ways. In the growing cities, with fewer animals to feed and less storage space, reuse became a problem. People with money paid cartmen to remove refuse from their property, while the poor threw it in the streets. After the Civil War, many household writers lashed out at American extravagance. Compared with the frugal people of Europe, who made soup from leftovers and conserved fuel, Americans were said to waste their vast resources. "We know nothing of the saving and careful economy of people of the Old World's thronged States," wrote Mrs. Julia McNair Wright in *The Complete Home: An Encyclopaedia of Domestic Life and Affairs,* a household manual explicitly addressed to the problems of maintaining genteel standards of living during the depression of the 1870s. "Lavish abundance of common things surrounded our ancestors, and they used it lavishly: we inherited the prodigal habit: but now our cities and some of our districts have a crowded population, and want is the result of waste." War, despotism, and centuries of urban life (as opposed to decades in the newer American cities) had taught foreigners economy. In other countries, Mrs. Wright went on, "the shops expect to sell in littles: a penny's worth of this, and two-pence worth of that. Exactly what is needed for use is bought, and there is *nothing to be wasted.* So many people live in 'flats' or in lodgings, and have little or no cellar and closet-room, that they must buy as they use."[4]

Some writers claimed that waste resulted from ignorance rather than extravagance. Christine Terhune Herrick, daughter of the widely read domestic-advice writer Marion Harland, expressed typical concerns in her first published article, "The Wastes of the Household: Watching and Saving the 'Left-Overs,'" which appeared in the inaugural issue of *Good Housekeeping* in 1885. Acknowledging "the well known saying that a French family could live with elegance on what an American housewife throws away," Herrick maintained that "it is also true that, in eight cases out of ten, this relegation of cold bits to the offal pail or ash barrel is not caused so much by extravagance as by the lack of knowledge of how to dispose of them in any other way."[5]

Such ignorance constituted the raison d'être of advice writers like Herrick, who dispensed thousands of suggestions for using up odds and ends and for most other problems of domestic life. No nineteenth-century housekeeper followed all or even most of the prescriptions to be found in advice books, any more than contemporary ones do everything prescribed in "Hints from Heloise" or *Martha Stewart Living*. Advice writing is a kind of reform literature, often more intent on correcting the behavioral norm than describing it. But some practices are mentioned so often in so many advice books that we may regard them as commonplace. Numerous mid-nineteenth-century manuals, for example, recommended lengthening the lives of thinning sheets by tearing them down the middle and sewing the outer edges together; "a double sheet can be made to *double* its existence," wrote Mrs. Wright in 1879, echoing advice given in print at least as early as Catharine Beecher's 1841 *Treatise on Domestic Economy*. "This is technically termed 'turning' sheets," Christine Terhune Herrick explained in her 1888 *Housekeeping Made Easy*, "and was more prevalent years ago than it is now." In fact, women continued to turn old sheets through the Great Depression and World War II in the United States, and even later in Europe.[6]

Like instructions for turning sheets, recipes and techniques for mending glassware and crockery appear in virtually every household manual. Catharine Beecher suggested in 1841 that broken earthenware and china be mended "by tying it up, and boiling in milk"; an 1884 manual reaffirmed the value of this method as "a very quick way of mending." "A glutinous property, doubtless caseine," the author explained, "penetrates the fracture and congeals with a firmness very tenacious." Beecher also offered recipes for cements, one (for crockery) made with white lead, glue, and egg white and another (for mending broken iron) with potter's clay, steel filings, and linseed oil; both may be found as well in other books. Crockery might also be fixed with lime or plaster of Paris mixed with glue or egg white, and glass could be repaired with a concoction of alcohol (Mrs. Child recommended gin) and isinglass (a kind of gelatine). "If the dishes do not look well enough to come to the table, they will yet do to set away things in the store-closet, or for keeping jelly, marmalade, or preserves," Mrs. Wright advised. An aquarium might be patched with a piece of glass, shellac, and turpentine. Marble could be repaired with a mixture of alum, plaster of Paris, and water; this cement could be colored, and when set, it could be polished. One book recommended mending glass with garlic juice ("stand the article upon a plate, or other level surface, and let it remain undisturbed for a fortnight"); another manual recommended garlic for china, as a "good cement [that] leaves no mark where it has been used."[7]

Many repair techniques were lessons in practical chemistry, requiring storerooms and sheds equipped with toxic and volatile materials: turpentine, white lead, sulfuric acid for bleaching ivory knife handles or removing fruit stains from white cloth, mercury for refinishing mirrors. "Benzole is often employed for removing grease-spots," explained the *Scientific American* book of household hints, on a page with "BOOTS, WATERPROOFING" and "BOTTLES, Sealing." "It is highly volatile and inflammable, so that the contents of a 4-oz. phial, if overturned, will render the air of a moderate-sized room highly explosive." Accordingly, manuals also included lists of antidotes, and instructions for rinsing out eyes, inducing vomiting, and dealing with fires. Some of the toxics, and other less dangerous chemicals for household use, were homemade from waste materials. Lye, pearl ash, and potash were all formulated from ashes, while ammonia was produced from urine, collected daily in chamber pots and sometimes used for cleaning without any aging or processing.[8]

The sense of stewardship with regard to objects may be seen not only in diligence about repair but also in the many processes that were recommended to protect new possessions and prolong their useful lives. Combs made from tortoiseshell or horn would last longer if they were rubbed with oil from time to time. Wooden tubs and pails would shrink less if first saturated with glycerine. A handful of hay boiled in new kettles would remove the iron taste; hay water could also sweeten tin and woodenware. New iron was seasoned by gradually heating it. Many manuals suggested seasoning glass and china as well, usually by placing them in cold water, bringing it to a boil, and cooling slowly. Mrs. Child and Catharine Beecher both advised bran water for seasoning new earthenware. Another book recommended salt. With or without additives in the water, the heating and cooling was said to toughen breakable materials against sudden changes in temperature. The process worked wonders for lamp chimneys, one writer claimed: "You can never break that chimney unless you throw a flat-iron at it."[9]

Spending time to prolong the useful lives of objects and to use up scraps was, of course, a way to save money. Household saving, the regulation of the only money that women had any control over, thereby became their special province. Thrift became ever more important as more people depended on factory wages and factory-made goods. It was essential for families with little cash; even for those in somewhat better circumstances, saving was a way for women to affect household budgets. Lydia Maria Child's *The American Frugal Housewife* went through seven editions in its first three years, suggesting that there was a market for a book whose title promised such advice. As Herrick pointed out in *Good Housekeeping* half a century later, most women's time had little market value. "With the average American housekeeper," she wrote, "it is far easier to save a dollar than to earn one." But thrift was not one of the central virtues of ideal middle-class womanhood, nor in itself a primary focus of most household writing, which was generally more intent on promoting other qualities of domesticity. Like system and neatness, wrote Catharine Beecher, thrift was only valuable insofar as it tended "to promote the comfort and well-being of those affected." Her 1841 chapter "On Economy of Time and Expenses" offered mostly practical advice for budgeting and spending; what little philosophy about the virtues of thrift it contained was largely edited out of the 1869 version she wrote with her sister Harriet.[10]

Indeed, much of what now seems like thrift in nineteenth-century housekeeping is better understood not as a conscious virtue or as self-denial but as a way of life. The *bricoleur* saves scraps not in order to get to heaven but because they may be useful. Even more surprising, some of what appears motivated by economy actually signified attempts at upward mobility, entry into the consumer lifestyle, and endeavors to keep up with fashion. Historian Katherine C. Grier, who has studied nineteenth-century parlors, has found much evidence of furniture made from packing crates and barrels, padded and covered with old quilts and other reused fabrics. Made and used by people who could not afford commercially made upholstery, these chairs and sofas are best understood, Grier suggests, not as emblems of thrift but as signals of "aspirations toward increased bodily comfort and the creation of self-consciously decorated rooms." Similarly, women of all classes took apart and remade old clothes in order to keep up with changing styles.[11]

Using Food Waste

The history of food preparation follows general trends in the history of housework: from home to factory, from production to consumption, from handcraft to purchasing. The history of food waste conforms to those trends: with canned and frozen vegetables, pea pods and corn husks have become industrial wastes, while metal cans, cardboard boxes, and plastic pouches fill trash cans at the curb. Kitchen garbage and table scraps, reused in the more productive household of the nineteenth century, are discarded with the packaging or ground up and washed down the drain.

But food and food waste also stand apart from other kinds of household production and household trash. Food puts cultural questions in relief; people from different cultures regard different foods and parts of food as edible, and throw different parts away. Food and food waste attain and lose value both as other products do—in the economic framework of production and consumption—and from the natural cycles of growth and decay.[12] Food has not generally been subject to technological or style obsolescence, though most food loses value with age. And food garbage smells, raising disposal and storage questions different from those generated by other trash.*

Early-nineteenth-century housewives typically stored food scraps in slop pails and grease pots. On the farm, leftovers and food scraps were useful byproducts of human cooking and eating, food for domestic animals or raw materials for making soap and candles—not waste at all. Farm animals grazed very close to houses, eating the scraps and bones that occupants threw out of windows and doors. (Even in the twentieth century, Willa Cather used the image of "gaunt, molting turkeys picking up refuse about the kitchen door" to depict the terrible isolation of Nebraska farm life.) Cows and hogs grazed near houses less often than poultry, but many farmers kept a swill barrel near the kitchen door, a fifty- or sixty-gallon hogshead for accumulating kitchen refuse and the sour milk left over from skimming cream. When full, it was removed to feed the hogs. Smelly and swarming with flies, it would be unattractive even to the most dedicated late-twentieth-century composter. But people were accustomed to the odors of chamber pots and outdoor privies and to the stench of manure on city streets as well as in the country. Even the most refined could scarcely have been squeamish about malodorous garbage.[13]

Urban dwellers' food scraps, too, were eaten by livestock. European travelers commented on the animals roaming the streets of American cities, eating from the gutter where unwanted food had landed, thrown from doors and windows. Scavenger pigs, goats, and stray dogs had

---

* Various words for discarded or worthless material—*garbage, rubbish, refuse, waste,* and *trash,* among others—are often applied interchangeably, both in general usage and in dictionary definitions. Those who write about the subject tend to be more precise. Rensselaer professor H. de B. Parsons, for example, differentiated between garbage (animal and vegetable matter) and ashes, sewage, and rubbish (all other household trash) in his *The Disposal of Municipal Refuse* ([New York: John Wiley, 1906], p. 19). For Parsons, the distinction was crucial. The offensive odor of decaying meat scraps, fish heads, and banana peels; their commercial value as fertilizer, hog feed, and marketable grease; and their high water content all distinguished them from other kinds of refuse. Like many other later writers, and because food waste has been treated in distinctive ways by households as well as municipalities, I have attempted to follow this distinction, using *garbage* for food waste and *rubbish, trash,* and *refuse* for mixed waste.

the run of the cities before the Civil War, along with the many cows and pigs whose owners let them loose to graze on the streets. Every city passed measures to control them. An 1819 ordinance in Washington authorized police and residents to kill "any animal of goat kind." New York dispatched carts to round up pigs in 1830, but to little effect. "Take care of the pigs," Charles Dickens advised Manhattan pedestrians in *American Notes,* published in 1842; that year the *New York Daily Tribune* estimated ten thousand hogs on the streets. The roaming pigs consumed so much garbage and furnished so much food for the poor that efforts to ban them ran into political opposition.[14]

Urban kitchen garbage continued to provide food for animals late in the century. Scavenger pigs were less common in American cities by the 1870s, but small pigsties were still permitted and New York tenement dwellers continued to keep pigs in their basements and even their rooms. In smaller cities such as Memphis, hogs and cattle were not driven from public roads until the late 1880s. Even where scavenger animals were banned, swill children toured late-nineteenth-century urban neighborhoods, gathering kitchen refuse to sell to farmers for fertilizer or hog food. Working-class families in factory towns like Homestead, Pennsylvania, and Manchester, New Hampshire, continued to feed kitchen wastes to chickens well into the twentieth century.[15]

Most households maintained a receptacle for cooking grease, which was reused in cooking or made into candles and soap, either at home or, as time went on, by commercial establishments that themselves purchased surplus fat from households. Tallow candles were commonly made from mutton or beef suets, both harder than pork fat; the animal fat was often supplemented with beeswax or bayberry wax and solidified with chemicals such as camphor, alum, and saltpeter. Candle-making was done after butchering, usually by dipping wicks hanging from poles into huge vats of hot fat. Molds made more uniform candles, but the process required more skill, and, in any case, no household had enough molds for a year's supply of candles. Molds were therefore used only for small amounts of fat, shared with neighbors at cooperative candle dippings or supplied by itinerant candlemakers who went from house to house, helping with the task.[16]

Tallow candles burned quickly and unsteadily, and they scattered grease. Those who could afford it burned whale oil for lighting in the decades preceding the introduction of kerosene made from Pennsylvania petroleum, discovered in 1859. But oil lamps were far from universal. Catharine Beecher provided instructions for making both dipped and molded candles as late as 1841. She suggested that "in places where pork abounds," lard could be used in large lamps, as "a less expensive and more agreeable material than oil." Revising her book twenty-eight years later, Beecher commented that kerosene had superseded sperm oil, lard, and tallow, but even so, she retained the candlemaking instructions.[17]

Even those who bought candles or burned oil did not throw grease away. Many used spare fat in making soap, combining grease with lye, which was produced by dripping water through another waste product, wood ashes. In 1841, Beecher proposed that all unused drippings and fat be saved for making soft laundry soap, one of three soaps for which she offered recipes. "Some persons keep a barrel, or half barrel, for soap-grease," she wrote. Making lye and soap were both tricky processes: lye required good ashes, while soap entailed the correct proportions of lye and grease. It was difficult to judge freshly made soap, another writer warned: it "sometimes appears to be good when put up, but changes entirely after standing a few days."[18]

In the cities, tallow chandlers bought fat from butchers and private households, to make both soap and candles. Lydia Maria Child recommended that her urban readers trade their ashes and grease with the chandlers in exchange for soap, "but in the country, I am certain, it is good economy to make one's own soap." In any case, as more city dwellers heated with coal instead of wood, they lost a critical ingredient, as lye could not be made from coal ashes. Like most other industries, commercial soapmaking remained essentially a small, local enterprise before the Civil War; in 1857, the United States had a remarkable number of soapmaking establishments—more than six hundred, each with an average of five employees. Cincinnati alone had twenty-five.[19]

In her 1869 manual, Beecher expected her readers to buy their soap and edited out the directions for making it. "Formerly, in New-England, soap and candles were to be made in each separate family; now, comparatively few take this toil upon them," she explained as an example of the merits of industrialization, recommending that Americans also let others bake their bread and do their laundry. Like so many other industries, soapmaking expanded and centralized after the war. Commercial soap production doubled between 1870 and 1890, with fewer companies. The biggest manufacturers—Colgate, Procter & Gamble, and Enoch Morgan's Sons, makers of the popular scouring soap Sapolio—developed into national giants. Mass production in their factories required immense amounts of fat, which they bought not from households or peddlers but from other large and expanding companies, the giant meatpackers and the producers of cottonseed oil.[20]

Household writers continued to suggest that soap be made at home throughout the nineteenth century, because ashes and grease were free, while soap cost money. Writing during the depression of the 1870s, Mrs. Wright even proposed soapmaking to the middle and upper classes, as an economy for hard times. "All that rough fat should be saved in a place secure from rats," she wrote, and the servant "should each month make up a little keg of soft-soap for scrubbing and dish-washing." This would preserve the more expensive commercial bar soap, so often left to dissolve in the wash bucket. As late as 1890, a prominent sanitary engineer claimed that "good and thrifty" country housewives still saved grease, some to make soap themselves, others to sell to peddlers along with rags, bones, and other refuse. But while many households continued to save grease for cooking until after World War II, only the poorest and most frugal made all their soap.[21]

Serving Leftovers

The best food scraps never saw the inside of the grease pot or the slop pail. Household manuals recommended serving them. As part of cleaning up after dinner, Lydia Maria Child advised, "all the good bits of vegetables and meat" should be collected and minced, "that they may be in readiness to make a little savoury mince meat for supper or breakfast." Catharine Beecher likewise recommended considering future use for scraps while clearing the table. "Put all the food remaining on the dishes, and which is good, on plates," she wrote in her 1841 *Treatise*, "and set it away for use. Scrape the grease into the soap-grease pot, and the scraps into the slop-pail; and put the tea leaves into a bowl for use. Save all bits of butter." (Household manuals gave instructions for purifying rancid butter, by rinsing it in boiling water, new milk, or a lime solution.) In her 1869 revision, Beecher was only slightly more refined about reusing what was left on the plates. "Scrape the dishes," she now wrote, "putting away any food which may remain on them, and which it may be proper to save for future use." Even though she now expected her readers to be purchasing soap, she still required them to save their grease and put scraps into the slop pail.[22]

Various utensils and devices facilitated the storage of leftovers, some commercially available and others homemade. Mosquito netting, wire covers, and perforated tin boxes offered some protection from bugs and rodents in pantries and cellars. But food still spoiled. Child explained what to do "if you have fear that poultry may become musty before you want to cook it" (stuff it with a peeled onion and some pepper and hang it in a dry, cool place) or if it was "injured before you are aware of it" (wash it thoroughly, cook it with pepper, and hang it up with a muslin bag of charcoal inside). Similarly, "loaf cake slightly injured by time" could be resurrected by cutting the mold off, wetting the cake with brandy and sugar water, and warming it in the oven. Tainted butter could be melted and purified with toast; rancid lard could be sweetened with potatoes. Child's biographer, who explains that *The American Frugal Housewife* came out of the author's own experience of poverty, reports that Child actually did all these things. "Even in old age, she would complain of spending an inordinate amount of energy battling mold, fermentation, and spoilage."[23]

Iceboxes—called refrigerators even before they were cooled by electricity and gas—became a realistic possibility after 1827, with technological innovations in the cutting and storage of natural ice, harvested from ponds and stored in icehouses. Beecher recommended commercially made refrigerators but described a homemade one fashioned from barrels in the 1840s, and ice carts made regular deliveries in cities by the 1850s. Ice was expensive, however, and remained a luxury for most people until the end of the century. In 1879, Julia McNair Wright discussed a wide range of practices for storing leftovers: using commercially made refrigerators, fashioning homemade substitutes from packing boxes insulated with sawdust (set on stovepipe legs "if your cellar has rats in it"), and forgoing ice entirely by putting food in earthenware basins covered with netting.[24]

Although refrigerators solved some problems, they created others. Iceboxes might be worse than going without ice, remarks one of the characters in Mrs. Wright's partly fictionalized *Complete Home,* because some people "crowded all manner of things into them, and were not careful to cleanse them thoroughly of all bits of food that might be scattered from the dishes." Christine Terhune Herrick described a problem that sounds familiar more than a century later. Into the refrigerator, she wrote, "are too often thrust odds and ends and scraps that are suffered to remain there long enough to become malodorous, and thus taint other food." Herrick told the story of a mistress returning to her refrigerator after a two-week illness, during which she had left kitchen affairs in the hands of the cook. A "nauseating" smell emanated from "a plate of refuse fish. . . . A couple of chops on another dish were white with mould, while a handful of vegetables rotted in the corner. And in the midst of all stood a plate of butter-balls and a pitcher containing the baby's supply of milk."[25]

Domestic writers suggested that leftovers be used quickly in new dishes such as hashes, mincemeats, bread puddings, meat pies, fish salads, cheese fondue, or Welsh rarebit. Industrious cooks might also render leftover fat for use in cooking or to soothe chapped hands, and turn bones and vegetable peelings into soup stocks. Beecher and Stowe advised emulating the French pot-au-feu, keeping a stock kettle constantly on the stove. Then as now, such enterprise depended on the skill and energy of the cook, whether she was a housewife or a servant.[26]

So did the quality of the remade dish. Beecher and Stowe contrasted "cunningly devised minces" made from leftovers by "the true domestic artist" with "those things called hashes . . . compounds of meat, gristle, skin, fat, and burnt fibre, with a handful of pepper and salt flung at them, dredged with lumpy flour, watered from the spout of the tea-kettle, and left to simmer at the cook's convenience while she is otherwise occupied." As for such unsavory concoctions, "Let us not dwell too closely on their memory," they wrote, using the occasion to campaign for domestic training in cooking.[27]

Unfortunately, cookbook writers had trouble describing exactly how to achieve a cunning mince instead of a forgettable hash. Cooking with leftovers was bricolage—a dialogue between the cook and the available materials—and without knowing exactly what was on hand, no writer could provide accurate directions. Mrs. Wright, who offered a recipe for mock macaroni made from broken crackers and even supplied directions for making jelly sandwiches from leftover bread, suggested that decoration might help. Garnishing such dishes as cold sliced meat or mashed codfish and potatoes with parsley or celery leaves, hard-cooked eggs, or lemon slices would make them more appetizing. "You can afford to economize," she advised, "if you can make your cooked-over dishes look handsomer than most people's first-hand dishes."[28]

Objections to leftovers were legion, a topic for jokes and the source of domestic insecurities. *The Family Save-All: A System of Secondary Cookery,* a British book reprinted in the United States in 1869, alternated witticisms and short tales with recipes that included pea-shell pottage and stewed artichoke stems. The quintessential leftover joke appeared on the first page. "Oh! Mary!" the Master of the House asks the maid, in a little dialogue printed below recipes for puddings made from cold meat. "What is there for dinner to-day?" "I think, sir, it's *cold meat*, sir," answers Mary. "Hm! tell your mistress, Mary, when she comes in, that I may possibly be detained in the City on business, and she is *on no account to wait dinner for me*."[29]

Friends and neighbors, too, might be put off. Therefore Christine Terhune Herrick reminded readers that though serving leftovers raised the "dread of appearing parsimonious," it could also make them look like skilled cooks. "Any one can go to the butcher and order a round of beef or a leg of mutton," she wrote, "but it takes judgment, taste and skill to prepare a ragôut, a salmi, or a really good scallop." But Herrick knew that cultivating those skills in her readers was an uphill battle, and she bemoaned the "reckless consigning of food that could be utilized to the garbage pail or ash barrel." Food is "constantly flung away with a lavishness that would bring the families to speedy penury, were the proverb that wilful waste makes woful want often or promptly justified."[30]

Some writers blamed waste on servants. One even suggested padlocking the ash barrel to keep the help from disposing of vegetable scraps. Indeed, many servants were unsure how to handle kitchen waste: migrants from the American, Irish, or German countrysides might simply not know what to do with garbage in the city, and like housewives who did their own cooking, many lacked the talent or training to create the cunning mince. Moreover, they had little reason to bother. Why would a servant care, asked Christine Terhune Herrick, "if those scraps of cold bacon left from breakfast are summarily disposed of in the swill barrel, or if that bit of corn beef—too small to appear upon the table again—is bestowed upon the first basket beggar who presents himself?" In this as in so much else, the mistress had to maintain control. Servants should not be given sole charge of the kitchen, and they must be supervised. "Human nature is not at so high a standard either above or below stairs as to justify the employer in expecting a hireling to feel an interest the owner herself does not manifest in saving the odds and ends."[31]

The good servant knew her kitchen well. Herrick, who told the story of the sick mistress and the nauseating refrigerator, also reported on a cook who called her mistress to task the morning after a party when the employer began giving orders for the marketing. "I followed her to the pantry, where she had set forth the remains of the last night's feast," the employer related. "It looked like enough to last us a week. The cook pointed to the shelf dramatically. 'Shure, mem, it would be sinful to be after buying anything more til that's all ate up. Don't ye know that wilful waste makes woful want?' " A more typical cook, Herrick warned, would not bother to alert the mistress. "Rather will she think that it's an ill wind that blows nobody good, and quietly appropriate cold vegetables and broken meats for the benefit of her particular friends; nor can she be severely blamed."[32]

The practice of taking food was consistent with the customary rights of servants in many cultures. In the South, taking leftovers, food scraps, and pantry staples was called "pan-toting," and it became standard practice—with and without employer consent—during the transition from slave labor to free. "I indignantly deny that we are thieves," one black cook declared. "We don't steal; we just 'take' things—they are a part of the oral contract, exprest or implied." Some employers did call it stealing; others used pan-toting as justification for paying low wages. "We know that most of this so-called 'food' is left-overs, cold scraps and the like which we would not use on our tables again," one employer admitted. "We know that our servants are paid a small wage." And some employers described pan-toting as gifts or charity. "There are hungry children in the cabin awaiting their mother's return," one explained. "When I give out my meals I bear these little blackberry pickaninnies in mind, and I never wound the feelings of any cook by asking her 'what that is she has under her apron.' "[33]

Charity was more clear-cut in the case of the basket beggar, who made the rounds asking for food at back doors. Begging and charity were both common in small towns and cities before public transportation separated poor from prosperous neighborhoods. Nineteenth-century household manuals almost routinely discuss responsibilities to the poor and ideas of Christian charity as part of the duties of the household and an essential element of the "woman's sphere." The benevolent act that opens *Little Women*—the girls donating their Christmas breakfast to a poor immigrant family—was obviously exemplary, but the incident that initiated it was not unusual. "Some poor creeter come a-beggin'," explains Hannah, the maid, "and your ma went straight off to see what was needed. There never *was* such a woman for givin' away vittles and drink, clothes, and firin'." By the 1880s, when Herrick published *Housekeeping Made Easy*, charity was being institutionalized, and housekeepers were advised to keep the poor at arm's length. "The indiscriminate giving away of 'broken victuals' at the basement door fosters a profession of begging, and should never be permitted," wrote Herrick. "It also breeds loose ideas of property in the servants."[34]

Despite all the options—the beggar's basket, the grease pot, the slop pail, and the hash or ragout—some food waste might remain. Most of it could be dried and burned in the kitchen range, the easiest alternative in the winter. It might also be dug into the ground. In either case it would not be wasted, providing heat on the one hand and soil nutrients on the other. "As long as there is sufficient garden space around the house," wrote a sanitary engineer in 1890, "the need of removal from the premises rarely exists." But people in the expanding cities did not have that space and their food waste did have to leave the premises, especially in the summer, when their stoves were cold. Thrown out the window or carefully set out on the sidewalk, it became food for stray animals and a pressing public health issue.[35]

The Long Lives of Old Clothes

At one time, it fell upon American women—virtually all American women—to do the miles of stitching required to keep their families and, collectively, the nation in clothing. In the language of their diaries and of the novels they read, sewing *was* women's work: "I took up my work," a woman might write, or "She brought her work with her." Girls learned to sew at a very early age, as embroidery samplers signed by five-year-olds attest. For some women, sewing was an art or a means of personal expression, for others a detestable chore. Women sewed for money, for love, or simply because they had to. They sewed alone, in organized sewing circles, and while visiting informally with friends. They shared techniques and ideas and admired each other's work. And because they sewed, they intimately understood the fabric and cut of old clothing—mending, patching, accumulating pieces that could be used again, and composing new garments from old ones. Like George Sturt's wheelwrights who understood the qualities of wood, they knew just what pieces would do for what purpose, and how to make what they had into precisely what they needed.

Hand-sewn clothes were extremely valuable; the plainest cotton shirt took a good seamstress half a day, while one with more complicated styling took a day or two. Wardrobes were small; only the wealthy had more than a few changes of clothing for each season, and many people had one change or none at all. The invention of the sewing machine in 1846 and the subsequent development of the ready-made-clothing industry eventually made it possible for some women to stop sewing or never even to learn, but not until the very end of the century. Even then, most women continued to make and to mend at least some of their own and their children's clothes.[36]

Before the sewing machine, sewing and mending were obligations even for the wealthiest women, who sewed at all but the most formal gatherings. Eleuthera du Pont, daughter of the first E. I. du Pont, frequently mentioned sewing in letters she wrote between the ages of ten and twenty-eight (1816–34). The Du Ponts employed a regular seamstress and patronized dressmakers in Philadelphia, but Eleuthera made her own underwear and nightgowns. She embroidered, made trimmings for handkerchiefs, collars, and cuffs, assembled clothing, created thread cases and pincushions for the Brandywine Manufacturers Sunday School, sewed baby frocks as presents, and supervised servants who stitched and mended household linens and the bags and other fabric items needed for her family's gunpowder business. Writing to her sister in 1832, Eleuthera described salvaging some old embroidery to use on a new garment. "I have disected half of your collar ready to transfer it to the lace when you have cut it out," she reported. "It is not very pleasant work as the muslin not being stiff it is not easy to cut it near the work."[37]

On Southern plantations before the Civil War, slave women and their white mistresses both sewed and mended. "Sewing women"—slaves assigned to work at sewing—made slave clothing out of rough homespun and fancy silk attire for their masters and mistresses; on smaller plantations they sewed in the slow season and worked in the fields during the harvest, while large operations had year-round slave seamstresses. Mistresses often supervised this work; some cut out the pieces in order to maintain control over the use of fabric. On small or unsuccessful plantations, where slaves were deemed indispensable for field work or heavy housekeeping chores, slaveholding women did all the sewing, even making clothing for their slaves. Like Eleuthera du Pont, prosperous white mistresses wrote frequently in letters and diaries about their sewing tasks. Even those who left the construction of their finery to expert dressmakers (black and white) often worked endlessly at darning socks, renovating old dresses with new trimmings, and mending apparel of all kinds for themselves and their families.[38]

While many if not most middle-class women in the North went to dressmakers or hired seamstresses, few could afford to buy all their clothes or hire enough help for the whole task of clothing the family. Consequently, most women worked with the dressmaker, usually doing the cutting out, hemming, and sewing of long seams themselves and leaving the more skilled labor to the seamstress. Only the wealthiest paid others to mend, darn, or do the plain sewing of household linens. Catharine Beecher called this division of labor "poor economy," recommending instead that her readers learn dressmaking and simple millinery and do "the more expensive and tasteful operations" themselves, "so that the plain work is given to the poor, who need it." More than forty years later, Christine Terhune Herrick discussed mending in a book addressed to readers with servants and summer homes. She advocated ready-made clothing, but even that eventually required repair. A woman without cutting and fitting skills, Herrick maintained, "should at least perfect herself in all branches of mending, from laying a patch by the thread to darning stockings well." Several pages of complete directions followed.[39]

Mending was frequently necessary for people who lived in houses heated by fireplaces and stoves and lit by candles and oil lamps. "I have a bad trick of standing before the fire," Jo March of *Little Women* explains as she stands against the wall at a party, "and so I burn my frocks, and I scorched this one; and though it's nicely mended, it shows." In a section of "Miscellaneous Directions" on how to clean combs, stuff cracks at the bottom of doors, and otherwise solve domestic problems, Catharine Beecher explained what to do if one's dress caught fire: "Do not run, but lie down, and roll over till you can reach some article, or the edge of the carpet, in which to wrap yourself tight, and this will put out the fire." More often, sparks burned small holes in clothing, as did the many corrosive solutions used in cleaning; caustic laundry soaps exposed fabric to additional wear.[40]

Holes created by burns or by fabric wearing thin could be either patched or darned. Patching entailed covering the hole with an extra piece of fabric, preferably one that matched the garment closely. "The Biblical prohibition against putting a piece of new cloth into an old garment should be carried into effect in modern mending," advised Christine Herrick. "If the patch must perforce be of new material, it should at least be washed and shrunk before it is applied."[41]

Slaves, poor people, and westerners on the frontier wore clothing that was patched over and over. One Georgia slave later remembered: "De clothes den wusn't but ol' plan white cloth. Most of em wus patched fum de legs to de waist. Some wus patched so till dey looked like a quilt." A South Carolinian concurred: "Make petticoat out of old dress en patch en patch till couldn' tell which place woave." One woman born in slavery insisted that, during her childhood, "patching and darning was *stylish*." Westerners, too, patched over and over: they were nowhere near stores, and large mail-order operations like Montgomery Ward and Macy's were not established until the 1870s. One woman, writing in a Kansas newspaper in 1869, suggested that the state flag should be designed in the "parti-colors" of the patches on Kansans' clothing. The author of *Emigrant Life in Kansas*, published in London in 1886, wrote, "You must not care much for appearances, and be reconciled to seeing patches on your clothes, and again think yourself lucky if they are of the same colour. I have seen brown overalls with patches of flour-sacking, with the brand and description of the flour in blue letters still on."[42]

In contrast to patching, darning was essentially a process of reweaving, filling the hole with a mesh made of thread. In general, knit clothing like socks and stockings was darned and woven garments were patched, but these were not inviolable rules. *Good Housekeeping* advised making patches out of old socks, as did Mrs. Wright, who also recommended darning table linen, towels, sheets, pillowcases, and handkerchiefs.[43]

Whatever the method, domestic writers counseled readers to keep on top of their mending tasks, both by working on thinning areas before they developed holes and by establishing regular times for inspecting garments and linens to see if they needed mending. Lydia Maria Child advised sewing "the heels of stockings faithfully; and mend thin places, as well as holes. 'A stitch in time saves nine.' " Eliza Farrar, who attempted to convince the fashionable readers of her 1838 *Young Lady's Friend* to take satisfaction in doing their own darning and doing it well, proposed working on stockings "at a stated time every week." Many writers recommended examining and repairing all clothing every week after it was washed; Mrs. Wright suggested examining one's "whole stock of household linen, napery and bedding" every spring.[44]

A commitment to mending required appropriate equipment. Here, too, household advisers set high standards for their readers. Catharine Beecher told the story of a wealthy lady who borrowed a needle from a visitor's sewing basket so well stocked that the borrower disdained it as "lavish and extravagant." But the wealthy lady hired out her tailoring, dressmaking, and most of her plain sewing, while the visitor made everything she and her family wore. "Each thought the other uneconomical," Beecher commented, leaving little doubt of her own opinion. Christine Terhune Herrick similarly characterized the typical mending basket—containing white cotton and black silk thread, needles, scissors, and thimble—as inadequate. Proper equipment, she maintained, would include several grades of white cotton thread, colored cotton threads, "3–4 spools of black silk of varying degrees of fineness, skirt braid, rolls of [cloth] tape both narrow and wide, pearl and porcelain buttons of different sizes, neat pieces of cambric, muslin, linen, and flannel for patching, a braid of variegated silks for gloves, a measuring ribbon, a wax, an emery ball, bodkins [pointed instruments for making holes] large and small, common and buttonhole scissors, thimble, shoe-thread, shoe needles, and buttons, hooks and eyes, etc. . . . A large piece box, near at hand, should hold scraps of dresses that may be needed to repair the gowns they match."[45]

Some observers predicted that the invention of the sewing machine would spell the end of patching. "The needle will soon be consigned to oblivion, like the wheel, and the loom, and the knitting-needles," the *New York Tribune* announced at the end of the 1850s. People "will dress better, change oftener, and altogether grow better looking. . . . Men and women will disdain the soupçon of a nice worn garment, and gradually we shall become a nation without spot or blemish."[46]

Making Clothes Over

Repairing garments and linens often went far beyond mending to "making over." The term covered a lot of territory: simple hemming, dyeing or treating worn fabrics, covering frayed cuffs and collars with handmade needlework or machine-made braiding, or completely disassembling a garment and using the pieces for some other purpose. Making over is frequently mentioned in nineteenth-century domestic literature of all kinds—fictional, descriptive, and prescriptive. Women who sewed were extremely conscious of the price of fabric and of their hours of labor; thinking like *bricoleurs*, they remade and remodeled clothing even as the magazines encouraged their fashion consciousness, and they saved their scraps for quilts, rugs, and other projects. As one fashion magazine explained in 1896, "The average woman, whether on the farm or in the city, wishes to use everything to the best advantage, consequently there are very few who do not renovate and make over their old dresses when they have grown too old fashioned to be presentable." Butterick and other manufacturers sold patterns for pieces of dresses—collars, cuffs, bodices, skirts, and sleeves. Until the very end of the century, paper patterns were more commonly used for restyling old dresses than for constructing new ones.[47]

Making over required more time and effort, and almost always more skill, than simple patching, darning, or mending ripped seams. It usually involved a combination of procedures. A green silk plaid dress from the 1850s, now in the costume collection of the Los Angeles County Museum of Art, for example, has had a panel removed from the skirt to repair damage under the arm and enlarge the back. The skirt of a two-piece blue striped dress from the mid-1880s, also at the museum, has been patched to cover a stain, while the jacket shows marks indicating that it was enlarged about an inch. Trimming on clothing in museums often covers the holes and marks left when a garment was remade, and is frequently sewed on lightly with big stitches, suggesting that it was removed for washing or changed frequently.[48]

Simple forms of making over put unworn fabric in the place of threadbare or heavily soiled areas. Cuffs and collars were "turned" by removing them and sewing the fraying outside edges to the sleeve or shirt. An entire garment might also be cut apart and "turned" if the reverse side of the fabric was attractive enough. Catharine Beecher recommended to a readership wealthy enough to own silk dresses that they rip out sleeves that were thinning at the elbows and switch them to the other side, so that the old insides of the elbows would be outside. Similarly, when pants knees wore thin, she wrote, "it is a case of domestic surgery, which demands *amputation*. This is performed, by cutting off both legs, some distance above the knees, and then changing the legs. Take care to cut them off exactly of the same length or in the exchange they will not fit." The resulting seam, Beecher explained, looked better than a patch or darn.[49]

Complete makeovers went beyond cutting out worn places. Clothing was disassembled and the fabric used to make new garments; braiding, new buttons, and other decorations were added. A double-quilted wrapper might be made out of two old dresses—"a great comfort, in case of sickness," wrote Beecher. Worn-out winter flannels could be turned into summer clothes or nightgowns by cutting out the collars and sleeves, binding the armholes and necks with muslin, and darning thin places. Shabby and worn-out dresses, wrote Mrs. Wright, "can be rejuvenated by ripping, brushing, sponging, pressing, adding new facing and braid, putting on fresh buttons and some other trimming, and reworking the button-holes. Shirts, given new neck and wristbands and possibly bosoms, will hold out an extra year." Remaking might even be planned into the original construction of the garment, with fabric set aside for patching or restyling.[50]

Making over clothing was the way that nineteenth-century women who cared about fashion managed to stay in style. The women of the

Huntington family, owners of a Rochester nursery and seed business, regularly wrote in their letters about remaking "cast off" clothes into "comely ones," during the decades after the Civil War. Meg of *Little Women,* packing for a two-week visit with a wealthy family, despairs that her "many-times pressed and mended" white party dress "isn't low-necked, and it doesn't sweep enough, but it will have to do." She would have preferred her mother's old violet silk dress, but "there isn't time to make it over." She has, however, remade her blue housedress for daytime, and it "looks so well, turned and freshly trimmed, that I feel as if I'd got a new one."[51]

Women who could sew—which meant most women—remade clothing themselves, but if they could afford to do so, they hired seam-stresses to remake their best dresses. Ida B. Wells, a teacher in Memphis before her fame as an antilynching activist, wrote frequently in her diary about the everyday sewing she did for herself, her sister, and her landlady. But when she was asked to serve as a bridesmaid in 1886, she hired a seamstress to remake a dress. "Bought $6.00 worth of lace to go on my dress last week & will have to pay about $4 to get it made over besides slippers, gloves etc—such a nuisance but it must be done, I suppose," she complained. The wealthiest women sent their clothes back to Paris couturiers for remaking. In Edith Wharton's *The Age of Innocence,* May Archer laments that she cannot wear her wedding dress to a dinner. "If I only had it here! But it's gone to Paris to be made over for next winter, and Worth [the most prestigious designer of the day] hasn't sent it back."[52]

An 1896 manual for dressmakers gave instructions for remaking but warned that it was generally far less remunerative than producing new clothing. "Does it pay? Yes and no. It pays if one has talent for re-making, and takes the stand of asking as much for making a whole dress out of old stuff as from new material, charging for 'fixing over' in proportion to the time consumed." The manual explained that some New York dressmakers earned good money specializing in making clothes over. One such dressmaker employed apprentices to rip the old clothes apart and press the pieces. "Patronage flows toward the dressmaker who can and will make over and who does it well," the manual concluded, "because she is a rarity and because 'making over' is an ever present burden of the feminine mind."[53]

Children too young to complain were frequently dressed in remade clothing. Indeed, refashioning adult castoffs for children was probably the most common use for fabric from disassembled garments; the most badly worn adult clothing might still have enough good parts to construct tiny pants and skirts or even stockings. "It is an economical plan," wrote Lydia Maria Child, "after [stockings] have been mended and cut down, so that they will no longer look decent, to color old stockings, and make them up for children." An 1885 article in *Good Housekeeping*, "Making Clothes for the Boys," argued that it was too much bother to make new jackets from old ones. "But the little pants are so easily made from the discarded larger ones that it is almost a pleasure to go about them," the article declared. The father's clothes should be ripped apart, the pieces washed and pressed, and the pattern laid on, "being careful to avoid the worn places, and lo, in a few hours the heart of the small boy rejoices in a pair of pants, which are equally as good as if cut from new cloth," it explained. "It seems quite as necessary that the mother of a family of boys should understand utilizing the cast off clothing for her sons as that she should understand breadmaking." The result of such ingenuity was maximum benefit to the household: "No forlorn tramp ever goes away smiling from our door hugging the cast off clothing of our lord and master to his shabby coat."[54]

Silk and wool garments particularly demanded makeovers, since they were expensive to begin with and because they had little useful afterlife. Cotton and linen were more practical as household rags, and neither silk nor wool could be sold to the ragman for papermaking. Black silk and wool clothes—worn during long mourning periods—were particularly troublesome because they faded and turned "rusty." Commercial dry cleaning was yet to come, but there were many formulas for renewing the fabrics. Aunt Sophronia, the heroine of Mrs. Wright's semifictional *Complete Home,* compliments her friend Miriam, whose husband's salary has been cut as a consequence of hard times, on a new black silk dress. "No, indeed," says Miriam, "it is the old one that I have worn this four years." Besides replacing the cuffs, collar, pockets, button covers, and other trimmings with velvet from an old blouse, "I sponged it with a teaspoonful of ammonia, mixed in half a pint of warm, weak coffee; then I pressed it." Miriam is also restoring an "old black cashmere: I ripped it up, washed it in warm water where soap bark had been steeped, and ironed it on the wrong side. I shall get a couple of yards of silk for trimming, and make it as good as new. Here, too, is my ancient brown merino [wool dress], ripped, sponged, and pressed, with a small investment in fringe and velveteen—it must come out a new gown; so I buy nothing this fall."[55]

Miriam's coffee-and-ammonia concoction was one of many suggestions for dyes, coloring agents, bleaches, and stain removers that might lengthen the lives of old clothes. Mixed with alum and cider or vinegar, the purple paper commonly used to wrap sugar could be used for dye. Chips of logwood, a tropical tree with dark wood, were boiled (sometimes a copper kettle was recommended) and used "To Renovate an Old Coat" or "To Revive Faded Black Cloth." A mixture of vinegar and iron carbonate could serve as well. Dealers in secondhand clothing were said to brush garments with water in which tobacco had been boiled. Ink could be used "if a black article of clothing gets rusty" or "if the shoulders look quite gray." Household manuals sometimes offered dozens of dye recipes, using both chemical and vegetable ingredients. Nearly every book of domestic advice told how to remove mildew and grease stains from clothing. They described methods of bleaching and of stain and spot removal that ranged from sunshine, water, and lemon juice to oxalic acid, which Beecher called "infallible in removing ink stains and iron rust"—warning, however, that it was "very poisonous, and should be kept with much care."[56]

The most straightforward and least creative form of making over involved household textiles. The clean white remains of torn or stained sheets and tablecloths, hemmed or simply cut down, served as pillowcases, napkins, bandages, diapers, sanitary napkins, dish towels, dusting cloths, and washrags before they were finally traded to peddlers and general stores for ultimate sale to paper factories. Factory-made fabric had almost entirely supplanted homespun by the eve of the Civil

War, but even cloth made by machines was valuable. The dirtiest rags, Lydia Maria Child maintained, "should never be thrown away because they are dirty. Mop-rags, lamp-rags, &c. should be washed, dried, and put in the rag-bag. There is no need of expending soap upon them: boil them out in dirty suds, after you have done washing."[57]

Toward the end of the century, rags began to seem like trash, at least to the middle and upper classes. Wood pulp was supplanting rags for papermaking, while dish towels and sanitary napkins could be purchased commercially. Domestic writers therefore redoubled their efforts to convince readers of the many uses of large pieces of fabric. Mrs. Wright suggested in 1879 that a worn-out double sheet could be cut down for a single bed or crib or made into pillowcases for servants' beds, or covers for food in the pantry, or dust rags. Old tablecloths should first be darned, but if they were too far gone, they could become napkins, soft towels for infants and invalids, or food covers. "Old towels, when darning them has ceased to be a virtue," might be made into dusters or washcloths. "The Philosophy of Dish-Towels," published in *Good Housekeeping* in 1885, spoke directly to the commercial competition: "An old, half-worn tablecloth, cut up into the right sized pieces, does as well as something bought out of the store for the purpose." Herrick, writing in 1888, insisted that "no fragments of [linen sheets] or of damask table-cloths or napkins should ever be thrown away. If the pieces of linen are not large enough to make full-sized cases, they may serve as covers to children's pillows, may be doubled and made into squares for babies' napkins or towels, or into wash cloths. The small bits that are impracticable for any other purpose are admirable for binding up cut fingers, or steeping in liniment to lay upon a burn or wound."[58]

Passing Clothes On

Not all old clothes were refurbished; then, as now, some were given away. Giving clothes to the poor was a common act of charity, practiced by individuals and by organized groups, some formed especially for the purpose, others organized by churches and benevolent societies. During 1837, the ladies of the New-York Clothing Society for the Relief of the Industrious Poor, for example, gave out 1,742 garments, 43 "comfortables" (tied quilts), and 169 pairs of shoes. Some of these they collected from their friends, but others they produced at their sewing meetings. Mrs. Bowles Colgate, whose family was wealthy from making soap and starch, was one of four "directresses" of the society and its most effective solicitor. She personally collected $135 (including $20 from the family company) and brought the group a bale of cotton, many pieces of fabric, a considerable amount of clothing, dozens of pairs of hose, and, from a single donor, fifty pairs of shoes. Forty years later, *Good Housekeeping* advised the affluent woman who had no need to remake her husband's old clothes to "cast her mind around to see on whom she can bestow them [so that] the small boys of some hard working, deserving mother will have their hearts gladdened and their bodies made warm and neat at slight expense and trouble." Churches collected clothes for foreign missions and the domestic poor. Early in the twentieth century, one writer recalled the clothing he had received from the missionary box throughout his childhood. "Those first old clothes received were donned with gloating and glory," he wrote, but in his teens ("that period so strangely composed for all of us out of spiritual shabbiness and spiritual splendor") his feelings "became uneasy, uncomfortable, at last unbearable. . . . I wanted raiment all my own, dully at first, then fiercely."[59]

Old clothes might also be given to servants. This practice was not widespread in the North, where mistresses worried that well-dressed domestics might be mistaken for women of their own class and where maids who wore nice clothes were faulted for putting on airs. In the antebellum South, where status lines were more clearly drawn, most slaves wore simple outfits made of homespun or cheap factory-made fabric, but some did get their masters' old clothes. Like decent food and humane working conditions, good clothing sometimes helped to define a "good" master. Historian Eugene Genovese asserts that "masters and especially mistresses took great pleasure in passing their used clothing on to the slaves, and understood this gift relationship as maintaining if not widening social distance." Advertisements for runaway slaves routinely described their clothes, which included many fine garments; whether elegant hand-me-downs or clothing stolen before fleeing, such costumes helped runaways pass as free.[60]

Nancy Williams, a former slave whose reminiscences were recorded by the Virginia WPA project in the 1930s, recalled a scene repeated every spring. "Missus would clean out de house . . . an' Ant Emma would come puffin' down to de quarters totin' 'cross her back a big bundle of clothes tied up in Missus' ole petticoat. Spread 'em out an' all de niggers scramble fo' 'em. Never could git nothin' to fit you. Arter de scramble de slaves go round tradin' each other, tryin' to git fittin's."[61]

But not all slaves had equal access. Cast-off clothes were part of a system of rewards, given to favorite domestic slaves and especially productive workers. In general, field hands wore rough clothing, while house slaves got castoffs, which were usually repaired, altered, or made over. "I wore pants made of Bosse' old ones," recalled Louis Hughes, a house slave, "and all his old coats were utilized for me. They rounded them off at the tail just a little and called them jackets." Even field slaves might get the master's old clothes for special occasions. A slave named Aunt Sally recalled that her mistress not only chose a husband for her and named the date for the wedding but provided "from her own stores" the wedding dress, "an old white muslin frock." Sally's new husband, a field hand, was also dressed for the occasion in "some cast off clothes of his master's, which made him look . . . quite like a gentleman."[62]

After the war, many black women received discarded clothing as "gifts" or partial payment from domestic employers; the women remade the clothes themselves, swapped or passed them on to others as material for bricolage, or gave them to their churches for the use of even poorer people. Because so many African American women did domestic work, the black working poor were in a better position to get old clothes than the European immigrant working poor, who were more likely to be employed in factories.

In England, old clothes were likewise a perquisite of domestic service, but servants often sold their masters' clothing. "For the employer it was an easy way of clearing a wardrobe and conferring a favour," writes Madeleine Ginsburg, a costume historian. For the servant, "there was merit as well as profit in selling, rather than wearing what was inappropriate and might be socially misleading." The used-clothing trade was active in England at least as early as the sixteenth century; infection from contaminated clothing was a concern of municipal authorities in times of plague, when the poor, looking for useful garments, scavenged the bodies of the dead. Eighteenth-century British purchasers of secondhand clothing "were mainly either the town mob or the underworld, the classless or the *declassé*," people attempting to appear to be other than what they were. By the nineteenth century, London's used-clothing trade was highly developed and highly specialized, central to the vast street commerce detailed in Henry Mayhew's *London Labour and the London Poor*, Charles Booth's *Life and Labour of the People of London*, and the novels of Charles Dickens.[63]

The United States, too, had a substantial secondhand clothing market before the Civil War. Used garments were frequently advertised in metropolitan newspapers. In the 1840s, New York City "fences"—buyers and sellers of stolen goods—considered used coats so valuable that they hired seamstresses to change the linings so that the owners could not make claims. Dealers bought up clothing and shipped it to the South (where many masters believed that slaves had more profitable things to do than sew slave clothing) and the West (where seamstresses were scarce). Frederick Law Olmsted, attending a black church in Virginia, commented that most of the people were dressed in white people's cast-off fine clothes, "received, I suppose, as presents, or purchased of the Jews, whose shops show that there must be considerable importation of such articles, probably from the North." He also reported that planters bought military clothing for their slaves ("who were greatly pleased by it") at auctions held in New Orleans after the Mexican War.[64]

As the Civil War drew to a close, Confederate finery was sold to finance declining plantations. "What a scene!" wrote diarist Mary Chesnut, who sold some dresses in Richmond in 1864. "Such piles of rubbish, and mixed up with it such splendid Paris silks and satins. A mulatto woman kept the shop, in an out-of-the-way old house. White ladies sell to, and the Negroes buy of, this woman." Six months later, Chesnut sold more clothing. "My pink silk dress I have sold for six hundred dollars, to be paid by installments, two hundred a month for three months; and I sell my eggs and butter for two hundred dollars a month. Does it not sound well? Four hundred dollars a month, regularly? But—in what? 'In Confederate money!' *Hélas!*"[65]

All over the country, clothes were among the household belongings and farm equipment offered at estate sales. Advertised on posters, such sales were sometimes known as "vendues," and in some parts of the country, the sale records were officially filed with the will and the estate inventory. Held in the spring, the sales were social occasions as well, featuring food, games for the children, and sometimes hard cider, to induce people to bid more freely.[66]

The value of old clothing to nineteenth-century Americans of all classes is difficult to grasp today, when even in Third World countries people sew with machines using cheap textiles made in factories. With economic development, the stock of textiles in the United States and in individual homes increased substantially. But even late in the century, after sewing machines and commercially made fabrics were common, wardrobes remained small by today's standards and all but the very wealthy used clothes as long as possible. Giving away and selling clothes; mending, patching, and removing stains; and making over by turning, trimming, or dyeing all kept old clothes in use. These practices embody the everyday regard for objects and materials bred by the "scarcity of objects" in an undeveloped economy, the value of objects created by hand, the working knowledge of a nation of seamstresses, and the bricolage of handwork. As one western woman wrote in 1867 of her new gray dress, "I finished my sacque and entered it to live therein till its last days arrive."[67]

Quilts

Besides selling and giving clothes away, mending and remaking them, and using them as rags for household tasks, women once regularly reworked textiles into useful and ornamental household furnishings, especially quilts, rugs, and upholstery. "Textiles recycled into decorative pieces demonstrated a woman's frugality and artistic skill," writes historian Harvey Green. "These activities and virtues were expected of all women, not just those with limited means." He cites the daughter of an important Rochester attorney who made old woolen curtains into sofa cushions stuffed with straw.[68]

It is of course impossible to know exactly how many women made quilts and rugs or created homemade upholstery from cast-off textiles. Not everyone enjoyed these crafts, and not everyone had the patience, time, and space where the materials for a partially finished task could sit without being disturbed by small children. But it is certain that, throughout the nineteenth century, virtually all women possessed the sewing skills basic to recycling textiles. As the sewing machine and the development of ready-made garments eased the task of clothing their families, many women applied their needlecraft skills to their accumulated scraps and rags, and tackled big projects so they could surround themselves with attractive things. In addition, quilts, rugs, and upholstery could provide income for women talented enough to make beautiful objects and enterprising enough to sell them. Working-class women and even slaves could earn money making and selling quilts, while middle-class women sold needlework as fund-raisers, at least as early as the antislavery fairs of the 1830s. Harriet Powers, probably the best-known nineteenth-century African American quilter, sold her first quilt for five dollars (she asked for ten) and the promise of more scraps; it was exhibited at the 1895 Cotton States and International Exposition in Atlanta, where it attracted the attention of a group of women who commissioned another one. Similarly, hooked and woven rag rugs were often made for sale. An 1876 article in *Peterson's Magazine* claimed that hooking had become "quite a domestic branch of industry in New England," practiced by farm women during winter evenings. "The rugs are, many of them, really beautiful and command a good price."[69]

Quilts are today the most celebrated of these projects. Although many of them were used until they were in shreds, they did not have dirt ground into them like rugs and upholstery, so many quilts have been preserved by descendants of their makers, as well as by collectors and museums. Art historians, women's historians, and serious quilt collectors have done extensive research on individual quilts and on regional styles, creating a rich literature about the craft. Despite the abundance of research, our ideas about quilts and quilt making remain shrouded in sentimental misconception. For example, contrary to common belief, quilts were rare in colonial America. Quilt historians agree that quilting represents not scarcity but the widespread availability of materials: few quilts were made of homespun, and large numbers of women began to quilt only when manufactured fabric became broadly accessible. Nor were the earliest quilts composed of patchwork—small pieces of fabric sewn together into quilt tops; the tops consisted either of one piece of white fabric or of colored fabrics appliquéd onto a single large piece. Since handmade fabric was so valuable, colonists favored "simple square-cut [clothing] patterns that used an entire width of cloth selvage to selvage, leaving no scraps to be incorporated into other projects." Only with factory-produced fabric could people afford the luxury of fitted clothing, cut so as to leave scraps. And only with factory-produced cloth could they afford the diverse fabrics required for patchwork.[70]

Quilting parties (also called quilting bees or frolics) have also been mythologized. There was a good reason for them. The actual quilting— sewing the quilt together with plain or fancy stitching—required keeping the sandwich of cover, filling, and backing taut and horizontal. This was best done in a frame that filled the major room of many houses. Quilting parties were intended to complete this final stage of quilt making: that way, the frame would not be in the way for long. The assembled women were often joined by their husbands and brothers for food and dancing afterward.

But quilting was not always sociable. Different women might work on a quilt at different times, especially if they lived together. One New York woman, Helen Davis Benton, sometimes quilted with a few friends or relatives, sometimes went to quilting parties, and sometimes quilted all alone. Women generally made the tops of quilts—the patchwork and appliqué work—by themselves. Because much of the work was done on relatively small patterned blocks, they could accomplish these crafts over long periods of time, in spare moments or during slack periods in their other chores. Even a nearly complete top was thin and relatively light and could be held in a needlewoman's lap. And many women preferred to secure the layers by tying them at intervals rather than by quilting. Tying was faster and easier than quilting, and could more easily be done alone. The resulting bedcovers—often called "comforters," "comforts," or "comfortables"—could be untied and taken apart for cleaning. Some women both quilted and tied, like Mary Ellen Schenck of Leavenworth County, Kansas, who wrote in her diary on February 21, 1876, that she "tied a comfort for Isaac and quilted till night."[71]

Jeannette Lasansky, a quilt historian, asserts that "the major myth about 19th- and 20th-century quiltmaking is about its role as a scrap medium." Not all material used for patchwork came from the scrap bag. The early appliqué quilt covers, especially the red-and-green ones now well represented in museum collections, were almost always made from purchased material. For patchwork styles as well, many women purchased fabric specifically for quilting, especially the large expanses of fabric necessary for backings and borders. Regional and class variations are of course important here: poor women, slave women, and those living on the frontier were more likely to use scraps.[72]

Buying fabric especially for a quilt allowed the quilt maker with money and access to a large dry-goods store much more freedom; she could choose materials with the project in mind instead of depending on what was at hand. The same woman might proceed differently as different resources became available. Martha Ogle Forman, the mistress of a Maryland plantation with some fifty slaves, wrote about making a number of quilts in the diary she kept between 1814 and

1845. She created her first one (as well as covers for six chairs) out of old window curtains. Seven years later, she received "a piece of material for bedquilts" from her husband, who did the household purchasing on trips to Baltimore, Wilmington, and Philadelphia. In 1831, Martha Forman paid for new quilt fabric herself with money from the sale of poultry and eggs.[73]

Many quilters combined scraps with purchased material. A quilt made in the late 1830s by Mary Magdalena Guss of Pennsylvania was preserved with a note about its creation. Some of the patches were begun "when she and brother Will watched cows together, when she was a very small girl from bits she gathered that other sisters discarded." Larger patches were made from "material her grandmother bought her for a dress." The backing was purchased when the quilt was nearing completion. Even slave women were able to add purchased fabric to their quilts, bought with money they earned for special tasks. A former slave from Mississippi treasured a quilt her mother made, partly from homespun and partly from red, green, and blue store-bought fabric. Another former slave recalled earning a dollar helping some women with their boarders. "I thot I wuz rich," she remembered. "I tuk dat dollar an' bot me some calico an' made me sum quilts." Nancy Williams, too, bought fabric with money she made selling quilts to her mistress and other white women.[74]

"The Patchwork Quilt," published in 1845 in the mill workers' magazine the *Lowell Offering*, sentimentalized both purchased and scrap fabrics. "How many passages of my life seem to be epitomized in this patchwork quilt," the author wrote. The quilt included pieces of "that bright copperplate cushion which graced my mother's easy chair"; her sister's dress, the first she ever saw cut with "mutton-leg" sleeves; some "old brocade-looking calico, presented by a venerable friend"; and "a fragment of the first dress which baby brother wore when he left off long clothes." She was also nostalgic about the material she purchased: "Here are pieces of that [which] I thought so bright and beautiful to set off my quilt with, and bought strips of it by the cent's worth—strips more in accordance with the good dealer's benevolence than her usual price for the calico."[75]

Such inventories of scraps were typical in quilt literature. Another story, entitled "The Patch-Work Quilt," published in 1846 by the popular writer Catharine Maria Sedgwick, shared many of the same themes. This quilt contained a bit of a wedding dress, a square of the bridesmaid's dress, a fragment of a dressing gown that the husband had brought from Philadelphia. Such "talismans" of the past, wrote Sedgwick, made quilts into "story-books—family legends—illustrated traditions." She explicitly described what most writers took for granted—that many of these talismans were not fragments of used clothing but sewing scraps left over from the garment's initial construction. "Being originally made of unwashed materials and wisely kept for show," she explained, the cherished quilt "has preserved its original gloss."[76]

In its plainer forms, patchwork was considerably less intricate than most nineteenth-century needlework and was therefore assigned to little girls for their first sewing projects. Many writers recommended that girls be charged with creating patchwork pot holders or blankets for their dolls' beds; many of the dolls themselves were also made from rags and scraps. To instill good habits, little girls were assigned an amount of work to do in each sitting, called a "stint." In "Mary's Patchwork," first published in 1853 and reprinted in an 1881 volume of sentimental tales, Mary's mother gives her some basted squares of pink and white patchwork. Every day she must do her stint: one patch. "When you have sewed squares enough for a quilt, I will buy you a new bedstead for your room," her mother promises. Mary soon gets bored, especially when her friend Alice comes by to "roll hoop." Lucy Larcom, a Lowell mill girl who became a well-known writer, learned to sew patchwork at school. She began a quilt with "scraps of gowns I had seen worn, and they reminded me of the persons who wore them," but eventually she quit and gave away all the pieces except for a swatch from a dress that had belonged to a beloved dead sister. Patchwork "is generally our first work and our last," wrote S. Annie Frost in *The Ladies' Guide to Needle Work* (1877), "the schoolgirl's little fingers setting their first crowded or straggling stitches of appalling length in patchwork squares, while the old woman, who can no longer conquer the intricacies of fine work, will still make patchwork quilts for coming generations." With the advent of the sewing machine, the straight, even stitching learned doing simple patchwork was no longer required for producing clothing.[77]

The patchwork quilt—today considered the epitome of intricate craftswork—was deemed coarse in comparison with the fine needlework that became fashionable once the sewing machine relieved women of their most mechanical tasks. Florence Hartley, author of *Ladies' Handbook of Fancy and Ornamental Work* (1859), liked "genuine old fashioned patchwork" and thought it "infinitely prettier than the bits of silk sewed together for parlor ornaments" but regarded it as unrefined, often put together by little girls, old women, maiden aunts with imperfect sight, or "over-tasked" mothers. Mrs. Matilda Marian Chesney Pullan, an English needlewoman who came to America as needlework editor for *Frank Leslie's Magazine,* was not so generous. "Of the patchwork with calico," she wrote, "I have nothing to say. Valueless indeed must be the time of that person who can find no better use for it than to make ugly counterpanes and quilts of pieces of cotton. Emphatically is the proverb true of cotton patchwork, *Le jeu ne vaut pas la chandelle!* It is not worth either candle or gas light." Mrs. Pullan's class bias is even more obvious when one notes that only extremely wealthy people used gaslights in their homes when she wrote; most people saw gaslight, if at all, only on the streets of the largest cities.[78]

Mrs. Pullan did approve of the English fashion of making decorative patchwork out of pieces of silk. Silk patchwork "is a favorite amusement with many ladies," she wrote, "as by it they convert useless bits of silk, velvet, or satin, into really handsome articles of decoration. . . . [W]ith a little taste and management, [such materials] make very handsome cushions, chair covers, and ottomans." Soon enough, the fashion crossed the ocean and became a fad. Silk patchwork "is again becoming very fashionable," *Peterson's Magazine* declared in 1877, at the beginning of what was to become the crazy-quilt fad. Intended not for beds but as thin throws for the parlor, crazy quilts combined silk, satin, and velvet fragments with ornamental embroidery stitches, often in random shapes and haphazard patterns. Women rushed to cut up their oldest silk clothing and used their fancy remnants, which were useless for papermaking and impractical for household work.[79]

Once the fashion caught on, few women had enough fine fabrics for the fancywork they wanted to do. At least six companies advertised packaged silk remnants on a single page of the February 1884 *Ladies' Home Journal.* Pieces might also be obtained by asking merchants for samples, but savvy storekeepers made their samples too small to be used, cut holes in them, or pasted them on cardboard, according to an 1884 story about two girls, Heloise and Marie, who were crazy about crazy quilts. The girls went to extremes in their zeal for sumptuous scraps, Marie begging a suitor for his necktie and cutting the lining out of her father's overcoat, Heloise posing as a representative of a dry-goods firm seeking samples. Eventually the urban magazines moved on to new fashions in fancywork. Crazy quilts became a topic for magazine articles addressed to farm women, who were advised to make them with old wool instead of new silk and velvet.[80]

Rag Rugs

Old wool clothing that was beyond making over was generally reused in rag rugs, probably a more widespread medium for reusing old fabric than quilts. Julia McNair Wright called carpet rags the "ordinary use" for "old woollen and flannel clothes." Many kinds of rugs and mats were manufactured from rags and waste materials such as corn husks. "It takes a great deal of material," one household writer admitted about an unusual design for a rag rug, "but that doesn't matter, for it can be made of what is good for nothing else."[81]

There were three dominant techniques. Weaving produced rectangular, striped rugs; braiding made round and oval ones; and hooked rugs could be created in any shape. Women wove and braided many beautiful rugs, and hooking was indisputably an art form. But few rugs survive, because they took hard wear. And they inspired less sentimental literature than quilts did; it was more difficult to differentiate the old clothes in a rug and less romantic to walk on memories than to be warmed by them.[82]

Rag preparation was simple, tedious work that could be done on a dark day without lamps or candles. "Cut and sewed carpet rags and patched Zenas' [her brother's] pants at night," Mary Ellen Schenck wrote in her diary one rainy March day in 1876. "Cut carpet rags till noon," she continued the next day. Two months later, she spent another two days at the task, again beginning on a rainy day. Cutting rags, one manual suggested, "will be found a nice task for children or for 'occasional' pastime work to 'pick up' at odd moments." Some poor women did the work for pay; an 1849 enumeration of African American women workers in Philadelphia revealed that thirty-three earned money sewing carpet rags.[83]

Old clothes were torn or cut into strips, about three-quarters of an inch to an inch wide, which were sewed end to end and rolled into balls. Usually the strips were quickly tacked together with big stitches made by hand, but some women used sewing machines. Hooked rugs required narrower strips than braided and woven ones, and rag preparation was easier for hooking because the strips did not have to be sewed together. Any fabric would do, and although some books advised separating cotton and wool, others advocated mixing them. Even old carpeting could be used. It produced an especially thick rug but was difficult to tear or cut; by the early twentieth century, a machine was being marketed for the task.[84]

Woven rag rugs were more popular than braided and hooked ones. Women either worked on looms at home or, as looms became less common in American households, prepared the strips and brought their balls of rags to a weaver, who charged by the inch. One writer warned against trusting the weaver to design the rug. "I believe there is no home-made article where such a lack of artistic skill is shown as in this," he wrote. "The rags may be cut well, and nicely colored, but the arrangement is too often left to the weaver, who will plan the stripe to suit her own taste, or so as to be most convenient for weaving."[85]

The basic weaving method used the strips of cloth as filler for the loom. Martha Ballard, a Maine midwife who with her daughters and daughters-in-law wove constantly during the early years of the nation, made bed coverlets this way. But rag rugs were scarce until factory-made fabric overtook homespun: there was limited fabric to make them with and few spare looms. A Connecticut man recalled that only a few families had rugs during the first years of the nineteenth century, and only in the best rooms. "They were all home-made: the warp consisting of woolen yarn, and the woof of lists [strips of material, especially from the selvage, or edge, of the fabric] and old woolen cloth, cut into strips and sewed together at the ends." As time went on, rag rugs became commonplace and domestic writers assumed that readers were familiar with rag preparation. "The pieces are sewed together (as for carpet rags)," one 1878 manual explained in its directions for making a different kind of mat.[86]

Weaving rag rugs was a source of income for women who owned looms. If they prepared the rags themselves, they could market the finished product through the normal channels for household produce, bartering with general stores or selling to city people at farmer's markets. The idea that farm women could make money from rugs and other crafts eventually became a central tenet of crafts revivals both at the turn of the century and in the 1930s. But many advocates of such home industry insisted that craftswomen spend extra time and money on articles intended for sale. Production for the market, they explained, demanded a refinement impossible to achieve with the materials and methods of household reuse. Rugs should be made out of new fabric, not rags; they should be carefully designed; the seams of the strips should be sewed, not tacked.[87]

Like patchwork, woven rag rugs had their counterpart in silk at the end of the nineteenth century, a genteel version of striped rag carpeting. Woven silk rags were used as curtains and table covers. They were also made into "portieres," large heavy curtains hung over doorways that might also be fashioned from other reused materials such as embroidered old woolen blankets. The procedure for silk portieres was identical to that for wool and cotton rugs: "Make a collection of all colors and kinds of old silk and satin which is not soiled, and the more new scraps the better. Cut or tear into strips, . . . sew these together and wind into a ball exactly as rags are prepared for a carpet. When a sufficient quantity by weight is thus prepared, take it to a carpet weaver and have it woven the width you desire the curtain." While not as widespread a fad as crazy quilts, woven silk portieres embodied the same new attitudes toward waste and reuse and created some of the same dilemmas. Women were said to destroy silk dresses that might still be made over; "the temptation is great," one writer cautioned, "to cut up what might be turned to better account."[88]

In contrast to woven rugs, braided ones required very little skill and no equipment beyond a needle. "After old coats, pantaloons, &c. have been cut up for boys, and are no longer capable of being converted into garments," wrote Lydia Maria Child, "cut them into strips, and employ the leisure moments of children, or domestics, in sewing and braiding them for door-mats." Many household manuals assumed that readers knew how to do this; one set of directions for chenille rugs, for example, ended with "then, on that another strip, and so on, just as you do braided mats." Complete directions were rarely provided. One exceptional book offered limited written instruction, with illustrations that compared the standard three-strand braid with a more complicated "quilled braid."[89]

The third method for making rugs from rags—hooking, or "pulling"—was employed by French and Scottish colonists in maritime Canada as early as the 1820s. These early rugs were generally hooked on linen backings, but the craft enjoyed its greatest popularity later in the century, when burlap sacks became widely available. In 1876, *Peterson's Magazine* provided complete directions for "the prettiest and newest way of using rags." The backing was "made of coarse canvas, known as 'Burlaps,' such as is used for packing bags. The pattern is roughly outlined on the burlap, and the rags, which are cut into little bits about half an inch wide . . . are drawn through the meshes of the canvas with a large crochet-needle." Hooked rugs had a considerable artistic advantage over woven and braided ones because they offered unlimited scope for patterns. Their creators designed geometric abstract compositions or representational ones such as flowers, animals, or landscapes.[90]

There were many variations in materials. Instead of rags, hooking could be done with yarn unraveled from old sweaters, scarves, and woolen stockings. (Conversely, rags in thin strips were sometimes used for knitting.) Some rug makers used special rug hooks instead of crochet hooks; one could be "manufactured easily by taking a parasol brace or a piece of wire and filing the end into a proper form." Rug hooks were first patented in 1868; by the mid-1880s several kinds were advertised. At least one early-twentieth-century woman used a can opener. For backing, one writer suggested that coffee sacks be "washed and ironed smoothly, or, if you prefer, buy the same material by the yard, which will be still better, as it will be clean and with the original stiffening." It was also possible to buy backing with ready-made designs. The Henry Ford Museum owns the stencils used by Edward Sands Frost, who stenciled patterns onto burlap and peddled them door-to-door in the 1860s; these are probably the earliest-known commercial patterns.[91]

Hooked rugs tended to be small because their production was very time-consuming. "In making rugs, two important points must be considered—the amount of work and time required," warned *Blakelee's Industrial Cyclopedia* (1884), which provided directions for many kinds of rugs, including hooked ones made on coffee sacks. "In these days, when quite handsome rugs can be purchased for a small sum, it does not pay a woman to spend all of her spare time for weeks and weeks over a rug, even if the materials do come out of the rag bag and therefore cost nothing. The drawn coffee sack rugs in figures of cats, dogs, bouquets, etc. . . . are open to this objection."[92]

Even though they were so labor-intensive, hooked rugs, like woven ones, were promoted as moneymaking crafts for poor women in the country. Mrs. Alexander Graham Bell, who summered on Cape Breton Island, Nova Scotia, brought in a crafts expert to stimulate handcrafts among her neighbors. They established a well-known hooked-rug industry, eventually selling rugs to decorators for New York mansions. Similar community industries were established throughout Nova Scotia and New England, some emphasizing particular designs and motifs, such as the Native American motifs of the Subbekakasheny Industries of Massachusetts and the Abnakee rugs from New Hampshire.[93]

Packing Crates and Old Quilts: Homemade Upholstery

Old clothing and household textiles could be put to yet another use. Books and magazines proposed many ideas for converting packing crates and plain wooden furniture into plush seating and heavily draped dressing tables. As Katherine C. Grier points out in her study of nineteenth-century parlors, the instructions were often minimal. They provided "simplified versions of upholstery" appropriate to the limited skills of amateurs, using waste materials or very inexpensive ones. No one, she points out, would have mistaken these homemade products for the craftwork of professional upholsterers. Nonetheless, making them was time-consuming. Such pieces were seldom sold or made for others. Rarely collected by museums and unappreciated by later generations—a padded chair was less likely to be stored than a quilt because it took up more space—few of these objects have come down to us. "Like most ordinary things," writes Grier, home-upholstered furniture "was used until it was used up, and then it was discarded."[94]

Ideas were abundant. An old rocking chair could be cushioned, a washstand made from "a common dry goods packing box," a toilet table from a flour barrel, a clothes hamper from a fruit barrel, a footstool from a box. Catharine Beecher and Harriet Beecher Stowe made upholstery sound easy in *The American Woman's Home*, where they gave directions for making many kinds of inexpensive furniture. "If you have in the house any broken-down arm-chair, reposing in the oblivion of the garret," they advised, "draw it out—drive a nail here and there to hold it firm—stuff and pad, and stitch the padding through with a long upholsterer's needle, and cover it with the chintz like your other furniture. Presto—you create an easy-chair."[95]

Good Housekeeping added details to the standard ideas in "Elegant

Home-Made Furniture" (1885): casters for chair bottoms, felt to cover the shelf of a washstand, velveteen flowers and a pickle jar covered with paint to place on the shelf. A seat cushion was covered with material from "an old broadcloth Prince Albert coat," and with such economies, "for the sum of twelve dollars—the price of an ordinary wicker chair, the parlor was prettily furnished." Mrs. Wright described a woman living near the Rocky Mountains who had equipped her house by covering boxes and barrels with remnants of fabric purchased at an auction. "In truth, the little four-roomed house was the tasteful home of a *lady*," Aunt Sophronia declares. "I never realized so completely the creative power of good taste."[96]

Women might call upon men to help them with such projects. "Let your menfolk knock up for you, out of rough, unplaned boards, some ottoman frames," Beecher and Stowe proposed. *Blakelee's Industrial Cyclopedia* suggested "a little mechanical aid from a man or boy" in making a barrel chair. But only a little. Instructions for remaking furniture appeared in a section of the book entitled "The Handy Housewife." Women were expected to do most of the work of varnishing, staining, and repairing cracked veneers on their own. Although some directions for making household items suggested enlisting male help with hammers and saws, many did not. Men who worked long hours in factories and offices might not be available for household tasks, and they were by no means universally skilled at so-called men's tasks. *Blakelee's Industrial Cyclopedia* warned that lawyers and merchants generally had "little idea . . . of mechanism" and performed handwork tasks in a "bungling manner." And certainly upholstery itself was textile work, definitively within the sphere of women.[97]

Used fabrics were excellent for stuffing, padding, and covering upholstery. "Any coarse fabric will answer," read one set of upholstery directions for stuffing chairs. "Bagging that has been used for packing goods, quite as serviceable as new, may often be had at stores for a trifle." Shredded newspaper, old clothes, or worn-out quilts would also serve the purpose, as would combinations of materials. Grier points to a piece of furniture, now in a New York museum, that was "padded with ten alternating layers of straw and quilts or coverlets."[98]

While homemade upholstery might cover old wooden furniture—ladder-backed chairs and rockers were especially popular—it also offered an opportunity for reusing wooden packing crates and barrels. An 1878 book on home decoration advocated buying new furniture for the parlor and dining room but championed covered boxes for more private spaces. A chapter on "Toilet-Tables, Wash-Stands, Etc." provided directions and engraved illustrations of small pieces of furniture, all draped and embellished with ornamental scrolling and other flourishes in high-Victorian style, and all constructed on bases of packing crates.[99]

The most common pieces of packing-container furniture were barrel chairs. Like braided rugs, these chairs were apparently familiar enough that many books gave only minimal instructions. The general idea was to make a horizontal cut halfway up the barrel and halfway through, and a vertical cut coming down through half of the top to meet the first cut; one of the top quarters of the barrel was thus removed. Wood was then nailed in to create a back from what was left of the top and a seat over the bottom. Some manuals illustrated relatively plain barrel chairs while others, writes Grier, "promised startling transformations of barrels into Turkish-style overstuffed chairs, a metamorphosis certainly beyond the skill and means of the amateur home upholsterer." The idea was appropriated commercially early in the twentieth century; manufacturers sold barrel-shaped chairs as part of the colonial revival although the style had actually originated in the nineteenth century. As Grier writes, barrel chairs had become "a symbol for all homemade upholstery. Perhaps it was a particularly attractive example because it seemed to be an emblem of Yankee domestic ingenuity and thrift. Perhaps the transformation of a coarse storage vessel also symbolized the possibilities of self-transformation contained within the activity of making refined furnishings for modest households."[100]

The reuse of packaging expressed the fundamental principles of household bricolage and the stewardship of materials. For most of the century, people paid for packaging: unless old bottles or sacks were brought in for reuse, new ones had to be purchased from the grocer, druggist, or flour miller. Businesses specializing in used bottles developed in most cities during the 1880s; middle-sized cities like St. Louis supported ten or more such concerns, and one New York City dealer was said to keep five million bottles in stock. Bottles and other packaging not brought back to the store had tangible value and could be reused for a number of purposes besides furniture: the hoop (from a barrel) that Mary wanted to roll when she was supposed to be doing her patchwork, the purple wrapping paper that came with sugar and could be used for dye, the brown overalls patched with flour sacks, the rugs hooked on coffee sacks, the paint-covered pickle jar. Many more examples could be cited, from ingenious ideas like table mats made from the cloth that covered oil flasks to commonplace practices like cutting and hemming the cotton bags that flour and salt came in, for use as kitchen towels.[101]

If no other uses came to mind, packages might be employed as wastebaskets. Catharine Beecher recommended covering a jar with prints and varnishing it, "to receive clippings, and any other rubbish" in a room used for sewing in summer, when the stove was cold. A later manual described a wastebasket made from a peach basket lined with fabric and covered. But wastebaskets were actually rare in households where refuse could be burned for fuel or sold to peddlers and where much of the clothing and everyday objects were still handmade by women who might put any scrap to good use. As late as 1882, a manual written for teaching children household economy had to define a wastepaper basket for its readers: "It is for collecting all the torn and useless pieces of paper, and should be emptied every day, care being taken that nothing of value is thus thrown away."[102]

CHAPTER TWO

Any Rags, Any Bones

One May day in the early 1880s, an itinerant peddler named R. S. Munsill penciled a postcard and mailed it from the town of Underhill, Vermont. "Sent in 3 sacks of rags & one small one of rubber from underhill to day," wrote Munsill to his employer, Morillo Noyes of Burlington. "Trade is fair please Send me a couple of sacks & half Doz Octagon Tea pots Send them to Waterbury Vt R S Munsill."[1]

Morillo Noyes, a manufacturer of tinware, hired as many as twenty-two salaried peddlers at a time over the years, providing them with wagons and horses from his stables. Noyes supplied his employees, as well as the independent peddlers he served as a wholesaler, with a wide range of products—pins and needles, bolts of cloth, tin-plated iron dishpans—that they sold from house to house. With the exception of the tinware made in his own shop, he purchased these goods in large quantities from the factories that made them. He wholesaled them also to general stores and dry-goods merchants in towns, usually shipping merchandise by rail and sometimes using his peddlers as salesmen and collection agents.

Noyes also obtained many goods *from* his peddlers, who bought them from households, and sometimes from stores, along their routes. A few of these goods (like eggs and butter) he sold at retail, but most (like the rags and rubber that Munsill sent him) he marketed to factories for use in industrial processes. Among his papers, now at the Harvard Business School's Baker Library, are printed lists for what Noyes called "barter," although he and his peddlers in fact assessed value at prespecified rates, handwritten on the printed forms. He used the lists to set those rates so that his employees would not bargain or exchange goods for other goods except at prices set by him in dollars and cents.

Many of the materials on the barter lists are farm products—grown, caught, or prepared by rural men and women: fruit, flax, mustard seed, woolen yarn, beeswax, butter, eggs, feathers, bristles, hair, horns, bones, and the skins of deer, sheep, calves, bear, mink, raccoon, and even house cats. Noyes sold most of the animal products to manufacturers. Paper mills, for example, cooked horns, hoofs, and scraps of hide to make sizing, the glaze or filler used on porous paper. All kinds of factories bought fat to render for lighting and lubricating.[2]

Also on Noyes's barter lists are many used products of previous manufacturing processes: old brass, lead, silver, gold, and other metals; rubber; glass; and above all, rags of many specified colors, fabrics, and qualities. These, too, he marketed to factories for use as raw materials. Just as he both shipped to and received from his peddlers, Noyes also acted as both customer and supplier to manufacturing concerns. Some factories sold him buttons, thread, silver spoons, and bolts of gingham cloth, while others bought and processed the many materials that his traveling peddlers took in exchange for their wares. The small memorandum books that Noyes carried with him throughout his business career recount his work in distributing his barter to factories—an enterprise apparently much more time-consuming (or more interesting to him) than the particulars of buying manufactured goods for resale. He was constantly searching for new outlets for the barter he took in, hoping to find manufacturing concerns that might pay higher prices, and he was always looking for new sources of sacks and bags to contain the rags and rubber.

Morillo Noyes distributed *manufactured* goods and collected raw materials for *industrial* processes in quantities large enough to supply factories. His peddlers bought small amounts of rags and old rubber from the farm households where they sold a few pins and spools of thread, but they bought huge sacks of reusable materials from the stores Noyes supplied with bolts of cloth and tin buckets. Although they drove horse-drawn wagons, the peddlers regularly lightened their loads by depositing freight at train depots. "I Shipped 2 Sks Rags from here to day Wt 520#," wrote C. C. Reynolds from St. Albans on June 27, 1883, enclosing also a draft for forty dollars and requesting dozens of brooms and pans. "Ship to Adams Dock," he continued. "Shall be there about Saturday." When Noyes bought rags from dry-goods merchants and general storekeepers, he sometimes demanded that they deliver the sacks to the depot themselves. Accumulating two or three sacks at a time from these shipments, he amassed tons of materials in his sheds and warehouses. In June 1859, he estimated he had a hundred tons of mixed rags and fifteen tons of white ones, ten thousand pounds of wool, six thousand pelts, and smaller amounts of hair, horns, and old metal. In April 1877, Noyes's bone shed was about half full; two years previously, he wrote, the thirty-foot storehouse had been "very well filled," with about twenty-seven tons of bones and some paper. Like other wholesale merchants, Noyes worried about keeping goods moving through his storage facilities, in this case to factories instead of to retailers. There was no more money to be made from bones that sat in the shed than from teapots or silver spoons that his peddlers carried around but did not sell.[3]

Noyes was particularly interested in developing new kinds of barter. On a trip to New York City in June 1877, while purchasing carpet tacks, scoops, preserving kettles, horse pails, mop sticks, and the like, he heard about a chemical used for coloring and derived from old leather, produced by a concern in Newark. The next day he went there to see the manufacturer, Josiah F. Dodd. "Had a full talk with E.R. Carhuff—bro in law of Mr. Dodd," Noyes wrote in his memo book. "He buys old Boots & Shoes at 35 cts per 100 lbs. They must be fairly clean. Does not want woolen or mixed cotten & woolen goods . . .

Wants leather, horns and hoofs & horn waste. Can send in bags, boxes, or other pkgs. . . . Mr. Carhuff assured me that what I might get and send up to this fall would be 35 cts per 100 lbs. . . . Why will not old harnesses & the like do, if stripped of the buckles, etc.? Only 4 manufacturers in the U.S. now."[4]

Noyes's extensive memoranda and barter lists provide a peek into the daily workings of the early industrial "recycling" system. Although the word did not yet exist, the process—the return of household wastes to manufacturers for use as raw materials—was inherent to production in some industries, central to the distribution of consumer goods, and an important habit of daily life.* Indeed, the disposition of waste products is an integral, if unrecognized, part of industrialization, linked to the processes of production, distribution, purchase, and use.

Recycling demands a relationship between households and manufacturers that is the opposite of the normal course of marketing: here households supply factories, rather than vice versa. Money changes hands: factories buy waste materials at a price determined by a marketing process, usually through a middleman. When households donate their discards to wartime scrap drives, Boy Scout newspaper collections, hippie recyclers, and—most recently—their own municipalities, the money goes to those institutions and organizations. They perform the first part of the recycling process, amassing large quantities of recyclables and converting trash into a raw material. It becomes an article of commerce, a commodity like cotton or corn, gathered into bales and containers, graded and sorted, and then traded for money. What once was valueless takes on value. In the second stage, the purchasers extract useful elements from a previously manufactured, used, and discarded product, and remanufacture them to create a new product.

---

* According to the Oxford English Dictionary, recycle originated in the oil industry during the 1920s, describing partially refined petroleum sent through the refining cycle again to reduce waste. Its use broadened during the 1960s, designating all kinds of reuse and reclamation, and the word became familiar during the early 1970s, as the burgeoning environmental movement promoted the separate collection of certain kinds of trash to promote their reuse in manufacturing.

As the United States industrialized, the same wholesalers, peddlers, and general storekeepers who introduced new manufactured goods to households acted as the middlemen in the marketing process for waste materials. Peddlers carried bales and sacks of recyclables in their wagons, general stores served as depots, and wholesalers doubled as junk dealers. These people—whose businesses are conventionally thought of as the distribution system for early manufactured goods— also amassed and processed large quantities of recyclables, transformed them into raw materials by sorting, sacking, baling, and grading, and sold them to manufacturing concerns. Trade in the new manufactured goods, then, was not simply a matter of money going one way, goods another. Materials literally cycled between households and factories, creating a *two-way* relationship between manufacturers and consumers.

From the very beginnings of consumer society, the exchange of new for old had made it possible for people short of cash to get consumer goods. In 1790 William Cooper, a storekeeper in Otsego County, New York, granted credit that could be used for cloth, tools, rum, and molasses to farmers who brought in bushels of the hardwood ashes they created by clearing land; he acted as a middleman between the settlers and the potash manufacturers who used the ashes. Soap boilers traded soap for ashes and fats in eighteenth- and early-nineteenth-century American cities. Pewter, brass, copper, and iron craftsmen took old metal for cash or barter.[5] As industries developed during the nineteenth century, they recycled numerous materials. Rags were in constant demand by the burgeoning paper industry; bones, rubber, and old metals also found markets, even in the small quantities individual households produced.

As time went on, peddlers—traveling with huge backpacks, hand-pulled carts, beasts of burden, and horse-drawn wagons—became a major institution of nineteenth-century distribution and took their place at the center of the recycling system. Traveling through territory where cash was scarce, they brought manufactured goods and took away barter. "All poor folks," a peddler from Dusseldorf hawking trinkets, calico, and patent medicines near Natchez, commented to

Frederick Law Olmsted shortly before the Civil War. "Dam poor; got no money; oh no; but I say . . . may be so, you got some egg, some fedder, some cheeken, some rag, . . . or some skin vot you kill. I takes dem dings vot dey have, and ven I gets my load I cums to Natchez back and sells dem, alvays dwo or dree times as much as dey coss me . . . Not bad beesness—no. Oh, dese poor people dey deenk me is von fool ven I buy some dime deir rag vat dey bin vear . . . But dey do n't know nottin' vot it is vorth. . . . Yees, I makes some money, a heap." Even with the cost of transportation from Natchez to the New England paper mills, barter was worth plenty.[6]

Peddlers and the small wholesalers who supplied them thus forged a new relationship between the home and the industrial world, a relationship not fully described by historians who have depicted the peddler as an agent of a developing consumer culture. David Jaffee writes that peddlers did not merely carry goods into remote places but "came to habituate people to the business of acquiring goods." Jackson Lears maintains that the "primal scene of the emerging market culture in the mid nineteenth century was the peddler entering the isolated village or rural community, laden with glittering goods." But attention to recycling heightens and complicates these descriptions. Women and even children transacted with peddlers—and thus with the industrial system they represented—not only as buyers but as sellers. The "primal scene" engaged potential consumers in two-way trade and offered them opportunities to purchase things even without cash. Provident saving of recyclable materials would do, and in this sense recycling may be understood as essential to the development not only of certain industries but of a consumer culture. In households grounded in habits of thrift and reuse, the congruence of conservation and consumption was surely part of the rationale for many women's apparent surrender to the wiles of the trickster peddler. For the historian, it suggests—like the chairs made from barrels and the elaborate dressing tables built on bases of packing boxes—that what looks like thrift may be understood as consumerism.[7]

Barter and Banter: The Peddling Economy

Although certain other goods made in New England—notably books and clocks—were sold by peddlers, the prototypical nineteenth-century peddler sold utensils fashioned from tinplate, thin sheets of iron coated with tin to keep them from rusting. Easily bent and shaped, and simply joined with solder, this material could be formed into a wide variety of items. One Philadelphia tinsmith advertised some forty different kinds of tin boxes, trays, pails, and other implements, a "partial listing."[8]

Tinsmithing and tin peddling originated in Connecticut before the Revolution, and the industry continued to be concentrated there for many decades, while the "Yankee peddlers" who sold its products became an institution throughout the South and West, as well as closer to home. Where roads were bad, peddlers tied up their horses and carried their trunks; where there were no roads, they took their goods down the rivers in boats. Establishing regular routes, they frequently spent the night with customers, and those with storytelling skills or musical instruments ingratiated themselves by entertaining. Contractual arrangements between tinsmiths and peddlers varied: some peddlers were employees, others used the tinsmiths as wholesalers. Some tin peddlers *were* smiths, making tinware during the winter and peddling it during spring and summer. Others worked for manufacturing concerns even larger than Morillo Noyes's that employed twenty, thirty, or even fifty peddlers.[9]

Peddlers and the selling organizations they worked for became essential as outlets for other industrial products. The tin manufacturers typically branched out into other wholesale business, like Morillo Noyes, whose business card listed his inventory in detail and at length: "FOREIGN AND DOMESTIC DRY GOODS, FANCY AND USEFUL ARTICLES," including wire, rivets, friction matches, many kinds of fabric and sewing notions, silver spoons ("warranted a prime article"), combs, "and a large assortment of useful and necessary articles, well adapted to the Peddling Trade." The card went on to explain that Noyes manufactured "a large stock of tin ware and stove pipes for Merchants and others" and that he would take many kinds of barter in exchange. To call Noyes and his colleagues "tin manufacturers," then, is an understatement. They were a hybrid form: both manufacturers and general wholesalers, of their own tin and of other manufactured goods, and the principal middlemen of the system that collected farm goods and recyclables for factories to process.[10]

The biggest tin manufacturers processed large amounts of barter. The Tracy Brothers of Ballston Spa, New York, operated a warehouse with a forty-by-eighty-foot rag room, where eight to ten women sorted rags and sent them down chutes to be baled on floors below. William Holbrook, a peddler who worked for Morillo Noyes, spent much of his time sacking barter to prepare it for shipping back to Noyes's headquarters in Burlington. "Bot and Sacked 1,289 lbs. [of rags] at three and a half delivered at Madrid Depot," he wrote in his diary on April 15, 1854. "71 lbs. copper @ .22 and 29 1/2 lbs. brass @ .15." For one 2,500-mile trip that lasted four and a half months, Noyes sent Holbrook more than two hundred sacks to fill with barter.[11]

At the other end of the scale was the solitary tinsmith and peddler like Michael Beasom, who peddled for several years in rural Pennsylvania with a pack on his back, carrying tinware he had made himself. "Beasom was a very skillful tinsmith. His wares made him famous throughout the valley and brought him many customers," a customer's son recalled. One year Beasom came with a two-wheeled handcart, painted bright red and divided into compartments. The next time, he drove a one-horse wagon. Finally, he arrived in a large wagon drawn by two horses, and announced that he planned to buy a store, marry, and settle down. Bigger vehicles, of course, offered capacity both for carrying more manufactured goods and for collecting more barter.[12]

Beginning with the German Jewish immigration of the 1840s, Jewish peddlers constituted the other type of nineteenth-century peddler. A common occupation among Jews in Europe, peddling involved skills and knowledge easily transferable to the new country. It required little capital, and sometimes none. Jewish peddlers rarely worked for the tin manufacturers. More often, a successful Jewish merchant, frequently a landsman, would loan a greenhorn enough for his first pack; some wealthy Jewish jobbers bankrolled any immigrant who was willing to work. Peddling was a low-status occupation in the Jewish community, in part because itinerant peddlers far from Jewish settlements had difficulty observing religious obligations, especially finding kosher food. Although subject to anti-Semitism, sometimes in the form of especially rigorous enforcement of license laws, Jewish peddlers learned quick lessons in American ways and retail trade. In places far from urban centers, peddling created links among small Jewish communities and helped pioneering sorts discover new places to build those communities. And it offered hard workers a chance to save enough capital to start their own stores. Although not all peddlers were successful enough to establish themselves in more stable businesses, many Jewish businessmen—especially retailers and junk dealers—began by carrying packs around urban neighborhoods or through the countryside.[13]

Both Jewish and Yankee peddlers were stereotyped as tricksters and confidence men. Like other trickster figures, peddlers crossed and recrossed boundaries, in this case the threshold between the farm household or the rural village and the increasingly cosmopolitan outside world. Their visits were diversions from the everyday. "His coming to our house was to me always a pleasant occurrence," recalled the customer who knew Michael Beasom in childhood, "because it broke the monotony of farm life and brought us in touch with the world beyond."[14]

In the South, where they were usually the only Yankees or foreigners that rural people met in a lifetime, peddlers represented Northern commercial interests, said to be draining money out of the region. They were stock characters in antebellum Southern novels, which propagated tales of the tricks they played and the unreliable goods they offered: the clocks that stopped running, the soldered tinware that melted in contact with boiling water, the "tortoiseshell" combs that dissolved, the "nutmegs" that turned out to be made of wood, the cigars made of oak leaves.[15]

Bartering sessions between the stereotyped peddler and his customers involved sharp dealing, seduction, and entertainment—banter, humor, and music. "Some forty to sixty years ago, the tin-peddlers traveled among the innocent Dutch people," according to an 1874 book about the Pennsylvania Dutch, "cheating the farmers and troubling the daughters. They were . . . tricky, smart, and good-looking. They could tell a good yarn, and were very amusing, and the goodly hospitable farmers would take them into their houses and entertain them, and receive a little tin-ware in return." Whether they "troubled" women with sexual advances or seduced them with tinware, peddlers were considered both exciting and dangerous.[16]

In *Farmer Boy,* a novel set in the late 1860s, Laura Ingalls Wilder offers a more balanced picture of the bargaining process. Tin peddler Nick Brown arrives for supper and entertains the farm family with news, songs, and funny stories. The next morning he drives his cart up to the house. "Mother brought the big rag-bags from the attic, and emptied on the porch floor all the rags she had saved during the last year," Wilder writes. "Mr. Brown examined the good, clean rags of wool and linen, while Mother looked at the shining tinware, and they began to trade. For a long time they talked and argued. . . . For every pile of rags that Nick Brown added to the big pile, Mother asked more tinware than he wanted to trade her. They were both having a good time, joking and laughing and trading. At last Mr. Brown said, 'Well, ma'am, I'll trade you the milk-pans and pails, the colander and skimmer, and the three baking-pans, but not the dishpan, and that's my last offer.' " Since Mother has only set the dishpan out "to bargain with," she agrees. "Mother was a good, shrewd trader. She had bested Mr. Brown. But he was satisfied, too, because he had got plenty of good rags for his tinware." Brown heaves the rags onto his cart and says good-bye until the next year, leaving the girls with little pattypans and the boy with a red tin horn.[17]

Rags and rag money were a gendered currency, a precursor to

"pin," "egg," or "butter" money, the small amounts of domestically produced cash that women would control later in the century. During the last decades of the eighteenth century and the first ones of the nineteenth—just before the peddlers began to ply their wares—women had generally set prices for their labor and the things they made, but they had traded in merchandise. Martha Ballard, for example, an herbal healer and midwife who practiced in Maine during this cash-scarce period, was usually paid for her services in cheese, candles, cloth, or other household goods. Historian Laurel Thatcher Ulrich describes a "women's economy" based in these goods and services separate from the emerging economy of men, who were generally paid in cash or with notes redeemable in cash.[18]

Peddlers were *men* who took stuff in trade—tricksters indeed. Usually (like Morillo Noyes's employees and unlike Mr. Brown) they followed the conventions of the women's economy, setting prices in dollars and cents but being willing to trade in goods. The cash and credit they offered represented supplementary income earned by women, set apart from the rest of the household money. Like other kinds of currency, rags and household waste served as a medium of exchange and a store of value. Unlike other kinds, they were a currency women had discretion over and could even make available to children if finances allowed. "I'm dreadfully in debt," complains Amy in *Little Women*, "and it won't be my turn to have the rag-money for a month."[19]

While the peddler dealt with women and sold primarily household goods, the store was the province of men. Some historians have described the peddler and the country store as rivals, citing merchant support for the poorly enforced license laws that nearly every state imposed on itinerant merchants. That support may be exaggerated. The Vermont legislature, for example, received an average of one petition per year requesting regulation of peddlers in the years from 1799 to 1835, "many with ten to twenty-five signatures" but some presumably with fewer—not necessarily evidence of massive shopkeeper opposition to peddlers if we assume that some individuals signed year after year. Much evidence, on the other hand, points to commercial dealings and friendly cooperation between peddlers and merchants.[20]

Many stories of Jews and Yankees alike suggest that the distinction between peddlers and retailers was an artifact of the life cycle: peddling was a life for young single men, shopkeeping one for older married ones. Most peddlers were under thirty years old, and they enjoyed the sympathy of storekeepers who had themselves begun as peddlers. Among Jews, merchants might offer transient peddlers a place to rest and worship on the Sabbath. Wilder's Nick Brown told his stories and sang his songs at Mr. Case's store in town as well as at customers' homes. Stores acted as agents or wholesalers for peddlers, providing them with goods on credit when they ran out of merchandise to sell. Peddling wholesalers like Noyes also dealt with storekeepers directly, further complicating the relationships. On a trip to Middlebury in 1859, for example, Noyes inquired about the reputations of its dry-goods merchants, then visited the stores, offering to sell bedsheet fabrics and, with one merchant, making arrangements to purchase about a thousand pounds of white and brown rags. He also used his employee peddlers as agents for this kind of business. William Holbrook whole-saled Noyes's goods to stores as well as peddling them to individuals, and he purchased (and spent many hours sacking) the barter that merchants had accumulated.[21]

"Ladies, Save Your RAGS"

Of all the materials collected for recycling in nineteenth-century factories, rags stand out as the most important household waste products. An industry depended on them, they were collected in much greater quantity than any other household recyclable, and they were the driving force of the other recycling collection systems. Initially, paper mill owners set up "rag routes," sending teamsters to collect rags gathered by country storekeepers, sometimes making agreements with other mills to divide up the surrounding countryside so they would not compete for rags. Businesses that used paper—newspapers, bookstores, stationers, and printers—also collected rags, with which they could pay the paper mills that supplied them.[22]

Households paid with rags for what they bought from peddlers and stores, who sold the rags to paper mills. Historian Judith McGaw describes "complex three- or four-way transactions" by which, for example, the Crane paper company of Dalton, Massachusetts, purchased rags from peddlers and country storekeepers; Pittsfield merchants bought paper from Crane; and peddlers, country storekeepers, and Crane's workers acquired goods from Pittsfield merchants—all without money changing hands. As one upstate New York printer and publisher wrote to a creditor in 1834, "If any part of the bill we owe you is going to be paid in money (which by the way we did not expect) there is no other way that we think of but for you to sue for it. . . . We have little to do with banks. Our business will not warrant it in a country where 7/8 of the business is done by barter."[23]

Thrifty housewives had considerable incentive for saving and using rags at home. Homemade clothing, valued for the labor it embodied, was often mended and patched many times before it was discarded; sewing scraps and old clothes were salvaged for children's clothing, patchwork quilts, and rag rugs; clothes beyond repair were saved for household chores. But papermaking required rags and scraps, and there were few industrial sources before factory-made clothing. As a result, entrepreneurs investing in paper mills, bookstores, and newspapers tried to make it worthwhile for housewives to give up their rags and scraps. They established systems for collecting rags from households and conveying them to the mills, and they propagandized households in an effort to get them to save rags.

The process for making paper, probably invented in China about two thousand years ago, was known to the Arabs by the eighth century and introduced to Spain by the Moors about three hundred years later. Paper manufacturing was established in England by the fifteenth century and in the American colonies before 1700, though America depended largely on British paper until the Revolution. In all of these places, the fundamental procedure was the same. Cotton and linen rags were washed, shredded, beaten to a pulp, and mixed with water. A screen was dipped into the vat, taking up a thin sheet of fibers that was then pressed, dried, and rolled to remove the remaining water and produce an even surface. Before the nineteenth century, the only part of this process to be mechanized was the preparation of the rags.

"Until well after the middle of the nineteenth century, the history of paper," according to one classic work on the American paper industry, "was, in one sense, a history of rag-gathering." Newspaper advertisements provide evidence of a perpetual rag shortage in the colonies and the new nation and of the papermakers' strategies of propaganda, education, and entreaty, aimed at gathering enough rags to keep new mills running. A Bennington, Vermont, mill invited ladies to visit and witness the papermaking process themselves so that they might be induced to save their rags.[24] A North Carolina mill, newly erected during the Revolution, when trade had been interrupted with both the northern colonies and England, tried a romantic appeal in advertising for rags, scraps, old stockings, and leftover warp from linen looms. "When the young Ladies are assured, that by the sending to the Paper Mill an old Handkerchief, no longer fit to cover their snowy Breasts, there is a Possibility of its returning to them again in the more pleasing form of a Billet Doux from their Lovers, the Proprietors flatter themselves with great Success." In 1807, a New York State mill combined eroticism and class distinctions in verse:

> *The scraps, which you reject, unfit*
> *To clothe the tenant of a hovel,*
> *May shine in sentiment and wit,*
> *And help to make a charming novel.*
> *. . . . .*
> *Each beau in study will engage,*
> *His fancy doubtless will be warmer,*
> *When writing on the milk-white page,*
> *Which once, perhaps, adorn'd his charmer.*[25]

Other advertising provided explicit instructions for saving rags. In essence, the idea was to sort rags from textiles that could be reused at home but not to define them as waste. A Sutton, Massachusetts, mill advertised during the Revolution for rags "be they ever so small." Its suggestion: "A *bag* hung up at one corner of a room would be the means of saving many which would be otherwise lost." An upstate New York mill recommended ways to make this practice more genteel: "The ladies in several of the large towns" of Massachusetts and Connecticut, it noted, "display an elegant work bag, as part of the furniture of their parlors, in which every rag that is used in the paper mill, is carefully preserved." Those too rich to care about the pennies the rags would bring should put children or servants in charge of the ragbag and let them keep the money. That way no rags would be "swept into the street or fire," faithful servants would be rewarded, and children would learn habits of "prudence and enterprise."[26]

Some advertisements offered prizes to those who collected the most rags. Hugh Gaine, publisher of the *New York Gazette and Mercury,* offered to pay "the highest price" for "all sorts of LINEN RAGS" when he and two friends opened a paper mill in 1733, "the existence of which entirely depends on a supply of RAGS which at present are very much wanted." He was still looking for rags three decades later, and offered premiums: ten, eight, and five dollars to the three people who brought him the most rags during 1765, to be paid on New Year's Day of 1766. In March of 1773, the American Philosophical Society offered prizes for the five families and the five individuals that saved or collected the most rags.[27]

The society wished to establish a paper manufactory near Philadelphia as a "means of affording employment to a number of useful persons, besides the advantage of saving large sums of money in America, which are now Annually sent to Europe to purchase paper." Such patriotic entreaties for the support of American manufactures were by far the most common arguments in rag advertisements, beginning long before the Revolution. "When Gentlemen have been at great Expense to serve the Public, as well as their own private Interest," a Boston manufacturer named Fry advertised for rags in 1734, "it is the

Duty of every Person, as much as in them lies, to help forward so useful a Manufactory; *Therefore I intreat all those that are Lovers of their Country, to be very careful of their Linnen Rags, and send them to* Joseph Stocker *in* Spring Lane, *Boston, and they shall receive* ready Money for the same."[28]

As the Revolution approached, the rag shortage became severe owing to increased demand for newspapers and to boycotts of British fabrics and paper. Legislative bodies passed resolutions in support of local paper manufacturing. The second provincial congress in Massachusetts resolved in February 1775 that every family save rags, "in order that a manufacture so useful and advantageous to this country, may be suitably encouraged"; a year later, the Massachusetts General Court resolved that citizens "be very careful in saving even the smallest quantities of Rags proper for making Paper, which will be a further evidence of their disposition to promote the public good." Once the Revolution began, even more paper was needed, to print money and make cartridge cases. Calls for rags took on revolutionary rhetoric. "It is earnestly requested that the fair daughters of Liberty," one mill advertised in 1778, "would not neglect to serve their country by saving . . . all Linen and Cotton-and-Linen Rags." The rewards were immeasurable: "If the ladies should not make a fortune by that piece of economy, they will at least have the satisfaction of knowing that they are doing an essential service to the community."[29]

The patriotic appeal persisted during the first years of the new nation. "The advantages accruing to our community from this addition to its manufacture will be very great," a western Pennsylvania mill advertised in 1796, "and it behooves every well-wisher to the community to contribute his mite toward the supporting it." Before opening his famous Dalton paper mill in 1801, Zenas Crane advertised in the *Pittsfield Sun:*

Americans! Encourage your own Manufactories, and they will Improve. Ladies, save your RAGS. As the Subscribers have it in contemplation to erect a PAPER-MILL in Dalton, the ensuing spring; and the business being very beneficial to the community at large, they flatter themselves that they shall meet with due encouragement. And that every woman, who has the good of her country, and the interest of her own family at heart, will patronize them, by saving her rags, and sending them to their Manufactory, or to the nearest Storekeeper—for which the Subscribers will give a generous price.[30]

American consumption of fabric rose steadily during the decades after 1814, when Francis Cabot Lowell organized the first American textile factory, but rags remained scarce, never sufficient for an expanding paper industry as demand for printed matter escalated. The shortage of American rags prompted international trade. Zenas Crane used foreign rags as early as 1822. Over the next six decades, as mechanization in the paper industry boosted demand, world trade in rags increased steadily. The value of rags imported by American paper mills also increased, by about one-quarter every year between 1837 and 1872. Most other countries regulated the trade, charging export duties or prohibiting rag exports to encourage their own paper industries. In 1850, about 98 million pounds were imported, twenty-five years later about 123 million pounds. About half of these came from the United Kingdom and British possessions. Most of the rest came from Italy, Austria, Turkey, and Germany, with smaller amounts from about twenty other countries.[31]

Good figures for the proportion of foreign to domestic rags are difficult to come by. In 1832, 75 percent of the rags used in the mills of Lee, Massachusetts, came from Europe, but papermakers in Dalton used 78 percent domestic rags that year. One estimate suggests that about 65 percent of the paper produced on the eve of the Civil War was derived from domestic cotton rags, which does not mean the rest was imports, since cheap paper was made of old rope, recycled paper, and other substitutes. What is certain is that, although manufacturers of the finest papers looked to foreign rags, imports by no means replaced household rag collection as demand for all kinds of paper continued to rise.[32]

International imports increased the dependence of the largest and most enterprising local mills on trade with New York City. As the paper industry expanded in the Massachusetts Berkshires, manufacturers could rely neither on local supplies of rags nor on local demand for their mounting production. Crane, who sold no paper in New York in 1819, was sending nearly one-quarter of his output there by 1826. Within three more years, the New York trade took more than 42 percent of Crane's paper. New York merchants dealt in both paper and rags, collecting castoffs from all over the Northeast as well as importing them from Europe. And, like the Massachusetts merchants, they carried both rag and paper transactions on their books, so Berkshire manufacturers could exchange the paper they produced for large quantities of rags—without any cash transactions.

European rags cost more than American ones, but they offered manufacturers higher quality, especially Irish linen. By 1850, few Americans dressed in linen, a fabric still made by hand. Used for the best paper, it had to be imported from less industrialized countries. Unlike silk or wool, cotton and linen both offered high cellulose content, but linen was particularly strong because of its long fibers. Cotton rags could be supplemented with more expensive raw cotton, but premium paper contained at least one-third linen. Linen was in such demand that some rag dealers imported exhumed Egyptian mummies so they could use the wrappings. A former Civil War captain who guided a tour of a Dalton paper mill, described in the *Atlantic Monthly* in 1867, emphasized that paper made wholly of linen rags was thin and strong but so "stiff and crackly" as to be useful for "hardly anything except banknotes and bonds." Showing his visitors a bale of "perfectly clean" prime Italian rags, the article reported, the captain "cut a great gash in the outer covering of the bale, and, drawing out a tattered garment, held it up for inspection. It was the white jacket of a peasant."[33]

Rags into Paper

Rag processing was women's work. "Dusting," the first stage, consisted of opening bales and pounding the rags to remove loose dust and debris. Sorting was the next step, sometimes to separate out wearable clothing. In Britain, sorters had the option to buy garments for themselves and their families or to sell them at secondhand-clothes stores; while this was probably true as well in some American mills, most American sorters were single women and their rural locations made access to secondhand markets more difficult. Sorters separated rags by type of fiber and coarseness of weave (to make beating more efficient, since different fabrics required different beating times) and by color and degree of cleanliness (for use with different bleaching processes and to make different colors and grades of paper).[34]

As the rag trade became better organized, more sorting was done before the bales arrived at the factory, and the few rough classifications gave way to many precise grades, some even trademarked, that varied in different parts of the country. Morillo Noyes listed three categories of rags on his 1854 barter list: clean whites, brown, and mixed. A Chicago rag dealer recalled that, before the Civil War, sorters produced "a good clean No. 1 white rag, a very good second rag, composed of large, clean colors, and soiled whites." He also noted some regional sortings: "a grade of culled 'colors' in New England" and one called "city seconds" in New York and "print rags" in Chicago. By the 1870s, firms that made cheap paper could even buy "muss" and "dustings," two distinct classifications of threads, lint, and rag trimmings from the refuse of higher-quality papermakers, who shipped such wastes back to the rag merchants who had supplied them in the first place. At the other end of the spectrum, makers of fine paper could by midcentury buy new white rags, scraps from ready-made-shirt factories, eliminating the sorting costs that came from processing household wastes.[35]

After the sorters were through, another group of women cut off seams, buttons, hooks, and other fasteners and removed patches and rotted sections of fabric. They cut the remaining fabric into uniform pieces two to four inches square. The *Atlantic* described the scene: "In a room partitioned off but not finished, stood several square frames, not unlike kitchen sinks, with a floor of coarse wire netting. Around the sides of these frames were set a number of scythe blades, with their edges turned inward; and behind each blade stood a young woman, her head swathed in a handkerchief, busily shredding handfuls of rags by drawing them down the keen edge of the scythe, the dust and finer particles falling through the wire floor, and the handful of shreds being thrown upon a heap." Herman Melville's portrait of a paper mill, "The Tartarus of Maids," offered a similar view in a more dismal tone. The rag room, he wrote, was "furnished with no visible thing but rude, mangerlike receptacles running all round its sides; and up to these mangers, like so many mares haltered to the rack, stood rows of girls. Before each was vertically thrust up a long, glittering scythe, immovably fixed at bottom to the manger-edge.... To and fro, across the sharp edge, the girls forever dragged long strips of rags."[36]

Lower-quality papermakers used mechanical rag cutters by 1867, when the *Atlantic* piece was published, but machines could not open seams or remove buttons and decomposed fabric. "Our boss is very particular, he is," explained a worker in the Dalton mill. "Every seam and hem and patch has got to be ripped up, so that the dirt underneath may soak out in the bleach; and every button and string must be cut off, and any piece that's badly stained thrown out. You won't find machines to do all that till they have eyes and fingers as well as knives." As late as 1885, manufacturers of fine paper preferred women to machines.[37]

Rag-room work was hazardous. Undoubtedly many women, especially beginners, cut themselves on the scythes, but there were other perils as well. "The air swam with the fine, poisonous particles," wrote Melville, "which from all sides darted, subtilely, as motes in sunbeams, into the lungs." A boy shows Melville around. " 'This is the rag-room,' coughed the boy. 'You find it rather stifling here,' coughed I, in answer; 'but the girls don't cough.' 'Oh, they are used to it.' " Again the *Atlantic* offered a cheerier but essentially similar description: "The air was heavy with dust; the women's clothes, faces, eyelashes, and even the backs of their hands were white with it." One of the tourists, "coughing and choking, asked a merry-looking damsel, 'Is not this very unhealthy work?' 'Well, I don't know. It pays pretty well,' was the philosophic reply." Because rags might be contaminated with infectious diseases, paper mills provided smallpox vaccinations to workers. Imported rags were embargoed in 1884 in response to a cholera epidemic, to the distress of the paper mills and importers and to the delight of nonimporting rag merchants in the interior, like S. M. Hunt, Chicago's first rag dealer. The embargo "set the craft wild," he wrote in a memoir published in the *Paper Trade Journal* three decades later, detailing prices that doubled and tripled until the restriction was lifted, when they dropped approximately 30 percent in a day.[38]

Leaving the rag room in small pieces, the rags were next transformed into pulp: beaten in a liquid solution, usually containing lime for better disintegration, until they were broken down into separate fibers that would mesh into a smooth sheet. As early as the twelfth century, this part of the process had been performed by animal- and water-powered mechanisms—essentially huge mechanical mortars and pestles, supplanted in the late seventeenth century by a new beater from the Netherlands called the "Hollander." Other stages of papermaking were not mechanized at all until around 1800, when a new method of screening—a continuous mesh belt moving over rollers instead of one screen dipped by hand—was introduced in Europe and soon afterward in the United States. The new process increased demand for rags and intensified the search for other papermaking materials. Mechanization was slow in part because rags were the paper mill's greatest expense, far surpassing labor. One Berkshire manufacturer in 1866 spent four times as much on rags as on labor, for a given amount of paper. As a result, money and effort for experimentation and invention went primarily toward maximizing the yield of the rags collected or finding alternatives to rags altogether.[39]

The cheapest option was to develop methods for bleaching and cleaning rags that were previously unusable. Chlorine was discovered in Europe during the 1770s and first used in America in 1804. Before that, bleaching was accomplished primarily by long exposure to sunlight. Dirty rags could be used for making wrapping paper and other cheap grades; blue rags were sorted out for manufacturing blue writing paper or tobacco wrappers. Other colors were more difficult to use. Chlorine and, after midcentury, new machinery made the cheapest, dirtiest rags of every color usable. Rotating "bleach boilers" used caustic soda, slaked lime, soda ash, and pressure. Despite the captain's claim that the Dalton mill's rags came out of the bales "perfectly clean," they were then soaked for ten hours in "a steam-bath redolent of chlorine," with an odor suggesting "the disinfectants scattered about a hospital." Because lime was cheap, manufacturers had little motivation to skimp on it, and they dumped it all—the grime removed from the rags, the caustic solution used to break down the pulp, and the bleach (lime chloride and sulfuric acid)—into the streams and rivers. Paper mills were therefore notorious polluters.[40]

Rag Substitutes

More mechanization, the ever-increasing demand for paper, and a worldwide rag shortage sent rag prices steadily upward decade after decade and inspired the search for rag substitutes. An effective fiber had to have more than the capacity to be pulped and formed into sheets; it had to be cheaper and more abundant than rags, and it had to produce good paper. Berkshire paper manufacturers received correspondence from people promoting arrowroot pulp, asbestos, wildflowers, and countless unnamed fibers from foreign lands. Investors put money into peat, bamboo, cotton stalks, sugarcane refuse, and the machinery for pulping such new fibers. During the Civil War when cotton was scarce, the Associated Press—concerned about the shortage, like everybody in the newspaper business—promoted corn husks, an idea revived during the 1920s.[41]

The real competitors were wood, straw, and the traditional rope fibers—hemp, jute, and esparto grass. Hemp was first used for paper in the United States in 1837, and the process patented six years later. Like linen, hemp had strong fibers with a high cellulose content, but hemp cost more than the cheapest rags. Because it could not be bleached very white, it was used primarily for manila paper and bags. Much of the hemp in use throughout the nineteenth century came not from new fiber but from old rope, purchased from dealers who made daily rounds in rowboats to buy rope and canvas sails directly from sailing vessels or from scavengers who gathered it on the docks. Straw, the waste product of local grain cultivation, was cheaper than hemp but had a lower cellulose content. It also had other disadvantages: excessive dirt, storage costs, and short fibers that were neither strong nor durable. Mixed with rags, however, it was widely used for newspapers, including the *New York Times,* by midcentury. Esparto, first used in England in 1857, was tried in the United States after the Civil War, but because it had to be imported from Spain and North Africa, it was expensive and did not find the large market in America that it found in Europe. The industry experimented with these fibers and many other substances throughout the nineteenth century; details may be found in every history of papermaking.[42]

Of all the possible rag substitutes, wood was the most promising, thanks to the vast North American forests. The first successful process for grinding wood and converting it to pulp was developed in Germany, where commercial wood pulp paper production began in 1847. Many American innovators worked on wood pulping, but none of them created a process that could compete in both cost and quality with the German method. Eventually, an American group composed of investors from Germany and German immigrants (including the piano manufacturer Theodore Steinway and the lithographer and art dealer Louis Prang) set up a company to produce wood pulp using German machines and methods. It shipped its first load of pulp to the Smith Paper Company in 1867.

Wood pulp paper was even less strong and durable than paper made from straw, but it was cheap. As it became widely available, newsprint prices dropped rapidly, from twenty-five cents a pound in the 1860s to two cents a pound in 1897; most newspapers adopted the new stock in the late 1870s and early 1880s. By 1885, wastepaper was mounting up and becoming a household problem. *Good Housekeeping* recommended sending old magazines to hospitals to keep patients occupied, making scrapbooks and decorating screens, ironing fine paper and covering shelves with it, insulating henhouses, putting paper in baking pans, and dozens of other solutions.[43]

By the end of the century, recycling paper itself was a common alternative to using rags. Once scarce in households, paper had been precious for the words it contained or useful as kindling for the fires that heated every room and cooked every meal. Fine paper for letter writing was expensive. People had used it carefully and fully, as historians know from the many handwritten documents in archives that are literally covered with writing, in all directions and with no margins. Old letters might be burned for privacy or saved for record keeping or as mementos, but they were rarely sold for recycling. Paper was usually not solicited in the many advertisements for rags, although there was a market for it. "Paper brings a cent a pound," Lydia Maria Child told readers of her *American Frugal Housewife* in 1835, "and if you have plenty of room, it is well to save it. 'A penny saved is a penny got.' "[44]

By the 1850s, the market was beginning to develop. Morillo Noyes paid one half cent a pound for newspapers in 1854, listing them under the category of rags, for which he paid considerably more: six cents for clean whites, three or four cents for mixed colors. Five years later, Noyes found an upstate New York firm that would buy "printing papers," probably a higher-quality stock than newsprint. "Want all they can get," he wrote in his memo book. "Will pay cash for them. Take them at Burlington." Later he added, "P.S. Will give 3 cts for them instead of 2³/4 cts, as above proposed! Are very *anxious* to get them." In 1857, forty tons of books and papers accumulated by the Bank of the United States—including ten tons of autograph letters of leading statesmen, politicians, and financiers—were sold in Philadelphia for recycling.[45]

Especially strong demand during the Civil War stimulated the market for used paper even further. "Think of folded newspapers selling for from 8 to 10 cents per pound, that now bring but one half cent,"

S. M. Hunt, the Chicago rag dealer, told his *Paper Trade Journal* readers many decades later. "This was before the days of wood pulp." As the wartime cotton shortage worsened, the price went up. In 1862, *Scientific American* expressed concern about the number of valuable documents being destroyed for papermaking, but over the next few years thousands of tons of books, newspapers, letters, and business papers were sent to the mills. By the 1870s, paper manufacturers were recycling all kinds of wastepaper, including used wrapping paper and the scraps and shavings left over from the manufacture of paper collars.[46]

The rag business endured and prospered despite the growing popularity of substitutes. "When wood pulp was first used I was more than ever convinced that very soon the use of rags for making paper would become obsolete," Hunt reminisced, recalling that he had been similarly alarmed by the introduction of straw paper. "Many years, however, have passed since then, and rags are still used." In 1894, the Holyoke Machine Company offered paper mills a complete line of equipment for processing rags. The Holyoke Rag Cutter—"compact, strong, durable—in short, the best rag cutter in the market"—could be adapted to all kinds of rag and rope stock. The Railroad Duster (so called because it cleaned rags in three to six cylinders arranged in a row, like railroad cars) could process rags, jute, old papers, and paper bags. Another machine was "specially designed for taking out buttons, pieces of metal, and other foreign material." The references to rope, jute, and paper suggest that the machines were intended for manufacturers of cheap stock, the papermakers most likely to seek rag substitutes. For fine paper, rags continued to be the only choice.[47]

Shoddy: Using Wool Rags

Despite all the experimentation in search of new fibers for papermaking, rags made of silk and wool were never developed for the purpose. "Silk won't make paper," the *Atlantic* article's captain declared firmly. "No more will woollen, although a small portion of either may be dusted in, without doing any particular harm. They used, for instance, to mix a small proportion of colored silk, bandanna hand-kerchiefs mostly, with the stuff for bank-note paper. It gave a peculiar complexion, and was a preventive against counterfeits; but, bless my soul! I should like to see any man make paper of all silk, or half or three quarters silk! It's no more than pepper in a soup,—flavor, but not stock." One British costume historian suggests that museum collections have so many more dresses made of silk than of other fabrics because cotton, linen, and wool could all be recycled.[48]

Whereas cotton and linen went into paper, wool was used in rugs and in stuffing for upholstery, mattresses, and saddles. Braided and woven rag rugs were made in factories as well as at home. Factories obtained scraps from the growing ready-made-clothing industry as well as old rags through dealers, who could not sell wool to paper mills. The Census Bureau reported production statistics for American facto-ries making rag rugs—both the rectangular woven variety and the braided oval style—as early as 1869. In that year, the value of rag carpets produced by factories and weavers reporting to the bureau was already over a million dollars.[49]

Above all, woolen rags came to be used in "shoddy"—a term applied to fabric made partially from reprocessed wool fibers, to the fibers themselves, and to the poor quality of goods made from reprocessed wool. The British were the world's leading manufacturers of the fabric. Samuel Jubb, in his *History of the Shoddy-Trade* (1860), gave 1813 as the date for the first industrial use of torn-up woolen rags; and indeed, this date is probably correct, since prices for new wool had climbed by the beginning of the century. In a time of high prices it made sense to economize by combining virgin fibers with the shorter and weaker ones obtained from old rags. And the process was already familiar, an adaptation of craft practices; as one historian of the British rag trade points out, women and men operating spinning wheels "would know very well how to teazle woollen rags and use the old fibres along with the wool." By 1860, the British imported consid-erable amounts of rag wool, especially from Germany and Denmark, two countries that permitted reprocessed wool to leave the country duty-free and whose own wool mills used primarily new fiber.[50]

Woolen fiber refuse that could not be used in textile manufacture found other applications. Seams cut out of fabric in the shoddy mills were left to rot and used as fertilizer, particularly on the hop fields around Kent; Jubb explained that it was principally the lanolin with which the clippings were naturally saturated that gave them their fertilizing property. Like old shoes, wool scraps could also be manufactured into the same chemical Morillo Noyes learned about in Newark. Even the dust created by shoddy manufacture could be used as fertilizer or converted into flock for fancy textured wallpapers. In short, wrote Jubb, "not a single thing belonging to the rag and shoddy system is valueless, or useless; there are no accumulations of mountains of debris to take up room, or disfigure the landscape; all—good, bad, and indifferent—pass on, and are beneficially appropriated."[51]

In the United States, interest in shoddy was the result of the Civil War cotton shortage, the consequent wool boom, and the rising demand for uniforms and blankets for the troops. Morillo Noyes paid two cents a pound for soft woolen rags in 1854, but they were probably shipped to England. S. M. Hunt wrote in his recollection of the Chicago rag business that "woolen rags were considered worthless" before the war. "I remember giving a farmer enough choice soft woolens to fill a car, to take them out of my way. He spread them on his land for manure." When Hunt learned of the English market for woolen rags, he shipped a few bales through Boston. After the war began, he was approached by a Chicago clothing firm making woolen uniforms to see if he would buy their tons of scraps. "I could sell old satinetts [mixed wool and cotton] at a small price to rag wrapping paper mills, but pure all woolens I was afraid of. Still I thought if there was a market for old seamed cloth, that the new certainly ought to be worth a little more. I told the clothing house I did not think them worth much, but decided to chance it and pay 1⅛ cents for what they had on hand. I shipped them to a Boston commission house, and when I got my returns I nearly fainted, as I got 19 cents per pound. How was that for a profit? I was nearly crazy as I went out to see if they had more." Unfortunately for Hunt, the manager of the clothing firm had recently gone to New York and discovered the value of his clippings on his own. During the war, Hunt remembered, "shoddy mills started up everywhere, and prices advanced rapidly." Indeed, the word *shoddy* became identified with wartime profiteers. It was applied particularly to Jewish contractors who furnished clothes and blankets for the Union troops and was frequently used in anti-Semitic cartoons representing these businessmen as unpatriotic for providing cheap materials.[52]

American fabric made from reprocessed wool was generally of even lower quality than European shoddy, which perhaps accounts for the difference in the meaning of the word as an adjective in British usage (where it refers to cheap material made to look superior) and American (where it simply means inferior). American shoddy was rarely used in home sewing; as *Good Housekeeping* counseled in 1885, "Give shoddy the cold shoulder." But demand from the ready-made-clothing industry revived shoddy making during the depression of the 1890s. "The one benefit the American manufacturer gained from the hard times," one manufacturer recalled, "was how to work shoddy. He had to do it to survive." Another, noting that 1895 saw a doubling in shoddy production, complained: "The fact is, that we find our European neighbors teaching us one lesson—namely, how to make a most miserable piece of goods."[53]

World War I spawned another revival. In April 1918, the government commandeered the entire supply of new domestic wool, and civilian production was dependent on rag wool. Three months later, the War Industries Board regulated even the shoddy trade. "The collection, sorting, and handling of about 250,000,000 pounds of woolen material . . . calls for much human labor," the Federal Trade Commission reported after the war. "To those unacquainted with the complicated gradings"—the fourteen pages of classifications the FTC provided in an appendix—"the scope of the woolen-rag trade to-day appears nothing short of amazing." And although the industry was considerably diminished by the time of the Great Depression, nearly seven thousand people were still employed in the recovered-wool-fiber indus-try in 1935.[54]

At the turn of the century, however, shoddy was a component of a less differentiated waste trade. The life story of Moritz Bergstein, a Hungarian Jewish immigrant who did business in the St. Croix River valley of Minnesota, suggests how shoddy manufacture intersected with dealing in junk of all kinds. Starting in business as a peddler based in Stillwater, Bergstein married around 1890 and purchased property near the railroad in the adjacent village of Oak Park. There he built a warehouse for wastepaper, rags, scrap metal, and wood shavings. During the next few years he developed a shoddy mill—a small stone building housing a machine for tearing up rags and a workroom where he employed local women to fabricate mattresses. Soon, however, Bergstein went into partnership with his brother Ignatz, a Minneapolis rag merchant, in a mattress-making firm. Moritz abandoned mattress making in Oak Park, but he continued to live there, buying and sell-ing waste materials, known to all as the Stillwater "junkman." After World War I, although he concentrated on scrap metal, he did some trade in rags and other refuse. When Bergstein died in 1923, he left "about 500 tons of old iron and junk," valued at about three thousand dollars, according to the probate records. "He bought and sold any-thing and everything," the *Stillwater Daily Gazette* reported in his obituary, calling Bergstein "one of the best known men in Stillwater" and noting that he "was always honest and straight forward in his dealings."[55]

Iron Rails and Scavenging Kids

Metal recycling is as old as metalcraft. Coins and jewelry made of gold and silver were melted down in ancient times to make new coins with images of the latest sovereign or to create new ornaments. Other metals, too, were reused in preindustrial societies; mining of new ore was dangerous and expensive, and moral and religious restraints against violating Mother Earth restricted mining through the sixteenth century. But melting and recycling metals were actions of last resort in preindustrial societies. Mending was as much a part of metal-craft as fabrication; goldsmiths, blacksmiths, and tinkers mended and remended broken articles. Metal objects were valuable, frequently sold or given away, rarely simply discarded. Many early court records mention iron cooking pots and even tin containers as material worth bequeathing and taxing. The 1775 inventory of the estate of Jacob Barr, for example, a relatively prosperous Philadelphia laborer with a wife and four daughters, included one saucepan, one skillet, a tea kettle, a spit, and one pewter plate.[56]

When things made of metal were beyond repair or otherwise unwanted, however, they were usually melted down. Craftsmen who worked with iron, copper, and the more easily recycled tin and lead customarily used as much old metal as they could. Lead has a melting point so low it can be heated over a wood fire in a plain iron pot. Plumbers regularly melted and recast it, and they were often paid in old lead. Plumbers and glaziers commonly owned stocks of old lead. But not all lead was recycled. Some was consumed as a constituent in a variety of products, especially paint, glass, pottery, and even women's makeup (lead-based skin whiteners that worked but that could and did sometimes poison their users). Morillo Noyes instructed his peddlers to pay three and a half cents per pound for solid lead in 1854, three cents for a pound of the lead sheets that usually lined tea chests.[57]

Tin melts at an even lower point than lead. Pewter, an alloy of the two, was typically remelted and recast when objects made from it wore out; early pewter ware is scarce and rare because it was so often melted down. This was true on both sides of the Atlantic, but especially in the American colonies. Britain protected the English pewter industry by prohibiting the export of raw tin to the colonies and by taxing unworked pewter but not finished vessels. New metal was therefore almost as expensive in America as imported pewter ware, so American craftsmen often imported British tankards and candlesticks to sell alongside the ones they fabricated from melted old ones. William Willett of Upper Marlboro, Maryland, advertised in 1756 that he would remold old pewter for nine pennies a pound, "or will return one half good new Pewter for any quantity of old, and to be cast in whatever Form the Employer pleases, either flat or soup Dishes, or flat or soup plates." Willett even offered pickup and delivery service to any customer within thirty miles. A New Hampshire pewterer advertised similarly during the Revolution: "cash for old pewter, brass, or copper, or one pound of new pewter for two pounds of old."[58]

Although pewter is now associated with colonial life, it was in common use throughout the nineteenth century. Traditional pewter gave way to its harder and more durable relative, Britannia ware, a more complicated alloy containing the customary tin and lead as well as copper and zinc, two metals often obtained by melting down old brass. Morillo Noyes's peddlers paid fifteen cents a pound for pewter in 1854. At the beginning of the twentieth century, pewter and Britannia ware were still relatively common. In 1908, Sears offered candlesticks, bread trays, sugar-and-cream sets, and other decorative items made from
Britannia ware, some of them plated with silver; four years later, the *Waste Trade Journal* listed two grades of pewter in its price listings for scrap metal.[59]

Many pewterers also worked in brass and copper, combining basic metals in a variety of alloys. Braziers, like pewterers, were dependent on reusing old metal. Though brass was cast in the colonies as early as 1644, the only sources for raw materials were imports from abroad and old copper salvaged from stills, kettles, and ship sheathing. American demand for copper increased as the country began to industrialize, but the United States continued to depend on old metal and imports until the opening of mines near Lake Superior in the mid–nineteenth century. Domestic copper production expanded during the 1860s and 1870s and, after 1880, with mining in Montana and Arizona. Zinc, the other major ingredient in brass, was likewise unavailable domestically until after the Civil War. Morillo Noyes paid fifteen cents per pound for copper, twelve and a half cents for brass in 1854; both had to be "free from iron and dirt."[60]

Noyes did not buy old iron, which was to become a staple of late-nineteenth-century industrial reuse, the central material of the industrial waste trade. Reuse of iron, like other metals, had ancient roots; blacksmiths' probate inventories in preindustrial England all listed old iron. Such scrap usually came from local sources, but old iron was traded internationally as early as the sixteenth century. This recycled iron was probably less significant in the American colonies than in Europe. Iron was produced from American ore in Massachusetts Bay as early as 1645; by 1700, American iron accounted for almost 2 percent of world production and about 10 percent of British production. In order to protect both its sources of raw materials and the market for its finished products, England decreed in 1750 that American iron could enter the mother country free of duty, but the colonists could not establish new ironworks to produce finished products. As a result, much of the colonial blacksmith's work was limited to mending. Smiths in Williamsburg fixed springs, locks, keys, axes, hinges, and chairs. They fabricated small parts—nails, nuts, keys, hooks, door latches and bars—but larger pieces of ornamental wrought iron like gates and balcony rails were imported from England. Americans did make some finished products without the knowledge of British authorities, and one historian estimates that on the eve of the Revolution the American colonies furnished as much as 15 percent of world production of unfinished iron, exporting more than they imported. But most of this was produced by old-fashioned methods, using new ore rather than scrap.[61]

Industrialization escalated the demand for scrap iron dramatically during the nineteenth century, and supply rose even faster. This marked increase in the sheer quantity of processed iron available was due to technological change. New furnaces used coke derived from coal instead of charcoal made from wood. These furnaces cheapened production by "puddling," refining pig iron into wrought iron by melting it, a more efficient method than the blacksmith's ancient practice of hammering hot metal. Puddling allowed the processing of large quantities of scrap. Most of it came not from household implements but from the new railroads, which were also the iron industry's biggest customers. Heavy railroad cars, frequent accidents, and sudden shocks regularly destroyed iron rails. By the Civil War, about half of new rails were rerolled from old ones. In addition to providing a source of scrap, broken rails stimulated the development of cheap steel, which lasted longer than iron. Steelmaking used even more scrap than the production of puddled wrought iron did. By the early twentieth century, the scrap metal business was well organized, with the industry associations and trade journals typical of the time. Dealers did accept large quantities of such small items as stove plate and horseshoes, but for the most part they traded in rails, train car axles, foundry castings, machine shop turnings, pipes, and the like.[62]

While peddlers and street scavengers occasionally collected iron, they had to carry their recyclables on their own backs or those of their horses, so they tended to concentrate on more valuable metals: copper, brass, and especially lead. Nineteenth-century discussions of ragpickers and scavengers offer vivid inventories of the contents of junk piles. "All the odds and ends of a great city," wrote Charles Loring Brace, describing a ragpicker's shanty in *The Dangerous Classes of New York* (1872), "seemed piled up in it—bones, broken dishes, rags, bits of furniture, cinders, old tin, useless lamps, decaying vegetables, ribbons, cloths, legless chairs, and carrion, all mixed together, and heaped up nearly to the ceiling." Iron was not often on such lists, as it was not on the one Noyes provided for his peddlers. Prices for scrap copper were on the order of twenty times those for scrap iron; scrap lead sold for about six hundred times the price of iron.[63]

The market that developed for small amounts of these metals toward the end of the nineteenth century depended on a base of scavenging children. In 1869, the *Atlantic Monthly* portrayed street children of both genders sifting through rubbish for fuel and items of value but did not mention metal other than the occasional silver spoon. In contrast, Jane Addams wrote in 1910 of her distress at gangs of "very little boys" who stole lead pipe from vacant houses. A 1919 publication of the Chicago Juvenile Protective Association described many instances of this practice and quoted juvenile-court authorities on its prevalence; the boys did hundreds of dollars' worth of damage, receiving only enough money for a few days' worth of candy and movies. The children in Betty Smith's *A Tree Grows in Brooklyn,* set in 1912, use jar lids to melt the lead tops of seltzer bottles and the tin foil from gum wrappers and cigarette packages. The junk dealer won't take an unmelted ball of foil "because too many kids put iron washers in the middle to make it weigh heavier"; he refuses to take unmelted seltzer tops "because he'd get into trouble with the soda water people." But the dealer pays a nickel for a melted top, substantial money to the kids.[64]

Recycling Rubber and Bones

Metal recycling extended ancient craft practices, the melting and remelting of already refined metal as a cheaper substitute for newly mined ore. Technological innovation enabled the iron and steel industry to utilize more scrap, but the physical process had long been understood. In contrast, rubber and bone recycling were the results of nineteenth-century experimentation. While rubber was a relatively new material, Americans were thoroughly familiar with objects fabricated from bone. But both materials were subjected to intense scrutiny by researchers aiming to increase the supply of scarce materials through reuse and remanufacture.

European travelers brought back as curiosities the rubber balls and molded bottles made by Native South and Central Americans. But there was little interest in using the material in Europe before 1770, when Joseph Priestley wrote that he had "seen a substance excellently adapted to the purpose of wiping from paper the marks of a black-lead pencil." In 1820, Thomas Hancock of London established England's first rubber factory, carving garters and other small personal articles from rubber imported from the Amazon. Hancock's enterprise eventually merged with one founded by Charles Macintosh, who in 1823 patented the process for waterproofing fabrics that gave his name to the rubberized raincoat. Because the raw material was valuable, both Hancock's and Macintosh's operations reused scraps and trimmings.[65]

In 1839, Charles Goodyear revolutionized the industry by heating rubber with sulfur and white lead. Vulcanization, as the process was named, solved a critical problem: untreated rubber softened in hot weather or even at body temperature and became hard and inflexible in the cold. Rubber-coated-fabric raincoats and rubber shoes ranged from stiff to sticky, depending on the season. Vulcanized rubber was tough and elastic within a wide range of temperatures, though it had one drawback: it could not be reused easily. Despite much experimentation, no successful chemical process for devulcanizing rubber was patented until 1881; the commercially efficient alkali process, which still accounts for half the reclaimed rubber in the United States, was not patented until 1899.

Instead, rubber was reclaimed for decades by mechanical means: women working at home were hired to strip it from cloth, and manufacturers combined ground-up old rubber with new rubber and other materials to make fillers of various kinds. A process for heating ground rubber, still used for about a third of American recycled rubber, was patented in 1858. Most nineteenth-century scrap came from shoes and boots, the most popular rubber consumer goods; as Munsill's postcard to Morillo Noyes indicates, these were recycled through peddlers and junk dealers. Noyes paid seventeen to twenty-five cents per pound for old rubber, more than for any kind of metal. Car springs—large blocks used as shock absorbers in horse-drawn carriages—provided another source; even today *ground spring* is a term used to describe ground-up fabric-free rubber.[66]

The market for bones, like that for used rubber, was stimulated by nineteenth-century research and development. Bones had been utilized without chemical alteration since prehistoric times, sculpted into knife handles, hair ornaments, buttons, and the dice and dominoes that are still called "bones" by devotees. By the nineteenth century, France and Germany both imported bones for making buttons. Marrow bones intended for button making were often processed first to render some of the pale fat valued in soapmaking and industrial lubrication, but excessive boiling softened them. Bones not meant to be made into buttons were processed longer and produced considerably more fat. In addition to fat, bones yielded gelatine—used in food processing, photography, glue making, and the manufacture of sizing for coating cloth, wall coverings, and paper. Bones were also processed to produce ammonia and a tar used in the manufacture of black varnishes.[67]

Fertilizer manufacture provided the most important market for bones. By the early nineteenth century, Americans—once heedless of soil fertility, thanks to scarce labor and plentiful land—had begun to take considerable interest in fertilizing practices. At first, agricultural reformers concentrated on teaching farmers the value of manure, educating them to attend to recycling in nature. During the 1830s and 1840s, agricultural journals began to publicize the successful use of ground bone abroad, and American farmers began to adopt it. Two Long Island mills were grinding and processing bones by 1833, and in 1841 bone mills had been established as well on the outskirts of Albany, Boston, Troy, and Baltimore. Although by the 1850s large fertilizer establishments were operating in New York City, most operated on the outskirts of towns because of their offensive stench.[68]

Advocates compared bones to manure, recommending them as a way of returning waste to the soil from which it had come; one British article reprinted in an American journal in 1838 described bone as part of the "great circle of revolving nature." A few years before the Civil War, another writer extended the concept of "divine economy" to human bone. "The bones left on the field of Waterloo," he wrote, "were gathered up to be put on the corn and grass fields of England to make other bones for the fields of Sebastopol and Balaklava." But despite growing American interest in fertilization, writers complained that large quantities of bones were exported to Britain, robbing American fields of their rightful nutrients.[69]

Bones were especially valuable to the soil for their phosphorus content. To make phosphates available, bones were ground and dissolved in sulfuric acid to produce "superphosphate," a process developed in Britain in the early 1840s. Initially, American farmers ground and acidulated bones themselves, but the machinery was expensive and the acid dangerous. Bone mills therefore expanded their services to include acidulation. As demand grew, bone prices rose, and limited quantities prompted manufacturers to seek other sources of phosphate. They turned to imported guano and eventually to rock phosphate, discovered in South Carolina in 1867. Soil enrichment now derived from resource exploitation rather than from waste recycling.[70]

Another bone market, however, continued to expand: "bone-black," charcoal made from burned bones, was increasingly in demand by the sugar industry as sugar moved out of the luxury category. Beginning about 1830, a sugar solution was run through huge cylindrical filters filled with bone-black, to remove mineral salts and coloring. The filters could be cleaned and reused for three to five years; once the charcoal was completely spent and no longer useful in sugar making, it could be used for its phosphates. Spent bone-black was recommended as fertilizer by a leading agriculturalist as early as 1851. It was especially convenient for farmers producing their own phosphates because the gelatinous matter had been removed in the burning; acidulation of raw bones often produced a viscous mass.[71]

In the middle of the nineteenth century, the bone trade included household waste. Much slaughtering was done on family farms; farmers ground their own bones or took them to the mills. City scavengers and ragpickers collected bones—thrown from windows or salvaged from the remains of dead animals—along with other detritus. Peddlers bought whatever bones households had for sale. Had there been no collection system for other domestic materials, it is unlikely that one would have developed for these small quantities of bone. But scavengers and dealers who built networks for recycling rags and bits of lead found it profitable to collect and distribute the bones that came their way. Still, even before the days of Swift and Armour—the mass meat processors that revolutionized the market by manufacturing their own fertilizer, glue, and bone-black—few of the bones collected for industrial use came from individual households. In the same way railroads dominated the market for old iron, commercial meat processors could provide greater quantities of bones than individual kitchens. Moreover, raw bones yielded more fat and gelatine than cooked ones. Besides slaughterhouse refuse, the bone trade depended on meat condemned by inspectors and on urban pigs slaughtered by official order. For several decades after the Civil War the northern Great Plains was the scene of a substantial commerce in buffalo bones. It was a profitable trade for the railroads, which would otherwise return from the West with empty boxcars, and bone picking offered relief to the impoverished farmers and Indians who cleared the plains of the masses of skeletons left after the extermination of the American bison.[72]

From Barter to Mass Market

Morillo Noyes's business was liquidated in 1883. Whether this was due to bankruptcy or death is not clear from his papers. A letter addressed to Noyes that August sympathizes with his financial misfortune; one sent in October to his assignee Henry Greene begins, "I see by your writing that you are settling the Estate of M Noyes." In the absence of further evidence, it is easy for the historian familiar with Noyes's extensive daily notes on his business to imagine the old man dying of heart failure in the face of an impending bankruptcy. But whatever Morillo Noyes's particular fate, his financial troubles were not entirely of his own making and they enhance his value as a historical example. Although individual peddlers continued to ply their trade into the twentieth century, countless systemic changes—in retailing, in wholesaling, in the tin business, and in the waste trade—account for Noyes's failure during the early 1880s.[73]

New technologies for making steel, plating it with tin, and stamping the tinplate into utensils all contributed to significant changes in the tin industry by 1880. One British tinplate maker commented on the demise of door-to-door tinwear sales. "Now, in all the large cities of the United States may be seen handsomely constructed factories of three and four stories, fitted with steam and hydraulic power," he wrote. They stamped out "pans and wash-bowls of every conceivable size and shape . . . which are as far superior to the old-fashioned, soldered up article as an express train is to the old stage-coach."

Of course, the new machines were too large and too expensive for small shops.[74]

Rural customers increasingly bought the new, mechanically produced tinware and other consumer goods by mail order, already a significant retailing method by the time Noyes died. Agricultural journals carried advertisements for companies doing business by mail at the end of the Civil War, and during the 1870s, "mail-order papers" (magazines depending chiefly or entirely on mail-order advertising) attained combined circulations "into the untold millions," according to the most definitive history of Sears. Montgomery Ward was established in 1872, and by 1884 its 240-page catalog listed nearly ten thousand items. City department stores likewise offered mail order; Macy's did as of 1874, putting out a 127-page catalog seven years later. Farm families who could scrape together the cash might well opt for the nearly immediate gratification of COD at the nearest railroad station, ordering from a catalog that offered hundreds or thousands of things, rather than waiting months for the peddler to show up with his dozens of items. Their incentive to accumulate rags and other barter dwindled accordingly.[75]

Nor could they necessarily use barter at the general store. Country storekeepers were being advised not to take barter—"it is often a great snare," according to an 1882 *Grocers' Hand-Book*—although most country stores did take eggs and butter (which they could resell to other customers) well into the twentieth century. Instead, the local stores offered credit, which became the keystone of the retailer-customer relationship and the most powerful weapon that local merchants had against the mail-order firms.[76]

Local businesses could offer credit because they got it themselves from new kinds of wholesalers. Wholesale trade had undergone its own revolution, leaving Morillo Noyes and his kind in the dust. By 1870, "full-line, full-service wholesalers" dominated regional distribution. These firms were huge, and they were growing. They sent traveling salesmen into the hinterlands to take orders, and they extended credit to general stores at country crossroads and to dry-goods stores and grocers on small-town Main Streets. Like the mail-order houses, these new wholesalers offered the entire panoply of manufactured goods. Some, like Marshall Field's extensive wholesaling division, were connected to big-city department stores and sold goods manufactured by their own factories.[77]

Such wholesalers did not deal in rags and bones. And unlike Morillo Noyes and the other tin manufacturers who kept stables of horses and supplied their peddlers with wagons, the new wholesalers shipped exclusively by rail and express companies. They did a one-way business, from manufacturer to consumer, and they paid for one-way shipping. Noyes paid his peddlers whether their wagons contained old rags or new teakettles; he had to maintain horses and wagons as they took goods in both directions, and he had a financial stake in keeping them full.

Like Noyes's wholesaling operation, the junk end of his business was increasingly controlled by large, specialized urban firms; by the end of the century, the waste trade would have its own magazine, and soon after that an organization. Dealers who traded in industrial waste dominated the organization process, as industrial waste now dominated the waste trade itself. The methods of mass production yielded not only massive quantities of consumer goods, but massive quantities of byproducts; large firms either developed new products that would utilize the waste—Armour even sold sandpaper that used glue made from hooves and bones—or looked for brokers who would market it. With the meat industry dominated by Armour and Swift, bones collected from house to house hardly mattered. As the remnants and scraps generated by the ready-made-clothing industry eclipsed those emanating from home production, specialized rag dealers could make a living handling exclusively new rags, or cotton, or remnants.[78]

The demise of the system that recycled waste materials from middle-class and even well-to-do households is an integral part of the history of American mass production and mass distribution at the end of the nineteenth century. Recycling—the marketing and remanufacture of household discards—was once inherent to production in certain industries, to the distribution of manufactured consumer goods, and to the habits of daily life. The very distribution system that brought manufactured goods to consumers took recyclable materials back to factories. By the end of the century, this two-way trade had given way to specialized wholesalers and waste dealers—a separate, highly organized trade built on a foundation of industrial waste, supplemented by scraps collected from scavenging children and the poorest of the poor. For the first time in human history, disposal became separated from production, consumption, and use.

CHAPTER THREE

Trash and Reuse
Transformed

Like the housekeeping books and magazines of the nineteenth century, the early-twentieth-century literature of household advice discussed habits of thrift and provided instructions for reuse. In chapters called "Saving by Taking Care of Things" and "Saving by the Homemade," a 1919 book called *Save and Have* reprinted many of the old ideas—keeping cake fresh by storing it with an apple and "turning" worn sheets by tearing them down the middle and sewing up the good sides. Like the old books, *Save and Have* recommended collecting grease until there was enough to make soap, though the recipe called for canned lye instead of the kind made at home from wood ashes. For removing painted lettering from cotton flour sacks in order to reuse them as dish towels, the book recommended either Gold Dust, a popular commercial cleaning product, or kerosene. A section entitled "Care of Containers" asked a modern question: not what to do with the food the reader preserved but what to do with the packaging she had saved. "White Dundee [marmalade] jars, jars from the 'Purveyor to the King,' screw-top candy jars, wide mouthed pickle and olive bottles, jelly glasses, seal-tight coffee and marshmallow tins, Educator [cracker] tins with nicely hinged tops, and even Sterno cans," the book suggested, could be used for canned, preserved, or dried fruits and vegetables.[1]

Advice writers still provided directions for mending china, darning, making over clothing, and removing spots, but now they warned that mending and reuse were associated with poverty and shame. "In handing down outgrown garments be merciful enough to change them so the new possessor shall not be taunted for wearing [them]," advised *Harper's Household Handbook,* published in 1913. "This is not hard; a new yoke, belt, and cuffs will transfigure a garment, to say nothing of the magic wrought by dyeing." Emily Holt's *The Complete Housekeeper,* originally published in 1903 and revised during World War I, warned that silk could not be successfully mended without "the usual appearance of premeditated poverty." Holt's book offered only a few paragraphs on clothing repairs; she admitted that "patching, darning, and mending deserve a separate chapter" but did not provide one. Housekeeping manuals had changed since Julia McNair Wright's *Complete Home,* which was full of ideas for rich women forced to economize by the depression of the 1870s and for upper-middle-class women who wanted to refurbish their silk dresses. Mending and reuse were still common practices and appropriate topics for housekeeping manuals, but their class associations had shifted.[2]

The old habits of bricolage and the stewardship of objects and materials had new meanings in a modern consumer society, according to the home economists whose concerns for hygiene and rationality by this time dominated household advice literature. Indeed, these concepts were used to argue against reuse. "The best use of all waste is a puzzling economic problem, but the housewife should consider no method economical which threatens health," warned S. Maria Elliott in *Household Hygiene* (1907), part of a series that bore the imprimatur of the leading lights of home economics. "Although we are taught that everything in the world has some use, . . . at some time each article loses its usefulness," she insisted. Accumulated objects threatened health. Stored bottles, iron, and furniture "interfere with the amount and purity of the air, they collect dust, they invite and encourage insect pests and they gradually deteriorate by the action of air, light and moisture." A 1913 home economics text for high school students assumed that its readers understood the basics of darning and patching, recommending that sheets be turned and linens "watched carefully and darned or patched in time." It assigned students to come up with "ethical reasons" for taking care of their clothing but warned them not to "spend too much time on old garments." Good judgment was imperative: "It does not always pay to cleanse and make over old clothes. Decide first whether the material is good enough to make the work worth while."[3]

Old-fashioned reuse and recycling did not disappear overnight. During the first few decades of the twentieth century, most people still threw away relatively little. But increasingly, new ways coexisted with old. Though most food, hardware, and cleaning products were still sold out of barrels and vats, companies like Heinz and Procter & Gamble were mass-producing and selling packaged products by 1900, and even workers' families began to buy some food and cleaning supplies in boxes and bottles during the next decades. Many Americans still heated with wood or coal stoves, burning their refuse as fuel, but some lived in apartment houses or installed central heating in their homes. As the consumer culture developed, rich people bought new products before poor people did, while people in the city adopted new ways before their country cousins. Then as now, young people took to modern methods and technologies, while their parents and grandparents lived as they always had.

Various options emerged for disposing of unwanted stuff, and middle-class people learned to toss things in the trash, attracted by the convenience and repelled by the association of reuse and recycling with a new class of impoverished scavengers. As cities and towns took responsibility for collecting and disposing of household refuse, it became easier to throw things out. Ever-increasing amounts of trash demanded complex systems and huge investments in sophisticated equipment, promoting the notion among citizens that refuse was a technical concern, the province of experts who would take care of whatever problems trash presented.

But even though reuse and recycling took a back seat to disposal, they did not disappear. Consumers who persisted in believing that their discards had value could donate them to a new kind of charity organization: Goodwill Industries and the Salvation Army would repair and resell them, providing both work for the poor and a store where even paupers could go shopping. Moreover, long traditions of reuse and active markets for salvaged materials shaped the development of municipal refuse systems; in most places, individual households were required to separate their trash so that their towns and cities could profit from the trade in recyclable materials. While many housewives abandoned their stewardship of materials for more convenient lifestyles, they did so in the belief that others would attend to reuse. The transition to a consumer culture was a complicated and gradual process, characterized by abundant continuities.

Street Scavenging

In 1900, when sixteen-year-old Rocco Corresca arrived penniless in Brooklyn from Naples, he lived with a padrone, or gang boss, named Bartolo, who supplied him with a bag and hook and sent him out on the street to pick up rags and other refuse. "On the streets where the fine houses are the people are very careless and put out good things," Rocco recalled two years later. His boss repaired some items to sell on the street, "but mostly we brought rags and bones." Rocco washed the rags in the backyard and dried them "on lines under the ceiling in our room. The bones we kept under the beds till Bartolo could find a man to buy them."[4]

Rocco and Bartolo and the work they did reveal the turn-of-the-century market for rags, bits of metal, and bones picked from the garbage. Such scraps were no longer sold by respectable people, as they had been in the days of bartering peddlers and patriotic rag collections. Instead, they were gathered by the urban poor and traded for cash through a series of middlemen: young children sold to older ones, small junk dealers to larger ones. Itinerant rag-and-bone men worked the streets of urban neighborhoods, offering cash to poor housewives and selling their wagons full of refuse to dealers with storage facilities. "The greater part of the rags now gathered are picked up in the large cities in poor neighborhoods and on the dumps by people who have to gather them from any source to get bread and butter," observed a Chicago rag dealer in 1912.[5]

Scavengers, especially the poorest immigrant women and children, combed city dumps according to well-understood rules. In Chicago's "back of the yards" community, for example, four city dumps were worked over by commercial pickers who paid the city as much as fifteen dollars a week for the privilege; in their wake came the neighborhood women and children. Historian David Nasaw suggests that scavenging and junking were nearly universal for working-class children, "as common a pastime as playing baseball or jumping rope." In *Junk Dealing and Juvenile Delinquency* (1919), the Chicago Juvenile Protective Association argued that, by providing a market, dealers encouraged children to steal and that boys went junking mainly to get spending money, not to help their families. Even relatively well-off children shared this motive. One home economics textbook cited the Chicago book, warning that, although there was "an educational value" in permitting children to collect and sell household waste, "there is danger here for an occasional boy."[6]

Street scavenging was not new at the turn of the century. Like the urban poor everywhere, indigent people in American cities had foraged for food, fuel, and marketable scraps as long as there had been cities. American urban life offered no chroniclers of street business to compare with Charles Dickens or Henry Mayhew, author of the four-volume *London Labour and the London Poor* (1861–62), whose descriptions of the London waste trade contain much to fascinate and revolt the modern reader. Nor were American ragpickers romanticized like those in Paris, who inspired a generation of painters and writers. Still, they show up in the shadows and the margins of all kinds of urban literature. George Foster, in *New York by Gas-Light* (1850), a sensationalist portrait of brothels, saloons, and other institutions of the slums, counts "the ragpicker with hook and bag" among a list of poor people "engaged earnestly at his or her regular occupation." Charles

Loring Brace lists ragpickers among *The Dangerous Classes of New York* (1872). At the end of the century, Frank Norris's San Francisco novel *McTeague* (1899) mentions them as part of the scenery, denizens of a border landscape: "Across the flats, at the fringe of the town, were the dump heaps, the figures of a few Chinese ragpickers moving over them."[7]

Midcentury writers occasionally described scavenging in more positive terms. When a paper mill was first established in Marin County in 1859, the *California State Register* commented that one benefit was "the clearing out of the cast-off garments which for years have carpeted the streets of San Francisco and every city and town in the state." A description of New York street children published ten years later in the *Atlantic Monthly* insisted that only the "hard-hearted builder—or unbuilder, rather" would harass the crowds of boys and girls who collected fuel at building demolition sites.[8]

Such sympathetic accounts of scavenging rested on the fact that the United States, with a labor shortage as opposed to Europe's oversupply, had not yet fostered a *class* of scavengers, ragpicker families with children who would probably become ragpickers themselves. For much of the nineteenth century, selling trash picked from the streets was more a matter of gender and age—the province of women and their children. Among poor New Yorkers in the 1830s, scavenging was the task of children too young for wage work or street selling. Waterfront junk dealers bought materials children collected from the docks: rags, scraps of canvas sails, loose cotton that had separated from bales, and fragments of metal, glass, and rope. Like the later authors of *Junk Dealing and Juvenile Delinquency*, early-nineteenth-century policemen and reformers connected scavenging with juvenile crime; New York passed an ordinance prohibiting junk dealers from trading with minors as early as 1817. But scavengers and the authorities might disagree about the fine line between finding things and stealing them, between what belonged to nobody and what belonged to somebody, though it was on the street, apparently free for the taking. Children's scavenging was often supervised by their mothers, who used the food and fuel their kids brought home and who regarded scavenging as one of the many ways to avoid spending scarce cash. Women, too, were frequently charged with stealing basic household goods that they might regard as found rather than stolen.[9]

By the last decades of the century, whole families scavenged for a living. The biggest cities had neighborhoods full of streets with names like Bottle Alley or Ragpicker's Row. "Anybody can tell you where the ragpickers live," declared one guidebook to the disreputable parts of New York. "There is no mistaking the place." In the courtyards of those neighborhoods, "one beholds a sight that cannot be imagined. Rags to the right of him, rags to the left of him, on all sides nothing but rags. Lines in the yard draped with them, balconies festooned with them, fire-escapes decorated with them, windows hung with them; in short, every available object dressed in rags." In *The Children of the Poor* (1898), Jacob Riis described New York boys "who ought to have been at school, picking bones and sorting rags." They were typically the children of Italian immigrant men who earned their livings "scow trimming"—leveling trash and sorting out resellable materials on the scows, the square-ended vessels that brought refuse out to sea—under the supervision of padrones who competed for city contracts. Their families lived in shacks built on the trash dumps or near the docks where the scows were loaded.[10]

Street scavenging may have kept poor families from succumbing to hunger and disease but it played less and less of a role in the waste trade. Like other industries, the salvage business was increasingly dominated by big companies, whose growth was stimulated by the sheer quantities of trash and scrap sloughed off by a developing consumer economy. Scavengers did not sell metal, rags, and bones directly to such firms, but to itinerant ragmen and small-time junk dealers who amassed larger quantities. The local and regional firms that bought from those dealers grew with American industry at the end of the nineteenth century, and the waste trade, like other industries, became more organized. The *Waste Trade Journal* began weekly publication in 1905, offering readers the latest quotations of prices in foreign and domestic scrap markets; advertisements for baling machines, iron shears, and burlap bags; solicitations from companies wanting to buy No. 1 Heavy

Melting Steel, colored rags, or scrap rubber; and news of the trade. The magazine's annual directory, eight hundred pages long by 1917, claimed to list the name, address, and credit rating for every waste importer, exporter, and consumer in the United States, Canada, and Europe. The magazine also published *Waste Trade Specifications,* a book that standardized the kinds and sizes of iron and steel scrap companies would accept; for wiping rags alone, it listed sixteen categories used by the majority of purchasers, and for scrap rubber it printed specifications adopted by the National Association of Waste Material Dealers.[11]

Founded in 1913 with a membership of twenty, this association numbered 450 by 1928. The organization offered its members credit information on businesses that bought or sold waste materials; an Adjustment and Collection Bureau helped members collect on accounts and settle controversies. In 1928, a Salvage and Surplus Material Division was established to bring large corporations into the association, assisting them in disposing of waste materials and of surplus or obsolete equipment. Western Electric, Du Pont, and General Electric were among the first to join. In addition to this general waste-trade organization, several specialized groups had formed by 1917, such as the American Cotton Waste Exchange, the National Scrap Iron and Steel Association, and the Rubber Reclaimers' Division. Such groups concerned themselves with massive quantities of industrial waste. Not surprisingly, the organized waste trade had little use for the quantities salvaged by the immigrant picker on the dumps or even the ragman who worked the streets of working-class neighborhoods.[12]

Municipal Trash Collection

The rationalization and institutionalization of the waste trade had a parallel in the development of municipal responsibility for refuse. The movement for sanitary improvements was typical of Progressive-era initiatives, and its participants were allied with those who took on other urban problems. Emphasizing cleanliness and rationality, sanitary reformers of the late nineteenth century demanded that cities undertake the eradication of public nuisances—the stinking piles of refuse that laissez-faire attitudes had failed to prevent. Of course, their demands were not new. For centuries, urban officials and reformers concerned about public health had attempted to clean garbage and rubbish from the streets of American cities. Throwing kitchen refuse out the door or window for animals to eat was as customary in villages and towns as it was in the countryside. Growing cities passed ordinances against tossing trash in the streets. Colonial Boston and New Amsterdam both outlawed the practice, hiring cartmen to pick up after lawbreakers. People dumped behind their houses as well as in the streets, especially broken crockery and glass, which animals would not eat. "These people had really messy back yards," an archaeologist excavating on the Mall in Washington, D.C., remarked in 1994 upon finding an assortment of bottles and dishes and a tiny porcelain doll missing an arm. "What they couldn't burn in the cookstove, they threw out back."13

Cities passed antidumping ordinances throughout the nineteenth century, but many people ignored them. Pittsburgh scofflaws prompted sarcasm in the local paper. "Some folks have no objection to the smell of warm tripe and garbage, to wading through puddles of green stagnant water, or to skating over dabs of ordure," wrote the *Gazette* in 1800. "What if a few citizens should be carried off by fluxes and fevers? It would be of no consequence, as our population is rapidly increasing." Periodic epidemics renewed the pressure on lawmakers to pass new regulations, to establish boards of health, or to make special appropriations for cleaning up particularly bad messes. The Washington, D.C., city council set aside fifteen hundred dollars during the summer of 1837, for example, intended (in the words of the resolution) for "purging the streets and alleys of the accumulated filth and garbage." But generally, debris simply piled up, the household garbage exacerbated by the excrement of horses and scavenger animals. In 1869, a writer in the *Sentinel* called Milwaukee's streets "perfect avenues of swill"; twenty-three years later, another writer described the "heaps of dirt" and "uninviting pools of filth" still to be found all over the city.14

As cities grew, these issues became cause for alarm. Piles of trash and garbage were perceived both as menaces to public health and as public eyesores, and the piles were becoming larger and more prevalent as urban areas increased in population and density. By the middle of the nineteenth century, both private citizens and public officials had become concerned about public health and convinced that sanitation obligations appropriately left to individuals in rural areas would have to be assumed by municipal governments in the cities and towns. "Urban America discovered the 'garbage problem' " in the late 1880s and early 1890s, writes historian Martin Melosi; addressing it was the second step in the sanitary reformers' campaign, after clean water and good sewers. Some believed that city workers should run trucks, dumps, and incinerators; others thought municipalities should contract for services or regulate private ventures. Despite these variations, American cities of all sizes embraced the Progressive position that government—and not free enterprise—was responsible for public health and should exercise that responsibility in the matter of refuse.[15]

The process was slow, however. Landowners and merchants resented what they saw as an infringement of their rights. They paid for contractors to remove their own refuse and were content to leave trash collection and street cleaning in private hands. Therefore they were unwilling to accept higher property taxes to pay for sanitary improvements. In deference to these moneyed groups, municipal authorities were initially reluctant to respond to sanitary reformers' suggestions. And the rich were not the only problem. Milwaukee aldermen reluctant to commit money to municipal refuse collection in the mid-1870s eventually agreed on a limited plan: individual wards could decide whether or not to contract for trash removal. But it soon became apparent that contractors could not fill their wagons, because citizens had relationships with the immigrant "swill children" who had been collecting their garbage and selling it for fertilizer. Residents "refused to give their refuse to the city collector," historian Judith Walzer Leavitt explains, "maintaining that they could 'give it to whom they please.' " This experiment in municipal collection failed within three years. Cleveland officials also lamented their "entirely inadequate" system, which depended on private collection. "No city of this size can be considered well taken care of which makes no public provision for this purpose," the officials declared.[16]

As late as 1891, the *Sanitary News,* a "weekly journal of sanitary science" published in Chicago, declared that "there is probably not a city of any size in the United States where the disposal of wastes is satisfactory or conducted in such a manner as to meet the demands of cleanliness and hygiene." Some towns had chosen the wrong methods; others hired contractors who did not perform. Most cities suffered from a lack of funds. In Cleveland, Milwaukee, and elsewhere, piles of garbage continued to accumulate, bringing with them rats, maggots, odors, and according to the prevailing theory, disease-causing "miasmas."[17]

In many cities, the call for sanitary reform became part of a more general attack on the inadequacies of municipal government. Reformers interested in municipal sanitation benefited from their connections with this broader urban reform movement, and they were in close contact with activists working on other issues of public health, personal cleanliness, and civic beauty, as well as with those attempting to deliver city governments from political bosses and their machines. In one historian's words, "sanitation was equated not only with the struggle against disease per se, but also with civilization, morality, and an orderly way of life." In 1906, the Civic Improvement League of Saint Louis, for example, had, in addition to a Public Sanitation Committee, groups concerned with playgrounds, smoke abatement, pure milk, free baths, billboards, trees and horticulture, and the restoration of Forest Park, site of the St. Louis World's Fair two years earlier.[18]

Sanitary reformers in government were stimulated and supported by women activists who flew the banner of "municipal housekeeping." All over the country, women's clubs took on sanitation issues in their communities, while other women formed organizations especially for the purpose. New York's Ladies' Health Protective Association, founded in 1884, was the first women's organization established specifically to clean up a city environment. It was followed by the Sanitary Protective League and the Street Cleaning Aid Society in Manhattan and by similar groups in other cities, such as Brooklyn's Women's Health Protective Association, Chicago's Municipal Order League, and the Neighborhood Union, organized among Atlanta's African American women in 1907. These organizations lobbied municipal officials and provided volunteer inspectors to make sure that municipal contractors did the jobs they were paid for.[19]

Women working in settlement houses also did trash-related work. Chicago's Hull House Women's Club laboriously documented more than a thousand violations of trash ordinances, forcing the transfer of three city inspectors out of the ward where the settlement house was located. Eventually the mayor appointed Jane Addams herself as the ward trash inspector. Hull House activists set up six alley incinerators and exposed the dealings of the contractor who was supposed to remove dead animals from the streets. "The one factory in town which could utilize old tin cans was a window weight factory," wrote Addams, "and we deluged that with ten times as many tin cans as it could use—much less would pay for."[20]

Helen Campbell, a writer and activist whose interests and projects spanned both urban poverty work and home economics, articulated the basic concepts of municipal housekeeping, which crossed and recrossed the border between the public and the private. In *Household Economics* (1897), she wrote about house sanitation and city sanitation as if there were no distinction between the two. After four paragraphs about dusting furniture and dealing with "insidious, all-pervading, unconquerable fluff," Campbell turned to a discussion of municipal solid waste—urban refuse—especially the merits of the St. Paul, Minnesota, trash system, offering no rhetorical transition other than the claim that the two were "in closest connection." It was housewife citizens' special mission to understand "what we must demand from the city government." Discussing a western university town filthy from coal smoke emanating from both homes and factories, Campbell again asserted "the interdependence of home and state" and the connection between cleanliness and ethics. "To keep the world clean—this is one great task for women. Not in the old sense of scrubbing away at her own steps, back or front . . . but in the newer one of making the whole world so clean that her own bit of it must perforce be the same." Many other writers concurred with the idea that women's sphere went beyond the borders of their households. A 1913 high school home economics textbook echoed Campbell: "It is not enough in these days for the housekeeper to see that her own premises are tidy. She must work in some way with the whole community to see that good methods are used in street sweeping, disposal of sewage, food waste, and all the rubbish that is thrown in the scrap heap."[21]

Despite the best efforts of the municipal housekeepers and their male allies, sanitary progress in most cities usually advanced two steps forward and one step back, or even vice versa. Colonel William F. Morse, a leading sanitary engineer, described the political procedure. "After the initial remonstrance and petition for a new order of things," Morse told a meeting of the American Public Health Association in 1898, "comes the somewhat tardy action of the Mayor calling attention to the subject; the tour of inspection by the council committee; a deluge of pamphlets, circulars and letters; the keen hunt of furnace builders and ambitious companies anxious to save the city all worry and trouble—for a consideration; the contradictory bids, tenders and offers that no man can reconcile; then the rejection of everything—and the repetition of these proceedings until everybody is sick and tired of the whole business." The contract, Morse continued, went eventually to "the longest winded, and the city gets a bad bargain that makes endless trouble in the future." Still, by the turn of the century, some form of municipal service had been established in most cities.[22]

And it was high time, because refuse was being generated on a scale never before known. The population was expanding rapidly thanks to massive immigration, and the middle classes were producing more trash per capita. Storage space was increasingly at a premium. Middle-class urbanites now lived in apartments and in suburban bungalows whose designers sacrificed space because of the expenses of plumbing and heating. Attics had been replaced by crawl spaces; basements were designed more for utility functions than for storage. Middle-class Americans now threw things out because they had nowhere to put them.[23]

Household refuse was neither the only source of the trash problem nor the biggest. Municipal solid waste—now sometimes called the waste stream—contained more ashes (produced by coal and wood heat, much of it from factories and public buildings) and more street sweepings (primarily composed of horse manure) than household trash. In 1906, New York employed 750 workers to load Manhattan's residential trash onto trucks, and 1,200 men to sweep its streets. The city collected less than half a million tons of household trash and over two million of ashes and street sweepings; ratios were comparable for the smaller cities of Buffalo and Washington, D.C. The Public Sanitation Committee of Saint Louis's Civic Improvement League similarly reported that household trash constituted one-quarter to one-third of municipal waste in the average American city.[24]

The street-cleaning problem alone was staggering. At the turn of the century, American cities were home to over three million horses. The ones that lived in Milwaukee produced 133 tons of manure every day, those in Brooklyn about 200. John McGaw Woodbury, New York's commissioner of street cleaning, explained in 1903 that street sweepings were often worthless as fertilizer because of the large proportion of newspaper—litter tossed on the streets—mixed with the manure. Stable manure was better, and there was plenty of that, too. When Woodbury tried to offer New York's Parks Department the manure produced by his own department's 800-plus horses, the parks superintendent accepted only on condition of free delivery: why pay when private stables regularly delivered manure to the parks for free? Manure was only part of the horse situation: the streets were littered with dead animals. In 1912—when horses were already sharing the streets with motor vehicles—Chicago removed ten thousand horse carcasses from public thoroughfares.[25]

As cars replaced horses and gas heat supplanted coal and wood, street sweepings and ashes declined but household refuse proliferated. Paradoxically, the more trash collection there was, the more trash was generated, especially organic garbage. Between 1903 and 1907, Pittsburgh's garbage increased 43 percent, Cincinnati's 31 percent, and Newark's 28 percent. One Milwaukee health commissioner was credited with increasing the quantity of garbage collected by 62 percent over four years, while the population grew by 12 percent. Some of these increases can be attributed to population growth, some to growth in consumption, and some to more efficient collection—sanitary engineers all agreed that reliable service encouraged households to throw away more. But the expansion came also from a new willingness to define leftover food, and used and surplus materials, as unwanted.[26]

Methods of Disposal

Even as municipal systems developed and experience accumulated, there was no consensus among professionals as to the best method of disposal. Much of the writing about municipal solid waste focused on New York City; because it was so large, New York handled more trash than any other city, and it faced problems years and even decades earlier than smaller municipalities. The flamboyant George E. Waring, Jr., a Civil War colonel who became commissioner of street cleaning under an anti-Tammany administration in 1895 and 1896, generated considerable publicity. Waring put sanitation workers in white uniforms, dubbed them "White Wings," and paraded them down Broadway; he published books and articles that told the rest of the country about his schemes for making money from selling refuse. His successor, John McGaw Woodbury, revived many of Waring's proposals almost a decade later and adopted his strategy of publishing descriptions of his work in general magazines.[27]

In fact, New York was too large and densely populated to be typical. Conditions varied from city to city, and so did each city's choices, especially for dealing with organic material. Southern cities had less ash and more organic waste than their northern counterparts because of shorter winters and longer growing seasons: Savannah collected twenty tons of watermelon rind daily during July and August 1915, constituting 20 percent by weight of the city's refuse. In Philadelphia, some garbage was collected for municipal hog feeding, some sold to farmers, and some buried. Brooklyn collected garbage from dwellings twice a week in winter and three times a week in summer, and from hotels daily all year; the garbage was dumped in the ocean. Cincinnati hired a private contractor who removed "all animal matters" three times a week from dwellings and hotels and daily from slaughter-houses, and it prohibited householders from mixing ashes and other refuse with vegetable garbage, which was used as hog feed. Many small towns collected garbage for hog feeding and dumped their rubbish on land, but sheer quantity rendered these methods impractical for most cities.[28]

Every year from 1889 to 1903, the American Public Health Association simply recommended that every city choose the method "best for itself." By 1911, Milwaukee had tried every known disposal method. Garbage had been fed to swine and used as fertilizer; trash had been dumped into Lake Michigan and used to fill land. The city had under-taken two expensive methods that required major investments in equipment—incineration and reduction, the latter a means of extract-ing grease, fertilizer, and other useful products. Some cities used one method in the summer, when there was more vegetable matter, and another in the winter, when more trash was burned and stoves pro-duced more ashes. Some cities employed several different methods at the same time. Enterprising municipalities tried all manner of experi-ments. Many of these, such as making fuel briquettes out of chemically treated street sweepings, were attempts to apply traditional ideas about reuse and recycling to massive amounts of municipal solid waste.[29]

Nevertheless, by far the greatest amount of American trash was dumped: the conglomeration of ashes, food scraps, street sweepings, and old mattresses was carted away to sites at the edges of towns. The bigger the city, the bigger the challenge: larger accumulations had to be hauled farther to reach the outskirts. Dumps bred rats, cockroaches, and wildfires. One Savannah dump was on fire continuously for several years. "In its simplicity and carelessness," a Florida physician told the 1912 meeting of the American Public Health Association, "the dump probably dates back to the discarding of the first apple core in the Gar-den of Eden, and its subsequent train of evils is ample testimony of the Eternal Wrath elicited by that act."[30]

Many of the largest cities also deposited at least some of their waste, especially organic garbage, into water. New Orleans and St. Louis used the Mississippi River, Chicago used Lake Michigan, New York used the Atlantic Ocean. Everywhere it was done, water dumping created controversy. Depositing refuse into rivers generated complaints and lawsuits from towns downstream. Ocean dumping fouled the beaches; Colonel Waring called it "barbarous." New York unloaded its scows beyond Sandy Hook, eliciting complaints from residents of Long Island and New Jersey. Milwaukee residents described dumping into Lake Michigan as "positively unbearable," protesting that it created a health hazard, endangered city water, and imperiled the fish supply. Still, the practice had its defenders. The 1898–99 report of the New Orleans Board of Health admitted that dumping a large city's trash into "a running stream from which is also derived the water supply" might seem "crude," "imperfect," and "unsanitary." But the Mississippi was "an immense body of water in constant motion," the report insisted—half a mile wide, fifty to a hundred feet deep, and with an average current of three miles per hour. "We may readily imagine how little influence a boat-load or two of garbage per day can have."[31]

Some dumping, into water and onto such "wastelands" as ravines and wetlands, was intended to create new land. The fill method was used as early as the 1880s, in cities as diverse in climate and geography as Seattle, New Orleans, Chicago, Oakland, and Davenport, Iowa. In 1893, the New York Dock Department built a crib around part of Rikers Island and tried to fill it with refuse, but the mixture of garbage, ashes, and rubbish fermented in the summer heat. Colonel Morse, the sanitary engineer, called it "a clear case of jumping from the frying-pan into the fire." The plan required even more hauling than ocean dumping, and the new earth was "of such character as to produce disease." Ten years later, New York's Commissioner Woodbury wrote that the experiment had "created so great a nuisance as to become a public scandal." Under his administration, the area was filled in with ashes, graded and leveled by convict labor. "Thus $630,000 worth of real estate has been added to the holdings of the City of New York," Woodbury wrote, "at an expense in construction equal to or less than the cost of throwing this material into the sea."[32]

The ashes for this project were collected by requiring households to maintain special barrels for them. Indeed, many of the municipal plans depended on householders to sort their trash, a practice now called "source separation" and then called "primary separation." Because he wanted to raise revenues by selling refuse, Colonel Waring instituted separation in New York in 1896, producing enormous publicity for the idea. Three receptacles were required: one for organic garbage, one for ash, and one for rubbish. Ashes had value as landfill and in concrete building blocks and pavement materials, but only if they were kept separate from other wastes, especially organic garbage. Cards were left at every house in the city, informing residents about the new program. The mayor assigned forty policemen to Waring's department, to call on every household and place of business to explain the system and, in some cases, to enforce it with fines and even arrests of citizens who were unwilling to go to the trouble. But the police were withdrawn in early 1898, and Waring lost his job when Tammany regained the mayor's office.

The home economist and urban reformer Helen Campbell, writing in the *American Kitchen Magazine* in 1900, urged housewives to agitate for primary separation. Wealthy urbanites were "apt to forget the existence of ashes," she wrote. "I thought everybody now had steam-heat and gas-ranges," Campbell imagined her readers remarking when they saw editorials debating the disposal of urban ashes, even if they themselves had "but lately come into this great deliverance." In the spirit of municipal housekeeping, Campbell advised the housekeeper instead "to look beyond the difficulties with her own range and furnace, and plan for the general good." Criticizing the politicians of New York, she called upon them to revive Colonel Waring's original plan for separating trash.[33]

By 1902, when John McGaw Woodbury took over from the Tammany commissioner, primary separation "had been practically undone." Woodbury restored it, and New York sold clean ash that year to a construction company that used it to make fireproof floors for department stores. The city produced over three million cubic yards of ash, worth twelve to nineteen cents a yard.[34]

Outside New York, most urban Americans separated their refuse during the first decades of municipal trash collection. In 1902, about four-fifths of cities with more than twenty-five thousand people required some separation of organic garbage or ashes so that these wastes could be recycled or reused; surveys conducted in various cities over the next two decades put the figure between 59 and 83 percent. Fewer than half of these, however, required the complete separation of all wastes that Waring had advocated. In the many places where primary separation worked, it did so—as it does now—with the help of civic groups, which popularized the attempts of sanitary reformers to run municipal trash collection and delivery at reasonable cost.[35]

Some smaller cities required separation because they made revenues by selling organic garbage for animal feed or even by establishing city-run piggeries and selling the pork. Hogs needed fresh garbage, so the practice demanded frequent collection; one government pamphlet advised daily collection in the South and three times a week in northern cities during the summer. In 1902, about a quarter of American cities fed garbage to livestock. Most were in New England, with its short, cool summers. Over the next decade or so, hog feeding became a disposal option for even more cities, including Grand Rapids, St. Paul, Omaha, Denver, and Los Angeles. Other towns adopted the method during World War I, when pork prices rose and the United States Food Administration encouraged garbage feeding as a conservation practice. After the war, the Department of Agriculture recommended it to farmers as "a practical means of pork production."[36]

Supporters of hog feeding expressed concern about careful separation, advocating strict ordinances to keep foreign matter—glass, oyster shells, or dishwater full of lye-based soap—out of the garbage. Public relations efforts suggested that citizens would sort more carefully if they understood the intent of the ordinances; the press might help by covering an autopsy report showing that hogs had died from eating foreign matter. "Surely very few phonograph needles would find their way into the garbage pail," one government pamphlet asserted, "if the householders could imagine the tortures suffered by the unfortunate animals."[37]

Not all separation for resource recovery was performed by individual households. In large cities, contractors hired immigrant workers to pick through trash and separate out marketable bones, rags, and bottles. Many cities followed the practice, although New York, with its abundant cheap labor and its media-savvy sanitary reformers, received the most publicity for its trash pickers. Colonel Waring explained to the readers of the *North American Review* in 1895 that the city received funds from fifteen padrones. Each supervised a gang that distributed the trash from an individual dump evenly over the scows.

Before 1878, the city had paid for this labor, but eventually authorities realized that contractors were making additional money by selling recovered materials. For the next four years, the city neither charged nor demanded payment, but after 1882, it required contractors to pay for the picking privileges and did not pay them for trimming the scows. "For some years," Waring wrote, "the city has received annually over $50,000 worth of labor and about $90,000 in cash as the value of the privilege of gleaning from its dust chutes." The amount received varied with the tonnage: in 1902, contractors paid $107,000 for the picking privilege in Manhattan and the Bronx, the next year, $71,000.[38]

Market prices for waste products determined how much was picked out. Some padrones concentrated on particular materials. At one New York dump in 1904, workers retrieved only rags, metals, and paper, a total of 31 percent of the whole; at another, they also collected wood, glass, bagging, carpets, shoes, hats, rope, and string, for a total of 49 percent of the trash. Twenty-five percent of the trash headed for a Boston incinerator was picked out and marketed. Writers describing the picking process liked to highlight the occasional treasures. "Often articles of value, silverware and jewelry are found," claimed one; another told of three pearl studs picked out in his presence. But "often" was an exaggeration; most of the materials recovered were the familiar ones of nineteenth-century recycling. A complete list provided to Waring by Carlo De Marco, the contractor in 1895, included fat and bones in addition to the rags, shoes, and other materials named above. If there were items of silver or pearls, De Marco did not report them.[39]

Officials tried to mechanize the picking process. An article in the *Metal Worker* described "a strange machine" installed at New York's Jackson Street wharf in 1884, designed to "turn street sweepings and house refuse of all sorts into money." Characterized as "a vast rag and bone picker of many Italian-power, working by steam," this gigantic sifter did not actually do the picking but separated materials by oscillation, screening, and floating or sinking them in water. Actual Italian immigrants stood on either side to pick out the usable bones and scraps of metal, glass, rag, and paper. Two decades later, incinerators in many cities—including Boston, Buffalo, Rochester, Washington, Columbus, Pittsburgh, and New York—were fed by conveyor belts. Pickers stood on either side, removing and sorting marketable materials. At least in New York, the pickers specialized: "One man picks only manila papers, another only spruce pulp papers, another the shoes, another the cloths and rags, another the bottles and cans and all metal substances. These are turned through the hoppers into large presses, where the papers are baled [and] the shoes are sorted and sold, many of them doing duty, after repair, on the feet of our poorer citizens." Mattresses and bedding, however, were burned as a sanitary precaution.[40]

Many sanitation authorities believed that the most hygienic and efficient way to deal with trash was to burn it, an approach that had the added advantage of eliminating the need to separate rubbish, ashes, and organic garbage. British and other European cities had experimented successfully with this method beginning in the 1870s; by the middle of the next decade, reports on these efforts were attracting considerable attention in America. A "garbage destructor" located in Leeds, for example, was described in a paper delivered to the American Society of Civil Engineers in 1887. The apparatus could destroy sixty tons of refuse in twenty-four hours. The chimney was originally eighty feet high, but after complaints about the smell, it was replaced by a 150-foot chimney equipped with a special flue designed "to mitigate the discharge of dust over the neighborhood." The paper recommended incineration for New York, comparing the method favorably with ocean dumping, although some contended that New York's refuse did not contain enough fuel to burn efficiently because poor New Yorkers extracted all reusable coal by washing their ashes.[41]

A model incinerator, fueled with crude petroleum and "always open for inspection," served as both infrastructure and exhibit for

Chicago's great Columbian Exposition. It was designed to dispose of "all garbage, sewage sludge, waste, refuse, manure and the bodies of animals," according to a paper that Colonel Morse delivered at the World's Public Health Congress, held in Chicago as part of the 1893 fair. He claimed that the incinerator discharged no odor, fumes, or smoke, thanks to a system of two fires: one burned the refuse and the second destroyed the smoke and gas. Morse was a longtime advocate of incineration, with financial interests in various companies that produced the equipment; at one time he served as New York manager for the company that manufactured the Columbian Exposition furnace, the Engle Sanitary Garbage Cremator.[42]

Speaking before the Woman's Health Protective Association early in 1893, Colonel Morse supported an expansion of New York's incineration program, then limited to a furnace for medical waste at the foot of East Sixteenth Street. If medical waste could be burned, why not other things? If Chicago and Philadelphia could spend money for such sanitary protection, why not New York? Morse claimed that the cost of constructing and operating incinerators was no more than that of building and operating the scows that towed refuse twenty miles out to sea. The ashes, he went on, could be sold as fertilizer.

In reporting on Morse's talk, the New York Times described the use of incinerators in a number of other American cities. "Considerable opposition" had initially greeted an incinerator erected in Lowell, Massachusetts, after a cholera scare, the paper reported, "but as day after day went by with no unpleasant odors or damaging effects to the health of the neighborhood, all opposition was withdrawn." Boston, too, was experimenting with various incinerators. "In the Southern cities," the Times went on, "garbage-crematories have become quite numerous, and are still increasing, owing to the greater danger of epidemic diseases in warm climates."[43]

Even in cities where initial attempts at incineration failed, its advantages—complete destruction of material that did not have to be separated—were enough to keep enterprising citizens investing in incinerators. In Milwaukee, the Phoenix Garbage Cremator Company won the city contract for both collection and disposal of all the city's garbage in 1887. But citizens complained as soon as the company began operations. One wrote to the *Sentinel* about "a killing odor . . . with strength enough to paralyze the man in the moon." Worse, the incinerator simply did not consume the loads, despite a series of improvements. By 1889, the city was experimenting with a reduction plant, a technology designed to produce marketable byproducts by means of pressure and chemicals. When that failed, Milwaukee went back to incineration; a successful furnace finally opened in 1910 and served until 1955.[44]

Incinerator ash was promoted as fertilizer, and at least one model furnace generated the power to operate and light the incineration plant. But to those who held on to the traditional view that organic garbage and other refuse had value, burning it was profligate. One American discussion noted that a proposed incinerator in London had been opposed as a "sinful extravagance" by neighborhood residents. "It is a wicked and wilful waste of money to burn indiscriminately all the valuable refuse from this the largest parish in London," wrote a representative of the ward's Conservative Association in an argument that went beyond its not-in-my-backyard roots.[45]

Bruno Terne, a chemist for a company that processed garbage chemically, presented a similar argument at Philadelphia's Franklin Institute in 1893. Natural fertilizers were being wasted, he insisted, while "we have fleets engaged in transporting phosphoretic and nitrogenous materials from continent to continent." Then he turned to urban garbage. "Unquestionably cremation is the most complete system for destroying all organic substances," he admitted, "and doubtless to the extreme sanitarian the only method that should be adopted. But what about the economical results?" He had analyzed incinerator ashes and found them valueless; moreover, operating the furnace required labor and fuel. A more rational process, Terne went on, would separate out the grease and dry the remaining material. Both products could be sold, making "a large figure in the housekeeping of a community," the chemist declared. "In this century of progress, with our knowledge of chemistry, and with the most complete machinery at our disposal, it seems to me like a lapse into barbarism to destroy this most valuable material simply for the purpose of getting rid of it, while at the same time we are eager to obtain these very same materials for our fields by purchase from other sources."[46]

Various machines and chemicals were devised to accomplish the two operations of extracting grease and removing water from urban garbage, which together were labeled the "reduction process." The rendering of grease was achieved by heat or with chemical solvents; the residue was called "tankage" and was composed of animal and vegetable matter that could be dried and (at least theoretically) sold as fertilizer. Although reduction originated in Europe, it enjoyed more success in the United States, where Colonel Waring publicized it and advocated it for New York. Only large cities that could afford the expensive equipment adopted the method. But as debates developed over municipal expenditures for new disposal technologies, reduction found proponents who believed that the sale of its products would offset its costs.[47]

Reduction offered a modern, urban, high-tech version of traditional agricultural reuse practices. The engineers and chemists who pioneered its development were part of a larger movement; their experiments aimed at creating marketable products from municipal waste were linked to those of industrial chemists searching for profitable ways to use byproducts and waste materials generated in a variety of industries. Chicago's big meatpackers led the way. As their operations expanded, they produced massive amounts of bones, horns, hair, fat, blood, and other substances, waste products to individual butchers but potential raw materials in such large quantities. Swift and Armour chemists created new versions of the soaps and fertilizers that had traditionally been made from the byproducts of butchering, but they also developed wholly new pharmaceuticals, explosives, lubricating oils, and cosmetics. With mass production in other industries, the massive quantities of waste products stimulated international research on their utilization. Interest in the reduction process for dealing with municipal solid waste benefited from these developments.[48]

One drawback of reduction was its pungent odor. When Milwaukee's new reduction plant opened in the middle of town, three hundred businessmen formed the West Side Anti-Stench Committee, protesting that the smell "robbed us of our sleep and our meals." Many of them vomited during a tour of the plant. After they threatened to sue the city, the plant was shut down and the garbage dumped into Lake Michigan. But lakeside residents complained about that, leading one newspaper to comment that "Like Banquo's ghost the garbage problem refuses to be downed." The reduction plant reopened temporarily when the weather got cooler, and a new company was formed to erect a plant outside the city. Still, after an extended political process, Milwaukee built another incinerator. Cities interested in reduction plants eventually learned to put them where only the poor would complain.[49]

By the end of 1914, forty-five reduction plants had been established in the United States, but only twenty-two were in use. Technical improvements had led to more complete extraction and less odor, but returns from the sale of materials were still debatable. "The costs of operating these utilization plants have not been made public, but the fact is that the returns from the sales do not meet the expenses," H. de B. Parsons wrote in his 1906 survey, *Disposal of Municipal Refuse*. "The question for settlement, before studying the reduction processes, is whether the material saved is worth saving after it is separated out by the process."[50]

Incineration, on the other hand, flourished. By 1914, approximately three hundred incinerating plants were operating in the United States and Canada. Of the eighty-eight built between 1908 and 1914, about half were in the South, where the hot climate made rapid disposal necessary. Incineration did not begin to decline until the late 1930s, when it began to compete with the sanitary landfill, a British innovation that was to become the preferred American disposal method for much of the rest of the twentieth century. Like the incinerator, the landfill did not require primary separation. Cities dropped regulations requiring citizens to separate their trash; as home garbage disposers gained popularity after World War II, such laws virtually disappeared. Although separation seemed novel when environmentalists reintroduced it during the 1970s, its long history encompassed not only traditions of household reuse but widespread municipal regulations. Primary separation was promoted at the turn of the century out of concern for the environmental health of the city rather than of the planet, and the materials to be sorted were usually ashes and garbage rather than plastic bottles and aluminum cans, but our contemporary sense that we are being asked to do something new in separating our trash is simply incorrect.[51]

Trash and Class

As public issues, poverty and trash were intertwined at the turn of the twentieth century: refuse was cast as an issue of poverty, not one of abundance as it is now. Progressive-era reformers and social workers took an interest in young scavengers as part of a more general concern for the poor, their quest for solutions to the "social question," as they called the tangle of problems created by industrialization. Lewis Hine photographed scavengers combing through the dumps; residents of Hull House wrote about these children; public and private organizations were formed to "protect" them; and Progressive debates about the responsibilities of government shaped the regulations that governed the dumps themselves. Reuse, recycling, and bricolage became identified as activities of the poor during a time of rising consumption and of new possibilities for convenient disposal.

The language of urban sanitary reform paid particular attention to the refuse of the immigrant poor. Before municipalities took responsibility for trash, more piled up in densely populated poor neighborhoods than in rich ones. The poor could afford neither storage space nor the private contractors that wealthier people hired to haul away their rubbish. Surveys and studies demonstrated that more affluent "Americans" actually produced more garbage, ashes, and rubbish than poor Italian, Polish, Bohemian, German, and Russian immigrants. But the rhetoric of refuse was intermingled with rhetoric about human refuse. In 1901, that language was inscribed in bronze on the pedestal of the Statue of Liberty, in Emma Lazarus's "The New Colossus": "Give me your tired, your poor . . . The wretched refuse of your teeming shore."[52]

A passage from Parsons's *Disposal of Municipal Refuse* is a more detailed case in point. Parsons explicitly stated that cities with the most poor people collected the least combustible refuse and waste from public markets. The poor ate rotting food left by the vendors, and burned what trash they could find for heat. In contrast, the most household refuse per capita came from neighborhoods with "large stores, private dwellings of the better class, and corresponding hotels and restaurants." Ashes from private houses in these districts contained especially high percentages of unburned coal.

Parsons's next paragraph took on a moral tone. "The tenement-house districts," he wrote, "especially those inhabited by the least educated of the Russians, the Poles, the Scandinavians, the Italians, and the Jewish element, often produce a careless and filthy class of waste, and one containing a low percentage of combustible materials, such as wood, paper, packing-boxes, etc., which is saved and retained for fuel." In truth, the trash of the tenements may have seemed especially filthy, since a low proportion of combustibles meant a high proportion of fish heads and melon rinds. But it was hardly careless. Unlike those who did not even bother to instruct their servants to sift ashes for usable coal, the poor took great care indeed to sort through the trash for heating fuel and other useful materials.

To counter the bad habits of the poor, Parsons advocated "rigid" inspection, "to educate and force the people to deposit their wastes in proper receptacles." Unfortunately, this was difficult to do, because of the ignorance of the poor, their crowded tenement apartments, and "their lack of order and reverence for things cleanly." Although Parsons referred to an "educational process," his approach, emphasizing force and inspection, seems closer to a policing process. And his description of ignorant people who lack "order and reverence for things cleanly" clearly conveys his belief that a "careless and filthy class of waste" was produced by a careless and filthy class of people.[53]

John McGaw Woodbury was more sympathetic. Two classes of people, "equally criminal," made trouble for the street-cleaning department by refusing to separate their trash, he wrote in *Scribner's* in 1903. "The criminally careless rich and their thoughtless servants" were as bad as the ignorant poor. "The worst mixed material thrown into the street may come from the teeming East Side," Woodbury wrote, "but the most scandalously mixed material that is hauled to the dumps comes from Fifth Avenue, and is handled by the private ash-cart man."[54]

In contrast to wealthy neighborhoods, where people did not throw garbage in the street, the department removed eighteen tons of garbage a day—tossed out windows and off fire escapes—from the streets of the Lower East Side. Woodbury explained that the neighborhood was inhabited by recent immigrants, "mostly from the Jewish pale of Russia. They bring with them their ideas of sanitation and habits of life, which are still those of the eleventh century." He described the garbage-filled cobble gutters of Russian and Polish villages and despaired of teaching sanitary habits to people accustomed to such arrangements. "Bringing to us a civilization whose sanitary aspect is of this character, it is exceedingly difficult to educate these newly arrived people to our idea of separation of garbage from ashes, and the placing [of] it in proper receptacles." Woodbury wasn't above a little self-aggrandizement: he made a point of telling his readers that his department posted the law requiring separation in a number of languages besides English, though this was standard procedure for municipal notices in New York and other large cities.[55]

Even the most sympathetic journalists and reformers had trouble getting beyond their prejudices. In his best-known book, *How the Other Half Lives* (1890), Jacob Riis set the tone for much urban-reform literature. "Look into any of these houses," he wrote about Bottle Alley in the Italian slums of Manhattan, "everywhere the same piles of rags, of malodorous bones and musty paper." He pointed to shacks erected in the yards of the tenements, "sheds built of all sorts of old boards and used as drying racks for the Italian tenants' 'stock.' " Riis cited a health inspector who visited a tenement in July. A sick baby lay among six people sorting rags and washing them on a hot stove; the temperature was 115 degrees. But what Riis called "piles of rubbish," his subjects perceived as salvageable materials and potential income; what he saw as child abuse, they understood as the lamentable but unavoidable consequences of their way of making a living.[56]

As in so many other areas, reformers' concerns blinded them to the needs and culture of the poor. This was especially so with respect to scavenging for food. Reformers believed that "children were without shame or taste when it came to picking through the discarded, spoiled, overripe, and ruined meat and produce," writes David Nasaw about Chicago's Juvenile Protective Association and the Massachusetts Child Labor Committee. "The reformers were a lot more squeamish than the children and their families could afford to be." Another historian, David Ward, points out how far the blindness extended. Throughout the nineteenth and early twentieth centuries, first in steel engravings and then in the photographs of the slums that illustrated sensationalist urban literature in midcentury and reform tracts at its end, perhaps the most common visual trope for poverty and squalor was a scene dominated by clotheslines, on which hung recently washed laundry. There were no clotheslines in middle-class neighborhoods, where people sent their laundry to washerwomen and commercial laundries.[57]

With preconceptions so powerful that images of cleanliness appeared to them as portraits of squalor, it is no wonder that sanitation reformers cared little about destroying people's livelihoods in the process of instituting municipal trash collection. In Milwaukee, municipal collection hurt poor immigrants who made their livings in the swill trade. Indignant about their loss of income, they downplayed the benefits to public health. In the words of a working-class newspaper, "it is a great pity if [our] stomachs must suffer to save the noses of the rich."[58]

Colonel Waring was blunt about his desire to take the city's lucrative waste trade away from poor people. "In the interest of the public safety, as well as of the public finances," he wrote, the city should "take up and carry on for itself, or through contractors whom it could control completely, the whole business of removing from houses whatever householders may wish to get rid of and will not take the trouble to carry for sale to a dealer." In his scheme, no rubbish would appear on the street ripe for entrepreneurial picking; householders who had paper, bottles, rags, cans, and other recyclable trash to dispose of would display a card in their windows that called for the special carts of the Paper and Rubbish Service. Writing about New York but philosophizing for all cities, Waring advocated "the suppression, or the public employment, of the push-cart man, who jangles his string of bells through the streets." No household should be allowed to sell its unwanted rags and other wastes to ragmen who appeared at the door. People should be required to take unwanted things to licensed second-hand dealers, "whose transactions can be held under proper supervision," and licenses should be granted only "to men who had fixed places of business." With a single stroke, the streets would be free of refuse and of the poor who made their livings spearing debris and pushing it on carts or hauling it around in bags on their backs.[59]

Salvage and Salvation

The very existence of municipal trash collection encouraged middle-class people to throw things out. Some were undoubtedly reassured that progressive municipalities' salvage activities would recover usable material and believed that little would actually be wasted. But some things were just too good to throw out, especially to people who were still making their own quilts and rugs. Household habits of reuse and belief in the potential value of discards persisted despite the demise of nineteenth-century recycling.

During the decades that municipal collection was being established, new kinds of charities began to accept donated materials. The personal relationships fostered by giving away leftovers at the door yielded to the institutionalization of a new sort of benevolence: giving things to organizations like the Salvation Army. Such organizations offered impoverished people jobs, spiritual salvation, and a chance to be consumers, and they provided the urban middle classes a virtuous outlet for unwanted things. Donating to charity, the better-off could free themselves from the social discomforts that might arise from identification or intercourse with beggars, scavengers, and ragmen or from worrying (as did people in small towns) about the embarrassment of seeing their things again. The organizations also fostered new ways of thinking about the sorting process: people could now avoid the trouble of repair and remaking and get rid of unwanted things without having to define them as worthless.

Led by the Salvation Army, Goodwill Industries, and the Society of St. Vincent de Paul, the new charities both benefited from and contributed to the identification of recycling and reuse with poverty. Because they derived most of their income from the customary materials of recycled trash—rags, paper, and metals—they were central players in the salvage markets, selling large quantities of those materials and competing with the biggest firms in the waste trade. The new salvage organizations fit contemporary ideas about assisting the poor, which regarded charity as degrading and emphasized self-help. They provided job opportunities: instead of receiving alms, poor people were set to work, repairing used clothes and furniture or sorting paper and rags, but now for an organization instead of a padrone. Moreover, they had to pay for the things that were donated to the charities, in turn (according to the theory) freeing themselves from humiliation. They could buy cheap clothing, an 1899 Salvation Army pamphlet explained, "at a nominal figure sufficient to cover working expenses, and at the same time avoiding the appearance of charity."[60]

There were precedents for this approach to poverty and charity. In Brooklyn during the depression of the 1890s, groups of middle-class women formed "Fragment Societies," collecting old clothing, paying indigent women to repair it, and selling it at low prices to the poor. But the Fragment Societies retained the relationships of old-fashioned almsgiving. "One comfortable home takes in its keeping one poor home," explained the prominent minister Lyman Abbott, "and the waste for the one, eked out by occasional gifts, or perhaps by some supplies from the Association for Relieving the Condition of the Poor, preserves the other home from want." Writing for a prosperous audience, Abbott denounced the modern tendency toward organized charity. He admitted that it was hard for busy people to find time for the poor, but he emphasized the importance of personal contact and recommended that his readers at least hire poor people to do tasks for them. "We cannot comply with the divine law by saying to ourselves, 'Go to! It is quite too much trouble to love our neighbor as ourselves. We will have a sec-retary to love him for us.' "[61]

Churches had for decades gathered clothes for local poor people and for domestic and foreign missions, but often these were new gar-ments, plain clothing stitched expressly for charitable giving by middle- and upper-class women meeting in sewing circles. Middle-class women remade their own clothing and considered even their old clothes too elegant for the poor. By the end of the century, hand sewing and sewing circles had both declined, but many organizations devoted themselves to clothing the poor. Often they were staffed by women or directed toward women and children as recipients, but men filled many leader-ship positions and some organizations had no gender focus. In San Francisco, for example, a number of groups were active. The Francesca Relief Society provided fabric, garments, and Christmas outfits to women and children. The Ladies of the Grand Army of the Republic gave clothing to needy Civil War veterans. The Mizpah Club fur-nished clothing to the worthy poor. The Young Men's Institute donated clothing to the needy during the winter. Some of these organizations collected old clothes, but others bought and distributed new ready-made ones.[62]

The Salvation Army, which created the model for charitable salvage work, was founded in London in 1865 by a renegade Methodist revival minister named William Booth. The organization adopted its military structure and titles in 1879 and the next year began operations in New York City, its first territory outside Britain. Its early approach was strictly evangelical, winning souls for both organized Protestantism and its own ranks. In 1890, Booth published *In Darkest England and the Way Out,* in which he described his "social scheme." The Army would develop "colonies" to lift souls from degeneracy. City colonies would provide food, shelter, and work in a Salvation Army factory. Individuals who demonstrated their willingness to work and their free-dom from bad habits would then be placed in rural colonies to culti-vate self-reliance and resourcefulness. Finally, converts would act as missionaries for the Army in overseas colonies.[63]

The Salvation Army's salvage activities, which were particularly successful in the United States, should be understood as part of this scheme. They began in New York in 1897 with "salvage brigades." A handful of unemployed men pushed handcarts through the city, collecting clothing and bearing a letter of explanation from the Salvation Army's American commander (and Booth's son-in-law), Frederick Booth-Tucker. The New York brigade soon folded, but others started up within months, in cities including Boston, Newark, Jersey City, and Chicago. The organization developed plans for brigades all over the country, one of the founders predicting accurately that salvage work would be "one of the strong features" of the Army's social work in the United States. Within two years, the Salvation Army Industrial Department was running nineteen Industrial Homes—salvage and workshop operations where men earned lodging, food, and a small wage for collecting and repairing goods. In Boston, collection baskets were placed with five hundred donor families. The highly successful Chicago operation handled twenty-five tons of wastepaper weekly and contracted with the city to keep the streets of several wards free of paper.[64]

Most of the Industrial Homes were three- or four-story buildings with space on the lower floors for the retail store, the receiving department, furniture repair and storage, an office, and the sorting and baling rooms. Upper floors housed the kitchen, the dining room, reading or recreation rooms, and dormitories. Longtime workers and Army officers slept in private bedrooms.[65]

The Industrial Homes multiplied rapidly. By 1904, forty-nine institutions accommodated about eleven hundred men and employed about seventy officers. They processed about a thousand tons of paper each month, in addition to clothes, furniture, and assorted bric-a-brac. Within three more years, they handled twenty-five hundred tons of paper every month. By 1909, the homes contributed substantially to the Army's nearly $2 million annual income in the United States, and their buildings were a large part of its $1.5 million real estate holdings. They were administered by the Salvation Army Industrial Homes Company; like the Army's other corporations—including a bank, insurance companies, and the Reliance Trading Company, which manufactured uniforms and other paraphernalia—it sought investments as well as donations from the public. Preferred stock was traded publicly, while the common stock was held by the Army in order to retain control.[66]

The Salvation Army was unusual among turn-of-the-century charities for taking virtually everybody who came to it, with no questions asked. Most charities investigated their clients, using either their own investigators or those of local umbrella institutions called Charity Organization Societies, which determined whether individuals "deserved" help and whether they were already getting any from other agencies. Such investigation was one aspect of an unsentimental "scientific" approach to poverty. Indiscriminate charity, in this view, would only produce a permanent dependent class. According to the Army, on the other hand, every soul could be saved. As one officer explained in 1898, "The Army does not waste either precious time or precious money inquiring into character. It divides the people into two classes only, the willing and unwilling to work."[67]

For those with the most potential, the Salvation Army operated an employment agency, sending laborers to outside employers and collecting a fee. But not everybody on the street was a capable worker, and the Industrial Homes took in men whose will was not matched by their ability. "Sometimes the victims of drink, sometimes of mere misfortune," Booth-Tucker explained, "weakened often in body, and with perhaps but little moral stamina to resist temptation—'Down on their luck,' as they would themselves say, they constitute largely the 'deadbeats' of society." These unfortunates were put to work in Army facilities: "The human wastage is employed in collecting, sorting, repairing and selling the material waste." The Army's New England annual report contended in 1903 that many of these men would otherwise be begging for food or stealing it, or in jail, "a prey and a danger to the community at large, besides being a burden on the taxpayer. They are now supported very largely from the *household waste of our city*. We confidently believe and are seeking to demonstrate that the *want* of our cities can be met from its *waste*!"[68]

An independent study of the Army provided descriptions of 109 men living and working at two Industrial Homes in New York City in 1908. Number 17, a forty-year-old widower of American parentage, was a carpenter. His wife had died, his child was living with a sister, his tools were in a pawnshop. "He looked like a very hard drinker," the investigator reported. Number 45 was twenty-five, a German without a trade who "looked bright and capable"; he "had people in Paterson but was ashamed to write to them." The study provided statistics but did not tell what proportion of the men in the two homes the sample represented or how they were chosen. Almost two-thirds of the men were of foreign parentage (mostly Irish and German), 84 percent single, half between the ages of twenty and thirty. Twenty-nine percent had regular trades. Nearly two-thirds had been out of work for more than three months, including those who had been working at the Industrial Homes during that time. Slightly more than one-third of the total were described by the investigator as looking "efficient."[69]

Army literature described the Industrial Homes more as business propositions than as soul-saving ones. Devotional meetings were held in the homes but were not compulsory. Booth-Tucker explained that the homes created temporary employment for unemployed men with skills in a variety of trades. "It would have required a vast amount of capital to employ each in what he might happen to know," he went on. "To collect and sell waste paper, clothing, shoes, old furniture, packing cases, bottles and articles of a similar character has been found to supply a maximum of work at a minimum of cost." A 1923 handbook for evaluating officers placed the "ability to secure business efficiency from men" above "spiritual results in dealing with men," and another official document concurred in 1929.[70]

By that time, the customers at the stores had become more likely recruits for the Salvation Army than the worker-residents of the homes. "It is safe to say that thousands of people who are now regular attendants at corps open-air and indoor meetings received their first impression of The Salvation Army in the industrial store," commented the head of Men's Social Work for the Eastern United States. "Through the stores we are making contact with a distinctly promising class of people, just the sort we seek for our constituency. They are not the desperately poor, but for the most part hard-working, industrious wage-earners who patronize our stores because their incomes do not permit them to buy new household and personal necessities at prevailing market prices."[71]

Besides the workers and the customers, the Industrial Home scheme depended on a third group, the people who donated their discards. These were generally not the truly wealthy—who were more likely to give castoffs to their domestic servants—but middle-class and even relatively poor people. "One may ransack the store and find little or nothing that could have come from a rich home," *Harper's Weekly* declared, describing the sorry merchandise at the Salvation Army's Chicago store, which told an "eloquent story of the poor helping those who are still poorer." Army officers described contributors not as poor but as "just the middle class." By 1909, the Army had established regular routes through middle-class neighborhoods. Many people collected odds and ends until the wagon called, one observer wrote, "often giving things away which they would not have thrown away or given any one else, unless it would be to sell them to an old-clothes man."[72]

In fact, there were other charities soliciting old clothes and household items. The Salvation Army's salvage operations were not yet established in 1895 when the Reverend Edgar James Helms arrived in an impoverished Boston neighborhood to run the Morgan Chapel, a Methodist missionary church that developed into Goodwill Industries. During the next few years, Helms started collecting old clothes and initiated a neighborhood sewing bee where poor women could work for credit to purchase the goods they worked on. In 1902, with the Army's example well in place, Morgan Chapel began to pay wages and to sell its small surplus of repaired garments for cash. "It is not good charity to clothe people in rags," Helms explained. "It is bad enough to have to wear your own rags without having to wear other people's rags. We, therefore, began to give work to those who could sew or cobble or repair furniture, to put these contributed articles into more serviceable condition. Prices were charged to cover the necessary expense of collecting, cleaning and repairing. No one has been pauperized by the process. The pennies of the poor folks who needed these things and could not afford to buy new articles helped to pay for the food, rent and medicine of the other poor folks employed to repair them."

Fred C. Moore, a tea and coffee merchant active in the cause, had the idea of placing discarded burlap coffee bags in middle-class homes so as to assure a supply of materials. Thousands of bags were eventually contributed by Chase & Sanborn, and the "Opportunity Bag," or "Goodwill Bag," became both a symbol and a central piece of strategy for the organization.[73]

The Morgan Memorial Cooperative Industries and Stores was incorporated as a nonprofit, charitable corporation in 1905. Like that of the Salvation Army, Morgan Memorial's salvage work was part of a broader program; it operated urban homes, summer camps, and other social service and religious education programs. Unlike that of the Army, Morgan Memorial's salvage operation offered employment to indigent women as well as to men. And it was considerably more liberal. Its Sunday afternoon "People's Forum" presented prominent speakers on such topics as woman suffrage, socialism, temperance, trade unionism, and child labor. From the start, the organization was explicitly interdenominational, and it was never primarily evangelical, out to create converts like the Salvation Army. The Morgan Chapel was endowed by a legacy to a Unitarian group, but with the proviso that a Methodist minister should serve there. As the organization branched out to other cities, many Protestant denominations were represented, and in some places Catholics and Jews served on the boards. Eventually the organization dissolved its formal affiliation with the Methodist hierarchy.[74]

Brooklyn, San Francisco, and Los Angeles were the first to follow the example of Boston's Morgan Memorial. The general plan in each city was to begin with the salvage work, which would provide funds for the other social services. In 1915, the Brooklyn group came up with the name Goodwill Industries. Three years later, the Methodist Board of Home Missions set up the Bureau of Goodwill Industries to encourage the establishment of Goodwills in other places and to foster coordinated planning and communications. Within a year, new workshops and stores were operating in Cleveland, Denver, and Buffalo, and the bureau was planning for New York, Philadelphia, St. Paul, and Pittsburgh. This organizing effort was enhanced by government contracts for training soldiers wounded in World War I, which fostered the organization's emphasis on providing work for the disabled.[75]

Goodwill of Southern California developed out of missionary work among Mexicans in Los Angeles. In December 1916, its founder, Katherine Higgins, inspired by a visit from Helms, asked the Latin-American Mission Board at the First Methodist Episcopal Church for permission to purchase two hundred old coffee sacks at eleven cents each. "Help us to help others to help themselves," the organization implored in a Spanish-language newspaper, appealing for clothing, furniture, and other discards, anything except broken bottles and tin cans. "The materials received in these bags will be repaired or made over by our Latin-American women and sold to them at a price low enough to enable them to keep their self-respect. Of course, in some cases it is necessary to give the articles away without charge." The store opened in March 1918, with first-day totals of 220 customers and $126 received in cash. The organization expanded rapidly, with plans to place ten thousand Opportunity Bags in homes. A branch store opened in June, advertised on handbills printed in English, Spanish, and Russian. In 1920, Goodwill moved into a large building, promoting further expansion: additional branches, more than a tripling of the workforce within eight months, and a sevenfold increase by 1923.[76]

The day started at Southern California Goodwill with a noncompulsory devotional period; the organization held Americanization and Bible classes for workers and conducted religious services in both Spanish and English. Americanization classes were held as well at Morgan Memorial in Boston. There, services for workers took place twice a day and even the stores offered a hymn and a prayer before lunch. But the real Goodwill gospel was work. In the midst of the Great Depression, the organization's leadership believed "that we should exhaust every effort to provide a maximum amount of labor in the repair and reconditioning of discarded materials." In truth, unemployment had always been high among the population Goodwill served, and this policy was well established before the economic crisis. "Work is the great tonic," the organization's official history explained in 1926. "The man, broken and discouraged, who is put to mending chairs, repairs his own fortunes and hopes in the process." The wage "brightens a man up, gives him new incentive and a new outlook. Work, says the psychologist, is the greatest godsend ever given for the restoration of men." Indeed, in the 1920s Morgan Memorial had two psychologists on staff to offer job counseling and guidance testing. Like the Salvation Army, the organization offered both temporary employment and an employment service that found permanent jobs.[77]

The donors and store customers who supported Goodwill and the Salvation Army could also choose these organizations' Catholic counterpart in the salvage of clothes and household goods, the Society of St. Vincent de Paul. This charitable organization of laypeople, founded in Paris in 1833 and established in the United States in 1845, initially got most of its funds from the poor boxes placed at the doors of Catholic churches. It began salvage work later than the other two large salvage charities, and it grew more slowly, but in some cities it came to rival them. The move into salvage work was compatible with the society's traditions. Its original rules called for a Keeper of the Wardrobe in each parish, "for the poor are as often in want of clothes as of food and to obtain them we must take trouble rather than spend money."[78]

The society's first salvage bureau was established in Philadelphia in 1911; although it was not a financial success at the beginning, its supporters enlisted the cooperation of the archbishop and the clergy, rented a small storehouse and hired teams of horses, and eventually produced profits that supported summer vacations for needy children, burial of the indigent dead, and a Seamen's Recreation Center. A Milwaukee branch opened a "clothing depot" in 1914. Taking up collections in parochial schools, the Milwaukee St. Vincent's did not limit itself to clothing but accepted paper of all kinds, metal, bottles, and furniture. "The waste is sold to defray the expenses of the office and the collection of articles," the local organization reported, "and although the income has not been quite enough the first year to cover all, it has increased from month to month."[79]

At the society's Los Angeles Waste Collection Bureau, which opened in 1917, poor women could pay for purchases with their labor; the San

Francisco salvage bureau, which started the next year, employed only disabled men and women. But unlike Goodwill, the Society of St. Vincent de Paul did not stress its function as a provider of work. Instead it emphasized charity: the needs of the poor as opposed to the excesses of the middle and upper classes. "Give to the Bureau your hidden treasures—that old dress, suit, overcoat or shoes you have not worn for a long time," the San Francisco group urged. "Somewhere in your attic, storeroom, or wardrobe may be just the article that will help send a child to school properly clothed, provide warm bedding for a family, make a man presentable and help him secure employment." The St. Vincent salvage work slogan was "Discarded by you— Treasured by others." Salvation Army and Goodwill rhetoric accentuated the transformations of people and materials that would be accomplished by work; the irony of charity was that the St. Vincent slogan suggested that poor people would be transformed by things.[80]

All the charity organizations that ran salvage operations came in for heavy criticism. Labor organizations complained about their substandard wages, which remained legal for nonprofit organizations even after minimum-wage laws were established. Junk dealers protested that they had to pay for the same materials these organizations received as donations, enabling the charities to undersell their competitors. Other critics pointed to funds and materials solicited for charity but not always used for the benefit of the poor.

Over the years, the Salvation Army received the most criticism. The press investigated the Army in its early days, and individual Salvationists were harassed frequently on the streets, both by people they were trying to convert and by the police. A number of well-known British thinkers criticized Booth's social scheme after his *In Darkest England* was published in 1890. Public figures who took stands included the agnostic and evolutionary biologist Thomas Huxley; the translator and philosopher Bernard Bosanquet; the founder of the English Social Democratic Federation, Henry Mayers Hyndman; and the secretary of the London Charity Organization Society, Charles Stewart Loch. In a series of letters published in the London *Times* and later as a book, Huxley described Booth as a despot. "The prosperity and glory of the soul-saving machine have become the end, instead of a means, of soul-saving," he wrote, calling the Army "an organised force, drilled in the habit of unhesitating obedience," and "mere autocratic socialism, masked by its theological exterior." Above all, he warned well-meaning people not to entrust the Army with their money.[81]

A committee of leading citizens issued an investigative report clearing the Army's name, but more controversy followed the 1906 publication, in both London and New York, of John Manson's *The Salvation Army and the Public*. Manson called the Army a "gigantic investment business" and criticized it for inadequate financial reporting that left potential investors and donors unable to appraise its work. Furthermore, he charged, by paying lower wages than other employers, the Salvation Army exerted downward pressures on both wages and prices.[82]

Edwin Gifford Lamb investigated Manson's points in a 1909 Columbia University dissertation. Although critical of the organization's religiosity, he was generally positive about the Industrial Home work and most of the Army's other activity in the slums. But he agreed that these efforts were weakened by the Army's business motives. Unsuccessful Industrial Homes were moved or shut down, even though they were beneficial to the poor. Lamb concluded that despite the Salvation Army's good social work, its critics were in general correct. "The movement," he wrote, "is drifting from its original purpose of uplifting the down-fallen humanity to the purpose of perpetuating and extending itself as an economic enterprise." The Army refused to cooperate with other organizations; it failed to disclose its financial dealings to the public and reported inaccurately on its accomplishments; it used money collected on the strength of its social work for religious propaganda; and its centralized military government had "disastrous consequences," including mutinies such as one led by William Booth's son and daughter-in-law, who left the Army to start Volunteers of America.[83]

Lamb acknowledged that junk dealers had reason to resent the Army for underselling its competition. Army officers, he wrote, admitted underselling in the retail stores, but justified this "by the fact that the regular second-hand men are tricksters and will rob the poor of their money." And whereas these officers insisted that the Army never undersold paper or rags, their claim was disingenuous, at best. As one rag merchant pointed out in 1912, the Army and the other church organizations that he called "a menace to the rag and old paper trade" benefited simply by getting donated materials, whatever price they charged. "The friends of these organizations give to them thousands of dollars' worth of old material annually, supposing they are giving direct to charity, but these institutions reap a harvest," the merchant insisted, by selling goods that legitimately belonged to the waste trade.[84]

Despite the critiques, the Salvation Army won general acceptance. Its activities in the slums, including the religious services it held in saloons, convinced the public that the organization and its activists took a genuine interest in people at the bottom. The Army's operations were in line with ideas that almsgiving should be replaced by self-support and that people should be taught—or forced to learn—how to take care of themselves. A more general move among Protestant activists to merge religion and social reform led to clerical backing; a group of New York ministers declared in 1886 that "the Salvation Army is worthy of the sympathy of all the Christian Churches in New York and the United States." Seven years later, the Congregationalist minister and social critic Josiah Strong commented on the large number of "thieves, gamblers, drunkards, and prostitutes" saved "through the heroic faith and labors of the Salvation Army." Turn-of-the-century Army literature bore testimonials from governors, newspaper editors, clergymen, and leading businessmen. As one newspaper quoted in a 1903 Army publication declared, "the once discredited and habitually ridiculed Salvation Army, by its steady, persistent and unflagging philanthropic work, has won the reluctant praise and admiration of the classes who denounced it." By the 1920s, the widespread criticism was virtually forgotten, replaced in the public memory by the Army's relief work in the 1906 San Francisco earthquake and by its kitchen, hospital, and ambulance work during World War I.[85]

Other salvage organizations heeded the lessons of the Salvation Army's experience. Edgar James Helms warned his movement not to use Goodwill money for the expenses of the church. Nor should contributions of junk from Jews and Catholics be sold to pay a Methodist minister's salary. If people sent clothes to help the poor, he insisted, they should be used to help the poor. Still, Goodwill, like the other organizations, was vulnerable to the labor critiques. It did use the law to its advantage to keep wages low. Inadequate pay led to considerable turnover: the Boston sorting and rug-weaving plant, for example, hired two hundred workers at a time, but three thousand different ones each year. At a national meeting in 1921, the supervisor of Goodwill of Southern California told his colleagues that critics had raised the question of minimum-wage requirements but that Goodwill got a ruling from the California Industrial Welfare Commission exempting the organization as a nonprofit benevolent corporation.[86]

Trash in War and Peace

During the relatively short time the United States participated in World War I, the steady upward trend in waste generation reversed. Prices were high, conservation propaganda encouraged reuse, and labor shortages cut municipal service. The quantity of trash collected per capita decreased by about 10 percent. More cities adopted conservation-oriented disposal methods, especially swine feeding, but conservation at the household level lowered the recoverable elements. Thirty percent less grease was recovered in reduction plants, for example, because Americans were eating less meat.[87]

The government encouraged but did not compel household recycling and reuse. Rationing was never instituted during World War I and no scrap drives were held, in part because the United States participated in the war so briefly. Still, consumers were affected by industrial conservation measures instituted by the Commercial Economy Board, later called the Conservation Division of the War Industries Board. The brainchild of a business publisher, Arch W. Shaw, the board worked through business organizations and trade journals, helping industries to establish standards that reduced styles, varieties, sizes, and colors. In most fields, standardization was highly beneficial to the manufacturers, since making fewer different products simplified both production and distribution. Over two years, 287 styles and sizes of automobile tires were reduced to 9, and 326 kinds of steel plows to 75. Instead of 150 colors of typewriter ribbons, American industry now offered 5. Rubber raincoats were discontinued completely. Clothing manufacturers were restricted to a limited number of models and to styles that minimized the use of fabric. They were encouraged to avoid needless decoration, to use shoddy instead of virgin wool, and to choose lightweight fabrics. The director of the Council of National Defense later claimed that a representative of the American government had called upon the French ambassador to discuss the 1918 Paris fashions, encouraging him to find a way to convince the designers to use less fabric.[88]

Women were called on to join in the war effort by conserving food, through the combined efforts of the U.S. Food Administration headed by Herbert Hoover, the Department of Agriculture, and the Council of National Defense. "While all honor is due to the women who leave their homes to nurse and care for those wounded in battle," the secretary of agriculture wrote in one propaganda piece, "no woman should feel that, because she does not wear a nurse's uniform, she is absolved from patriotic service. The home women of the country, if they will give their minds fully to this vital subject of food conservation and train themselves in household thrift, can make of the housewife's apron a uniform of national significance."[89]

Hoover himself urged Americans to eat wheatless and meatless meals, conserve sugar, toast stale bread, and make washing soap out of leftover fats. Half a million people went door to door during two pledge drives in 1917 to encourage women to sign cards promising to "carry out the directions and advice of the Food Administrator in the conduct of my household as far as my circumstances permit." The pledge was promoted as well by the Four-Minute Men, volunteers who gave brief propaganda speeches in movie theaters before the show. Despite some resistance from individuals who feared they would have to give up half their canned food or who resented the government's intrusion into their kitchens, and despite political opposition from German communities and antiwar socialists, more than ten million women signed the pledge and received buttons to wear and cards to put in the windows.[90]

The Department of Agriculture issued the Food Thrift Series, pamphlets that explained principles of food conservation, with recipes and advice for home gardening and canning. American households wasted $700 million worth of food annually, the pamphlets claimed. Food spoiled due to careless handling and storage; burned or undercooked food got thrown out. Americans wasted food in preparation and serving, and they did not know how to use leftovers. The Food Thrift Series taught them to keep food cool, to cover it, and to store it safe from mice and weevils. Recipes explained how to make soups and stews from leftovers, to use stale bread, and to make cottage cheese from skim milk.[91]

Cookbooks published during the war offered similar instruction. Alice Gitchell Kirk's *Practical Food Economy* (1917) included an admonishing section headed "Waste No Fats!" based on a bulletin produced by the Ohio Branch Council of National Defense Agriculture. The 1917 revision of Emily Holt's *Complete Housekeeper* provided recipes for the standard hashes and croquettes and taught how to make "Save-the-Wheat Breads." Holt herself rehashed the conventional complaint that European housewives knew how to make appetizing and nutritious meals from leftovers. "Indeed," she wrote at a time when the war had created particularly dramatic and well-publicized differences between European and American lifestyles, "it is a common saying that a European family can live on what the average family in this country throws away."[92]

Clothing was another topic for conservation propaganda. In one of the Food Thrift pamphlets, the secretary of agriculture pointed out that fabric was an agricultural product. "Whenever a useful garment is needlessly discarded, material needed to keep some one warm or dry may be consumed merely to gratify a passing fancy. Women would do well to look upon clothing at this time more particularly from the utilitarian point of view." He concluded with a warning: "Make economy fashionable lest it become obligatory." The threat fell on ears that, if not deaf, were already well attuned to the habits of consumer culture.[93]

The Department of Commerce designed an elaborate plan for continuing reclamation and salvage activities after the war. The U.S. Waste

Reclamation Service was to cooperate with other government departments and national organizations, including the Salvation Army, the United States Chamber of Commerce, and the American Federation of Labor, in establishing local Waste-Reclamation Councils. Paper, wool, rubber, cotton, leather, and a variety of metals would be collected; junk dealers would be guaranteed prices for their cooperation. Mass meetings and other educational activities encouraging people to continue conserving and reclaiming despite the armistice would employ the slogan, "Don't waste waste. Save it."[94]

The plans never got off the ground, and despite other suggestions that wartime thrift might make peacetime sense, Americans returned to learning the habits of consumerism and waste making. The war had momentarily suggested a different direction, but the crisis had passed. Middle-class waste generation renewed its upward trend, municipal collection and disposal were well established, Goodwill and the Salvation Army prospered, and reuse and recycling were firmly associated with the lower classes. Patrick Hart, an elderly junk dealer in Newburgh, New York, told a magazine reporter in 1923 that country-women and immigrants accounted for most of the household waste handled by junk men. Hart had given up house-to-house collection decades before to concentrate on contracts with businesses.[95]

Salvation Army literature urged potential donors to search their homes for junk. "There is not an old newspaper in the family trash basket, or a disused garment inviting the moths in the family closet, or a three-legged chair which has about given up trying to keep its equilibrium in the domestic economy but what in the hands of the Army alchemist it may help some submerged man to rise above his engulfing circumstances," one 1926 pamphlet implored. Everybody had such things; the point was to define them as having some value somewhere but none in the context of the middle-class home. The Army therefore used language implying that goods to be donated were both trash (already in the trash basket, perhaps deteriorating in the closet, missing a leg) and not-trash ("inviting moths" but not eaten by them, "about given up trying" but not quite yet).

Like Frederick Booth-Tucker's earlier prose, the pamphlet featured a rhetorical link between "waste material" and "waste lives." As rubies and diamonds were formed from clay and soot, the pamphlet declared, "Divine and human love working together has fashioned things valuable and precious" from "humanity's scrap-heap." It offered an example, scarcely typical: a "man of education and refined birth" found picking over garbage pails for food. Brought to an Industrial Home, he was soon back to his old self. When a former employer and friend of his father's heard of his conversion and offered him his job back, the man chose instead to stay with the Army.[96]

In an effort to increase the income from their stores, Salvation Army leadership encouraged modern selling techniques. The stores had been organized into departments as early as 1909, but now the emphasis was on hanging clothes on hangers, displaying goods on racks and in bins, and collecting bric-a-brac and furniture, which brought in the most money. Some clothing that formerly would have been baled and sold as rags was separated out for sale. The Army opened a bookstore in New York City, where it ran thirty-five more general stores. By 1929, store sales had surpassed paper as a source of income for Industrial Homes east of the Mississippi. There were few successful Industrial Homes in the South, however, where most middle-class white people "gave" cast-off household goods and clothing to their black domestic servants as partial payment or pressured servants to buy their discards. Even used newspapers brought no income in the South, because there was no local market for recycled newspaper.[97]

Goodwill was operating in twenty-six cities by the mid-1920s, providing jobs for between fifteen and twenty thousand workers a year, most of them old or disabled. About half a million households contributed Goodwill bags, and an equal number patronized the stores. In the Boston area, regular truck routes collected discards from more than a hundred thousand homes in sixty towns; workers at a six-story factory sorted rags and paper into fourteen classifications and wove old rugs into new ones. In southern California, Goodwill prospered, collecting 9,500 bags in 1920 and 218,000 in 1929. Overall sales—$8,700 in 1919—had multiplied to more than a quarter-million dollars on the eve of the Depression.[98]

Local Goodwills looked for new ways to collect, process, and market materials. In one city, Boy Scouts placed bags in three thousand homes in a day; in others, Goodwill women's auxiliaries distributed bags. Some Goodwills operated "tinker shops," which resilvered mirrors or repaired pots and pans. In Jersey City, Italian immigrant women made what were touted as "exact reproductions of the Italian linens of the 15th and 16th centuries" in the organization's workshops. Southern California Goodwill manufactured underpants from old cotton shirts, babies' caps from bits of fancy fabrics, and boys' suits "from the wide-gored skirts of styles now extinct." Additional fabric came from new remnants and unfinished garments sent in by frustrated home seamstresses. And like the Salvation Army, Goodwill tried to modernize its stores with contemporary business methods, sales conferences, and classes in salesmanship.[99]

A 1922 national meeting approved the idea of manufacturing new items and starting paper mills. Suggestions were made for manufacturing articles like boys' suits, men's trousers, and other garments not often donated and for establishing rug and carpet factories and shoddy mills, where the organization could use rags instead of selling them. There was much discussion about what to do with surpluses of old shoes. Baltimore donated them to the needy in the Middle East, St. Louis sold them by the bag, Buffalo provided them to the Methodist Home for Children to use as fuel, and Cleveland sold them "as is" for twenty cents a pair.[100]

Growth and institutionalization had drawbacks for the salvage charities. During the business slump of 1921, the Milwaukee salvage bureau of the Society of St. Vincent de Paul found that it was collecting less material and prices were falling in the waste markets. "Yet we had to keep on collecting the same," the president complained in his annual report, "in order not to offend our well-meaning friends and supporters." The operation recovered; St. Vincent's, like Goodwill and the Salvation Army, flourished during the 1920s. By 1924 the Milwaukee group had opened a new building, with space for storage, a workroom for furniture repair, and the retail store. They started another branch the next year, and a third store the year after. "Call Grand 8208 and the Waste Bureau truck will call," the Milwaukee office appealed to those with excess to give away.[101]

With the support of the public and the protection of the law, charitable organizations had become central to the disposition of unwanted items. In southern California, for example, at least thirty-four different charities solicited salvageable goods. Household-advice literature, which once taught readers how to renew and reuse old clothing and furniture, now recommended selling and giving them away. Benjamin R. Andrews's *Economics of the Household,* a widely used college home economics textbook first published in 1923, insisted that all waste should be used somehow, by somebody, but offered the option of giving unwanted things "to a charity such as the Salvation Army's industrial department." Only as a final resort should material be turned over to the municipal garbage collection system, which "should be so handled as to extract whatever values the waste may still have." Andrews, who taught at Columbia University's Teachers College, one of the leading home economics graduate schools, also urged readers to sell unwanted items: just as businesses tried to make money selling wastes, so should households. The exception was clothing. Andrews asserted that people had "a social responsibility" for using old clothes, but while there was "every reason" to recover their economic value, there was "an odd feeling" about selling clothes, he insisted, almost a taboo. Charity giving, whether to the occasional church rummage sale or to the more permanent Goodwill or St. Vincent's thrift shop, was just the ticket.[102]

Andrews offered images for reuse appropriate to postwar prosperity. Lamenting that wooden packing crates and barrels ended up in city dumps, he suggested that they "might at least be saved for kindling and for the children's Fourth of July celebration." He described "a Ford car carrying a bundle of wood on the running board, evidently parts of old boxes destined to serve as fuel at a day's picnic fire." As fuel for recreation, Andrews suggested, household trash might serve "transcendental" purposes.[103]

CHAPTER FOUR

Having and Disposing in the New Consumer Culture

Lillian Gilbreth, a management consultant later memorialized by two of her children in *Cheaper by the Dozen* and played by Myrna Loy in the film of that title, usually worked from her home and office in New Jersey. In late September 1926, though, she traveled into New York City to talk with R. W. Johnson, of the Johnson & Johnson company, about doing some market research for a new product, Modess sanitary napkins. After the conversation, she went home and proposed a study that entailed an analysis of the literature of menstruation and interviews with an assortment of experts.

Its centerpiece was a survey, concentrating on college girls but also investigating women in full-time jobs and "women in the home," to find out what kinds of napkins they used, how they used them, and what they wanted in a sanitary napkin. With three staff members and some student assistance, Gilbreth sent questionnaires to Radcliffe, Vassar, Wellesley, Smith, New Jersey College for Women, Johns Hopkins Medical School, Antioch College, and the Detroit Normal School. They collected data from more than a thousand questionnaires, conducted personal interviews, and organized what would now be called focus groups, where college women discussed the napkins on the market and helped design better ones. Johnson paid Gilbreth six thousand dollars for her research.[1]

Market research was not Lillian Gilbreth's specialty. With her husband and partner, Frank, she had previously studied efficiency in the industrial work process, refining Frederick Winslow Taylor's theories of scientific management. Unlike Taylor, whose principal tool was a stopwatch and whose concept of efficiency was based on saving time, the Gilbreths had emphasized "motion study," seeking to increase productivity by minimizing exertion, strain, and wasted motion. Now Lillian Gilbreth turned to market research because she needed work. Frank had died two years before her discussion with Johnson, and other companies had canceled their contracts with Gilbreth, Inc., the management consulting business the couple had created together.[2]

Commercial sanitary napkins had been available for decades, but they were by no means universal. Many women continued to fold linen or cotton cloth into sanitary pads, a traditional product of the *bricoleur* sensibility, constructed at home and often from scraps. Some purchased fabric for the purpose, especially a textured material called "birdseye" that was also used for diapers. Others selected cloth from the rag bag. They pinned these homemade pads into their underwear or held them to their bodies with belts and suspenders; they soaked soiled napkins, washed the blood out, and reused them. Some women who could afford it concocted homemade disposable pads instead, from cheesecloth, gauze, and surgical cotton.[3]

There were dozens of sanitary napkins on the market, but a single brand—Kotex—dominated the field. Montgomery Ward had advertised a disposable sanitary napkin as early as 1895: "more absorbent, antiseptic, no washing, burned after using, invaluable while traveling, cheaper than laundering." New concerns about sanitation and germs, long-standing taboos about menstrual blood, and the privacy of mail order made these pads attractive, but at fifty cents a dozen, they were expensive, especially compared with reusable rags. Widespread use of disposable pads did not begin until Kimberly-Clark introduced

Kotex in 1920. It was fabricated from cellucotton, a material the company had developed for bandages during World War I. Early Kotex advertising claimed that army nurses had pioneered the use of cellucotton dressings as menstrual pads, but at least one historian suggests that Kimberly-Clark was left at the end of the war with warehouses full of the stuff and developed the product to exploit the surplus. As *Fortune* told the story in 1937, the market for cellucotton had collapsed after the war and Kimberly-Clark, "geared to produce it in large quantities, had to create a new market in a hurry or else lose the money invested in it."[4]

Wallace Meyer, a copywriter from the Chicago firm of Charles F. Nichols, was responsible for the first Kotex advertising. He presented the *Ladies' Home Journal* with a portfolio of tastefully designed advertisements intended to crack the taboo on public discussion of menstruation. The *Journal* declared that it would accept the ads if they "continued on the same high plane, and provided this acceptance be not construed as a precedent for other products of a similar nature." It *was* construed as a precedent for other magazines: *Harper's Bazaar, Good Housekeeping, Redbook, Vogue,* and a number of newspapers immediately followed suit and accepted Kotex advertising. Meyer next fashioned a campaign for trade journals devised to convince pharmacists they should carry the product and to suggest that, by mounting prominent displays of Kotex, they could sell it without embarrassment to customers. In 1922 and 1923, Kimberly-Clark placed vending machines in public rest rooms, and thereafter the advertising incorporated pictures of the dispensers. In 1924, the company moved the advertising account for its now successful product to the well-known Lord & Thomas agency, headed by Albert Lasker. According to his biographer, Lasker personally courted Kimberly-Clark, telling the inventor of cellucotton, "The products that I like to advertise most are those *that are only used once!*"[5]

By 1927, Kotex advertising claimed that "*80% or more better-class* women have discarded ordinary ways for Kotex," copy that implied that old habits could be disposed of as easily as soiled napkins. Lord & Thomas made the same claim in advertising its services to clients, calling the Kotex campaign a "Simon-Pure Advertising success," proof that people read advertising. But while Kotex could boast of impressive market share, the market as a whole was still undeveloped. In fact, the old ways were still the ordinary ones, and advertising copy still compared Kotex with reusable fabric: "No laundry," it promised.[6]

The "modern college and business women" Gilbreth interviewed did for the most part use commercial napkins. Not only were these women "better-class" and less sensitive to the price difference between rags and commercial napkins, they were also young and more likely to try new products. Gilbreth speculated that most had made their own napkins when they lived at home and had turned to commercial ones at college or when they moved away to take jobs. College and business women had less space, less time, and less opportunity for making sanitary supplies. They could not easily store materials in their single rooms and small apartments, they did not accumulate extensive supplies of rags and sewing scraps, and many simply considered themselves too busy. Nonetheless, describing and analyzing dozens of brands of napkins, Gilbreth asserted that no product on the market was really satisfactory. Women accustomed to homemade napkins thought they could make more comfortable menstrual protection than anything they could buy.[7]

Because they knew how to assemble pads according to their personal preferences and their individual bodies, these women did not simply accept a standardized product. Instead, they treated the pads they bought as materials, not finished products. Eighty-one percent of Gilbreth's respondents altered commercial napkins before using them. They shortened tabs, cut corners, and shifted the padding around— removing excess, adding filling from another napkin, or changing the shape by transferring filling from the ends to the middle. As Gilbreth pointed out, "various sizes are needed by various people or by any one person at various times." Drawing on the skills and temperament that they had acquired doing other kinds of handwork, women in the 1920s approached this purchased product as something malleable.[8]

Gilbreth's report to Johnson & Johnson was sharply critical of

Kotex, the company's most formidable competition. Kotex was inexpensive and widely available, she wrote, but "entirely too large, too long, too wide, too thick, and too stiff." Mrs. V. V. Davidson, a West Virginia woman who corresponded with Johnson & Johnson, spelled out the competition's problems: "The sides of the Kotex are square and harsh so that fat women cannot wear them on account of chafing. And on account of the width and the square sides small women and young girls cannot wear them. . . . On automobile trips where such pads are indispensable the Kotex is very uncomfortable because of its harshness." According to Gilbreth, Johnson & Johnson's own Nupak was not much better: "The materials . . . are very good and it would be very soft and comfortable, but it is entirely too large and bulky."[9]

But whatever its discomforts as purchased, Kotex was easy to modify. The gauze could be opened up and the filling readily trimmed; the layers of cellucotton could be moved neatly from one napkin to another. This feature concerned R. W. Johnson, whose new Modess used a shredded filling. "One question we are very anxious to settle is, the necessity of a napkin being subject to adjustment," he wrote to Lillian Gilbreth as they were negotiating for the study. "We have worked for years on the MODESS product, which . . . can not be made thicker or thinner as can be done with a KOTEX or MAKETT. We want to know if this is an important feature. If so, we will have to work on the problem from a new angle." Gilbreth's response suggested that Modess had nothing to fear from Makett, or (as she spelled it) May Kit: "This consists of gauze and a paper filler to be made up by the purchaser, but we feel that most girls or women who were going to make their own anyway, would buy other materials." The Kotex competition was another story. Johnson was hoping to capture market share from the leading sanitary napkin, and Gilbreth's respondents stated clearly that they liked the fact that Kotex was easy to alter.[10]

Modifying sanitary napkins did not, however, satisfy consumers fully. Many of the grievances they expressed centered on an issue they could not affect so readily, their desire to conceal menstruation. The very act of purchasing a commercial product generated a new predicament in what had once been a private interaction between a woman and her ragbag. Before self-service, customers had to ask clerks to retrieve merchandise from shelves behind a counter, and clerks in pharmacies were usually male. Moreover, college women attracted to the thin fabrics and form-fitting fashions of the 1920s wanted "a new product which will be completely invisible no matter how tight or thin their clothes are." (Tampax, the first major brand of tampon, would be introduced in 1936.)[11]

Gilbreth's respondents also worried about how to hide the fact that they were having their periods when they were generating soiled napkins. They stated that they cared about "disposability," and they did not mean merely that they preferred to burn or throw away napkins instead of washing and reusing them. They wanted a product they could flush down the toilet. Kotex advertising stressed disposability as a major selling point. The same feature that allowed women to take Kotex apart to alter them made it possible to take them apart for disposal. A pamphlet packed in the Kotex box explained how to put a used napkin through the plumbing: remove the gauze, tear apart the filler, and soak for a few minutes before flushing. Ads in the product's early days declared that it was "cheap enough to throw away" and "easy to dispose of by following simple directions found in each box." Lord & Thomas's 1927 advertising proclaimed "Easy Disposal" in large type. "Disposed of as easily as tissue," read the text under a small inset drawing of an elegant woman standing in her bathroom, perhaps whiling away the requisite time until she could flush the toilet.[12]

Some women apparently followed the instructions successfully. Mrs. Davidson, the West Virginia woman who wrote to Johnson & Johnson, called easy disposability "the only real convenience about Kotex." A respondent for another Gilbreth survey complained that she had tried the Kotex method to discard Johnson & Johnson's experimental disposable diaper pads but found that they dissolved less quickly. Dozens of women, however, complained to Gilbreth's investigators that Kotex was not really disposable. "Yes, supposedly," one wrote, "but practically, no." To flush Kotex successfully, they had to follow the instructions, and pulling apart the lining required handling bloody napkins in a procedure no less distasteful than soaking rags. Hanging around the bathroom waiting to flush the toilet made the procedure even more impractical.[13]

Not hanging around was worse. One young woman described her humiliation at a boyfriend's family home. "I had heard that Kotex was easily disposed of and when I dressed for dinner, threw one into the toilet. Halfway through the dinner, the corner of the dining room ceiling developed a large wet spot. Everyone jumped up from the table and the father of the house went up to investigate. It ended by a plumber being called to fish out the napkin. I nearly died of embarrassment." College women attending dances at men's colleges usually knew better than to flush Kotex, so they wrapped them up and hid them until they left. "As a result," Gilbreth wrote, "many are forgotten, and there is embarrassment for both the men and the women."[14]

College officials testified to perpetual difficulty with pipes clogged by sanitary napkins. Likewise, after a great deal of plumbing trouble, the head nurse at Metropolitan Life Insurance decided against Kotex for her office building's fifteen vending machines, which dispensed forty-five hundred napkins per month. She told the interviewers that the Kotex disposal method worked in theory, but few of Metropolitan's women workers read the instructions and even fewer took the time to follow them. She chose instead a brand that did not claim to be flushable; moreover, she declared, it was softer and less irritating, and the company provided a better dispenser.[15]

Gilbreth advised Johnson & Johnson not to claim that its napkins were disposable. No napkin could be disposed of easily, she stated firmly, criticizing the claims of a brand called Flush Down Ideal as "absolutely misleading" and giving "a false impression." Her final recommendations to the company included the suggestion that "many hygiene authorities, heads of dormitories, etc. would welcome an advertising campaign stating that under present usage, sanitary napkins clog plumbing." Such educational work, she believed, would be better than misleading consumers, as Kotex did. "The chief grievance against Kotex," she wrote, "is not that the napkin is not disposable in this way, but that its manufacturers advertise it as being easily disposed of when it isn't."[16]

Armed with Gilbreth's advice, Johnson & Johnson launched Modess, advertising it as softer and more absorbent than other napkins and backing it with a big enough budget to present Kotex with its first serious competition. A decade later, when Consumers' Union rated nineteen brands, its magazine commented that "the old style cloth napkins are now so obsolete that the WPA Division of Social Research—even in its basic maintenance and emergency budgets—allows for the cheap, disposable napkins." Women had exchanged long-standing habits of reuse for a disposable product that offered concrete advantages. Although sanitary napkins might not be tailored to individual needs, they were clean, they saved time, and they made it easier to be out in the world.[17]

Modern Products, Modern Trash

The history of the sanitary napkin demonstrates the complexities of a developing consumer culture. As historian Roland Marchand suggests, early Kotex advertising provides an excellent example of the way that advertising men served as "apostles" or "town criers" of modernity. From the start, Kotex ads stressed that this was a modern product. "Just as the coming of telephones and electric lights changed old habits of living," one 1922 ad read, "so too Kotex warrants the forming of a new sanitary habit." Another set up contrasts. "Study lamps instead of pine torches," read the copy. "Printed books instead of written parchments. Women welcomed instead of barred at schools of higher learning. Habits and customs change. Living conditions improve. Grandmothers and mothers used birdseye and other bulky sanitary pads. Today a new sanitary habit has been made possible by Kotex." The campaign in druggists' trade journals struck the same note: "People used to have leeches applied to suck their blood as a cure for ills of every description. The fever-stricken were forbidden a drink of water, consumptives were kept in closed rooms. But that day is passed and with it has gone the period of home-made wearing apparel of every description."[18]

Kotex advertising focused specifically on modern ideas about women. Unlike most other advertisements in women's magazines, the ones for Kotex never showed pictures of women doing housework. This product helped women live outside the home. Some ads portrayed travel, showing upper-class women or their maids packing Kotex into luggage, or simply picturing women riding trains. Others showed groups of women at the theater or gathered for a club meeting. One early Kotex ad even depicted women's employment in offices. "Kotex is as essential to the modern woman's toilette," asserted the copy accompanying a picture of Kotex in an open desk drawer, "as typewriters and stenographers are to modern business."[19]

During its first few years Kotex limited its advertising to the "better" magazines, but by 1928 it was advertising in *True Story*, a publication that targeted young working-class women. While immigrant women might not embrace social workers' "scientific" information and modern advice about personal hygiene, their American-born daughters were more responsive to the idea of what was in effect billed as "an 'American way' to menstruate." In *True Story* as in upper-class-women's magazines, writes Marchand, the company "bluntly and repetitiously" claimed that its product had been adopted by "better-class women." Like many other companies, Kotex implied that consumers would gain social status, or the qualities of fastidiousness and discrimination supposedly characteristic of the wealthy, by choosing particular products.[20]

But the advantages of the sanitary napkin are more tangible than "modernity" or some illusionary identification with the upper classes. Few contemporary women, even dedicated environmental activists, would give up this product or its successor, the tampon, for a return to reusable rags. Given its advantages, Kotex's achievement in building a market could be described as an example of the triumph of the product itself rather than of its advertising. Advertising practitioners, who often claim that all they do is educate the public about the availability of products, might take the sanitary napkin's success as evidence that advertising genuinely serves this "educational" function rather than the ideological ones that Marchand outlines so effectively.

The success of the sanitary napkin is better understood, however, as a demonstration of the principle that products depend on cultural context for success, let alone triumph. The successful introduction of the most obviously desirable new product rests on groundwork laid by other products and cultural practices. New needs emerge where none existed before, and time-honored habits change. It is true that women bought sanitary napkins, not modernity. But the product exemplified, and was made possible by, modern attitudes and practices. Its success relied on a general acceptance of relatively new ideas and practices relating to cleanliness and convenience, which supported the notion that throwing things away not only was all right but could make a positive contribution to the quality of life. In contrast to bricolage, ever more the province of the poor, the modern relationship to the material world linked products made to be used only once, municipal waste collection, and attitudes that equated handy new inventions with ease and prosperity.

A technological and organizational revolution in production and distribution constituted the basis for this modern relationship. The physical volume produced by American industry nearly tripled and the horsepower of industrial machinery quadrupled between 1899 and 1927. American industry spewed out a wealth of standardized, uniform goods that cost money to replace the makeshift, the home-made, and the handmade. New products and technologies made old ones obsolete, as, for example, electric lights replaced oil lamps. A wide variety of packaged foods and cleaning products were advertised and distributed to a national market. Heinz and Campbell's prepared sauces and soups; Quaker and Pillsbury sold packaged oats and flour; Colgate and Procter & Gamble offered toothpaste and soap. Exploiting the economies of mass production, these firms offered goods at low prices, and by the 1920s, packaged products and small electrical appliances could be found in working people's homes.[21]

Formerly *customers,* purchasing the wherewithal for daily life from craftspeople or storekeepers whom they knew, Americans became *con-*

sumers, buying and using mass-produced goods as participants in a complex network of distribution that promoted individuals' relationships with big, centrally organized, national-level companies. They purchased many of the new goods from mail-order houses and chain stores. They got their information about products not directly from the people who made or sold them but from advertisements created by specialists in persuasion. These changes, though by no means universal or complete on the eve of the Depression, had taken a firm hold on the American way of life. In 1890, Robert and Helen Merrell Lynd argued in their 1929 study of Muncie, Indiana, people lived "on a series of plateaus as regards standard of living." Their vision limited to people they knew, they had little opportunity to examine how others lived. By the late 1920s, thanks to movies, magazines, and all kinds of advertising, "every one lives on a slope from any point of which desirable things belonging to people all the way to the top are in view."[22]

Marketing produced its own ephemera: boxes and cartons, newspapers and magazines thick with ads, mail-order catalogs, showcards created for temporary window displays—all designed to be used briefly and then thrown away. The 1897 Sears catalog was 786 pages long, and the company supplemented it with twenty-four special catalogs aimed at particular markets. Dutch Boy paints sent a regular magazine to ninety-five thousand dealers and housepainters in 1911. Coca-Cola grew outside of Atlanta by sending letters to two million people at a time, enclosing coupons for free Cokes at a local soda fountain. Heinz used its five-hundred-man sales force to change window displays in grocery stores with every new magazine advertisement; a 1911 Thanksgiving advertisement featuring mincemeat was supported by twenty-five thousand store displays, each to be trashed with the next round of advertising.[23]

Decades before Kotex, throwaway packaging was promoted for its convenience and cleanliness. Beginning in 1899, National Biscuit sold its Uneeda Biscuits in its In-Er-Seal carton, a patented creation of cardboard and waxed paper that protected crackers from dirt and claimed to seal out moisture. In 1905, the Pro-phy-lac-tic company advertised that its toothbrushes "reach you clean and sterilized, the *yellow box* protects and guarantees. Do not buy from a fingered pile of dusty, germ-laden tooth brushes, handled by nobody knows who." In the grand scheme, the cracker barrel and the toothbrush pile were doomed. In a more immediate sense, every yellow box and In-Er-Seal carton was headed for destruction, to be burned in the kitchen stove or apartment house incinerator or left in the trash can for municipal pickup.[24]

Some manufacturers suggested uses for their packaging to consumers who had not yet developed the throwaway habit. Tobacco tins were designed for reuse as lunch boxes. Paterson Parchment Paper could be washed and used again. "By wrapping your products in this paper, printed with your advertisement," the company told butter makers, "you improve your products by keeping them free from germs and you advertise your business by giving the housewife a nice piece of parchment paper that she will use and appreciate." At the same time, however, Paterson championed disposability. It sold parchment paper in rolls, promoting it for a variety of household uses. For dishwashing it was "vastly more hygienic than a rag that is kept over from day to day, as parchment paper is so cheap that after once using, it should be burned up."[25]

The Paterson paper company and National Biscuit—one company and its product now forgotten, the other still significant—sold products to households that were in the process of a fundamental technological transformation. Electricity, plumbing systems, and gas lines literally connected the private household to the public world and extended the range of communication. These technologies transformed people's everyday relationship to the material world. Electricity, gas, and water systems eliminated the work of making fires, cleaning lamps, and hauling wood, coal, and water. They made possible a level of cleanliness unthinkable for most people when heat and light came from open fires and every drop of water had to be carried in from outside.

At the same time, the new utilities fostered new trash and encouraged new attitudes about throwing things away. Technological obsolescence, still a relatively new idea even in most industries, now came to the household as modern appliances replaced old stoves and fireplace equipment, and aluminum and enameled steel pots and pans supplanted iron ones. Used paper, kitchen waste, packaging, and scraps of wood could not be burned as fuel in radiators or central gas furnaces, as they could in fireplaces or cast iron stoves. Used lightbulbs did not simply burn up, like kerosene and its wicks or gas and its incandescent filament mantles. In the trash, they joined the other refuse of a developing ethos of disposability: chewing gum, cigarette butts, razor blades, and paper products.

Well-established habits of reuse persisted, partly because not everyone had all the new products. In the rural Midwest, for example, many families chose to buy automobiles rather than install running water. Electricity was simply unavailable in most rural areas until the government programs of the Depression. Among urban workers, consumption practices varied according to income and ethnicity. But movies, magazines, and radio had begun to set standards for everybody everywhere. Advertising propagandized values, ideas, and ideals that were eventually to affect people of all classes, all over the country.[26]

No longer did the habits of reuse and the methods of the *bricoleur* frame the ways people perceived the objects they used and used up. Now articles could be declared obsolete because new technologies had made them so or for reasons of style and fashion, preoccupations not only of the wealthy. Like style, cleanliness and convenience were touted as reason enough for throwing things away. The selling points of modern products—styling, technological superiority, convenience, and cleanliness—all amounted to arguments for disposing of things rather than seeking ways to reuse them. Together they fostered a new kind of relationship to the material world, to production, and to disposal.

Cleanliness and Paper Products

When Gilbreth reported to Johnson & Johnson in 1927, she could assume that the college women she interviewed bathed frequently and changed their underwear daily, but such habits were still new enough to merit her commentary. The younger generation had "a passion for clean garments and the feel of personal daintiness," she told her clients. Bathrooms, washing machines, commercial laundries, cheap and effective soap powders, and affordable ready-made clothes had developed in the modern woman "standards of hygiene far higher than those of her ancestors."[27]

The marketing of the sanitary napkin rested on a foundation of ideas about cleanliness well in place by 1920, when Kotex was introduced. Personal cleanliness had signified moral superiority among middle-class people at least since the Civil War, and dirt was a sign of degradation. Industrialization made both cleaning and keeping clean easier and cheaper. Cleanliness became big business, as manufacturers of washstands, basins and tubs, towels, plumbing parts, and the large-scale devices necessary for urban sanitation all flourished. Soapmaking became a major industry, no longer the province of the housewife or the tallow craftsman. The germ theory of disease, popularized in newspapers and magazines and by home economists in colleges, high schools, and settlement houses, raised Americans' awareness of the dangers of dirt. Comfort and morality united with science as the public learned that dirt and dust carried tiny creatures that caused illness. After the 1890s, articles about health matters in popular magazines focused primarily on germs and the many ways people came in contact with them.[28]

By the time of Gilbreth's report, paved streets and automobiles had alleviated the most offensive dirt in the cities. Electricity and gas had reduced the staggering amounts of grime from wood and coal heating and kerosene lighting. Household plumbing and commercial laundries had made it possible to keep bodies, clothes, and houses considerably cleaner. The housing boom that followed World War I had brought bathrooms—already typical in middle-class homes—to many in the working class as well. The number of bathtubs in the United States doubled between 1921 and 1923; per capita expenditures for cleaning supplies more than doubled between 1900 and 1929.[29]

Disposable paper products had fostered the idea that it was acceptable to use throwaways rather than durable products, at least in the service of cleanliness. Some disposables were commonplace by the turn of the century: paper collars, toilet paper, and—in public places—paper cups and towels. Such products were prohibitively expensive until paper prices began to decline beginning in the late 1860s, as wood pulp and other nonrag papers were developed. By 1868, paper was being molded into pails, spittoons, washbowls, buckets, and barrels. It was also used for cuffs, collars, and shirt bosoms; buttons; hats and bonnets; tapestry, curtains, and carpets; and belting for machinery. According to a classic history of the paper industry, "It was not now so much a matter of inquiry of what paper could be made, as of what could be made of it." Some of the new paper goods were advertised as durable, others as expendable.[30]

Japanese manufacturers were particularly inventive. Trade with Japan developed after the Meiji restoration in 1868, and within a few years the Japanese were known in the United States for hundreds of kinds of paper, suitable for pocket handkerchiefs, waterproof overcoats, and even saucepans that could be used over charcoal fires. One American importer advertised Japanese paper pails, slop jars, cuspidors, pitchers, bowls, and alms basins printed with Bible texts. But all these products were essentially novelties. For the most part, people continued to use handkerchiefs, bowls, and saucepans made out of the traditional cloth, ceramic, and metal.[31]

The first disposable paper products to enjoy widespread use were paper cuffs and collars. Detachable collars were buttoned onto the old-fashioned collarless man's shirt, lengthening its useful life and saving the labor of laundering whole shirts. In 1860, with paper still quite expensive, 600,000 collars were manufactured in Boston alone. The Northern cotton shortage during the Civil War stimulated the market. Shortly after the war, a writer in the *Atlantic Monthly* claimed that America "wears about her neck annually nearly as many reams of paper as she uses to write upon." By 1872, the trade organization for the paper-collar industry reported annual production of 150 million paper collars and cuffs. Paper collars were widely worn until the 1920s.[32]

Another commonplace benefit of cheaper paper was the broader availability of toilet paper. Many people reused newspaper to serve this function, but because old paper could be sold, even that practice was costly before the 1870s. In the following decades, mail-order catalogs—made from cheap paper and utterly disposable—fit the bill. Anna Sorensen of North Dakota remembered an outhouse her family built in 1904. "We were lucky if we had a good Sears, Roebuck catalog," she recalled. "And if we had a Sears and a Montgomery, we always took the Sears, 'cause the Montgomery was so stiff and scratchy." Minnie Ness, another North Dakota woman, remembered her family using catalogs, but "we'd save apple wrappings and whatever peach wrappings we had for our company to use."[33]

Toilet paper, its makers insisted, was softer and cleaner. In 1885, the Albany Perforated Wrapping Paper Company declared in boldface type that the use of printed paper was a "direct cause of Hemorrhoids," anticipating by nearly half a century the scare campaign that sold Scott Tissue in the early 1930s ("In countless households someone is suffering in silence from troubles caused or aggravated by inferior toilet tissue"). For those already ailing, the Albany company offered medicated paper. The company's advertising claimed that all its paper was formulated to dissolve in water, insinuating that reusing printed paper clogged the plumbing.[34]

By the turn of the century, toilet paper was common, though still manufactured primarily by relatively small companies and distributed locally or regionally. George C. Mather & Company of Phoenix, New York, in 1903 offered at least ten brands in flat sheets and sixteen in rolls, some for commercial use in public places and some for retail sales. Medicated papers were still available. One company offered a pine tar toilet paper, good for hemorrhoids and because "its aromatic exhilations permeates and purifies the atmosphere from malarial and miasmatic vapors, disinfecting the toilet, closet, soil pipes, etc. [sic]"[35]

While the sanitary advantages of toilet paper might have been obvious, those of the paper cup required a belief in germs. The widespread use of paper cups was a direct result of a public health crusade educating people about the invisible organisms spread by the common drinking cups once standard in public places, especially trains and railroad stations. Manufacturers of paper cups teamed up with public health authorities to campaign for federal and state regulations banning common drinking cups from use in interstate traffic. Succeeding in 1912, they then competed for the business of the railroads and train stations.[36]

Stone & Forsyth, makers of the Hygienic Paper Towel, offered the Finback Drinking Cup, with "mahogany bronze" dispensers that matched railroad car interiors. "This cup," the company informed one prospective client railroad, "is designed to be used many times, and can be carried in the vest pocket or bag." The New York Central, this small railroad was told, ordered ten million at a time. The Individual Drinking Cup Company, manufacturers of Health Kups, had a more profitable idea: sell more cups by making them difficult to reuse. The "Cup Beautiful," the company boasted, "is destroyed if you try to fold it for a second use." By 1914, Health Kups had been adopted by Lord & Taylor and other stores, and in the office buildings of National Cash Register, U.S. Steel, Armour, American Can, and J. P. Morgan & Company. In 1919, the Health Kup became the Dixie Cup.[37]

Disposable paper cups met significant resistance. Most public places offered them in coin-operated dispensers, and some people were not willing to pay for what had once been free. Respectable travelers carried their own cups, available in metal and celluloid in a variety of collapsible and folding designs. Others reused paper cups from the trash or drank out of the public tanks, putting their lips to the faucet or using the cover of the tank as a cup. Some people protested against the vending machines: soldiers smashed paper cup dispensers in Washington's Union Station during President Wilson's inauguration in 1913. And some public places installed drinking fountains instead of paper cup dispensers, although at first these, too, were attacked as unsanitary because people could touch the nozzle with their lips.[38]

Paper cups were next marketed to replace drinking glasses at drugstore soda fountains, even though these were washed after every use, unlike the common cups on trains. In 1910, during the original crusade against the common cup, there was almost no demand for paper cups at soda fountains. By the mid-1920s, a druggists' trade journal commented on "an ever enlarging conviction that in the public drinking glass constantly lurks [sic] the elfs and gnomes of communicable diseases." Microscopic examinations sponsored by boards of health and publicized in newspapers disclosed evidence of bacteria. In time, the writer warned, glassware would be outlawed. It was already on the decline. The Vortex Manufacturing Company, which made the cone-shaped paper cups that eventually became ubiquitous at drugstore soda fountains, claimed in 1925 that its cups were in use at over 60 percent of American fountains. For druggists, cleanliness was only part of the story; paper cups saved on breakage and on dishwashing labor.[39]

Drugstore soda fountains also offered another disposable product, the paper straw, patented in 1887 by M. C. Stone. Natural straws (usually rye stalks) might break, some came clogged with dried mold, and even good straws were so thin that three or four had to be used with every drink. Stone advertised that his paper straw was "sweet, clean and perfect," and big enough "so that one will always suffice." Even better for his business, they could be used only once, "as they will always show the marks of use," Stone warned. "To any who want to use a straw twice over, I will say that I do not want your custom." But one-time use of anything, even so small as a straw, was still a novelty. He therefore suggested that used ones, cut in half, would "make an excellent taper for lighting cigars." In 1895, the *National Bottler's Gazette* called Stone's straws a "curiosity" and the phrase " 'paper straw' . . . rather a misnomer." Twenty-three years later, the magazine recommended wrapped straws as a good advertising medium for bottlers of soft drinks, and suggested four firms (including Stone's) that made straws and printed advertising on their wrappers.[40]

Like paper straws and cups, paper towels were promoted as a sanitary measure for use in public places. Some victorious crusaders against the common cup chose the common towel as their next battlefield, but they did not achieve as decisive a victory. Nearly a century later, the cotton roller towel may still be found in a few public washrooms, while the common cup is a historical curiosity. It was not so easy to comprehend how towels spread germs, and it took a long time to develop paper that was soft, strong, and cheap enough to substitute for cloth. An advertisement for the Hygienic, a well-known brand, suggests the drawbacks of most early paper towels; the Hygienic, it promises, "will absorb, and dry the face or hands without going to pieces." But whatever their faults, paper towels were increasingly adopted for public washrooms during the first decades of the twentieth century. Production of paper towels more than tripled during the 1920s.[41]

Few paper towels were yet used in homes. The Scott Paper Company advertised them in the *Literary Digest* as early as 1912, and by the 1920s *Good Housekeeping* carried advertising for at least four different brands. Christine Frederick, who wrote books and articles on efficient housekeeping, recommended paper towels for draining fried foods, wrapping food, wiping up, "and in general, taking the place of unsanitary 'rags.' " Paper towels would reduce laundry labor and foster cleanliness. "No one group of minor kitchen furnishings has done more to make for neatness and sanitation," Frederick declared, "than the increasingly popular group of paper products." But most women continued to drain fried foods on scraps of wastepaper, they wrapped food in old butter wrappers or damp cloth, and they wiped up with rags. Paper towels were expensive. As late as 1938, only about 19 percent of fifty-three thousand households inventoried in one market study even had them in their kitchens.[42]

Facial tissues, too, were used sparingly, although germ theory had fostered suspicion for some time that handkerchiefs were not safe. In 1913, *Good Housekeeping* warned that commercial laundries, widely used for household linens, might contaminate healthy people's laundry by mixing it with that of consumptives. Six years later, the magazine gave instructions for home laundering: soiled handkerchiefs should be separated from the rest of the wash load and dropped "carefully" into the washtub, to which salt had been added. Paper handkerchiefs, imported from Japan as early as the 1870s, were expensive. They remained virtually unknown until Kimberly-Clark introduced Kleenex, its second cellucotton product, in 1924.[43]

At first, as both "Kleenex" and "facial tissue" suggest, the product was promoted for cleaning, the face in particular. A 1927 ad, "Right and Wrong Ways of Removing Cold Cream," declared that only Kleenex did this task properly and that it "costs less to use than soiling and

ruining towels—*Less than laundering them.*" In a small box headlined
"For COLDS—Never again use a Handkerchief," the ad claimed that
"many doctors" recommended Kleenex instead of handkerchiefs for
people with colds. The company revised its advertising after market
research revealed that people used Kleenex to blow their noses more
than to wipe their faces; in repositioning the product as a handkerchief,
it increased the market to include men and children as well as adult
women. Like Scott, Kimberly-Clark conducted a scare campaign during the 1930s, warning, "Germ-filled handkerchiefs are a menace to
society!"[44]

Nonetheless, people continued to use and launder cloth handkerchiefs. Kleenex dropped its price during the Depression and facial
tissue sales nearly tripled between 1935 and 1939, but per capita consumption was still less than one box per year in 1940. It was easier to
convince Lord & Taylor and U.S. Steel to adopt sanitary innovations
like paper towels in the rest rooms, since these saved labor, than to
change people's intimate habits. In the store or factory, the cost of laundry service could be calculated. At home, the laundry had to be done in
any case, and neither handkerchiefs nor kitchen towels added enough
bulk to make a labor-saving appeal very effective.[45]

Paper napkins, like paper towels, were used mostly in public places,
but by the turn of the century they were being advertised for domestic
use, available in a rainbow of colors with ornamental designs, and promoted as party and picnic items. The Dennison company began manufacturing them in 1897; Sears offered paper napkins in its 1900
catalog. Advertising in the posh magazine *Country Life in America* in
1911, Dennison recommended them for hunting trips. Mechanization
of the manufacturing process prompted further market development: a
folding machine, introduced in 1912, was eventually improved so that
it also embossed the napkins. In 1920, "household engineer" Christine
Frederick recommended "fine quality" paper napkins, and tablecloths
"exactly resembling damask." But until after World War II, paper napkins were primarily used in cheap restaurants and at soda fountains,
often printed and supplied as advertising matter by bottlers of soft
drinks and beer.[46]

Christine Frederick also recommended paper plates, which did not appear in the Sears catalog until 1914 and which remained novel for decades. They reduced dishwashing, could be used in the icebox, and might even serve for baking pies. Frederick claimed that some looked "just like china" and that they were "no longer confined strictly to picnic use" but could be employed for children's summer meals, and even on occasion for adults. In fact, paper plates were so expensive that Frederick suggested using them more than once by lining them with disks of waxed paper, another new product that "is developing daily new uses." Generally purchased in rolls, waxed paper also came folded into bags (which could be used to line garbage pails) and cut into disks to fit cake pans. "It is possible by using a fresh disk at each course, to serve an entire meal (except soup of course) on the same paper plate," Frederick asserted. The china finish plates she recommended cost twenty-five cents a dozen; that quarter would buy a thousand waxed paper disks.[47]

The Lure of Convenience

Christine Frederick's regard for disposable paper products followed directly from her primary passion: household efficiency. Frederick built her career on this idea, writing articles and books that tried to apply to the home the principles made famous in industry by Frederick Winslow Taylor and his followers, including the Gilbreths. In a column in the *Ladies' Home Journal* and in two books, *The New Housekeeping: Efficiency Studies in Home Management* (1913) and *Household Engineering: Scientific Management in the Home* (1919), Frederick taught women to plan and schedule their work, separating their manual labor from their mental labor. She never resolved the fundamental incongruities between household life and industrial efficiency: the absence of the profit motive, the impossibility of a division of labor in a workplace with a solitary worker, and the unavoidable inefficiencies of living with small children.[48]

Whereas Taylor restructured tasks by shaving seconds off the time it took to perform them, Christine Frederick's close connections to the advertising world prompted her to advocate consumption as the means to efficiency. She was the founder in 1912 of the League of Advertising Women. Her husband, J. George Frederick, was at various times the editor of the advertising industry's two leading journals, the weekly *Printers' Ink* and the monthly *Advertising and Selling.* Eventually Christine Frederick turned from advising housewives to counseling businessmen on "Selling Mrs. Consumer," the title of her 1929 book.

The banner of household efficiency was taken up during the 1920s by none other than Lillian Gilbreth, whose background qualified her uniquely. "This book applies to the home the methods of eliminating waste that have been successful in industry," Gilbreth declared in *The Home-Maker and Her Job,* published in 1927, the same year she delivered her Modess report to Johnson & Johnson. The book's central chapters outlined ways of applying the Gilbreths' methods of time and motion study to the household. As an innovator in the field of industrial efficiency, Lillian Gilbreth understood and communicated the technical aspects of Taylorism far better than Christine Frederick, and she promoted consumption less directly. But like Frederick, Gilbreth attacked only particular kinds of "waste": squandered time and the dissipated energy of wasted motion. Gilbreth's book, Frederick's *Household Engineering,* and the industrial classics, Taylor's *Scientific Management* and Frank Gilbreth's *Primer of Scientific Management,* are all concerned with the labor process, and strikingly silent on the subject of wasting materials.[49]

Translated into the language of advertising, household efficiency became "convenience." Convenience was a feminized—or at least home-based—efficiency, a feature of products promoted as worth paying for, a value expounded by publicity for a wide range of goods. Like efficiency in the factory, convenience in the home was intended to save time and wasted effort, but the concept went further. Factory efficiency offered the "one best way" to do a job from the employer's point of view. It never promised freedom from work itself. Convenience, on the other hand, was used to suggest that products could liberate housewives from troubles that ranged from annoyance to hard labor. Modern products offered release from the responsibility of caring for material goods, the stewardship of objects and materials that characterized the traditional relationship to the material world. Advertising proposed that purchasing those products—rust-free aluminum pans or throwaway handkerchiefs—offered consumers the leisured lifestyles once accessible only to wealthy women with servants.

Philosopher Thomas F. Tierney proposes that convenience is a function of technological culture, central to "the hold which technology has on modernity" and "an integral part of the modern self." Assisted by technology, Tierney suggests, the modern household focuses not on satisfying the demands of the body for food, clothing, and shelter but on satisfying them quickly. Indeed, in the modern world, the needs of the body are understood as limits—"inconveniences, obstacles, or annoyances" that impinge on time. The products of modern technology appeal to consumers because they alleviate inconvenience and allow them to satisfy their bodies' needs in as little time as possible.[50]

Certainly time was central to convenience as it was interpreted by advertising, which was only slightly more subtle about speed than it was about germs. "Women, whose time must not be wasted, value the simplicity and reliability of the Hotpoint Vacuum Cleaner," that company declared in 1923. Packaged food products counted minutes. Wheatena could be prepared in "just 2 minutes of boiling and bubbling." Borden's condensed milk furnished the wherewithal to whip up hot chocolate and macaroons "in just nineteen minutes," and thereby to win the heart and hand of a man. Grape Nuts did not have to be cooked at all, a welcome solution for the special problem that breakfast posed in the modern household. A 1927 ad for the product depicted the chaos of morning with a modernistic drawing juxtaposing a frantic couple at the table with fragments of clock faces. "Is there no hope?" read the headline. The copy began: "When the clock hands aren't where they ought to be . . . When time and trains are up to their old tricks of waiting for no man . . . When she-who-gets-the-breakfast shows signs of getting hysterics . . . What then? What then? Is there no hope?"[51]

One way to save time was to make things accessible or handy, saving steps, as the Gilbreths demonstrated in their industrial time and motion studies. This aspect of convenience sometimes had the particularly profitable feature of requiring duplicates of a product rather than only one. "Telephones near at hand," AT&T suggested in the late 1920s, "for Comfort and Convenience." The company's campaign for extension phones sought to break down an attitude that the telephone was a utility rather than a consumer good, a necessity, not to be used for frivolous conversation. Like so many other advertisements for household products, this one employed upper-class imagery. The drawing showed a well-dressed woman with a maid near at hand. The text recommended extra phones in rooms that most people didn't even have: the dressing room, the library, the sun porch.[52]

Many advertisements suggested that products could stand in for the servants that most women could only wish for. Hotpoint actually called its line of small appliances—iron, toaster, curling iron, chafing dish, and the like—"Hotpoint Servants." The naphtha in Fels-Naptha made it seem "as if you had hundreds of tiny helpers doing the rubbing for you." Procter & Gamble's naphtha laundry soap could be thought of "as a laundress—not merely as soap." Advertisements for laundry products promised emancipation from the care and responsibility that washing clothes had required in a previous era, and time released for other pursuits. And indeed, even without washing machines, women whose mothers made soap and carried wash water from wells or creeks to heat on the stove might well regard running water and commercial laundry products as liberating.[53]

Beyond efficiency, then, convenience was a synonym and a metaphor for freedom, a form of well-being that products could provide, an amalgam of luxury, comfort, and emancipation from worry. In this sense, convenience was much like the satisfaction that historian William Leach describes as a goal of the service offered by the turn-of-the-century department store. Leach uses the German *gemütlichkeit,* "a term meaning something like 'pure comfort,' " to convey "a sense that, in the world of goods at least, men and women could find transformation, liberation, a paradise free from pain and suffering, a new eternity in time." The concept of convenience suggested that *gemütlichkeit* might emanate not from service but from products. "Give Your Home the Convenience of Frigidaire," the Delco-Light Company, a subsidiary of General Motors, recommended in 1925. "It is entirely automatic—nothing to replenish, nothing to worry about." The Frigidaire offered "freedom from the possible annoyance of outside ice supply—automatic day-after-day, week-after-week operation, without any attention on your part."[54]

Indeed, convenience meant freedom from work itself. The general claim was applied to all kinds of products. "What a convenience electric light is," General Electric captioned a picture of a colonial woman dipping candles in a 1925 ad. "The early settlers had to learn to make candles themselves—the most arduous of their women's tasks. *Your* light comes at a finger touch." Women who covered their wood floors with Armstrong linoleum made trouble for those who bought their houses half a century later and wanted to remove it, but at the time they installed their new floors, they could "forget that a floor ever had to be scrubbed." Linoleum would "keep spotlessly clean with just an occasional dusting," saving "time and endless labor."[55]

Although candlemaking was actually not the colonial woman's most arduous or most frequent task, General Electric's history lesson was credible because the readers of women's magazines ran houses equipped with a wide range of technology in the mid-1920s. Nobody was dipping candles, but everybody understood that most household tasks could be done with more or less labor. "A single home may be operated in the twentieth century when it comes to ownership of automobile and vacuum cleaner, while its lack of a bathtub may throw it back into another era," the Lynds wrote of Muncie. "Side by side in the same block one observes families using in one case a broom, in another a carpet sweeper, and in a third a vacuum cleaner." The advertising for laundry products made washday look easy and pleasant whether a woman labored over a washboard or used a machine (still generally a hand-cranked model unconnected to plumbing). Chipso, a flaked soap that Procter & Gamble introduced with considerable fanfare in 1925, "cuts work in half," bringing "washday relief" to women whether or not they used a washing machine. "Please don't make a mistake," one ad insisted. "CHIPSO is not a *special* soap for a special method. It doesn't say 'Change your method and I will help you.' It says, 'Wash as you like—I will make your work easier.' " LaFrance bluing and cleansing agent used the same appeal. "Some women use a washing machine, some women use a tub, some women use a boiler," the ad was headlined. But every woman who redeemed the coupon for a free package "will save half her washday work."[56]

The point was that every woman should have her work cut in half—indeed, that no woman should really have to work very hard, whatever laundry technology she used. The fundamental assumptions about life and labor that had prevailed everywhere before the twentieth century, for all but the aristocracy, were now regarded as arguments for drudgery, a word repeated endlessly in the ads. "Free from the drudgery of 'oven watching,' " promised a company that made thermostats for gas ranges, as if checking the oven temperature had once been seriously burdensome or time-consuming. "The woman of today has far too much use for her time and strength to waste it watching an oven in a hot kitchen. . . . Already it is just as out-of-date to buy a range without a Wilcolator, as it would be to buy an automobile without a self-starter. In both cases, the manufacturers have planned to save you from hard work and annoyance which should never be yours." According to the company that made the Vacuette, even electricity could be inconvenient. "What a convenience is this non-electric cleaner!" the ad read. "The Vacuette has no motor—no cords—no connections of any kind . . . it takes the wearying drudgery out of cleaning."[57]

Advertisements in summer issues of the women's magazines claimed that products could turn women's workaday lives into vacations. "A real vacation for you," Shredded Wheat announced in August 1925. "Of course a man must have a vacation—but how about the wife, the mother, the home-maker? Managing a country home, or cooking meals in a bungalow, is not a vacation. A month out in the open under sunny skies, with no kitchen worry or work—that's a real vacation. You can have it with Shredded Wheat. It is ready-cooked and ready-to-eat." An ad for the Hoover vacuum cleaner admitted that such product-generated vacations might be brief. "Why not a 'vacation' for wives?" the headline read, over a drawing of a woman and her children picking flowers in the country. "The leisure hours you've always wanted—the little 'vacations' so inviting in summer—they're yours, when The Hoover comes into your home." The machine would bestow many benefits: "An immaculate home; longer-wearing rugs of enduring beauty; freedom from drudgery—these are yours, with a Hoover. But the thing you'll enjoy most is the leisure hour or two The Hoover brings you."[58]

Convenience—brief "vacations," easier work, and freedom from attention, care, and responsibility—joined cleanliness as a selling point for a wide variety of products; both became prerogatives of American life. Convenience was promoted as a potential benefit of so many products that it became one of the goals of modern living, an attribute of the new lifestyle and of the entire panoply of consumer goods that contemporary experience required. Spotlessness and ease, once attainable only with servants—if at all—could now be achieved by buying things and by throwing things away. With Kleenex, you could always have a clean handkerchief.

The Empire of the Ephemeral

Kleenex, Kotex, and Shredded Wheat boxes—the literal throwaways—represent the most extreme form of a relationship to objects that was new at the beginning of the twentieth century. More and more things were made and sold with an understanding that they would soon be worthless or obsolete. A French social critic, Gilles Lipovetsky, calls contemporary consumer culture an "empire of the ephemeral," arguing that its central feature is the extension of the principle of fashion—obsolescence on the basis of style—to material goods other than clothing and to a broad spectrum of people, "a society restructured from top to bottom by the attractive and the ephemeral." Fashion's "abbreviated time span and its systematic obsolescence have become characteristics inherent in mass production and consumption," he writes, and "consumers spontaneously hold that the new is by nature superior to the old." In Lipovetsky's view, this generalization of the fashion process defines consumer society, which depends on ever-expanding needs and organizes production and consumption along principles of obsolescence, seduction, and diversification.[59]

The expansion of fashion into new realms was part of a more general development in the history of marketing. By the beginning of World War I, manufacturers understood that markets were not shaped by preexisting supply and demand but could be developed and extended. In the pages of their trade journals, marketers spelled out the principles for selling more. Repositioning a product could increase the market: thus Carnation milk, once sold for use on camping and mining expeditions, moved into the home as "The Modern Milkman." Markets could be expanded by suggesting more uses for products: the makers of Shredded Wheat, Baker's chocolate, and nearly every other successful food product gave away recipe booklets full of ideas for using more chocolate or cereal, while Procter & Gamble advertised that Ivory soap could be used in both the bath and the laundry. Year-round demand was created for products previously considered seasonal. And manufacturers found that they could sell more of products as different as phonographs and canned foods if they offered a range of options, different grades at different prices.[60]

Encouraging people to buy new goods before the old ones were used up was another strategy for increasing markets, and fashion a means for doing so. A wide range of consumer goods could be sold according to the principles that the French critic Roland Barthes describes as fundamental to fashion. "If the garment is replaced as soon as it is worn out," he explains, "there is no Fashion." If it is kept much longer than that, there is "pauperization." But "if a person buys more than he wears, there is Fashion, and the more the rhythm of purchase exceeds the rhythm of dilapidation, the stronger the submission to Fashion." Lipovetsky adds that products "are never offered in just one unique form"; consumers choose among models or decide among optional accessories. "Like haute couture," Lipovetsky insists, mass consumption implies more versions, diverse alternatives, and "the stimulation of a personalized demand."[61]

Americans learned the concept of fashion through clothing. The idea that perfectly good clothes might be outdated, or at least the perception that this was how people might think if they could afford to, was introduced to middle-class American women in magazines of the 1850s. *Peterson's, Frank Leslie's Lady's Magazine,* and *Godey's Lady's Book* published "fashion plates"—engravings showing the latest designs—and rudimentary diagrams to help in constructing them. But most followers of the fashion plates stayed in style by making their clothing over. In contrast, Americans of both sexes and all classes commonly bought most of what they wore by the 1920s; if they cared about fashion, and if they could afford to, they followed the trends by buying new clothes ready-made. Making clothes—once a task that occupied most women's every spare moment, a source of craft satisfaction, and the foundation for bricolage—had become a choice, and it was on its way to being a hobby. Women no longer valued the labor of sewing, and they lacked the skills and the scraps that once enabled so many to regard old clothing as worthy of remaking. A ready-made dress, cut and stitched in an unknown sweatshop, could more easily be discarded or given to Goodwill than one made by its wearer or by somebody she knew.[62]

Critics of fashion complained almost from the start that it was reaching beyond clothing. "If fashion would rest satisfied with just controlling our dress, we should find less fault with its encroachments," one writer protested in 1867. "But I should like to see the thing that it does not meddle with. Like the frogs of Egypt, it forces itself into our bed-chambers." She described some stylish bedroom furniture, complaining that the owners had disregarded the sentimental associations that went along with the old set in order to "shiver with poverty under a brilliant and stylish exterior." Half a century later, academic analysts described the extension of fashion beyond the wardrobe as a feature of contemporary consumer culture. In his 1923 text *Economics of the Household,* Benjamin R. Andrews listed the characteristics of modern fashion: "(1) The immense number of objects to which it extends; (2) the uniformity of fashion, which knows no territorial or class limit; and (3) the maddening tempo of the changes of fashion." Economist Hazel Kyrk concurred. "More and more of our consumption goods," she commented, "must include in their bundle of necessary utilities this quality of 'up-to-date-ness,' must evidence the particular feature which has received current approval."[63]

Roland Marchand has shown that the process of extending fashion to a wide variety of objects was well under way in the 1920s, especially with respect to color, which could be varied without redesigning products or retooling factories. Color offered manufacturers a way of converting staple goods, purchased according to Barthes's "rhythm of dilapidation," into fashion goods, purchased on the basis of desire. Many products that had once come in standard black or white were now available in rainbow hues. Parker offered a pen with a red barrel; Willys-Overland pioneered the colored automobile during the early 1920s. Over the next few years, Marchand writes, "major break-throughs in both color and design occurred at an accelerated tempo," and by 1927 "a writer in *Printers' Ink* had enthroned color as 'the sex appeal of business.' "[64]

The Crane Company, which made plumbing fixtures, suggested color in the bathroom in 1925; soon even Montgomery Ward adver-tised sinks, tubs, and toilets that met "the modern demand for COLOR in Bathroom Fixtures." To coordinate with the plumbing—or for those who wanted to spruce up their bathrooms but could not afford new fixtures—Cannon Mills and Martex, both manufacturers of towels, introduced color and decoration in their products, previously available only in white. "The plain vanilla, so to speak, of the modern bathroom is turning pistachio and orange!" Cannon rejoiced in the *Ladies' Home Journal* in 1927, recommending towels to match the soap. "If you are fond of color schemes—and what woman is not?—try having the bathroom appear in towels bordered with blue and orange one week, lavender and green the next." The ad claimed that accommodating to seasonal and weekly rhythms in bathroom fashion would not cost more, but of course it did.[65]

Most women could never afford new bathroom fixtures or even "Vanity Kodaks" (cameras that came in Cockatoo Green and four other colors named for birds and "designed to echo the color scheme of a particular costume"). Many women continued to fill their hope chests with hand-embroidered kitchen towels made out of flour sacks as well as with colored bath towels from the department store. But they were learning the principles that were to make perfectly good refrigerators outdated because of their avocado exteriors. As Christine Frederick put it in 1929, "The same thrill that women have always had over new clothes, women are now obtaining over replacements, changes, reconstructions, new colors and forms in *all* types of merchandise."[66]

Obsolescence: Technology and Styling in Product Design

Manufacturers of the many consumer products that depended on new technologies were not confined to creating new styles and colors: people also replaced goods before the old ones were used up if they had become obsolete because of technological change. Before the twentieth century, technological obsolescence had been a concern of manufacturers faced with decisions about replacing workable production machinery with the latest innovations. By the 1920s, it was an ordinary concept in everyday life, familiar to people who had thrown away old kerosene lamps first in favor of advanced models and then because they had electricity. Major consumption decisions almost always involved technological improvements. All over the country, families chose between indoor plumbing and automobiles, expensive purchases that became widely available during the same decades. Moreover, new technologies were improving. Like computers today, automobiles, radios, and phonographs got better from year to year. Technological obsolescence became as much a concern of people buying things for their houses as of industrialists investing large sums in factories.

Many writers have tried to make the distinction between technological obsolescence and style. In 1908, Edward A. Ross, one of the founders of American sociology, described change "made because it is *better*" as progress and other kinds of change as fashion. Half a century later, Vance Packard denounced style and celebrated technological change in *The Waste Makers*. But the distinction is not so easy to make: Ross's examples of utilitarian products—fountain pens, alarm clocks, telephones, and bathroom floor tiles—had all become objects of styling by the 1920s. Most were also made of new materials or used new technologies. In practice, stylistic and technological obsolescence have gone hand in hand throughout the twentieth century. Avocado refrigerators notwithstanding, Americans have been tempted to replace many products because new ones worked better *and* looked more up-to-date.[67]

By the end of the 1920s, this combination of technological and stylistic obsolescence was part of daily experience for the many Americans who owned or hoped to own radios. Radio had once been a two-way medium, a hobby for a small core of technically oriented, mostly male enthusiasts who listened on headsets; amateur radio operators both transmitted and received radio signals. Now it was a major commercial enterprise, broadcasting entertainment and requiring no skill or knowledge on the part of an audience who tuned in to particular programs, on sets with loudspeakers. Christine Frederick, describing the radio as a consumer product in 1929, commented that progress and obsolescence were at first exclusively technological. Keeping up with the Joneses had entailed "working up from a three tube to a nine tube set," upgrading "as often as twice a year" as new improvements appeared. Later, manufacturers combined radios with phonographs or desks and promoted stylistic change. "Radio sets fitting the particular scheme of furnishings were then bought; and this is the principle operative now," Frederick wrote.[68]

Automobiles provide the most prominent illustration of the workings of obsolescence in the decades before the Depression. The automobile was the single most important product in the new culture of consumption. It dwarfed other items in the family budget, and it changed the physical, economic, and cultural landscape, stimulating highway construction, the development of new communities, and new approaches to everyday activities like shopping, entertainment, and travel, in supermarkets, drive-in movies, and motels. For manufacturers of all kinds of products, the automobile was the ultimate test case for the principles of consumer marketing: if people could learn to discard cars that still worked, for reasons of style or new technologies, they could certainly come to think of anything else as disposable.

The triumph of obsolescence in the automobile industry has been told by a number of historians as part of the explanation for how Henry Ford—tenaciously and ideologically opposed to obsolescence, as a concept and in practice—forfeited his dominant share of the market. The story of Ford's decline and the rise of General Motors, the company that instituted the yearly model change, stands as a parable of the importance of style and change to consumer culture. Henry Ford believed that he was selling basic transportation and opposed model changes on principle. His focus on production efficiency, both before and after his celebrated introduction of the assembly line in 1913, had the effect of continually lowering the price of his product. The price of a Model T Ford—$950 in 1909—dropped to $290 by 1924. Price was Ford's sole focus in marketing, a spectacularly successful strategy for many years.

In contrast, General Motors staked its success on stylistic change. Introduced in stages beginning in 1923, GM's yearly model change was "the innovation no one wanted," according to one historian, Richard Tedlow. Even the company's president, Alfred Sloan, who championed the new policy, acknowledged its drawbacks. Changing models, as many critics have pointed out, increased costs. It pressured production facilities. It committed the company to style and fashion, more difficult to predict and control than other factors of auto design. It required GM constantly to educate its dealers and their salesmen about new models and their new features. But Sloan and his staff were intent on competing in new ways and had the skills to meet these challenges, establishing manufacturing plants and sales organizations capable of adapting to and fostering the annual model change. Indeed, the perpetual production of new models created advantages besides the obvious benefit of generating annual publicity. The system as eventually implemented enabled the company to schedule regular innovation and restyling. To control costs, major technological changes were limited:

they were implemented every three years, the life expectancy of the dies used to stamp the metal. In between, remodeling was confined to matters of surface and style.[69]

Ford initially refused to compete in this way and began to lose market share: the company sold 55 percent of new American cars in 1921 and 30 percent in 1926. By the spring of 1927, a single GM brand—the Chevrolet—had overtaken the Model T, "one of the most startling reversals of brand preference in merchandising annals," in Roland Marchand's words. Henry Ford eventually caved in, shutting down production entirely in 1926 to overhaul his product. The next year, he introduced the Model A, with fanfare organized by a leading advertising agency, N. W. Ayer and Son. The Model A was a perfect example of Lipovetsky's tenet that "the increasing of models, the diversification of series, the production of optional differences, the stimulation of a personalized demand" are central to ephemeral consumer culture. It came in colors and in twelve different body types—sedans, coupes, a roadster, a station wagon—as opposed to the Model T's six. "Note the wide variety in type and color," the Ayer copy crowed.[70]

Still, Henry Ford insisted that a Ford was forever. He described the new car as "so strong and so well-made that no one ought ever to have to buy a second one." At the same time Ford and Ayer were promoting the new styles, they promoted the services of Ford dealers for reconditioning Model Ts. "Protect Your Investment in Your Model T Ford," read one ad. "The Ford Motor Company is making a new car, but it is still proud of the Model T. It wants every owner of one of these cars to run it as long as possible at a minimum of expense." Many of the more than eight million Ts on the road, the ad explained, would still last for "two, three and five years and even longer." Their owners were urged to take them to Ford dealers for estimates on the cost of replacement parts. Another in this series of advertisements, "It Costs Very Little to Recondition a Model T Ford," detailed labor charges for overhauling engines and transmissions, tightening doors, and taking dents out of body panels.[71]

Many car owners, however, preferred to get rid of old cars rather than recondition them. The development of a substantial resale market for secondhand cars made old cars available to people who could not afford new ones, further broadening the influence of the automobile. Indeed, it kept the new-car market afloat. Few automobile owners would buy the latest models, however attractive, if they could not get money for the cars they had. Dealers gave trade-in allowances on old ones, but as time went on, their stock of used cars mounted and trade-ins ate into their profits. Because they were required by the manufacturers to sell their quotas of new cars and because they could only do so by taking cars in trade, considerable friction ensued between dealers and the auto companies, which intensified as the used-car market expanded. To stave off this conflict, the manufacturers developed the used-car market as consciously as they did the one for new cars. It was a delicate balance, as Alfred Sloan recalled in his autobiography. Model changes had to be "so novel and attractive as to create demand for the new value and, so to speak, create a certain amount of dissatisfaction with past models as compared with the new one, and yet the current and old models must still be capable of giving satisfaction to the vast used car market." By the late 1920s, used-car sales exceeded new-car sales, and most new cars were bought with trade-ins.[72]

The automobile market served as a model for manufacturers and dealers of other consumer goods. An emphasis on styling and the yearly model change became selling points for products of all kinds. Philco redesigned radios annually, offering new technology along with new looks. "Decide now to trade-in your out-of-date radio," the company urged in 1934, recommending improved shortwave reception on its "forty-nine magnificent models," encased in "gorgeous, costly woods." Sears asked a noted industrial designer, Raymond Loewy, to redesign its refrigerators in 1932. His first Coldspot appeared in 1935, and he introduced yearly model changes thereafter. Other manufacturers followed suit. Even Kotex offered the "1934 Wondersoft Kotex," improved by three new patented features and packaged in a "smart-looking" box.[73]

Manufacturers and dealers of radios and refrigerators debated in their trade journals about what to do with old appliances. "Are Used Sets Like Used Cars?" *Radio Broadcast* asked in 1929. Its article asserted that "the radio industry is beginning to meet exactly analogous problems" to those in the auto industry and explained various plans for cooperation among dealers in used cars. Similarly, *Electrical Merchandising* discussed the ins and outs of reconditioning trade-in washing machines and other major appliances. The formation of markets in used radios, washers, and refrigerators raised issues for readers: what should be junked and what reconditioned, how much to give for a trade-in to keep from losing the sale, the high costs of trade-ins, and the kinds of guarantees that should be offered.[74]

New and Different

Constantly changing models of refrigerators and automobiles encouraged Americans to venerate the new and repudiate the old and the customary. As pistachio-colored towels and the latest-model radio supplanted still-usable items, the old ones might be classified as trash, moved to the basement, given to a friend or relative, or sent to the Salvation Army, to be used by someone poorer. In a larger sense, incessant novelty battled tradition and custom. "Newness and change themselves had become traditional in America," writes William Leach, commenting on the "cult of the new," which "readily subverted whatever custom, value, or folk idea came within its reach."[75]

The extension of fashion beyond the arena of clothing and beyond the well-to-do supposedly meant that everybody could join the cult of the new and apply its tenets to an ever-growing list of household items. Christine Frederick asserted that the principles applied to everyone, "on successively lower levels of American life until we reach 'hardpan,' or those approximately 93 millions who are too close to necessity to dispose of their purchases much before the last usage is out of them." And even these people bought fourth- or fifth-hand autos and radios. The accelerated obsolescence exercised by the wealthy increased the standard of living of the poor. Now, Frederick claimed, nearly everyone's purchases exhibited a new element, previously available only to the rich: "indulgence, luxury, fancy, excess and pleasure, in addition to plain necessity." Frederick's statement is striking, given a population of 122 million; more than three-quarters of the American population was "hard-pan" by her estimation, even before the Depression started. Her general thesis that virtually everybody participated in the consumer culture is difficult to substantiate solely in terms of luxury and fancy; the owners of most fourth- and fifth-hand autos had to spend too many hours on their backs underneath their cars, trying to fix the machines that were supposed to be raising their standard of living. But the used radios did a good job of keeping working-class Americans tuned in to that consumer culture, and while the "hard-pan" did not live indulgently, they had more stuff—and threw more away—than their parents and grandparents.[76]

Christine Frederick and her husband, J. George Frederick, were leading celebrants of this state of affairs. In her *Selling Mrs. Consumer* (1929) and his *A Philosophy of Production* (1930), both published by his own Business Bourse, they coined and defined the phrase *progressive obsolescence*. She enumerated its characteristics: first, a suggestible state of mind, "eager and willing to take hold of anything new"; second, "a readiness to 'scrap' or lay aside an article *before its natural life of usefulness is completed,* in order to make way for the new and better thing"; and third, a willingness to spend money, "a very large share of one's income, even if it pinches savings," in order to have new things and new experiences.[77]

Christine Frederick claimed that this set of attitudes was distinctly American and that progressive obsolescence was the source of American achievement. She attacked "European cultural domination" and "the Old Antique-Worshiping Standards," and the people who insisted that cultured and civilized people lived in antique-filled homes, "treasuring the old" and "disdaining the new." The time had come, Frederick insisted, for "a parting of the ways with Europe." Progressive obsolescence was "the very knife-blade which is carving this cleavage." Europeans thought it wise to "buy once and of very substantial, everlasting materials," like long-wearing English tweeds, "and you never buy again if you can help it." But that kind of buying, Frederick explained, slowed the rate of progress.[78]

Americans did the opposite. They believed that "Mrs. Consumer is happiest and best served if she consumes goods at the same approximate rate of change and improvement that science and art and machinery can make possible," instead of consuming them until they were no longer usable. "If designers and weavers and inventors of rapid machinery make it possible to choose a new pattern of necktie or dress every few weeks, and there is human pleasure in wearing them, why be an old frump and cling to an old necktie or old dress until it wears through?" Frederick asked. "To cling to the old one will discourage designers from designing new ones, discourage inventors from making fast machinery, and discourage business men from offering new things. There is nothing civilized or cultured in this."[79]

The year after he published his wife's *Selling Mrs. Consumer*, J. George Frederick's *A Philosophy of Production* made the same point. A third of the book was his own writing; the rest consisted of essays by others, including such captains of industry as Henry Ford, Bernard Baruch, and the president of AT&T. In a chapter entitled "Obsolescence, Free Spending and Creative Waste," Frederick described obsolescence as "the spearhead of a sound philosophy of production." In "Obsolescence and the Passing of High-Pressure Salesmanship," the executive director of the American Institute of Steel Construction declared that progressive obsolescence was the new basis of business. "What do I mean by 'progressive obsolescence'?" he asked. "I mean *our readiness to scrap half-worn goods for new.*"[80]

There were other voices and countervailing arguments. Academics still read the work of Thorstein Veblen, whose *Theory of the Leisure Class* (1899) analyzed and satirized the rise of consumerism and the expansion of "pecuniary emulation." Engineers continued to promote standardization, insisting that vast resources were being wasted because products came in too many styles and sizes. The American Society for Thrift, established by a mortgage banker in 1914 and active well into the 1920s, was the hub of a network of thrift evangelists who organized school lessons on saving. And in *Middletown* (1929), their best-selling study of Muncie, the husband-and-wife team of Robert and Helen Merrell Lynd observed many of the same phenomena that the Fredericks celebrated, but with a critical eye. Nonetheless, savings lessons represented an old ethic, and even the strongest advocates of standardization and thrift had to make those concepts palatable to readers steeped in the new consumer culture. Nearly every discussion of standardization included an obligatory reassurance that nobody was advocating standardized sofas or women's hats. In 1925, the editor of the *Journal of Home Economics* even redefined thrift to mean "wise spending of money."[81]

Toward the Throwaway Culture

"The Roaring Twenties" may have a reputation for prosperity, but it was not a time of conspicuous consumption. Economic indicators rose, but Americans did not share this good fortune equally. Wages increased only modestly, especially for the unskilled and semiskilled workers who still dominated in industrial employment. Unemployment was high in such major industries as agriculture, coal, and textiles. The "fully employed" got laid off frequently, for even skilled industrial work was often seasonal.

Nonetheless, most families were moving toward a modern relationship to the material world. People made fewer things and bought more than their parents and grandparents had. They saved and fixed less and threw out more, for the habits of reuse had always been intertwined with the skills of household production. Within any particular family, neighborhood, or community, individuals held to old ways, modified new ones, and found ways of doing a little of each. Few people adopted the ideas of progressive obsolescence all at once. Many grandparents did as they had always done; most children coveted new products and the lifestyles they represented even if they only saw them in the movies. Some old ways survived longer in the country, others in immigrant neighborhoods. But despite this uneven development, contemporaries saw the changes as fundamental, and so they appear with the historian's hindsight.

The new consumer culture changed ideas about throwing things away, creating a way of life that incorporated technological advances, organizational changes, and new perspectives, a lifestyle that linked products made for one-time use, municipal trash collection, and the association of traditional reuse and recycling with poverty and backwardness. Packaging taught people the throwaway habit, and new ideals of cleanliness emphasized swift and complete disposal. Paper cups, towels, and straws in public places, and Kleenex and commercial toilet paper at home, reinforced that habit. Nor could the new throwaways serve as fuel in houses with radiators and gas furnaces; they went in the trash, along with the lightbulbs.

In the empire of the ephemeral, Americans got rid of things sooner. Everyone could be fashionable, or at least large numbers of people paid attention to new styles and to the idea that wearable clothes might be outdated. The extension of fashion concepts to many goods beyond clothing encouraged people to replace things before they were used up, even as diversified models and colors encouraged consumers to buy more of what they already had. Technological obsolescence became a concern of ordinary households as Americans replaced their old lamps and stoves with gas and electric heating, hot water, and lighting systems. Purchasing radios and automobiles, consumers exchanged old for new because the old—even the not-very-old—was both stylistically and technologically obsolete.

The taste for novelty, the conviction that new things represented progress, and the belief that products were desirable because they represented modernity contributed to the celebration of the modern way. It all added up to well-being, a luxurious life without annoyance or worry, in which even women without servants could have time for leisure, good works, and what would later be called "quality time" with children. The propaganda was effective in part because fundamental household technologies had in fact brought life in the average household closer than it had ever been to the life of the wealthy. The benefits were tangible, saving women time and labor, freeing them from lengthy processes like making soap and candles, from the innumerable smaller tasks involved in caring for goods, and from work created by making, and cleaning up after, open fires. New products raised standards, and consumption itself became a new form of work, but as the example of the sanitary napkin suggests, it never rivaled the burdens of the old ways.

In this context, the rhetoric of convenience, luxury, and cleanliness was potent. It sold a wide variety of products that transformed Americans' relationship to waste and, in general, to the material world. In a few decades, the ideal of the durable and reusable was displaced by aspirations of leisure and luxury, ease and cleanliness. The new ways were entrenched by 1929, in principle if not always in practice, and neither a depression nor the material shortages of a world war were enough to reverse what most people saw as progress.

CHAPTER FIVE

Making Do and Buying
New in Hard Times

Writing in *House & Garden* in 1930, Richardson Wright, the magazine's editor and the author of the recent *Hawkers and Walkers in Early America*, reminisced about peddlers and tinkers. "According to contemporary economists," Wright asserted, the thrift represented by the "picturesque itinerants" who once bought and repaired the castoffs of middle- and upper-class households would be "the worst sort of citizenship" in Depression America. "We live in a machine age," he explained. "To maintain prosperity we must keep the machines working, for when machines are functioning men can labor and earn wages. The good citizen does not repair the old; he buys anew. The shoes that crack are to be thrown away. Don't patch them. When the car gets crotchety, haul it to the town's dump. Give to the ashman's oblivion the leaky pot, the broken umbrella, the clock that doesn't tick. To maintain prosperity we must keep those machines going."[1]

Wright used the phrase *factor of obsolescence*, suggesting that, as the editor of a leading home magazine, he was familiar with Christine

Frederick's recent *Selling Mrs. Consumer* or that he had picked up the terminology from others who were. But the larger position Wright was pointing to—that economic growth was fueled by what had once been understood as waste—went beyond Frederick's formulation. It got to the heart of prevailing theories about the causes of the Depression.

Common sense suggested that hard times would get better if people would just spend their money. "This whole depression business is largely mental," an Indiana newspaper wrote in a 1930 editorial. If every person would just "unwind the red yarn that is wound about his old leather purse . . . the whole country could join in singing, 'Happy Days Are Here Again.' " Professional economists, blaming the Depression on "underconsumption," made essentially the same point.[2]

But if people were "underconsuming" during the years before Wall Street crashed, they were nevertheless doing so as consumers. Few people made soap anymore; most bought clothing, and sewing was becoming a hobby. When hard times came, most younger people, at least, were already thoroughly consumerist. Their versions of "making do" and watching their wallets when the effects of the crash hit home were framed by consumer concerns and consumer possibilities. People with jobs—three-quarters of the workforce—continued to apply for and receive the credit they had learned to use during the more expansive 1920s, when many bought cars, bedroom sets, and clothing on time. Now they bought refrigerators on time with the excuse that they would save money on food. They stayed home in the evenings to save money but amused themselves with hobbies that cost money, like making quilts from kits.

Depression-era consumers were courted by advertisers and tempted by industrial designers, who set out to loosen the yarn around their purses, vanquishing underconsumption with new colors and designs, new ideas for using products, and better packaging. Industrial design was a "depression baby," in the words of historian Jeffrey Meikle. Advertising agents and department store executives may have cared about the way products looked in the 1920s, but most manufacturers did not become interested in product styling until after the crash. They were willing to try designers' radical ideas—the streamlining and the Art Deco styles that became identified with the 1930s—"because they had nothing to lose," whether that amounted to optimism or desperation. "Within a few years industrial design became a fad among manufacturers."[3]

Many companies hired designers to revamp their packages. Kotex boasted that women praised its "smart-looking" new package, grateful for the privacy it offered, since it no longer was shaped like all the other sanitary napkin boxes, which imitated the previous Kotex design. Bon Ami offered scouring powder in two packages, one an Art Deco–style black-and-gold "deluxe" container "so smart in appearance that you'll be proud to keep it out in plain sight, anywhere. It harmonizes perfectly with any bathroom color scheme."[4]

Fortune declared that, although nobody could agree about whether to change packaging subtly or dramatically, everybody recognized that new packaging could save money or sell more goods, perhaps both. The American Management Association held yearly packaging expositions beginning in 1931, with presentations by leading lights of the packaging field. The trade press trumpeted the success stories. Hanes reduced its costs by repackaging hosiery in a transparent bag; sales at one Brooklyn department store tripled the first day, then settled down at double their previous rate. A food company repackaged more than fifty products and increased sales by 10 to 700 percent.[5]

People in the advertising business were explicit about their intent to get consumers "to abandon the old and buy the new to be up-to-date," in the words of a top advertising agent, Earnest Elmo Calkins, writing in 1932. "Does there seem to be a sad waste in the process?" he asked. "Not at all. Wearing things out does not produce prosperity, but buying things does. Thrift in the industrial society in which we now live consists of keeping all the factories busy." Aldous Huxley simplified and satirized this catechism in *Brave New World,* published the same year. "I do love having new clothes," whisper the recordings played to sleeping babies in the anti-utopian nurseries. "Old clothes are beastly. . . . We always throw away old clothes. Ending is better than mending." But Calkins insisted that the only option besides promoting spending was to "turn back the page to earlier and more primitive times when people got along with little and made everything last as long as possible. We have built up a complicated industrial machine and we must go on with it, or throw it into reverse and go backward."[6]

Roy Sheldon and Egmont Arens, both industrial designers for the Calkins advertising agency, justified the work they did in the language of obsolescence, "the barometer of progress for the consumer." People who focused on "the scrapping process and the junk-heap" instead of on new, attractive products, the designers explained, were prejudiced against advertising and afraid of fashion. Obsolescence was "the thrusting force which clears the way for the more desirable product, the more convenient article, the more beautiful object." Obsolescence released the consumer "from the shackles of tradition, from outworn equipment and ideas." There was plenty of waste, Sheldon and Arens admitted, "but let's put the responsibility where it belongs. The workings of obsolescence by themselves do not create waste. It is the manufacturer who attempts to oppose changing fashions, who defies obsolescence or attempts to halt its march, who creates the waste." They offered the definitive example: Henry Ford shutting his factory to convert to the Model A.[7]

Sheldon and Arens, their boss Calkins, and others in the advertising business may have been alarmed by unemployment rates as high as 25 percent, but their job was to influence the majority who did have some money to spend. Throughout the Depression, people bought less, did without, and practiced countless small economies in their daily lives. Nationwide, retail sales dropped 48 percent between 1929 and 1933 and then rose slowly during the rest of the decade. But some kinds of consumption changed more than others. Sales in food stores remained constant, in general-merchandise stores nearly so. The statistics suggest that people who did have money to spend sacrificed luxuries, in order to assist family and friends who had lost their jobs or to save for their own security. In Muncie, for example, jewelry stores were the hardest hit, with a decrease of 85 percent in sales between 1929 and 1933, followed by lumberyards, car dealerships, and candy stores.

Restaurants suffered a drop of 63 percent in sales as people stopped going out to eat.[8]

At the same time, the definition of luxury continued to change along lines that had been developing since before World War I. By the time of the crash, electricity and automobiles—luxuries a generation earlier—while not yet universal, had become commonplace. Residential use of electricity and consumption of gasoline both went up during the Depression. Purchases of new cars went down, but not overall car registrations; people drove older cars, but they continued to drive. And two major consumer durables—radios and electric refrigerators—actually moved out of the luxury category during the Depression.[9]

In the world depicted by the home magazines, homeowners were even remodeling, though some concessions to economy were usually part of the process. *House Beautiful* featured a large Massachusetts house, newly equipped with a modern gas range and contemporary cabinets. The old soapstone sink and drainboards were retained and reused, raised to a comfortable height and equipped with a sliding towel rack. For other remodelers who wanted to cut corners, "knotty pine," once considered cheap in both senses of the word, was now marketed as stylish.[10]

The government provided an incentive for remodeling by including renovations in the federal home-building program. Under the National Housing Act of 1934, homeowners could borrow up to two thousand dollars at 5 percent interest, with five years to pay off the loan. A major nationwide survey had suggested that more than half of American houses were in need of repair. At least a quarter of urban homes lacked plumbing, gas, electricity, or central heating. The government-guaranteed loans would pay for upgrading housing stock and channel money into local economies. "Home renovating," a writer explained in *Good Housekeeping*, "is being put up to the home owner as a patriotic duty—something for which he will get one hundred cents on the dollar in value and personal satisfaction, but also a comparatively small and easy thing that he can do to aid industry to move and to help bring his country back to normal spending." *Good*

Housekeeping offered an added incentive, five-hundred-dollar prizes for the best interior and exterior remodeling jobs. But most readers of home magazines, then as now, could only dream of remodeling. The small government loans—granted to one out of eight American homeowners between 1934 and 1937—typically paid for exterior paint, a heating system, or electric wiring. The act authorized much larger and longer-term loans for new housing, and as the program developed, it favored—and shaped—new suburban developments rather than renovations.[11]

Home remodeling exemplifies the high end of Depression consumption, but the salvaged sink in the remodeled kitchen represents a common thirties phenomenon: the ways of modern consumption mingled with the ways of making do. Most families juggled priorities, economizing on items that were less important to them while spending and even splurging on others. One midwestern farm woman, Anna Pratt Erickson, made clothing and household linens from flour and sugar sacks during the Depression, canned a good deal of her family's food, and disconnected the phone to save money. But she also bought many things: clothing, a new stove, a radio, a pressure cooker, and a new Maytag washer for her daughter Dorothy, purchased on time.[12]

Anna Erickson's radio was one of many sold during the Depression, a purchase that could bring many hours of entertainment for the small additional cost of electricity. In 1936, a market research firm that studied fifty-three thousand households in sixteen cities found that 91 percent of Americans owned radios, compared with fewer than 20 percent nine years earlier. Radios were marketed during the Depression as they had been during the 1920s, on the basis of annual styling and technological obsolescence. Manufacturers slashed prices after the stock market crashed, and over the next few years they introduced smaller models, with pressed-metal and plastic cases instead of fine wood cabinets. By 1933, the average radio cost $35, down from $133 in 1929. About half the sets sold were small models that most families could afford.[13]

Refrigerators: Saving by Buying

Refrigerator prices, too, were reduced once the Depression started, and their sales were even stronger than those of radios, although refrigerators were much more expensive. Only very wealthy people owned electric refrigerators in the late 1920s: less than half of one percent of the homes in one midwestern city had them in 1927. Nine years later, 60 percent of the households in the sixteen-city survey cited above had refrigerators. Their phenomenal popularity during the Depression was achieved by marketing that acknowledged hard times. Even in the posh *House Beautiful,* General Electric advertised that "most people buy on our easy time payment plan."[14]

Refrigerator advertising went beyond arguing that Depression-era consumers could find a way to afford this major purchase. It claimed that they could scarcely afford not to buy refrigerators. "Invest in an Electric Refrigerator," GE counseled in *Cosmopolitan* (then an upper-middle-class magazine featuring fiction by well-known authors), as if there were money to be made by purchasing consumer goods. "Have the enjoyment of General Electric convenience now. Each month's delay means dollars wasted. Your G-E will actually pay its own way into your home. It can save from 20% to 30% of your monthly food bills. . . . A small down payment will put a General Electric in your kitchen tomorrow." Norge asserted that its product would save households up to eleven dollars a month. "You don't have to save *for* a Norge—you save *with* it," read the headline. The explanation was partly technological: "the Rollator mechanism—exclusive with Norge." Magazine editorial copy echoed the advertising vocabulary: "Generous food compartment space in the refrigerator will prove a worth-while investment," *Good Housekeeping* claimed in 1934.[15]

To actually achieve the savings, the housewife had to change her buying and cooking habits. Depression editions of the cookbooks that came with new refrigerators explained the mechanics of money saving. Before the crash, these were hardbound books adorned with color drawings, befitting the luxury status of the refrigerator. Economy appears in them only as a secondary reason for using leftovers. The home economist Alice Bradley's 1929 book for GE emphasized the dainty possibilities of using odds and ends of food in new kinds of recipes made possible by the refrigerator: jellied and frozen salads, fruit creams, jellied soups, and aspics. These dishes employed the refrigerator not only to store ingredients but to "cook with cold." Similarly, *Frigidaire Recipes* (1928) contained a chapter on leftovers that concerned primarily the proteins and vitamins that made food too good to throw away and the labor and time that could be saved by reusing it.[16]

The Depression-era softbound revision, *Your Frigidaire* (1934), made a strong appeal to economy, offering explicit instructions for quantity buying and for menu planning with leftovers. "New Thrift in Marketing," one section was headlined. "Because Frigidaire preserves foods for such long periods, it enables you to save surprising sums of money each month." Again, technology provided the foundation for the housewife's craft. Because food would keep for as long as a week in the Frigidaire, the maker claimed, the housewife could "keep leftovers long enough to have them come to the table with fresh appetite appeal"; her family would barely remember having eaten them before. She could purchase in quantity and take advantage of sales. By consulting advertisements, she could buy chuck roast and strip steak on sale, freeze the steaks for use during the week, cook the roast on Sunday, and use leftover juices and meat in soup, stew, or croquettes during the week.[17]

Instructions for saving on canned goods were even more explicit, phrased like a schoolbook word problem. "A No. 2 can (20 ounces) of crushed pineapple was purchased for 15 cents, while a No. 2-1/2 can (30 ounces) of the same brand was purchased for 19 cents. The cost of the extra 10 ounces was only 4 cents! Half of the pineapple was used for a salad on Sunday, and the balance was used for a sherbet which was frozen in the Frigidaire for Thursday evening dinner." Milk and cream could be purchased in larger bottles, lettuce bought at three for a quarter instead of ten cents a head. "Good things" could be made "out of odds and ends which would otherwise be wasted. This means a large saving and a great contribution to better living." But lest any-one misinterpret better living to be the equivalent of frugality, these lessons in saving were printed opposite the first page of a chapter devoted to appetizers for formal luncheons and fancy dinners. The first four recipes called for caviar, probably not on the shelves of most Depression-era Frigidaire buyers.[18]

Storing leftovers in a new electric refrigerator was one instance of a new consumerist bricolage that linked modern consumption with tradi-tional habits of making do. There were other manifestations. Cotton sacks from flour and animal feed were made into dresses and embroi-dered tea towels, not always because of poverty but in response to commercial tactics. Quilts were commonly made from purchased pat-terns during the Depression, filled with nationally advertised cot-ton batting, and pieced from fabric purchased expressly for quilting rather than from sewing scraps or old clothing. Home repair became the occasion for trips to the store. And people who could not afford to shop in regular stores remade clothing bought at Goodwill and the Sal-vation Army.

Flour Sacks and Other "Dual-Use Packaging"

"I think that's a flour sack dress I'm wearing," the subject of one of Marion Post Wolcott's famous Farm Security Administration photo-graphs commented to Wolcott's biographer nearly half a century later. "I remember how Mama would boil and bleach the lettering out. They could turn about anything into something else, they set their minds to it." In fact, the Depression-era flour sack dress is not a straightforward symbol for the making do that conquered grinding poverty. Many—probably most—rural women reused flour and feed sacks during the Depression, not only the wretchedly poor. Nor was sack reuse simply the product of individual women's ingenuity. It was the result of a mar-keting campaign that lasted for decades.[19]

Information on reusing cotton bagging appeared first in the col-umns of magazines addressed to farm women during the 1910s and

1920s, amidst much other material about reuse and thrift. During the Depression years, a number of companies and organizations—including the Textile Bag Manufacturers Association, the National Cotton Council, Sears, Roebuck, and the 4-H Clubs—published booklets variously titled "Sewing with Cotton Bags," "Sewing with Flour Bags," or "Bag Magic for Home Sewing." These books provided instructions for turning sacks into everyday articles like aprons, housedresses, and dish towels, and into gift items like broom covers and "toast pockets." At least one booklet even suggested saving the string the sacks were fastened with, for tying comforters or crocheting doilies and table mats. The promotions continued for decades; the National Cotton Council was still sponsoring bag-crafts contests at state fairs during the 1950s.[20]

Sugar and flour companies made bag reuse part of their advertising. One large miller broke into the market in an immigrant mining district by changing the cotton he used for sacking, labeling his sacks with washable ink, and helping grocers decorate their windows with displays of garments created from flour bags. In 1933, the Savannah Sugar Refining Corporation mounted a major campaign based on bag reuse. Print advertising offered free copies of a booklet about making clothing from Dixie Crystals sugar bags. The company sent letters about the campaign to retail grocers and county demonstration agents. Grocery stores were urged to donate bags to the Red Cross and local parent-teacher associations; company representatives worked with these organizations to set up programs that made clothing for the poor. Georgia's governor was photographed wearing overalls made from sugar bags.[21]

Reusing cotton bagging was a long-standing practice, especially on farms, which used seed and animal feed that came in sacks, in addition to considerable amounts of flour and sugar. Plain, coarsely woven cotton muslin bags were first produced in the 1850s, shortly after the invention of the sewing machine, and women naturally adapted them to their traditional sewing habits. Reused sacks were sometimes called "chicken linen" after chicken feed sacks, but they came from products of all kinds. Sugar, salt, flour, animal feed, seed, and fertilizer containers might be turned into all kinds of clothing, as well as into diapers, sanitary napkins, table linens, or towels. Bags were also used in quilts. They were usually dyed and used to make quilt backings, but there was a fad during the 1930s for quilt tops made from flour sacks with the printing left on and embellished with embroidery.[22]

Printing first appeared on sacks in the 1880s; instructions for removing it were central to the published information about how to reuse sacks. Sometimes these directions were printed on the bag as part of the labeling. Other manufacturers printed their trademarks on paper bands; sewn into the seam or pasted onto the sacks, they could be removed by soaking in water. Margaret Lien, a North Dakota woman, remembered her flour sack underwear. Her mother was good at bleaching out the printed label. "She didn't leave parts of the name. Some people had Pillsbury on their seat."[23]

Manufacturers who used paper labels or printed reuse information on their bags were explicitly creating "dual-use packaging"—designed to serve other purposes after its original contents were used up. Advertising and packaging trade journals promoted this practice vigorously throughout the early 1930s. A leading packaging expert, C. B. Larrabee, explained that the dual-use package had two advantages: it might induce customers to buy a product, and it remained in the home as an "ever-present advertisement for the product."[24]

The ideas were endless. National Biscuit packed crackers in a container that could be used as a child's lunch box. Ocean Spray cranberry sauce came in a savings bank. The boxes from Pepperell sheets turned into backgammon boards. Borden's sold malted milk in an emerald-green glass jar that made an attractive container for sugar or coffee. Bouquet Lentheric cologne came in decanters on an ivory plastic tray; filled with cocktails or cordials, they made "a logical, sensible, transition 'from boudoir to banquet.' " Hickok packaged garters and suspenders in a simulated-leather book cover, cuff links and tie pins in plastic cigarette boxes and miniature ashtrays, belts in a zinc cocktail-shaker head. The General Pencil Company offered ink in a triple-purpose bottle—cocktail shaker, lamp base, or refrigerator water jar—and, for twenty cents in postage, supplied the accessories to make the conversions. (The enthusiastic article in *Modern Packaging* that touted this advance did not explain why consumers would want ink in bottles big enough for lamp bases.)[25]

From the marketers' standpoint, dual-use packaging had drawbacks and pitfalls. The advertising trade journal *Printers' Ink* warned that elaborate containers might make consumers believe they were "paying for the package rather than for the contents." Larrabee suggested that the dual-use package was excellent for gifts but warned manufacturers of staple goods to offer a regular container as well because there were limits to how many lunch boxes or ashtrays any one family needed. And some products simply did not foster dual use, as Lillian Gilbreth pointed out to Johnson & Johnson. Her respondents stated clearly that they had no interest in saving sanitary napkin boxes for other purposes, so Modess packaging need not be decorative or sturdy. "Their answers," Gilbreth wrote, "ranged from a disgusted, 'Hell, no!' to the satiric, 'I use them for sending Christmas presents.' "[26]

But cotton sacks provided the exception to Larrabee's rule about staple goods and dual use: women who sewed could always use more fabric, especially in hard times. Manufacturers of textile bags therefore promoted dual use by introducing bags with floral or geometric designs, especially as new kinds of paper began to compete with cotton for bagging. At least one manufacturer claimed that it made a thousand different patterns of bag cloth. Virgie Bowers, an Indiana woman, remembered printed feed sacks woven to look like linen. "We made everything from them," she recalled. "Another thing that made lovely table covers at that time was the seed corn sacks. That was a little heavier sack, but four of them made a nice square for a square table or a card table. We put them together with single tatting or a little crocheting, then around the edge put an edging on to match. And they made beautiful covers." A Pennsylvania woman remembered "the excitement I felt on Saturday mornings when I was allowed to go to the feed mill with my dad. While we were waiting for the grinding to be completed, I'd look at feed sacks and dream about a new dress."27

Fifty million printed flour and feed bags were sold every year by the end of the Depression, and one writer claimed that three million farm women and children "of all income levels" were wearing garments made of bagging. A hundred-pound sack provided a yard and a quarter of fabric for a nickel, the cost of the deposit. One sack made a pillowcase, four a tablecloth or sheet. Feed stores and grain elevators bought the sacks back from those who did not want them, selling them to those who did. Sacks could also be purchased from bakers or obtained from friends. Eventually even Macy's and Sears sold laundered flour sacks for use as dish towels. "They made some nice things," recalled Pearl Laffitte, a retired home economist who had given demonstrations on using sacks. "The only fault I ever found with it was on washday. You had to starch and iron them. You couldn't wear it without."28

Quilting: Handcraft as Hobby and Moneymaker

In the depths of the Depression, the Sears, Roebuck company (which had previously sponsored contests for the best ear of seed corn and the best stalk of cotton) offered a thousand-dollar prize for the best quilt in America. Newspaper advertisements announced the contest. The final round was to be exhibited at the modernistic Sears Pavilion at the 1933 Chicago Century of Progress exposition; a two-hundred-dollar bonus would go to the winner of the grand prize if the quilt commemorated the theme of the fair. The winner would meet Eleanor Roosevelt at the White House. The ad announcing the contest in the *Chicago Tribune* also promoted quilting materials: "serviceable" white muslin for backings at ten yards for seventy-nine cents, fashionable pastel sateens for twenty-nine cents a yard. The ad invited women to the main Chicago store for a quilt show and a demonstration of the craft by Mae G. Wilford, a "national authority on quilts" who would answer questions, give each visitor a free pattern, and help pick fabric and plan entries for the Century of Progress contest. "Once grandmother's pastime," the ad read, "quilt making becomes the pleasure of the present generation. . . . Don't wait until your friends show you their beautiful hand made quilts . . . start yours now."[29]

The Sears contest was the biggest quilt promotion of its day, one of many manifestations of a Depression-era quilting fad. The company received more than twenty-four thousand entries and displayed many of them before the fair started, in hundreds of local and regional quilt shows. Five million Century of Progress visitors came to see the thirty quilts on display at the Sears Pavilion, which also featured dioramas representing the history of merchandising, an exhibit of furs, and photographs of some of the 102,000 contestants in Sears's national baby contest. After it was all over, the company published a special catalog, *The Quilt Fair Comes to You,* with patterns and instructions for the prizewinning quilts and advertising for Sears yard goods.[30]

Quilting had been a dying art in the 1910s and early 1920s. Quilt entries dropped dramatically at the Minnesota State Fair, for example, and more came from old women living in rest homes than from younger farm women or small-town clubwomen. But the craft was revitalized during the 1920s. Traditional American handcrafts were given the imprimatur of high culture with the 1924 opening of the American Wing at the Metropolitan Museum of Art, which inspired one of a series of colonial revivals. Quilts became fashionable among stylists for home magazines and women who hired decorators. Books addressed both to collectors and to craftswomen stimulated considerable interest in the traditional reuse arts, rugs and quilts; the best known were Ruth Findley's *Old Patchwork Quilts and the Women Who Made Them* (1929), Carrie A. Hall and Rose G. Kretsinger's *The Romance of the Patchwork Quilt in America* (1935), and Ella Shannon Bowles's *Handmade Rugs* (1937).[31]

The fashion spread. Like Sears, newspapers and magazines sponsored quilt contests with cash prizes. In big cities, shows displaying as many as eight hundred quilts attracted crowds of up to twenty-five thousand people. Women of all classes could participate. Wealthy women could study and collect quilts if they did not choose to sew;

poor ones could produce them for sale; middle-class women could make quilts for their own beds and their daughters' hope chests. Any of these levels of involvement was legitimate to Sears, whose contest did not require that entries be submitted by their makers; indeed, the winning quilt was entered by a woman who did none of the work and did not even identify the women who did the intricate quilting. Most women worked with published patterns. Kits were available for those without the patience or the skill to cut out the pieces for patchwork or appliqué. From the marketers' standpoints, this, too, was a legitimate way of being part of the quilt craze: Sears and other stores sold materials for quilters of any skill level. The fad finally ended with World War II, when fabric was restricted, paper shortages put pattern companies out of business, and women working in factories had little time for quilting.[32]

Many of the patterns—Double Wedding Ring, Grandmother's Flower Garden, Sunbonnet Sue—were themselves fads. Few Depression-era quilts were designed by their makers; creativity and mental labor were often limited to varying the colors suggested in printed patterns. One quilt collector and historian maintains that "it is rare to find a quilt made between 1925 and 1970 that cannot be traced to a published source." Companies all over the country—many of them one-woman businesses—sold patterns through the mail. These written directions and paper templates for appliqué and pieced quilts were promoted in magazines and newspapers throughout the Depression. One quilt supply company claimed that at least four hundred newspapers published quilt material regularly, mostly in syndicated columns. A Gallup survey showed that the quilt article was the most popular Sunday newspaper feature, read by nearly a third of all women. Quilters also took patterns from the packaging of commercial quilt fillings, especially wrappers from Stearns & Foster's Mountain Mist cotton batting. This company published more than 120 patterns over the years and advertised them in national magazines.[33]

Many Depression-era quilt designs incorporated elements of contemporary life. President Roosevelt's dog Fala inspired Scottie quilts. A

1934 pattern was based on a stylized airplane, to be pieced in orange and blue; "the airplane will take its place in historical quilts," declared the newspaper that promoted it. "Letha's Electric Fan," to be made in blue and white, appeared in 1938 in the *Kansas City Star,* which published a new pattern every week. "As the churn dash was a motif for quilts 100 years ago, today the electric fan becomes conventionalized for that use," the newspaper explained.[34]

Quilt making as it was publicized during the Depression was an activity for consumers. The newspaper columns suggested that quilts be worked in new fabrics such as cotton sateen, not in cloth recovered from discarded dresses. They promoted modernistic color combinations such as orange and green, and entirely new colors such as the pastels made possible by chemical dyes developed during the 1920s. The traditional designs that were particularly effective for using scraps—especially the crazy quilt and the log cabin, which could be done without patterns—became old-fashioned. Bricolage survived, of course: women who could not afford new fabric adapted published patterns to whatever fragments of material they had on hand. But as in the nineteenth century, most quilt makers purchased as much fabric as they could.

For the ultimate convenience of the modern quilter-consumer, quilt kits, with precut and presorted pieces, were sold through the mail and in department stores. "Seventy-five years ago the world moved more slowly, and they had to find things to occupy their time," *House Beautiful* explained, promoting kits from the Patchcraft Corporation. Now there was never enough time, but if, "more than anything, you'd like to hand down to posterity a patchwork quilt, you can very easily do so by purchasing the patches ready cut, and sewing them together on a machine." The Patchcraft quilt, at $7.50, not including backing or filling, "is as fine as anything your grandmother could have made." Sears sold "World's Fair" ready-made quilt patches through the catalog for twenty-five cents. Quilters could also buy fabric squares stamped with patterns for embroidery or appliqué; the most popular appliqué patterns of the 1930s, like Sunbonnet Sue, were available this way.[35]

To really save time, quilts could be bought fully made. "Day by day, the magic and beauty of Colonial America is making its way into the modern house," declared the Louisville Bedding Company. Purchasing its Olde Kentucky Quilts, "a delightful result of this desire to recapture the charm of Early American house furnishing," made more sense than running around to antiques stores looking for bargains, because "few of the old quilts remain." Macy's sold newly made quilts. At its 1938 "Second Annual Show and Sale of 115 Superb Hand-Made American Patchwork Quilts," prices ranged from $19.98 to $64.54.[36]

Quilt making still offered opportunities for socializing, since women still worked in a group to do the actual quilting—sewing the cover, filling, and backing together. "For the winter I think I shall make a quilt to keep from getting lonesome," a Minnesota farm woman wrote in a letter in 1931, "for some of the women around here are real interested in quilting again." Rose Tekippe of Fort Atkinson, Iowa, was one of the thirty national finalists in the Sears contest, with a New York Beauty quilt she pieced from the design on a Mountain Mist package. Her sister Ada marked the quilting design in pencil; their mother's club, the Twelve Faithful Quilters, did the final stitching.[37]

Among middle-class women, quilts and other handcrafts had become a hobby, a category of activity that became publicly acceptable for the first time during the Depression. Historian Steven Gelber has suggested that hobbies "served to expand the work ethic in a period when work itself was at risk." Although they paid nothing, they looked very much like work and reinforced the value of work. From another point of view, hobbies structured leisure time into consumer activities. Most hobbies required purchasing materials and equipment, and the market for these things expanded as the Depression went on: sales of power tools increased, as did sales of books and equipment for bridge, Ping-Pong, and backgammon. Gardening grew, and more people kept pets. Expenses for hobbies like carpentry and quilting, which created tangible products, could even be justified as ways to save money. Women bought materials for quilts, added their time and their skill, and could produce bedcovers worth much more than they had spent, at least if their time was not taken into account.[38]

Middle-class men, too, were exhorted to save money by spending it on hobby materials. Home maintenance and repair became a hobby during the Depression, offering men opportunities to save money but also to develop a sense of self-reliance in hard times by "doing it themselves." Home-maintenance books of the period contributed to a new definition of manliness, requiring that middle-class husbands have skills as handymen. Even rich people supposedly understood the appeal of such character-building activities, and popular magazines pictured wealthy businessmen and actors in their home workshops; similarly, some wealthy women were said to love quilting.[39]

Like quilting and other handcrafts, Depression-era home maintenance was based in consumption. In magazines like *Popular Mechanics,* historian Joseph Corn has found, men learned "how to reconfigure coat hangers to permit the hanging of a hat as well as a coat . . . or how one might use bobby pins to hold an electrical extension cord in place along the top of a baseboard." This was know-how based on the fact that even poor households were now "veritable warehouses of manufactured products." The man who could fix or make things without spending money, practicing what the magazine called "good homecraft," had, paradoxically, to be a consumer. To follow the directions in the magazine, readers had to have consumer goods on hand. The skills explained in *Popular Mechanics* required trips to the five-and-ten, the hardware store, and the lumberyard.[40]

Advertising practitioners believed that, while most people could not afford travel or nightlife, they would spend some money to help occupy their time at home. "People may not have as much money to spend as in the good old boom days," *Printers' Ink* commented in 1933, "but they have more *time* to enjoy what they spend." In *The Care and Feeding of Hobby Horses,* a publication of the Leisure League, Earnest Elmo Calkins, the ad man, promoted hobbies as keeping the unemployed from idleness and offering respite from work for those who did have jobs.[41]

Many rural women looked to handcrafts not as hobbies but as income-producing activities that were compatible with child care and the seasonal rhythms of farming. Sears encouraged this perspective. "Not only are hand made quilts decorative," the advertising announcing the quilt contest suggested, "but your idle hours can be turned into money." Government-sponsored home economists working in the programs overseen by the federal Agricultural and Home Economics Extension Service also taught quilt making, but only as a response to persistent requests. This program, founded in 1914, offered farm women instruction intended to parallel the agricultural information available to their menfolk from county extension agents, land grant colleges, and the Department of Agriculture. Home economists visited farm homes and offered courses; they introduced farm women to new products and labor-saving devices and provided instruction in the latest methods for such tasks as raising and canning vegetables.[42]

When state and county extension services began to offer recreation programs such as drama and music appreciation in 1921, rural women responded by pressuring extension home economists to teach them crafts like basketry and chair caning. Some obliged. The Alabama extension service declared handcrafts beneficial for developing industry in rural counties and an appropriate activity for women at home and children at camp. At Cornell, however, the home economists resisted demands for classes in subjects that they had not studied and that they considered beneath them. One Cornell home economist expressed surprise that "it wasn't always the ones with the low IQs" that asked for handcrafts, but even "some of the women who might well study the chemistry of food." In 1928, Cornell finally offered rug-hooking classes and provided some help with marketing, setting up outlets for rural crafts near urban centers. The home economists insisted on "proper" color combinations; one explained that rural women's standards were set by "cheap commercially-minded magazines and limited small-town stores" rather than by museums, and therefore "guidance is wanted where one might expect spontaneous natural skill and taste."[43]

During the Depression, many extension services formed hobby groups that sponsored exhibits at state fairs. At the 1935 Iowa State Fair, thirty-six farm women exhibited quilts and braided rugs alongside their oil paintings, poems, wedding cakes, and collections. Two years later, the federal extension service sponsored a national traveling Rural Arts Exhibition, which included handcrafts. The Works Progress Administration, recognizing the moneymaking possibilities in quilts and other handcrafts, joined the quilt craze by publishing thirty different quilt posters and a training manual for home economics teachers that stressed the importance of "keeping weaving, handicrafts, and sewing crafts alive." The idea was that stimulating traditional American home crafts could create employment in community industries. Even Eleanor Roosevelt took an interest in community industries established in Appalachia, the Carolinas, and the Midwest.[44]

Salvage Charities: Discarding as Donating

Thrift stores extended the possibilities for consumerist bricolage to those who could not afford to shop for new materials. "I sewed most of the children's clothes and I did not have new fabric," remembered Vi Cottrell, a rural Washington State woman who belonged to an extension service homemaker's group. "I would go down to the Salvation Army and buy an adult person's second-hand coat, take it apart, wash the fabric, cut it out and make the coats and things for the children." In Alaska, Evie Foster's husband "went to the thrift store in town there and he got a beautiful tomato-red coat trimmed in fur and brought it home to me. I made my oldest daughter a snow suit out of it, and a little bonnet, and she wore it until she outgrew it. Then my second daughter wore it. When she outgrew it, I gave it to my nephew who was just a year younger, and he wore it until he wore it out. And my husband had paid 25¢ for that coat."[45]

Beautiful fur-trimmed coats were available in thrift stores because of an ethos of middle-class *oblige* that Goodwill, the Salvation Army, and the other salvage charities promoted during the Depression. Their marketing campaigns encouraged people with jobs to donate new kinds of discards: not worn-out belongings suitable only as rags for paper-making, but good-quality items that middle-class people might discard because they were out of fashion. The charities argued that these contributions would help people of the lower classes to be more like the middle class, both as consumers and as workers.

Selling to the ragman—still an option, but only in the poorest neighborhoods—had always been a way of earning a few pennies, not an obligation of class. Now, according to the salvage charities' publicity, anybody who still had a job was obliged to get rid of things for a good cause rather than fixing or selling them. Even people with no extra cash could clean out their closets and gain the opportunity to be charitable to those poorer than themselves. "To most families," an article about Goodwill explained in 1932, "the contents of their attics is a burden, contributing nothing to their welfare or happiness." Goodwill could put those things to better use: fifteen dollars' worth of junk lay in the average attic, and Goodwill's repair work would more than triple that value.[46]

In appeals to the middle class, the salvage charities stressed as always that they did not offer charity: poor people had to pay for their thrift store purchases. But their solicitations carried a special charge in hard times. "In these difficult days we are greatly in need of clothing," Boston's Morgan Memorial Goodwill exhorted in its newsletter in 1939. "Men desire clothes to present a neat appearance as they seek work and employment." Contributions of clothing also provided jobs, "as our workers repair and press these garments in preparation for their shipment to our Stores and service centers."[47]

If middle-class people thought they had nothing to give, Goodwill beseeched them to look further. "With winter coming closer each day, men and women are becoming more desperate in their feverish search for work," Morgan Memorial's newsletter exhorted one Depression autumn. "Surely we may expect our friends to be able to fill a bag at least twice a year for the Spring and Fall housecleaning times." What to put in it? "Just take a look around your house and sort out those articles of clothing and household goods that you no longer need."[48]

The language of Goodwill's national operations manual insinuated that anyone who contributed once had an obligation to do so again. "A contributor *delinquent* more than six months should have a special call," it recommended, "in addition to the regular calls." It would help to solicit these people "at the height of spring or fall housecleaning," but getting castoffs from them took a selling job. "The person selected for this work should be the best salesman from either the district visitors or telephone solicitors."[49]

As the Depression wore on, and more people were fixing and reselling things instead of giving them away, the salvage charities had to intensify their campaigns. They sought the help of local businesses. Radio stations donated advertising time; department stores held trade-in sales and gave items taken in trade to the charities. For a week in 1937, the Syracuse phone company played a brief Salvation Army message when the time number was called. The Army advertised in newspapers and on posters—one ad asked, "If a Poor Man Could Eat Paper, Would You Burn It?"—and published pamphlets to be distributed door-to-door, entitled "Hidden Treasure in Your Trunk" and "Spring! Just around the Corner: House-Cleaning Time." Local Goodwills were instructed to put out monthly or quarterly newsletters, to be sent to every contributor and to noncontributors in wealthy neighborhoods during spring and fall housecleaning seasons. The key to a successful Goodwill, the operations manual insisted in boldface type, was to "Promote! Promote! Promote!"[50]

Salvation Army officers redoubled their efforts to emphasize sales in the stores rather than bulk sales of paper and rags to dealers. Stores generated much more income per unit of labor, and store income depended less on uncertain markets and unfriendly paper and rag dealers. By creating stores so cheap that virtually anyone could shop, the salvage charities kept the poor from dependency and integrated them into consumer culture even in Depression conditions. Memoranda urged stores to spruce up, and officers to encourage clean stores and attractive presentation. The Army sponsored talks on salesmanship, clear pricing, neatness, advertising, and display (which generally meant little more than hanging clothes on racks). Goodwill administrators, believing that newspaper advertising was too expensive, recommended that local stores get newspapers to write about them instead. The Goodwill manual, like the Salvation Army memoranda, offered advice for creating window displays, tracking inventory, and checking stock. Both organizations sorted out antiques that would attract dealers and collectors; they sold these treasures in special sections, and sometimes even special stores. The Goodwill manual recommended opening outlets for the best merchandise on good shopping streets instead of in the slums.[51]

But actual house-to-house solicitation was increasingly problematic. In 1939, Morgan Memorial complained that its bags were being " 'hijacked' and 'kidnapped' in alarming numbers. Unscrupulous persons persuade our contributors that they represent Morgan Memorial." Contributors were reminded that genuine Goodwill trucks would not come unless they were called. The organizations also struggled against the attitude that giving to a good cause was a form of disposal. They pleaded continually for good-quality castoffs. "REMEMBER!!! Every filled Goodwill Bag gives work and respectable wages to those who seek only an opportunity to provide for their dear ones! Doesn't such a purpose transfigure and glorify your cast-off material? Can you think of any finer use for your gifts?" Such rhetoric served not only to make donors feel transfigured but to encourage people to donate better things.[52]

The charities did still accept the completely irreparable; at Goodwill, for example, the Salvage Department sorted paper, rags, and metals for sale in the waste trade. Its 1935 operations manual stressed that such salvage created jobs and could be a good source of income for local Goodwills. To make it pay, administrators had to keep abreast of the markets for these materials and not allow junk dealers (to whom they sold the salvage) to dominate the bargaining process. But Goodwill, as always, saw itself primarily as a labor program, and its goal was to fix things, not sell them as salvage. Labor programs distinguished the salvage charities from local charity resale shops, which sold what they got, as was. Goodwill insisted on the distinction between

Goodwill stores (where everything for sale had been repaired) and other secondhand stores and rummage sales. The manual declared that "we should exhaust every effort to provide a maximum amount of labor in the repair and reconditioning of discarded materials." Every article should be used to this end, if possible. "We should eliminate for salvage only that which is unfit for use or will cost far beyond any possible price that would be fair to ask."[53]

By the end of the Depression, Boston's Morgan Memorial Goodwill was in trouble. Never in its history, its newsletter declared in the spring of 1940, had the organization been so "short of cast-off materials of every kind." It would have to downsize its workforce "unless our friends come to our rescue and send us their filled Goodwill Bags, furniture, etc." By the fall, supporters had responded, but mostly with paper and rags. "The crying need now is for BETTER clothing, BETTER household goods and BETTER shoes," the newsletter implored. In the winter of 1940–41, the appeal reached fever pitch: "An EMERGENCY EXISTS," caused by "conditions beyond our control." Too many people were giving clothing to poor friends and relatives; too many churches were holding rummage sales. Goodwill had enough waste materials, paper, and fabrics; it needed good clothes and furniture. The organization offered to pick up even partly filled bags. "You responded wonderfully to our appeal," Morgan Memorial declared in the next newsletter, but by the summer of 1941, the complaints about quality reappeared. Middle-class *oblige* could go only so far, even though the Depression had finally begun to recede.[54]

Soon enough, Goodwill and the Salvation Army were to benefit—along with the larger American economy—from World War II. The first major drive to collect household scrap was an aluminum collection held that summer of 1941, even before the United States entered the war. It was a public relations disaster, but Goodwill saw its promise. "Salvage for Victory, though a new slogan," the organization commented in its 1941 annual report, "has indeed a very old significance at Goodwill Industries." The management expected that agencies like Goodwill would be called upon when the war was over, because of their experience both in salvage and in rehabilitating the disabled. In fact, they were called soon after the war started. Their workshops did considerable contract work for the government, providing unskilled labor for tasks such as assembling survival kits and sorting nuts and bolts. And along with other established purveyors of junk and salvage, they were mobilized in the scrap collection effort, which transformed the discarding of old things into patriotic behavior.[55]

CHAPTER SIX

Use It Up! Wear It Out!
Get in the Scrap!

A month after the Japanese attack on Pearl Harbor, the high school students of Prosser, Washington, collected ten tons of paper in a drive sponsored by the Rotary Club. Sophomores gathered paper that farmers dropped off at the Prosser Motor Service; the school's Hi-Y Club collected bundles left on doorsteps in town. The Stitch and Chatter Sewing Club filled a dairy truck with nearly thirteen hundred pounds of newspapers and magazines. The U.S. government class loaded nine tons onto a larger truck bound for Yakima, where the paper was sold; proceeds went to the local defense council. As a result of the enthusiastic drives held throughout the area, the Rotary chairman announced at the end of April that the market for newsprint was glutted and the paper collectors would accept only magazines. Four months later, not even those could find a market. Tons of paper sat in sidetracked railroad cars.[1]

Even so, Prosser exceeded its quota in the national rubber drive that began during the summer of 1942, and the town's high school students geared up that fall for "the greatest of all salvage drives," an intensive campaign for iron and steel, rubber, and rags, with the motto "Get in the Scrap!" Prosser students collected 153 tons of scrap in October, hoping to raise enough money to pay for new athletic uniforms. The senior, junior, and sophomore classes competed with one another. The drive began with a rally featuring the high school band, a girls' trio, and a saxophone solo; it ended with a dance, sponsored by the juniors and sophomores for the winning seniors. Their victory was assured by five senior boys who pulled a 1,380-pound motor from the Yakima River.[2]

Scrap drives figure importantly in home-front memories of World War II, along with rationing and shortages of nylon stockings and other consumer goods. For two years, Americans participated in hundreds of national, state, and local efforts to collect materials that had sustained the waste trade for a century: scrap metal, rubber, paper, and fats. Short-lived programs gathered other materials. Milk and beverage bottles were collected in some places, as were furs. Utah women collected jewelry to ship to the Pacific so that GIs could barter with "South Sea natives." For a while during 1943, old silk and nylon hosiery were collected at department store hosiery counters. The silk was ideal for gunpowder bags, used to shoot shells from big guns; it burned fast and clean, so no burning fragments would ignite the next bag of powder. Nylon stockings were made into cloth. All over the country, people in big cities and in small towns like Prosser came together to express their community spirit and support husbands, brothers, and uncles overseas.[3]

Scrap drives strengthened other home-front programs like rationing and government-mandated production restriction by fostering public perception of the fundamental materials necessary to fight a war. Early in 1942, the government prohibited the manufacture of nearly six hundred consumer products in order to conserve raw materials. It became impossible to get things people had come to depend on every day: things like stockings or rubber pants for the baby. Rationing controlled how much individuals could legally buy of certain things like gasoline, shoes, and meat. Government regulations dictating what could be produced for sale deprived consumers of new cars and washing machines; the factories that once made them now manufactured tanks and weapons. Conservation measures in the clothing industry outlawed double-breasted suits, full skirts, and cuffs on trousers. The government explicitly opposed fashion; one War Production Board press release sought to "assure the women and girls of America" that "their present wardrobes will not be made obsolete by radical fashion changes." Regulations also limited the materials manufacturers could use, encouraging innovations in plastics, plywood, and concrete. Scrap drives bolstered the point that the government and industry were short of basic materials; consumers were not the only ones unable to get things they wanted.[4]

The rationale for this extraordinary level of government intrusion into the rights and opportunities of manufacturers and consumers was that sacrifice and deprivation were necessary in order to protect the American Way of Life. The American Way was not presented as an abstraction; it consisted of "Four Freedoms" specifically named by President Franklin D. Roosevelt and painted by Norman Rockwell. Defending "Freedom from Want" meant fighting for the fundamental guarantee of the New Deal state. But Rockwell's vision for that freedom—the abundance represented by the Thanksgiving feast—was not possible to achieve during wartime; it would have to wait until the enemy had been vanquished. Wartime sacrifice was linked to this emergency version of consumerism: a positive future without scarcity, an expectation of what American industry would provide consumers after the war. This prophecy was explicitly developed in campaigns for war bonds, which promised that saving now would pay off in the future, when the factories would again be producing consumer goods.[5]

Presenting the war as a crisis to be resolved at least in part by civilian regard for materials, the government urged a return to old habits. "*If you don't need it,* DON'T BUY IT," the Office of Price Administration told citizens on the back cover of War Ration Book No. 3, issued in 1943. On the theory that Americans might still be mobilized to practice thrift in an emergency, they were exhorted to forsake prewar luxuries for spartan ways. "Use It Up, Wear It Out, Mend It, and Make

Do," went another slogan; a more severe version urged, "Use It Up, Wear It Out, Make It Do, or Do Without." The Consumer's Pledge for Total Defense promised, "As a consumer, in the total defense of democracy, I will do my part to make my home, my community, my country ready, efficient, and strong. I will buy carefully. I will take good care of the things I have. I will waste nothing." Government posters were more succinct. "Food is a Weapon," read a typical one; "Don't Waste It! Buy wisely—cook carefully—eat it all."[6]

Popular magazines reinforced the message. "Don't Throw Away the Best Part," Pearl Buck told her *Collier's* readers in August 1942, describing everyday life in China, where nobody wasted anything. Garbage pails were unknown there: leftovers were eaten, fed to chickens, cats, or dogs, or returned to the earth as compost. *Real Story,* addressed to working-class women, suggested that patriotic women try to make the things in their homes "last almost indefinitely, thus eliminating the necessity of buying new ones." Floors, radios, and tables should all be protected with wax. "In short, along with buying War Bonds, working for the Red Cross and saving waste kitchen fats, protect everything in your home, too, and get the best possible wear from them." In its "Clothes Salvage Course," the magazine admitted that mending, patching, and hemming dresses and skirts "may not be a very exciting way of winning a war, but it's a very real way." Reminding readers of "today's great slogan for the consumer," *Real Story* asserted that "it's much more sensible to learn how to make it do, and not have to do without." The magazine carried an advertisement for a tool that would mend runs in stockings.[7]

Better-off women paid others to mend their stockings. "On South Washington in downtown Lansing a store opened to mend women's hose," a Michigan woman remembered in the 1990s. "I mentioned that to one of my daughters not long ago and she could not comprehend such a thing." *American Home* (whose readers were mainly buying rather than sewing their dresses and skirts) offered patterns in 1942 for making men's undershorts from worn-out shirts and crocheting a floor mat from package twine. "Last year we called them waste," the article remarked about the materials to be reused. "How times change!" *American Home* readers were also encouraged to melt down old candles and store silk stockings in glass jars in a dark place to protect them from deterioration. The husbands could make sturdy outdoor tables out of wagon-wheel rims or mend punctured garden hoses with rubber disks and ball bearings. Men might also make compost from yard waste, a project advocated in books on victory gardening, to produce a soil amendment preferable to the commercially produced fertilizer available at seed stores.[8]

On the surface, the shortages and propaganda of World War II seem to have induced Americans to retain a consciousness of waste and a desire to save money, ideas diametrically opposed to the consumerist lessons that had encouraged people with spending money to stop making do. Indeed, American households continued to practice thrift of all kinds, as they had done throughout the Depression. Most women mended at least some clothing. So many reused cooking fat that the government had difficulty getting them to part with it for the sake of the boys overseas. Without washing machines or new cars to buy, Americans did save money: the liquid assets of individuals nearly tripled between Pearl Harbor and the end of the war. To young women reared on consumerism, the frustrations and sense of sacrifice on the home front must have been great, whatever their satisfactions from contributing to the war effort. After a decade of depression, people with money to spend were being told not to spend it. Women working full-time in factories or volunteering for the Red Cross or the Victory Bond drive were expected to find time for scrimping and mending.[9]

War Preparations and Strategic Materials

Throughout 1941, American business seemed to be rehearsing for the sacrifices the war was sure to bring. Preparation for war dominated American discussions of economic policy. The Office of Production Management (OPM) was organized in January of that year to mobilize the economy and manage strategic materials; in April, the Office of Price Administration (OPA) was set up to regulate wages and prices, prevent inflation, and develop rationing plans.[10]

With the economy recovering from the Depression, articles in popular magazines at first implied that frugality might be relaxed. The *Atlantic Monthly*'s tongue-in-cheek "We Never Threw Anything Away" sentimentalized habits that sprang "not from avarice but from caution." The author fondly recalled his family's saving odd skates and shoes and gloves, bits of broken china, and half-full medicine bottles. "We were afraid we might be sorry later," he wrote. "Some day, perhaps, such a terrible calamity would descend that we should be grateful for the old golf cape and the raccoon coat, too bare in strange places to be given away." In "I Married All Three . . ." *Better Homes and Gardens* divided women into three types: "women who save things because they might come in handy sometime, women who save things because it seems a shame to throw them out, and women who save things because you never can tell." The author made fun of his wife's glass jars, her string and paper, her old medicine bottles. He lampooned bricolage, dividing the "because you never can tell" women into "1. Women who save little pieces of cloth. ('You never can tell when you're going to want to patch something.') 2. Women who save buttons. ('You never know when you'll need a button.') 3. Women who save one left-handed mitten. ('You never can tell when you'll have a right-hand mitten.')" But he concluded by confessing that he, too, had a hard time letting go of old hats, pants without knees, empty cigarette tins, and cigar boxes.[11]

Meanwhile, in the business press, the talk was of shortages. Advertising to packagers, the Aluminum Company of America admitted in May 1941 that "many regular users of aluminum are having to do without" its product but promised that "your aluminum is on the way." *Business Week* was not so sanguine. "For some time," the magazine declared, "there hasn't been enough aluminum left over for anything like normal civilian needs." *Modern Packaging* put a good spin on the situation: packagers faced problems obtaining brass, nickel, and bronze as well as aluminum, but paper, glass, plastic, rubber, and cork could be made to supply their needs. The magazine predicted lavish gift giving for the 1941 holiday season because mobilization had so improved business conditions. Despite material shortages, the packaging industry would be sustained by gifts for the two million men in the service, like the khaki-banded Ingersoll "Warrior" watch, packaged in red, white, and blue.[12]

In June 1941, the government mounted experimental salvage drives for aluminum in Madison, Wisconsin, and Richmond, Virginia. Six hundred Madison Boy Scouts, assisted by members of the American Legion and the Veterans of Foreign Wars, went house to house collecting nearly fifty thousand pounds of pots and pans. *Life* magazine warned that such efforts would not suffice. Americans would have to drop "the national illusion that America can with a comfortable business-as-usual half-effort compete with a fanatic Germany," the magazine declared. For eight years, Germany had been "stripping its homes and streets of every scrap of metal that could be spared." Its aluminum production had passed the United States by 1934 and it "now has the resources of all Europe to draw on."[13]

In July, the aluminum scrap campaign went national. U.S. troops were stationed in Iceland, American ships were escorting British ones, and trade with Japan had been cut off. The aluminum drive at first seemed wildly successful. Millions of people contributed pots and pans, kettles, ice cream scoops, and hair curlers. New York City salvaged a damaged two-ton gate from the Triborough Bridge; in New Jersey, a piece of the German zeppelin *Hindenburg* was scrapped. The violinist Jascha Heifetz donated an aluminum violin. Detroit nightclub patrons paid one old pot each to see the famous stripper Gypsy Rose Lee "clank around in (and finally out of) a bizarre costume of aluminum kitchenware," reported *Time* magazine, adding that the New York *Daily Mirror* called her dance the "pan-pan." The aluminum drive was "a lot of fun," according to *Life*, "the first chance most citizens have had to participate directly in the defense program."[14]

But by the beginning of September, people were starting to complain that their pots and pans "were still stacked high around courthouses and fire stations." *Time* blamed Fiorello H. La Guardia, mayor of New York and head of the Office of Civilian Defense. La Guardia had

vetoed the OPM's original plan, which entailed the collection committees' selling the scrap to junk dealers, who would in turn sell it to
smelters—in other words, using the normal channels for gathering and
melting down scrap, regulated with price controls. He accused junk
dealers of bootlegging aluminum for nearly four times the ceiling price
and insisted that collection committees sell direct to smelters. But the
smelter operators balked. They normally bought aluminum scrap
that the junk men had sorted, while the drives brought them whole
refrigerators and baby carriages, items containing as little as two
ounces of aluminum in fifty pounds of bulk. Obliged to pay freight on
material they could not use and compelled to hire men to do the sorting, they soon began to run out of storage space and stopped buying
from the collection committees. Despite the scrap piled up in plain
view in public places, President Roosevelt declared the drive a success.
The House Military Affairs Subcommittee criticized the methods but
praised the results. In November, the Office for Emergency Management assured *Woman's Home Companion* readers that "Uncle Hiram's
coffeepot" really would be used. But months later, *Business Week*
called the aluminum roundup a disaster. "It is alleged that some of the
pots still lie piled where the last photographer snapped them, that it
became too much of a political publicity stunt, that anyway there isn't
enough household aluminum scrap left to worry about."[15]

Meanwhile, another experimental salvage campaign was mounted
in Appleton, Wisconsin. In October 1941, the mayor informed a group
of prominent citizens that "certain responsible Washington officials"
had asked him to make Appleton a demonstration city for the continual salvage of paper. About a quarter of Appleton's paper was
already collected for reuse—some by dealers and the rest by the Salvation Army, the Boy Scouts and Girl Scouts, and an assortment of regular collections and special drives sponsored by churches and clubs. Still,
the average home had no convenient arrangement or special incentive
to save paper. The mayor requested the civic leaders to meet and create
a strategy for doubling paper reuse. Each Scout wore a button declaring him or her an "Official Appleton Plan Paper Collector." House-

wives got pamphlets. Buses carried placards. Every Appleton merchant received a rubber stamp, to imprint on packages and statements, "SAVE THIS AND ALL WASTE PAPER." A radio program explained that paper and wood pulp had to be saved for plane and battleship blueprints, food containers, explosives, and cellulose bandages. The first collection was scheduled for Saturday morning, December 6, the day before Pearl Harbor.[16]

Even before the Japanese attack, people believed that mobilization required them to cut back. *House Beautiful* warned its wealthy readers in its December issue that they would have to "Live on Less and Like It." With taxes and prices going up, materials scarce, and working-class men being drafted, they had to change their habits. "Even during the depression we have been living the soft life of the historic southern planters," the magazine asserted. Readers would need to learn building and repairing and how to do things themselves. Fuel would have to be conserved, houses kept in good condition. "Often we shall have to make old things do. No longer shall we throw out something merely because it is slightly worn, old hat or tiresome. Instead we shall refinish to transform it into something new. We shall make old Victorian bureaus into dressing tables and desks. We shall paint badly battered beds. We shall save old draperies, dresses and suits and fashion them into hooked rugs and patchwork quilts." Gardeners were urged to make compost, cooks to "cherish leftovers as the basis for stews and soups." The article was not a typical one for the Christmas issue of a posh home magazine, but days after it appeared on newsstands, the United States was at war.[17]

The attack on Pearl Harbor killed twenty-four hundred Americans and turned American public opinion firmly in favor of war. Immediately, the government moved to control materials and facilitate war production. In mid-January, Roosevelt established the War Production Board (WPB) to replace the OPM and its bureaucratic rival, the Supply Priorities and Allocation Board. Donald M. Nelson, a former Sears executive and a popular "New Deal businessman," was chosen to head the new agency. The WPB had authority to convert factories, set quotas for war production, determine the supply of materials to industry, and issue orders for conserving materials and limiting industrial production. Most WPB orders affected manufacturers and wholesalers; the Office of Price Administration, with ninety-three district offices, continued to deal with consumers, regulating prices and rationing consumer goods. For relationships with ordinary citizens, both agencies relied on the network of state defense councils, already set up before the war. The OPA used the councils to organize rationing boards, while the WPB employed them to coordinate scrap drives in American communities.[18]

The WPB set to work immediately, issuing a series of L (limitations) and M (materials) orders, limiting production of individual items, and prohibiting the use of essential materials. Cellophane was forbidden in the packaging or manufacture of 245 classes of consumer products, for example, and copper could not be delivered to anyone except a scrap dealer or brass mill. The most sweeping regulations came in May 1942, halting the production of more than four hundred products containing iron and steel. But the rules could be bent: with sufficient protest from the trade, the War Production Board would modify or rescind its restrictions. The agency, one historian writes, "prided itself in being flexible and responsive to manufacturers' needs."[19]

The packaging industry was seriously constrained by WPB regulations. Not only were packagers required to reduce the amount of material they used, but they were limited as well in the use of machinery and labor. Early restrictions on metal led to attempts at standardizing can shapes and sizes. In March 1943, more drastic limitations on tin-plated steel cans forced food packagers to replace them with glass and paper containers. As much as they could, packagers used the L and M orders as occasions for marketing. Companies that did not create patriotic products like the Warrior watch could still make the best of adversity; Pebeco tooth powder, for example, came in a "new wartime metal-saving container," with an assurance on the label that the package contained the "same generous amount of tooth powder as in former metal container."[20]

Eventually paper, too, was regarded as a strategic material; it was in seriously short supply by 1943. Paper was used for containers to send food and supplies overseas; goods headed for the Pacific required extra packing for protection against weather and insects. There was a manpower shortage in the forests, and pulp was used in making explosives. Although paper piled up in some places as it had in Prosser, national drives called attention to the need for it throughout the rest of the war. Schools held Paper Doll dances: a pound of paper bought a vote for the queen who would rule over the event. The radio program *Truth or Consequences* sponsored a nationwide contest in December 1943 and broadcast the show from the small midwestern school that collected the most paper. The Girl Scouts held a paper drive in the fall of 1944; the Boy Scouts' national campaign the next spring awarded its Eisenhower medal to Scouts collecting a thousand pounds or more. The Double VV program during the summer of 1945 ("V for Victory—V for Veterans") anticipated the final days of the war, with proceeds from paper collections to be used for projects in veterans' hospitals.[21]

"Let's Junk the Jap"

With increasing pressure on supplies of raw materials after Pearl Harbor, demand for salvaged ones mounted. So did discussions about collecting them. Because the government was not prepared to perform the actual tasks of gathering scrap materials, sorting them, and transporting them to factories, established collection agencies and dealers became involved immediately. In January 1942, the OPM asked Goodwill to increase its salvage collections; the charity stepped up its effort in more than a hundred cities, until by summer Goodwill—like the wastepaper dealer in Yakima—had a surfeit of wastepaper that the mills would not take. The public was urged to sell junk to dealers and buy defense bonds with the proceeds or to give it to a charitable organization; the government officially recognized the Boy Scouts, Boys Clubs, the Salvation Army, Volunteers of America, the Society of St. Vincent de Paul, Goodwill Industries, and the American Legion.[22]

But defense salvage was not the salvage charities' primary interest. Boston's Goodwill continued to remind its contributors that it also needed "better things." Wastepaper, scrap metal, rubber, and textiles were of course necessary for jobs and defense, the organization explained in its newsletter, but repairable shoes, clothing, and furniture were required "for jobs, defense and *handicapped people*." In any case, relationships between the government and the charities were not always smooth. In San Diego, the general salvage director for the WPB threatened to commandeer city-owned trucks to collect salvage, intimating that the Salvation Army, Goodwill, and Volunteers of America were not doing the job. City officials joined the organizations in resisting that plan.[23]

The major players in the scrap metal industry insisted that collecting enough scrap for defense was a big and complicated job, not to be achieved by collecting household scrap. In February 1942, six hundred scrap dealers attending a meeting of the Institute of Scrap Iron and Steel in Chicago reported their biggest volume in history for 1941, forty-seven million tons. But it wasn't enough; they estimated a demand for sixty million tons in 1942.[24]

Leading citizens tried to stimulate interest in the need for salvaged materials. FDR had the White House cellar canvassed, yielding half a ton of scrap; the Library of Congress turned in 150 tons of wastepaper and metal; the War Department microfilmed its World War I records and scrapped both the paper and the filing cabinets. *Life* reported on a party given by Boston socialites. Guests had to bring a minimum of twenty-five pounds of scrap, and some joined the "scrap tease," peeling off and contributing old clothes they had worn over their party attire. The mayor of Boston spoke. Governor Leverett Saltonstall sent his regrets, along with a rowing machine and a radio.[25]

Household scrap collection began in earnest during the summer of 1942. President Roosevelt announced a nationwide drive for rubber on the radio in mid-June, explaining that neither the United States nor its allies had access to raw rubber. "Modern wars cannot be won without rubber," he explained, and "92 percent of our normal supply of rubber has been cut off by the Japanese. . . . We do not want you to turn in essential rubber that you need in your daily life—rubber you will have to replace by buying new things in the store. We do want every bit of rubber you can possibly spare—and in any quantity—less than a pound—many pounds. We want it in every form—old tires, old rubber raincoats, old garden hose, rubber shoes, bathing caps, gloves—whatever you have that is made of rubber. If you think it is rubber, take it to your nearest filling station."[26]

As *Time* pointed out, the "painful and recent memory" of the aluminum drive suggested that "only experienced junkmen can make a scrap drive work." The campaign for rubber was particularly hard since "much of the rubber scrap lies in out-of-the-way places, in small quantities, in widely separated rural areas, costly and time-absorbing to reach." The government had indeed enlisted experienced junk men—the four biggest scrap rubber dealers. They signed an agreement that they would no longer trade in scrap rubber except as agents for the government's Rubber Reserve Company. In this capacity, they handled industrial collections as well as buying rubber for the government from local junk men. As the president explained, filling stations served as collection depots for small quantities of rubber. The major oil companies agreed to gather it up and were authorized to pay the public a penny a pound, although donations were encouraged. The Rubber Reserve Company paid the oil companies twenty-five dollars a ton if they pledged to charity whatever profit they made above the costs of collection. The drive produced 454,000 tons of scrap rubber, at least a year's supply.[27]

Business Week called the 1942 rubber drive a "smoke screen," charging that it was intended to distract the public from the imminent fact of gas rationing, which was being planned to save rubber more than gasoline but would not be announced "until it seems absolutely necessary." Industry, the magazine pointed out, was "under the heel," referring to the L and M orders. "Now comes the job of kicking the public around." The public relations effort "will move faster, more clearly, when the military situation looks bad. A resounding defeat right now would bring a flood of rationing orders. Lacking such a defeat, officials attempt to dispel current optimism by issuing warnings, and they're none too successful."[28]

Only rubber was collected in a national campaign during the summer of 1942, but municipalities across the country held drives to collect other materials—salvageable metal, paper, and kitchen fats— often in cooperation with local businesses and civic organizations. By September, every county in the United States had had at least one scrap collection. The American Industries Salvage Committee ("representing and with funds provided by groups of leading industrial concerns") published a WPB-approved pamphlet explaining how to run a salvage campaign with regular collections, using municipal trucks and employees. In Worcester, Massachusetts, where scrap collection was organized by the Bureau of Sanitation, a drive brought eleven hundred tons of scrap. "The people have it and it is up to our municipal governments to see that they disgorge," American City asserted. A photograph showed not household collections but fraudulent scales, seized from grocers and other retailers by the Philadelphia Bureau of Weights and Measures, being smashed up for scrap. The magazine warned cities not to keep the money they made from selling scrap to dealers but instead to turn the proceeds over to charity or to let Boy Scouts keep the money if they helped with the scrap drive.[29]

Other local drives were coordinated by specially organized state and local salvage committees. In Boston, the mayor headed a salvage campaign planned by a committee representing the wastepaper industry, the junk dealers and collectors, the Boy Scouts, and the schools. Streetcar and billboard advertising publicized the program; circulars were distributed to 200,000 households. Households received window cards to display when they wanted a junk dealer to call; salvage boxes were set up around the city for depositing small amounts not worth selling. In Clinton, Missouri, the mayor proclaimed "Scrap Collection Day" on Memorial Day, mandating that businesses be closed and their workers devote themselves to scrap collection. The chamber of commerce offered an encyclopedia set to the rural school sending in the most scrap. The local Allis-Chalmers dealer sponsored an ad showing Uncle Sam's arm depositing an Asian man into a trash barrel full of cans. "Let's Junk the Jap," it read.[30]

The next national scrap drive—for iron, steel, tin, rubber, and rags—was slated for the fall of 1942. In preparation, the steel industry sponsored a 1.5-million-dollar advertising campaign in July, with full-page ads in "virtually every publication," according to the *New Republic*. Young & Rubicam, a leading advertising agency, conducted a nationwide survey to determine how much scrap could be collected. Responses were used to create regional, state, and local quotas for the fall campaign. Approximately half the respondents had already disposed of some metal for war salvage in a local scrap drive, but more than two-thirds still had salvageable metal. Almost four million tons of metal were available, 83 percent of it in rural areas. The situation was much the same with rubber. Two-thirds of the respondents had already salvaged rubber, and a third still had rubber they were willing to give up. Again rural areas held most (73 percent) of the salvageable rubber. Farms had more scrap to begin with—old tractors and plows as well as automobiles and irons—and rural people had more space for storage than urban ones. Rural people still mended and reused more than urbanites, whose culture was based more in consumption; scrap drives destroyed materials for bricolage.[31]

Once the fall 1942 campaign was under way, criticism mounted. The *New Republic* charged that the government's confused scrap policies were causing deaths in steel mills. In August, working without an adequate supply of scrap iron, the Carnegie-Illinois Steel Corporation had changed the proportions of ingredients in an open-hearth furnace. According to the article, this "probably" caused a reaction in the huge steel-pouring ladle: molten steel "shower[ed] out of the ladle like a geyser." Two steelworkers had died and a third was seriously burned. The magazine blamed the shortage—and by implication the accident—not on the company but on "the scrap collectors in Washington." Even if the analysis of the tragedy was overwrought, the complaints about confusion were certainly convincing. At least four different agencies handled scrap; connections among them and between the government and the big scrap brokers were very unclear. "No coordination. No singleness of purpose. No single seat of authority. No final agency of responsibility."[32]

Some of the problems were more procedural than political, but they, too, contributed to confusion. Tin cans, for example, were actually made of tin-coated steel and could not simply be melted down but had to be processed to separate the tin from the steel. Tin was as critical as steel: it was used in submarines, battleships, tanks, trucks, bombers, binoculars, hand grenades, tubes for medicinal ointments, and Syrettes, kits for self-delivery of morphine. As one WPB pamphlet put it, "Tin 'Fights'!" The United States had no tin ore, and the Japanese controlled 70 percent of the world's resources. But detinning capacity lagged far behind demand for tin, and detinning facilities were unevenly distributed around the country. Many detinners did not take cans, preferring industrial scrap, which usually came flat; cans were often rusty, and tin was hard to recover from their folds. As a result, cans were collected in some places and not in others, and they piled up in towns around the country. The Young & Rubicam study found that only about a third of the people who saved cans knew what to do with them. Even many people who lived near detinning facilities had no arrangements for getting rid of the cans they were saving. Some local and national scrap drives solicited cans; some did not. The big national scrap drive in the fall of 1942 did not collect cans; more detinning facilities were built during the next year and the 1943 drive did collect them.[33]

Scrap drive propaganda rarely acknowledged the piles of cans or the chaos. Instead it incessantly reiterated "wash and squash" processing instructions—remove the label and ends of a can, wash it out, put the ends inside the can, step on it to flatten—directions frequently echoed decades later by people calling up home-front memories. Despite the disorder in collecting cans, the government harangued a confused public about their importance. "Throwing a tin can away represents a waste of critical war materials which is unpardonable," declared one

War Production Board pamphlet, which estimated that two-thirds of salvageable tin cans were discarded.[34]

Business Gets Scrap-Happy

Nationally advertised and locally mobilized, scrap drives during the first years of the war represented attempts to make sacrifice in the service of the nation a community value. With great hoopla, organizers claimed they were uniting communities against common foreign enemies. In towns and cities across the country, scrap drives—along with bond sales and civil defense councils—brought together individuals and businesses of all sizes and tied neighborhood groups to city and state organizations. But these alliances usually represented and reinforced long-standing power relationships. In Chicago, civil defense activities were an arm of the political machine: the civil defense block captain was the party precinct captain; the party's ward office served as neighborhood civil defense headquarters. All over the country, leading local merchants initiated scrap drives and bond drives, and wealthy businessmen served as officials on the state and local defense councils. Union members and others complained that these people had no experience with normal everyday life. One midwestern official reported "definite evidence of a lack of public confidence in local Defense Councils." Some council members were said to be too busy to do the work; councils were criticized for "not represent[ing] enough of the interests in the community" and for "the dominance of people whose names appear frequently in the social columns of the newspapers."[35]

Some observers asserted that business-citizen cooperation in the service of the country helped build communities and counteract a decade of misgivings about business, fostered during the Depression by militant unionism and a mobilizing consumer movement. A University of Chicago sociologist declared that scrap drives and bond sales, organized by building, block, and neighborhood, had counteracted urban anomie. The "new sense of solidarity and community consciousness" these patriotic activities created had "in many cases, been strong enough to bridge economic, racial, religious, and ethnic barriers" and made strangers in adjoining apartments into neighbors.[36]

If that community existed—and some denied that it did—it did so at the expense of privacy. The borders and margins of the public and private spheres—the attics, basements, alleys, and outbuildings where people stored things they were not ready to discard—became sites for public scrutiny. People were asked to tell on their neighbors. In Clinton, Missouri, a committee of leading citizens "agreed to call on any farmer or industrialist who has not sold or made arrangements to sell his scrap," a local paper reported. "Anybody knowing the location of a large pile of scrap iron should notify some member of the salvage committee." Investigators for Young & Rubicam, studying scrap for the government, were hired to inventory homes and farms for metal and rubber goods. "In asking for a *complete* inventory," the director of market research told his field-workers, "we do *not* mean that you are to sit in the living room and ask the housewife what she has on her property! We mean that you are to go up in her attic with her, go through her kitchen with her, go down in her cellar with her, go out to her garage, barn, outbuildings, back lot, etc., *with her*." If the housewife declined to have her house searched, the investigator was to explain firmly that many people believed they had nothing to offer, "but that when you actually came to look, there *were* lots of things." The interviewers were warned, however, not to be too persistent. "Although this is a job for the Government, you are not empowered with any direct authority to order anyone to do anything they are unwilling to do. In other words, you are not a member of the FBI, or a policeman or an air-raid warden."[37]

A successful scrap drive required the cooperation of businesses of all sizes. Small businesses had access to the facilities that made local campaigns work: the trucks, the newspaper space and radio time, the restaurant equipment for the windup supper. Big businesses had the advertising experience and the organizational power that the national scrap drives demanded. The biggest oil companies participated, as did the smallest local butchers who collected kitchen fats and the St. Louis mom-and-pop store that offered free ice cream cones to kids who brought in rubber.[38]

In February 1942, for example, months before the first big national scrap drives, International Harvester enlisted its more than ten thousand dealers in a crusade that was both scrap drive and advertising campaign. Every dealer received a booklet explaining the plan, along with posters, ads, and publicity copy to place in local papers. Radio stations were asked to donate time; International Harvester dealers were to persuade local junk men to participate. Farmers were exhorted never to drive an empty truck to town. Dealers who brought equipment to the country were to bring back a load of scrap rather than return empty. A poster showed a farmer and a dealer, their sleeves rolled up, dumping a barrelful of metal into a War Industries machine spewing trucks and tanks. International Harvester supplied receipts for its dealers to give to the farmers; the dealer sold what he collected to the local junk man and distributed the proceeds to the farmers according to the stubs in his receipt book. All that the company and its dealers got out of the drive, *Business Week* contended, was "the closer bond resulting from their mutual work with the farmers."[39]

Expanded into the "National Scrap Harvest," this campaign became part of the big general scrap drive of fall 1942. Other farm machinery companies joined in. The Farm Equipment Institute, a trade association, published a handbook for workers, declaring the drive "an all-out, every-farm effort especially on metals and rubber." Some farms had been missed in both local metal collections and the national rubber drive, the booklet explained; others had not given everything they had to donate. To counter farmers' suspicions that scrap dealers were hoarding salvaged materials and holding out for higher prices, the pamphlet explained the price ceilings and described the costs of processing and grading scrap.[40]

The Farm Equipment Institute prescribed for local campaigns only in general terms. It suggested establishing state and county organizations, setting dates and quotas, and coordinating activities and publicity, but it did not dictate. "Let the enthusiasm of the county committee, the facilities available, and the estimated scrap to be gathered be the measure of whether it shall be a 3-day, a week-long, or a 2-week campaign," the booklet suggested. Parades of loaded trucks and huge community scrap piles would generate publicity; piles should be in or near the junk dealer's yard for easier processing and loading. Proceeds should be invested in war bonds and donated to churches, the 4-H, the Red Cross, or the United Services Organization (USO), which ran recreation centers for servicemen. Teams could compete for who brought in the most scrap; "a wind-up supper with chicken for winners and beans for losers" would build interest.[41]

Trade associations like the Farm Equipment Institute were critical to scrap drives because they could muster the money and the people in the field—the salesmen and dealers—to make collections work. The American Iron and Steel Institute (with help from trade organizations representing the auto, rubber, and gasoline industries) underwrote the two-million-dollar advertising bill for the 1942 general salvage campaign, planned and executed by the McCann-Erickson agency. The kitchen fats drive was sponsored by the Glycerine and Associated Industries with help from the American Meat Institute and the Association of American Producers of Domestic Inedible Fats. The Packing Institute of America and the Collapsible Tube Manufacturers Association organized the "Tube for a Tube Program," a 1942 campaign for collecting tin tubes from toothpaste and shaving cream, using drugstores as salvage depots; customers had to turn in empty tubes to buy full ones. "It should be a great good-will builder for druggists," *Business Week* declared, "since it gives them a front seat on the salvage band-wagon, and brings in tube donors who will pause in the stores to buy new tubes of this and that."[42]

Publicity for scrap drives was coordinated by the War Advertising Council, a consortium funded by advertisers, advertising agencies, and media and dominated by the agencies; it turned into the Advertising Council and later, after the war, the Ad Council. The council's initial goal was "A War Message in Every Ad." It offered the government free advertising space and donated the skills of the advertising agencies to help implement government programs. Typically, the government agencies contacted the council, which recruited people in the advertising industry to write copy and plan layout, and corporate sponsors to underwrite the advertising; the sponsor chose an advertising agency to place the ads. The Treasury Department was the War Advertising Council's first client, in February 1942, seeking help in promoting a payroll deduction plan for buying war bonds.[43]

Donald Nelson of the War Production Board was one of the council's early supporters. Coming from Sears, he was more sophisticated about consumer marketing than the many businessmen in government, whose experience was with production in the basic industries. In preparing for the big fall campaign of 1942, Nelson called a meeting of 140 leading newspaper publishers to talk about scrap needs. "From this meeting have flowed miles of words in the daily press about the importance of scrap iron and steel to the war effort," the *New Republic* reported. "The slogans are good, too. 'Slap the Japs with the Scrap!' 'Hit Hitler with the Junk!' "[44]

Even with the best publicity, however, scrap campaigns often faltered because the WPB insisted that collections be handled through the regular salvage industry, and the public mistrusted junk men. "I could have sold this aluminum many times to junk men," declared Frank Hogue of Paterson, Washington, who donated six hundred pounds of aluminum castings to the infamous 1941 aluminum campaign, "but I have been afraid it would be sent to Japan and I would rather throw it into the river." Most people resisted junk men for a simpler reason: they did not want anybody making money off their contributions to the war effort. Early in 1942, before any of the major drives, *Business Week* expressed concern that widespread suspicion of people in the waste trade might make it impossible to collect much household scrap.[45]

Many believed, as La Guardia had when he ran the aluminum campaign, that junk dealers and big scrap merchants were trying to manipulate the situation, holding out for higher prices. Automobile graveyards—which were highly visible, storing old metal in public view—were particularly suspect. At the end of January 1942, the government, threatening army takeovers, ordered graveyards to sell their scrap. The graveyards held back, asserting that they dealt not in scrap but in used auto parts, which would be in big demand now that Detroit was making tanks instead of cars. In the middle of February, steel industry and steelworker officials charged that major scrap dealers, too, were holding metal off the market, hoping that a continued shortage would induce the OPA to raise the ceiling price. As the government began to actually requisition scrap, compelling dealers of all sizes to sell, the tug-of-war brought publicity to the hoarders. Alan Dick, of Shelby, Ohio, got his picture in *Business Week,* along with the four-acre pile of iron he had built up over thirty years and refused to sell until requisitioned. Such stories did not inspire housewives to give away their skillets and kettles for free.[46]

Scrap campaign promoters insisted that the public failed to understand dealers' crucial contributions. "The junk dealer does more than simply buy and sell," a WPB official told *Business Week.* "He collects, sorts, grades, processes, packs and ships." The scrap dealer's work was "a most necessary cog in the wheels of War Production," according to an industry-sponsored pamphlet on scrap collection. Too many people overvalued their junk. Others believed that they should receive the full ceiling price for their castoffs, without considering that ceiling prices were paid *to* dealers for sorted material delivered to the reprocessing plant. The *Saturday Evening Post* featured Jim Mouro, a longtime junk man, an American Legionnaire, and an air-raid warden. "An experienced junkie can appraise your salvage quickly and with astonishing accuracy," the *Post* asserted. "Neither a profiteer nor a philanthropist, he knows at a glance what there is in it for him. The price he offers must make allowance for his own time." A picture caption reiterated the lesson. "Don't feel cheated if he offers you only a few cents," it read. "Government ceilings limit his prices."[47]

Suspicion of junk dealers threatened to undermine scrap efforts, but it was countered with community enthusiasm, the key to wartime scrap drives. In essence, the people on the home front were propagandized to "kick" themselves and one another around. Local businesses volunteered financial and logistical support. Millions of individuals donated their time. Newspapers and radio stations spread the word. People applauded as big piles of scrap got bigger; contests and community suppers added to the fun.

The Home Front

Scrap drives—along with victory gardening, rationing, and shortages—literally brought the war home. The private details of housekeeping were declared to have public significance, indeed to be matters of life and death to the men overseas. As the *Seattle Times* put it, "the kitchen and the sewing room are the housewife's battleground." Rationing limited what people could consume, including people who had money to spend. The metaphor of the home front encouraged Americans to interpret scrap drives, rationing, and frugality as participation in the war effort—almost as participation in the war itself—and to regard women as a fighting force even if they did not join the Women's Army Corps.[48]

In gearing up for the national scrap campaigns, conservation and salvage administrators decided that women should be formally mobilized to collect scrap. "Minute Women," identified by stickers on their windows and credentials in their wallets, would disseminate information about salvage drives and other war programs, including rationing and ride sharing to save gasoline. In August 1942, officials set a goal: a Minute Woman on every block in every community in every state, within eight weeks. Utah, the first state to organize, was the only one to retain its entire organization, with eight thousand block leaders, until the end of the war. The Utah women donated the proceeds of their scrap drives to hospitals, schools, and the Red Cross; at the end of the war, they endowed a scholarship at the University of Utah.[49]

Utah was relatively easy to mobilize, since the dominant Mormon community was already organized down to the neighborhood level. Women participated in scrap drives elsewhere—in Boston, for example, women calling themselves Salvage Commandos went house to house explaining the fall 1942 campaign. But most women had little time for scrap drives. Women played many parts in World War II, and they were all time-consuming. Rosie the Riveter worked forty-eight hours a week; she took crowded public transportation to and from work; she shopped during her lunch hour, because few stores had evening hours. Many of her sisters committed themselves to workweeks of thirty-two hours and more, without pay. Women volunteers ran the Red Cross office, the local hospital, the day care centers. The national bond drives were administered by a Washington staff of forty, with women volunteers at the state and local levels. Unpaid women staffed government agencies, including the Selective Service, the Office of Price Administration, and the U.S. Employment Service. More than three-quarters of the workers in the Seattle OPA office in 1944 were women volunteers. Rationing depended on more than 300,000 volunteer women, many of them "price panel assistants" who checked prices in their neighborhood stores, helping uninformed retailers and reporting those who intentionally broke the law. In California, these volunteers were recruited and organized by women who had long been volunteering for labor unions and for organizations like the League of Women Voters, the Community Chest, and the Red Cross. Even women's iconic roles as sisters and sweethearts to be protected by American fighting men were translated into volunteer work at the USO, where they staffed recreation centers for servicemen.[50]

Housework, too, took more time. Cooking was more complicated because some foods were rationed and others unavailable. Soap was scarce. It was impossible to buy new appliances, and nearly as hard to get old ones repaired, because replacement parts were difficult to come by; ownership of washing machines, refrigerators, and vacuum cleaners declined for the first time. Shoe repair shops and commercial laundries had all the business they could use and no equipment to expand with, so those services, too, became scarce and expensive. Domestics charged twice as much as before the war, and many quit being servants to get better jobs. Propaganda urged women to take up even more work—mending or victory gardening. And with the exception of day care, there was no effort to relieve the burden. Housework remained the individual task of individual women, working alone to maintain the private sphere.[51]

With such constraints on their time, women were not easily mobilized for salvage campaigns. Their participation in scrap drives was further limited by assumptions about what tasks were appropriate for women. While they might do the clerical and organizational work, they were not actually called upon to handle scrap. The one real "women's campaign" for scrap was the largely unsuccessful attempt to collect kitchen fats. "This is a woman's job," explained a pamphlet published by the American Fat Salvage Committee. "It is her job for the duration. And is one way in which women whose family responsibilities prevent their taking an active part in the war effort can make a real and vitally important contribution to Victory."[52]

"The kitchen fats make glycerine," Helen Hayes explained in an advertisement depicting the actress in her suburban New York home, "and glycerine makes the powder charge that drives millions of shells." In fact, glycerine was used in making nitroglycerine, a component not of ordinary gunpowders but of double-base propellant powders. These were not explosives of major importance, according to one physicist who worked at a government arsenal, remembering his skepticism at the time about the strategic importance of the fats campaign, as opposed to its propaganda value.[53]

Fats were first collected in July 1942, after campaigns had already been mounted for metals, wastepaper, rags, and rubber. Over the next three years, officials created innovative programs for fat collection, assisted by seventeen thousand local fat salvage committees. The Utah Department of Fish and Game sponsored deer fat collection; hunters left contributions in receptacles at checking stations, and fat salvage committees picked them up. In July 1943, the Brooklyn Dodgers, the WPB, and the local fat salvage committee offered ten-cent admission to the baseball game to anyone who brought a half pound of fat to the gate; the *New York Times* called the idea "a new variation of Ladies Day with a war angle."[54]

For the most part, however, collecting fat was an everyday matter, not just part of cooking but part of shopping, as it was collected by 250,000 retail meat dealers and 4,000 frozen-food plants, which in turn passed it on to renderers and independent collectors. The fat had to be in clean tin cans, which the renderer or independent collector was supposed to salvage. Everyone got paid. The public got four cents a pound, and in December 1943, the government began to pay two ration points per pound in addition to the cash. Renderers and independent collectors registered with the OPA to receive ration points, which they paid to butchers, who paid them to consumers. Money, too, changed hands down the line.[55]

The fat salvage program was not a "campaign," a concentrated effort announced for a limited period of time. An ongoing program, it required housewives and butchers to change their habits. Both had to be trained to collect fat and told what to do with it. A 1943 WPB pamphlet suggested quotas for families: a tablespoon of fat saved per day would add up to a pound a month. Any fat would do, no matter how black it was or how it smelled, the American Fat Salvage Committee stressed. If women believed that the government wanted only fat good enough to use at home, "we are in direct competition with the family's ration books, and that's a pretty tough row to hoe." Nor should housewives consider making soap from excess fats, as so many of them had seen their mothers and grandmothers doing. "It is wrong to make soap at home," the committee warned despite a shortage of commercial soap, "because all the glycerine contained in the fat is lost in so doing, and the country needs every ounce of glycerine."[56]

Payment was not sufficient to make many women turn in their household fats, which they saved for cooking and which some still used for soapmaking. Fat supplies were limited to begin with, since the United States could not import oils from Pacific islands in enemy hands; demand was incessant. The Young & Rubicam study, conducted when the fats campaign had barely begun, found that almost three-quarters of households saved grease for reuse; of those, 88 percent used all the grease they saved. Southerners saved the most grease, but even in parts of the country where the practice was least common, nearly half of the households used all their grease. After March 1943, when lard and butter were rationed, they needed it even more. According to another study, nearly every American woman knew that fat was being collected and why. But only about half ever turned in any at all.[57]

The fat salvage program was supposed to involve women in the war effort in the course of their everyday activities at home and at the butcher shop. It was quite different from the scrap drives collecting metal, paper, and rags, which fed on short-term community excitement and depended less on the participation of women than on that of businessmen and of children, the foot soldiers of the scrap drives. Indeed, children did most of the work of the drives, because they could be readily mobilized. Kids were already organized into homerooms and Scout troops, elements of larger hierarchies; they had less autonomy than adults and could be more easily pushed around. Younger children were good at exploring for scrap in their neighborhoods and tended to believe enthusiastically in the war. The oldest high school students could drive and were capable of most of the administrative tasks.[58]

Confined to the home front by age, kids were mobilized in military style to gather scrap and disseminate information. Collecting materials for salvage, in their schools and as an extracurricular activity, was only one aspect of their unpaid work for the war effort. Children served as intermediaries between their homes and neighborhoods and the civil defense hierarchy. Kids grew victory gardens and distributed literature for the Red Cross. They sold war bonds through the Scouts, the Camp Fire Girls, the 4-H Clubs. The High School Victory Corps sponsored classes for girls in first aid and child care and prepared boys for military service. The Treasury Department's Schools at War Program sold children savings stamps in denominations ranging from ten cents to five dollars, which they pasted into books until they had enough to buy a war bond. In the 1943 "Buy a Jeep" campaign, schoolchildren "bought" more than ninety thousand Jeeps for the army by purchasing bonds.[59]

A month after Pearl Harbor, *Scholastic* magazine began to devote space to scrap collection; over the course of the war, it published more articles on scrap than any other popular magazine. *Scholastic* explained how to scavenge in attics and garages for scrap metal, wastepaper, old rubber, and rags; described the mechanics of organizing scrap drives; and encouraged schoolchildren to put on a skit called *War against Waste Day,* its script available in a government pamphlet. *Jack and Jill,* a magazine addressed to younger children, published a six-part story called "The Scrapper's Club," about a group that found an abandoned trolley car. In these magazines, in their classrooms, and on the radio, kids learned that scrap drives offered them the opportunity to participate in the war effort. The comic strips' Little Orphan Annie was the commander in chief of the Junior Commandos, a hierarchical scrap-collecting organization that recruited children who were not already collecting for their schools or Scout troops. Organized by Annie's creator, Harold Gray, and her syndicator, the *Chicago Tribune,* the Commandos enlisted nearly twenty thousand members in the Boston area alone.[60]

As part of the major fall scrap drive in 1942, the "Get in the Scrap!" campaign mobilized schoolchildren in imitation of the army, to collect iron and steel, rubber, and rags. The WPB issued a pamphlet for teachers, bearing letters from the president and the U.S. commissioner of education. It explained the military organization: county and city school superintendents were to be colonels, principals would be majors, teachers captains, and students would serve as lieutenants, sergeants, corporals, and privates, "eligible to promotion for meritorious performance of duty." "Every school yard in the land will become a salvage depot," *Scholastic* explained two weeks before the drive started. "In every room of every school, you students will be the active soldiers and non-commissioned officers of the scrap drive."[61]

Each school district was to be mapped, with children assigned to particular streets, using "the methods of commercial sales organizations, which strive always to avoid overlapping of effort." The WPB's pamphlet explained that "householders must not be annoyed by having too many children calling indiscriminately at their homes to ask for scrap." Children were to write letters explaining the drive to their parents and their immediate neighbors. Three days after the letters were delivered, the children would canvass for junk, taking small items away with them and making lists of larger ones. The pamphlet outlined plans for meetings and for poster and slogan contests. Prizes would be awarded to groups of children bringing in the most scrap; lieutenants (older boys) would do the weighing and give receipts. Proceeds from the sale of scrap to dealers could be used for athletic equipment and other school needs or distributed among the students, preferably in the form of war savings stamps, not cash. The WPB also offered many publicity ideas, most involving local businesses. Photo equipment stores might provide film and print pictures for a window display. Other merchants could trim their windows with scrap and pictures of guns, shells, and tanks.[62]

The next year, the beginning of October marked another major campaign mobilizing students, this time to collect metal, fats, and paper. The motto was "Salvage for Victory." For this campaign, the WPB offered teachers an entire salvage curriculum. Students might write essays for English class on "The Romance of a Tin Can" or "How Fats Become Explosives," create science exhibits showing how waste materials were converted into essential products, learn how to salvage fats and prepare cans for collection in home economics, make posters in art class, or practice arithmetic by keeping records of collections and funds. "Pupils also like to work out 'conversion' figures to determine how many tin cans it will take to supply the tin needed for a bomb, a machine gun or a torpedo," the government explained to teachers. The WPB continued to encourage contests but warned that *"pupils should never be allowed to lose sight of the fact that the object of the salvage effort is, not honors, not money, but materials with which to fight and win the war."*[63]

In general, younger children were more easily enlisted than high school students. In one rubber campaign, held in a city with ninety-six schools, a single junior high school brought in more than 10 percent of the total. Senior high schools gave less than elementary schools. "Are high school students really so blind, so stupid, so snobbish, so indifferent to their country's welfare in its hour of mortal danger?" *Scholastic* magazine asked in 1942. "Wake up, high school students— this is war, and you're part of America! And when the American people decide to fight, or to buy bonds, or to collect scrap, believe us, it's socially OK! We're doing these things because we want to, not because the government will put us in a concentration camp." If they were willing to assume the responsibility, high school students could virtually manage a drive, but they were old enough to be bound by the gender conventions: boys were encouraged to participate as leaders, drive trucks, handle scrap, and oversee the weighing; "older girls can manage the fats collection campaign through their domestic science departments."[64]

Parents' Magazine called children "great little scavengers." They were particularly good at locating scrap because they knew their neighborhoods well, including the borderlands and marginal places, the vacant lots and alleys where scrap could often be found. Children had no sense of the old habits of reuse and recycling; outmoded things had no nostalgic value to them. Kids added human interest to community scrap campaigns. "Local radio stations will almost certainly give spot time for the appearance of a child," the War Production Board pointed out in an instructional pamphlet. And kids liked gimmicks and challenges. In Giddings, Texas, scrap metal could be used for admission to the Saturday matinee at the local movie theater; in Denton, children were asked to contribute their weight in scrap metal. Kids who were particularly competitive or patriotic contributed a lot more than that. Joan Petsch, for example, collected 1,220 pounds of scrap in a week, more than any other child in St. Louis.[65]

Above all, children were receptive and susceptible to propaganda. "Children strive to exceed their elders in patriotism," the Chicago superintendent of schools declared. Younger children naturally saw the world in black and white; they responded enthusiastically to the notion of a war between good and evil, in which God was on the side of the United States. Their days began with the Pledge of Allegiance; many classes added a prayer for the boys overseas. They put on patriotic plays at school and sang patriotic songs. Reading groups were divided into privates and sergeants instead of bluebirds and robins. As Little Orphan Annie explained, she and her friend Loretta "have somethin' to do lots more important than playin'. We're doin' war work. It's our war, just as much—or maybe more—than anybody else's."[66]

A Return to Old Ways?

By the end of 1943, the major national scrap drives were over; only local efforts were launched in 1944 and 1945. With the development of synthetic substitutes, the rubber situation was no longer critical; on December 31, 1943, the government terminated its agreement with the Rubber Reserve agents and reprivatized the industry. The public was weary of the war, impatient with home-front programs, and increasingly mistrustful of the government. The conservative Seventy-eighth Congress was attacking programs Roosevelt had instituted during the New Deal. Public complaints about rationing were commonplace; newspapers described black markets not only in the most coveted commodities (especially tires and gasoline) but in ration coupons themselves. In Chicago, officials admitted that people had stopped coming to neighborhood civil defense meetings. Bond drives had to go door-to-door to meet quotas. Scrap drives had been subject to serious criticism since the first disastrous aluminum campaign, and they were increasingly difficult by definition: with each drive, more people had already thrown their old pots and pans into some previous scrap pile.[67]

The tremendous efforts required to mobilize Americans to "make it do" and contribute scrap to the war effort contrast sharply with nineteenth-century habits of reuse and recycling, which were intrinsic to the work of daily life. Like Depression-induced thrift, World War II scrap campaigns did highlight the value of waste materials. But they do not represent a reversion to an older way of life, nor did they significantly slow the American embrace of consumerist ideals of convenience, fashion, and obsolescence. The scrap drives stand out in public memory because they brought communities together in the service of patriotism, but the memory disguises how much the culture had already changed.

In fact, saving and making do went on mingling with consumerism, as they had done for decades. Consumer spending actually increased during World War II. Consumption rose with employment as the United States mobilized for war and the Depression ended. Consumers spent 10 to 15 percent more in 1941 than in 1939, and another 16 percent over the next three years. Purchases of automobiles, radios, washing machines, and other electrical products—goods not being manufactured "for the duration"—did go down. But production and consumption of virtually everything else increased: clothing, cosmetics, toys, jewelry, and many household goods. Americans used increasing amounts of electricity and, despite rationing, even of gasoline throughout the war, as they had throughout the Depression. Although meat, too, was rationed, consumption rose from 134 pounds per capita before the war to 162 pounds in 1944. More people went to the movies than ever before. Pearl Harbor Day 1944 was the biggest day ever at Macy's in New York. "People want to spend money," one department store manager remarked, "and if they can't spend it on textiles they'll spend it on furniture"; otherwise, "we'll find something else for them." People on the home front consumed despite the propaganda to save and mend instead.[68]

Indeed, consumerism not only persisted but prospered. The mechanisms of the consumer culture—advertising and public relations—were used to sell war bonds, promote scrap drives, and explain rationing. The War Advertising Council bolstered the advertising business, keeping agencies busy at a time when corporations were thriving thanks to a government mobilizing for war but had little—and in some cases nothing—to sell to consumers. Corporate managers continued to advertise because they believed in advertising per se and because they were anxious to maintain name recognition. Food companies advertised to keep their brands in the public eye, although the government bought much of their output and consumers faced shortages in stores. Automobile and refrigerator manufacturers advertised to remind consumers that, even though they were currently making tanks, civilian production would resume once victory was achieved. The work of the council directly associated war bond sales, blood drives, and scrap campaigns with corporate names. Even Kotex intertwined a salvage story with discussion about its product as the nation geared up for the fall 1942 scrap drive. "How can a girl deal with trig and trivialities when her brother's out there fighting for freedom?" the company asked in *True Story*. "Why not organize an all-school treasure hunt for the scrap material Uncle Sam needs for his win." With Kotex, Sis could get in the scrap even though she had her period.[69]

In ads like these, the council offered the advertising industry an opportunity to make a public contribution. Wartime advertising rescued the industry from the bad reputation it had acquired by the end of the Depression, when Consumers' Union and other similar groups had raised issues of ethics and taste and had questioned whether advertising should be considered a legitimate business expense, deductible from taxes and factored into government contracts. The advertising industry's propaganda work, historians believe, got it an exemption from wartime excess-profits taxes.[70]

Wartime consumerism was wrapped in the language of patriotism. Scrap drive propaganda, for example, frequently used a consumerist metaphor, juxtaposing household items with war material. "An old bucket will make three bayonets," one typical pamphlet explained. "Two pounds of kitchen fats makes enough glycerine to fire five anti-tank shells. The aluminum in a washing machine will build 21 four-pound incendiary bombs." A similar list appeared in *Scholastic* magazine, among many other places: "One flatiron equals 2 steel helmets or 30 hand grenades. . . . One lawnmower equals 6 three-inch shells. One set of golf clubs equals one .30 caliber machine gun." The Kotex ad used the same technique: "*Hey look*—one worn-out tire makes 8 gas masks!" It was almost as if scrap drives offered consumers an opportunity to "buy" grenades and machine guns with their castoffs. Certainly they gave people an opportunity to buy the respect of their schoolmates or communities.[71]

Scrap drives had more utility as propaganda than as a means of collecting strategic materials, and their importance has been exaggerated in public memory. Not all materials were donated; the government paid for rubber, fats, and some scrap metal. Furthermore, industrial salvage was simply of much greater significance: more materials could be collected more efficiently. Even with extensive volunteerism the cost of household scrap collection was high and the volume of material collected minor, compared with the efficiencies of gathering huge old machines from industrial plants or salvaging abandoned bridges and sunken ships. After a decade of depression, there was plenty of abandoned equipment, and with business reviving, many companies bought the latest technology to replace decaying machines. The wartime memoir of Donald M. Nelson, the chairman of the War Production Board, offers only one paragraph about household scrap. Nelson discusses it solely as a public relations issue, commending "the wholehearted co-operation of the press, the radio, and the movies."[72]

Scrap drives offered Americans a way to contribute to the war effort without sacrificing too much. The child who threw a favorite toy truck on the scrap pile was photographed for the local paper, but most people contributed trash. Indeed, government pamphlets stressed that they *should* contribute trash, not things they would want to replace by buying new items. The days of the traveling tinker had passed; there was no reason to save that old bucket. The 1920s electric iron might not make it through the war, but nobody used flatirons, which had once been heated on the coal or wood stove. They might as well be thrown on the scrap pile. Indeed, they were symbols of an old culture that was to be scrapped in favor of the new. Paradoxically, the very emphasis on scrap reinforced not the traditional stewardship of objects but the newer habits of throwing things away.

By the end of the war, Americans were fully ready to favor consumerism over reuse. Rationing, shortages, scrap drives, and homefront propaganda had grown stale. The language of sacrifice and the community participation that initially sustained the campaigns could scarcely compensate for more than fifteen years of thwarted consumption, constrained by depression and war. Scrap drives left many American households without spare pots and pans or aging baby carriages to pass on to young couples. And people had money to spend. In the new peacetime economy, they were ready to cash in their war bonds and satisfy what economists called "pent-up consumer demand."

CHAPTER SEVEN

Good Riddance

Next time you take out the trash, why not go out in style?" The 1994 magazine advertisement depicts a zany old woman, preening in hot-pink pants and a flowing pink print blouse. Her outfit matches her 1950s-style kitchen: its pink refrigerator, pink metal cabinets, pink dishes, pink walls, and pink trash can. She carries a full plastic trash bag. The bag is pink. Color Scents, "The Designer Bag from Ruffies," deodorized with "potpourri scents," could also be purchased in green, blue, and yellow.[1]

Scented, colored plastic trash bags, nondegradable and headed for the landfill, epitomize a contemporary attitude about trash—a far cry from homemade soap, darned stockings, turned sheets, and Morillo Noyes's warehouse full of bones. Still on the market in 1999, Color Scents illustrate distinctively late-twentieth-century ideas and attitudes about products and about disposal, rooted in a way of life remote from hand production. Old-fashioned habits of reuse and recycling have been virtually abandoned in the United States; disposal has been disengaged from whatever is left of household production and assigned to the technocrats who oversee sewers and sanitary landfills. Plastic liners—adopted by virtually all businesses as an efficiency measure— defend against wet, smelly garbage. Color Scents and their advertising propose that disposal is a positive affair: it is fun to purchase things, use them briefly, and throw them out. With Color Scents, materials for handling waste—like clothes, dishes, and other kitchen equipment— may be seen as part of the ever-changing assemblage of consumer goods that makes up a personal image in the empire of the ephemeral.

Of course, the Color Scents perspective is not the only contemporary attitude about trash in consumer culture. As always and everywhere, poor people sell and reuse what they can, while a broad movement to protect and restore the environment has encouraged some who do have money to adopt ways of life that acknowledge the effects of trash on the global ecosystem. If the Color Scents bag symbolizes the prevailing course of wasting and wanting, other symbols highlight many varieties of contemporary reuse: the baby carrier at the suburban garage sale, the recycling container at the curb, the shopping cart full of bottles and cans that the homeless man wheels down the street, the dustpans made from Mexican license plates in the collection of a North American museum. But at least for now, Color Scents is winning.

Disposing for Pleasure and Freedom

The idea that the act of disposing is a good thing is not new, nor is it simply emblematic of postwar consumerism. Convenience, cleanliness, and disposability have been effective selling points for products since paper collars in the 1860s. But the Color Scents ad epitomizes an actual celebration of trashmaking that only emerged after World War II. Postwar innovations, many based on war research, made possible qualitatively new levels of household cleanliness and quotidian ease. Postwar households bought goods in multilayer packaging and products made for one-time use, threw it all out to be collected by trucks employed or regulated by municipalities, and confirmed the association of recycling with poverty and backwardness. New materials, especially plastics of all kinds, became the basis for a relationship to the material world that required consumers to buy things rather than make them and to throw things out rather than fix them. Nobody made plastic at home, hardly anybody understood how it was made, and it usually could not be repaired. Prepared frozen foods substituted modern food waste—paper, plastic, and aluminum—for corn husks and chicken bones.

"Disposability" became a selling point for postwar consumer goods, especially things made out of paper and, later, lightweight plastics. It was not a hard sell to people who could remember scrubbing diapers, handkerchiefs, and kitchen towels on washboards. Disposable products made cleanliness possible without considerable effort or hired help. Kitchen slops came to have zero or negative value. Although the stubborn and backward might accumulate cupboards full of disposable aluminum potpie pans or plastic microwaving platters on the chance that they might come in handy, most people threw them out, preferring consumption to making do.

During the decade after the war, disposability was promoted particularly by the manufacturers of paper napkins and towels (previously common only in restaurants, public rest rooms, and other commercial enterprises) and aluminum foil (previously a packaging material used by manufacturers). Consumers had to be taught how to use these products; Reynolds Wrap came with instructions for "1001 Kitchen Miracles." Women's magazines also gave lessons, even promoting foil while it was scarce and expensive during the Korean War. Illustrated articles and advertisements adopted the instructional photographic format popular in step-by-step cooking instructions. ScotTowels advertising pictured women's hands using paper towels to drain fried chicken, wipe up spills, collect vegetable peelings, and clean sinks. *Better Homes and Gardens* illustrated how paper towels could come in handy, draining salad greens, drying pots and pans, soaking up spills, and wiping the dog's feet. The *Woman's Home Companion* showed how to use paper towels to gather up vegetable scrapings in the sink ("then all go straight to the garbage can"), waxed paper to roll cookie dough and pie crust, and aluminum foil to waterproof the bottom of a paper garbage sack. ("An already much-used piece of foil will serve this purpose as well as a new one," the article acknowledged.)[2]

Like foil and paper towels, food packaging was promoted as something to throw away after it did its job, generating freedom from unpleasantness. "With quick-frozen foods you throw away nothing," *Good Housekeeping* applauded in 1946, pointing out that fish heads, pea pods, and other trimmings never even entered the house. In fact, you threw away the packaging, now apparently less than nothing. But only apparently. Packaging may have been disposable, but it was hardly worthless; the costs of packaging research and development, marketing, and raw materials were often equivalent to the cost of the contents. New materials and new combinations of paper, foil, and plastic went into food packaging, ranging from coated paper boxes to the three-section foil tray and six-color laminated box developed for the Swanson TV Dinner. These packages were fundamental to marketing prepared foods. "Packaging has grown from a mere way of covering and shipping a product into a market force all its own," *Business Week* declared in 1958. As the title of a 1967 American Management Association publication put it, *Packaging* Is *Marketing*.[3]

Frozen-food packaging served new functions. Like ancient covered pots, the boxes and foil pans from potpies and TV dinners protected food and gave the purchaser something to carry it home in. Like Heinz ketchup bottles, Shredded Wheat boxes, and Campbell's soup cans, they also branded the products, identifying the manufacturer and making the packages suitable for self-service supermarkets. In addition to these long-standing functions, the new frozen-food wrappings replaced the vessels and utensils once used for cooking, serving, and eating. By encouraging consumers to throw away paper, foil, and plastic, frozen food saved the time and labor not only of food preparation but of washing pots and dishes as well.

Disposable products, food packaging, and the convenience, cleanliness, and labor savings they represented were understood to distinguish the freedom of modernity from the drudgery of old-fashioned life. The tedium of cooking contrasted with the modern virtue of convenience, and commentators noted that consumers were willing to pay for the latter, in dollars and in flavor. "These platters are not filled with examples of culinary art at its best," *Consumer Reports* commented about frozen dinners in 1959, refusing to rate any of them Excellent, a stance it had previously taken on cake mixes. "For what they offer in convenience, however, and at current prices, frozen dinners are certainly a good buy."[4]

Advertising and publicity frequently used the word *freedom* to connote convenience: ease and emancipation from the limits of the body and the physical labor once required of everyone without servants—that is, of most people. "Is Your Grandmother Standing between You and Today's Freedom?" asked a headline in *House Beautiful* in 1951, inaugurating a section of the magazine explicitly devoted to teaching women to use the products of the food and appliance industries. "Prejudice about processed foods is keeping millions of women chained to old-fashioned, unnecessary drudgery," declared one article, explaining that processed food did not necessarily taste good but might be improved with a little work. In 1959, *Look* described the "kitchen freedom" made possible by "a revolution in food packaging and processing"—foil and plastic pouches, aerosol cans, and squeeze tubes. "Miracles in packaging and processing are radically simplifying U.S. cooking," declared the headline. The article quoted Secretary of Agriculture Ezra Taft Benson, who called the new packaging concepts "built-in maid service."[5]

Although advertising rarely appealed directly to the capitalist ideology of freedom in the marketplace, the idea that the act of disposing signified liberation became, in the language of the Cold War, a distinction between the freedom of capitalism and the bondage of communism. Historian John A. Kouwenhoven explained in 1959 that waste, abundance, and American democracy were interrelated. "A commitment to democracy—and a certain indifference to waste and untidiness—are prerequisite to abundance," he declared, and conversely, waste was "as much a result of democracy as abundance."

Kouwenhoven's view fit into a larger argument about democracy and consumption. Consumer goods were often described as weapons in the Cold War, and consumption became a vehicle in the political and ideological clash of capitalism and communism. Buying became a surrogate for liberty, and freedom of choice a matter of purchasing. The 1959 American National Exhibition in Moscow—scene of the "kitchen debate" where Soviet Premier Nikita Khrushchev and U.S. Vice President Richard Nixon expressed their opinions on these matters—was only the best-known of the many displays of American products that the U.S. government mounted at fairs and exhibitions throughout Western and Eastern Europe and Latin America.[6]

Disposability was a kind of convenience, and a metaphor for freedom. It could liberate modern housewives from aggravation and work, providing a respite from drudgery that could be purchased for the price of a roll of paper towels. Disposable products offered deliverance from the obligation to care for things, the stewardship of objects and materials inherent in the nineteenth-century relationship to the material world. They saved time by obviating the need for maintenance work: filling, washing, and sorting. Disposability rested on the ideas that somebody else would carry away the trash and that used materials were worthless. As the *Woman's Home Companion* told its readers in 1951, disposable products offered the opportunity to "chuck your dishwashing and laundry problems in the wastebasket."[7]

It was fun to do. *Look* featured doggerel by the comedian Victor Borge as part of a two-page paean to "the miraculous multiplication of throwaways in U.S. homes" in 1954:

> *The modern way of living*
> *Has fulfilled a woman's wishes*
> *Since, after she has used them*
> *She can throw away the dishes!*
> *I think, and I am almost sure*
> *The world will be completed*
> *The day when we can all dispense*
> *With food before we eat it!*

Twelve years later, the Scott Paper Company kicked off what would once have seemed an equally unlikely phenomenon: a fad for paper dresses. The company bought seven-page spreads in women's magazines to introduce its new paper towels and toilet paper, "fashionable disposables triggered by the Color Explosion." The ads included a coupon for a paper dress "created to make you the conversation piece at parties. . . . Wear it for kicks—then give it the air." Scott received half a million orders and spawned numerous imitators. *American Home* described paper dresses, pillowcases, and furniture as "inexpensive, decorative, gay, immediately available and easily disposable. . . . Because they are not forever, just for fun, paper furnishings can be bought on impulse without the usual lasting commitment." But if the paper dress was a fad, disposable garments were not. They were immediately adopted by hospitals and medical facilities, and over the next three decades disposables supplanted cloth garments for patients, nurses, and surgeons.[8]

Out of Sight, Out of Mind

At one time, ignorance about trash was a luxury. People with many servants were liberated not only from physical labor but from thinking about the most basic issues of daily life and bodily care: how to stay warm, get sustenance, and rid their living spaces of wastes. By the early 1950s, most American trash was collected by public agencies or by private companies overseen by municipalities. Refuse was dumped in the country, hidden in landfills, or destroyed in incinerators. Kitchen garbage was ground up and flushed down the drain, as far from most people's minds as it had once been to the wealthy with servants. Most people were fundamentally oblivious to what happened to household trash once it left their sight. It had been turned over to technicians, as a problem to be solved by refuse collection and disposal.[9]

Sanitary landfills, which were introduced in the United States during the 1930s and became increasingly popular after World War II, differed from the common dump in two important ways. First, refuse was not simply dumped but covered over with dirt every day. Second, "controlled tipping"—dumping things in a sanitary landfill—cost money. Whether landfills were publicly or privately owned, the operator controlled where dumping would be done, covered the trash, and charged for the privilege. For those responsible for refuse, landfilling created fewer problems than options such as swine feeding and open dumps: the daily layer of earth reduced odors, vermin, and fires. But the trash did not actually go away. The city engineer of Bismarck, North Dakota, discovered in 1965 that paper had scarcely decomposed in the landfill he excavated in the course of building a new highway to the airport. "Print and pictures in old catalogs were still very clear," he reported to his colleagues. "We also uncovered sales slips for groceries that dated back to the 1920's and were still legible." Archaeologists now analyze American disposal habits using artifacts preserved in landfills. And if landfills put trash out of sight and out of mind for most people, they did neither for the poor. In most cities, landfills—like incinerators—were placed in the poorest neighborhoods. But the poor could no longer benefit from scavenging, which landfills discouraged: the trash was covered daily, and entrance to the fill was patrolled so that the landfill operator could charge for tipping.[10]

By the 1970s, a considerable amount of organic waste from American households bypassed the trash collection system and the landfill, instead entering the sewers through garbage disposers, or disposals, as they became widely called after the original brand, General Electric's Disposall. The appliance epitomized the midcentury ethos of disposing as freedom. It offered the ultimate "convenience," contributed to a level of hygiene previously impossible, and turned food that would once have been reused into sewage. It answered the problem of what to do with smelly stuff now that the family pets ate commercially prepared foods, and it was a lot less trouble than making soup. Water served as a purifying solvent, and the municipal sewer acted as a servant. Emptying private trash directly into public sewers, the disposer joined garbage to the public realm as soon as the waste left the kitchen. It bypassed the curb and the alley, those marginal spaces between the public and the private where household refuse retains its identification with the household where it originates. Grinding food waste into particles too small for reclamation, the disposer took it underground.

Although it was invented in 1935, the garbage disposer's commercial development awaited the country's recovery from World War II, like so many other consumer products. But unlike most other products, its marketing required the cooperation of sanitary engineers and municipal policy makers, some of whom believed that ground-up garbage would clog sewers. Opponents moved to forbid the devices in some cities; supporters got it required in others.[11]

Not only were garbage disposers overseen by experts, they were purchased and installed by them. Most disposers were bought not by consumers but by builders, plumbers, and electrical contractors; people purchased houses that had disposers in them, not disposers themselves. As one California housewife told an interviewer in 1963, "Our disposer came with the house, and I thought it was just a gimmick to increase its cost." Direct advertising to consumers was minimal. Businessmen were the targets of disposer marketing campaigns.[12]

Disposers were also installed in older houses as elements in remodeled kitchens. Kitchen remodeling businesses kept old housing technologically in line with houses built after the war and made entire kitchens into ephemeral products. The remodelers promoted not simply painting the room, laying a new floor, and buying new fixtures but installing prebuilt cabinets and continuous work counters. Garbage disposers were relatively inexpensive appliances that one Chicago plumbing and heating contractor described as a "perfect door opener." Once people had considered a disposer, he explained, "the whole idea of a real, complete modern kitchen takes hold of them and then anything can happen."[13]

The disposer became a hallmark of the modern clean kitchen, and the garbage can "a symbol of the past." With a disposer and easy-to-wipe counters, modern cleanliness could be achieved without domestic servants or very much work. As an electric-appliance trade journal explained, consumers had become "ultra-conscious of 'clean' as a way of living." Freezers that defrosted themselves, ovens that cleaned themselves, and machines that not only washed dirty dishes but kept them out of sight had made the ideal of the antiseptic kitchen attainable.[14]

Once the market for garbage disposers was saturated—and in the midst of the environmental debates of the early 1970s—appliance manufacturers introduced a second machine for dealing with refuse: the trash compactor. Trash compactors were expensive—they cost two or three times as much as garbage disposers—and the few consumer magazines that took notice of them made grudging recommendations at best. *Consumer Reports* was blunt: "Who, then, needs an expensive appliance that does nothing but reduce the volume of household trash?" *Popular Mechanics*, which featured a kit-built compactor to assemble "in a weekend or two," was the most enthusiastic: "For the man of the house, it eliminates the annoying daily trips out to the garbage pail and the horsing around of heavy trash cans." But five months later, the magazine described a fifteen-dollar homemade, hand-powered "masher" that did the same thing.[15]

From the start, compactors came in trendy colors—avocado, copper, and gold in 1971. In 1999, they could be bought to match dishwashers and stoves or finished to look like custom cabinets. But they were still a luxury, found in only 5 percent of U.S. homes, according to one manufacturer. With undercounter space routinely taken by dishwashers, cupboards, and drawers, it took a big kitchen to accommodate a trash compactor. They were most often found on luxury yachts or used for industrial and commercial purposes—in apartment houses, in nuclear-waste facilities at the Department of Energy's Rocky Flats facility in Colorado, and on the space shuttle *Columbia*.[16]

Planned Obsolescence

Although the idea of planned obsolescence had been widely publicized during the 1920s, Henry Ford's capitulation to the principles of styling made it look like a necessary aspect of progress under capitalism. The phrase was probably not used until 1955, when *Business Week* described the expansion of "planned obsolescence" from the auto industry to the marketing of consumer goods in general. The appliance industry, for example, had begun to emphasize color as well as styling; dealers accepted trade-ins, whether or not they had plans to recondition them. "This is anathema to many, who see a planned assault on the American character and peace of mind in the feverish effort to create new designs, in order to make old ones look old-fashioned," the magazine remarked. "Nevertheless, planned obsolescence is here to stay in the auto industry and it is moving into more and more fields."[17]

Under other names, the concept was discussed in trade magazines over the next few years. A provocative editorial about "product death-dates" in *Design News,* for example, sparked a debate over engineering ethics among the magazine's readers and writers. Martin Mayer, the author of a mostly uncritical best-seller about advertising, took up the subject again in 1959, in an article for the general business audience of *Dun's Review.* Mayer acknowledged that some products—he cited fountain pens and cigarette lighters—still offered lifetime guarantees and unlimited repair service. But he described a trend toward three kinds of planned obsolescence. The most objectionable, "planned failure of materials," could not be studied reliably, Mayer claimed, because it was "so highly charged emotionally." The second type, "functional obsolescence," characterized products outdated by new technologies like frost-free freezers or larger-screen TV sets. The third, "style obsolescence," Mayer condemned as particularly American, comparing the yearly automobile model change with the practices of the European auto industry. American car advertising applauded obsolescence, he charged, quoting the slogan for the 1959 Dodge, "The old must make way for the new." In the end, however, Mayer defended obsolescence as inherent to big business. Using the introduction of stereo as his example, he insisted that planned obsolescence was not really planned, and asserted that the concept of planning was rigid and socialistic. "The more one studies the question of 'planned obsolescence,' " Mayer concluded, "the more certain it seems that the phenomenon occurs because business men react to changing conditions, rather than because they plan."[18]

Vance Packard's *The Waste Makers* (1960), which quoted the

business and engineering journals, brought the discussion of "planned obsolescence" to the general public and made it a household phrase. This was the third book of a popular trilogy, following *The Hidden Persuaders* (1957) and *The Status Seekers* (1959). Each stayed on the best-seller list for at least six months; each hit number one; each was translated into more than a dozen languages. The three books offered a sharp critique of business institutions and the experts who worked for them, manipulating Americans into coveting things they didn't need and pursuing those spurious desires. Packard's first two books put the blame on business, but in *The Waste Makers* he criticized consumers as well, describing them as credit-dependent hedonists. He noted the proliferation of stuff: Americans by the late 1950s had more houses and more of everything in them—from wall-to-wall carpets to his and hers deodorants—than ever before. One swimsuit or pair of eyeglasses was no longer enough for many people. Packard warned about "the throw-away spirit" with a quotation from Aldous Huxley's *Brave New World,* whose dictator explains, "We don't want people to be attracted by old things. We want them to like the new ones."[19]

Packard denounced the waste represented by gas-guzzling cars and throwaway packaging, but at the core of *The Waste Makers* was a discussion of planned obsolescence. Packard followed Mayer's categorization scheme, if not his exact terminology. "Obsolescence of quality" described planned product failure; "obsolescence of desirability" was style obsolescence. Like Mayer, he described new technology as "obsolescence of function"—"an existing product becomes outmoded when a product is introduced that performs the function better." He agreed that functional obsolescence could be good: jet planes were better than propeller-driven ones, and the twenty-one-inch TV was an improvement over "the hard-to-see twelve-inch television screen." But he balked at Mayer's stereo example, charging that there had been "overtones of manipulation" in the introduction of additional speakers, new amplifiers, and replacement records. And unlike Mayer, Packard had quite a lot to say about shoddy products designed for quick replacement, citing problems at all levels of manufacturing: engineering, craftsmanship, inspection, and quality control.[20]

Business reacted strongly to *The Waste Makers*. *Fortune*, *Barron's*, and the *Wall Street Journal* responded with articles; the advertising industry trade journal *Printers' Ink* ran a seven-page cover story, "Is 'The Waste Makers' a Hoax?" Du Pont retaliated with "Waste-Maker Nonsense," a wordy newspaper advertisement. "The latest critique scornfully charges us with advocating waste, with somehow inducing consumers to throw away perfectly good articles for replacement with new items of dubious utility," the ad complained. "Well, sir, what sometimes seems like waste is economy of the most stringent kind." Real thrift meant abandoning things when an improvement came along; *not* discarding outmoded products was truly wasteful. "Du Pont, like other large units of American industry, has had a hand in this process and the national scrap-heap is crowded with things rendered obsolete through constant research." And obsolete was good: Grandma no longer had to darn socks, thanks to nylon yarn.[21]

Academic sociologists attacked Packard's books as "kitsch sociology." Seymour Martin Lipset argued that the problems Packard described were not the result of evil business practices but were inherent in American institutions based on democratic values; conspicuous consumption, Lipset claimed, was a way for successful people to announce that they had made it. Packard failed to propose institutional reforms— taxes on advertising or gasoline, for example—that would solve the problems he described. Lipset called Packard an "old-fashioned conservative" who celebrated "the simple, primitive, almost poverty-stricken life." His book, far from being a "radical critique of American capitalist commercial civilization," was nothing but "a nostalgic rejection of a materialistic culture written for those who believe that the only good society was the pre-industrial, pre-commercial, agrarian civilization."[22]

Soon after *The Waste Makers* appeared, a trio of economists from MIT, the University of Chicago, and Harvard tested the meaning of planned obsolescence by calculating the cost of model changes in the auto industry since 1949. They concluded that new models accounted for more than a quarter of the purchase price of the car. But consumers had mostly gotten what they wanted, the economists declared; people buying cars "thought model changes worth most of the cost." When a writer in the *Nation* used the economists' figures to compare unfavorably the amount of money spent on model changes with that spent on foreign aid, schools, mass transit, and the arts, an officer of the Automobile Manufacturers Association responded indignantly. "There is no doubt that the cars offered to the customer today are much improved over their 1949 counterparts," he insisted.[23]

Packard's priorities now seem outdated. His emphasis on shoddy products appears misplaced in a consumer culture characterized by continually evolving audio formats and computer technology—the functional obsolescence that he applauded. Manufacturing defects are surely less systematic than the inexorable parade of new features that stimulate dissatisfaction with things that work perfectly well and make products obsolete before they have left the store. Indeed, the life spans of televisions and automobiles, arguably the two technologies most central to American daily life, have increased.

But Packard was the first to popularize a critique of the throwaway society. In the face of Atomic Age gee-whiz attitudes, he questioned technology; in the midst of the Cold War, he opposed business. Packard's social criticism helped to shift American thinking; his best-selling trilogy thus contributed to the development during the late 1960s and early 1970s of a widespread critical analysis of American business and business-dominated culture. In publicizing the idea of planned obsolescence and in suggesting that business might not be providing goods in the best interests of consumers, Packard laid the groundwork for later debates about consumer issues. In calling for independence from the values of status seeking through possessions, he encouraged the creation of oppositional lifestyles among hippies and cultural radicals. And in calling for attention to waste, he fostered a negative view of a disposable society that became central to the new environmental movement.[24]

"Still Perfectly Good"

In 1974, Carol Stack, a white anthropologist who did fieldwork among African American welfare families, described secondhand shopping as a kind of work, a frustrating task that poor women and their children did daily toward the end of the summer, looking for school clothes. The children seemed resigned to acquiring clothing in ways that accommodated their families' poverty. Two decades later, sociologist Carl Nightingale asserts, poor African American children in inner-city neighborhoods were thoroughly immersed in the imagery of abundance and a "moral culture" that equated "conspicuous consumption, personal identity, and status." He comments on the cynical assumptions of children raised poor in this culture, and he describes the insults that those kids inflicted and received. "Hand-me-downs," Nightingale writes, were a "favorite target; 'Hey y'all,' Chauntey used to yell when he dribbled up to the basketball hoop, 'Georgie got his cousin pants on. His cousin pants and his uncle underwear!' " Without the sewing skills that poor women once used for altering and transforming castoffs, their contemporary counterparts had little hope of making secondhand clothing acceptable to children. The irony was that during those same years, secondhand shopping was becoming acceptable, even fashionable, across the wide spectrum of Americans who defined themselves as middle-class.[25]

Poor people have been buying used clothes and household goods for a long time, first in the stores run by the Salvation Army and Goodwill and, beginning in the 1920s, in thrift shops run by Junior Leagues and the women's auxiliaries of hospitals. "We turn your trash into cash," the Junior League's Thrift Shop in Washington, D.C., told its potential donors; it divided the proceeds (sixteen thousand dollars in 1931) among four institutions serving sick children. By the 1950s, such shops were common. The customers were poor, a Columbus, Ohio, hospital auxiliary leader reported to a national conference; they ranged "from burlesque girls looking for formal gowns with 'makeover' possibilities, to parents searching for shoes that will be a 'close enough' fit."[26]

Charitable groups also sponsored occasional or periodic rummage sales. To help buy seven new oxygen tents, the Dallas City County Hospital System Women's Auxiliary borrowed a building on the state fair grounds for its "Trinkets, Trash and Treasure" sale. The auxiliary for the Norwegian American hospital in Chicago held annual sales.

Many church bazaars featured "White Elephant," "Almost New," or "Flea Market" booths among the craft items, food, games, and prizes. Some organizations held sales irregularly. Any suburban group could "set up shop at a local farmers' market or in the parking lot of a supermarket," a manual for church- and clubwomen explained. In one "very good rummage-sale town," the *Saturday Evening Post* reported in 1961, sales were held at least every two weeks. They sent needy children to college, supported Christmas celebrations in hospital wards, and raised money for sororities and church groups.[27]

In general, middle-class people donated goods and ran these sales but did not buy, and the pricing was intended to be charitable. Donations included defective merchandise from retail shops, discontinued goods from factories, uncollected dry cleaning, and household furnishings from estates, in addition to unwanted goods collected from members of the congregation or club. Individual donors benefited by clearing out storage space; "they can now fill the cupboards with newer vases and relish dishes, the garage with brand-new fertilizer spreaders and snow shovels," the *Post* explained—"all potential fodder for another rummage sale next year." Goods that failed to sell were donated to the old salvage charities, Goodwill and the Salvation Army.[28]

Some women with entrepreneurial energy and a lot to sell held clothing sales to clean out their closets at least as early as 1963, and heirs held private sales of furniture from estates. By the early 1970s, these yard, garage, porch, and driveway sales had developed into competition for the charitable rummage sale. They were public events at—or, usually, outside—private homes, generally one or two days long and open without appointment. Most of the merchandise was used. The sales were attended by middle-class bargain hunters and collectors as well as by the poor.[29]

At first, many people believed that garage sales were a fad, fostered by an economic slump in 1969 and a recession in 1973–74 and by the eccentric styles of the counterculture, which sanctioned secondhand shopping and "vintage" fashions. But the sales were not a passing thing. By 1981, according to one estimate, Americans held over six million garage sales a year, generating nearly a billion dollars. Surveys suggested that more than half of Americans attended these sales at least occasionally, mostly in their own neighborhoods or within a few miles. Most people thought garage sales were fun, and few supported regulation or believed that the sales hurt local merchants. By the 1990s, garage sales were a well-established institution even in wealthy suburban neighborhoods.[30]

Rather than a sign of a troubled economy, garage sales were a function of affluence, a response to the proliferation of stuff that Packard had described. Buying and selling at garage sales were consumerist pastimes; bargain hunting was a consumerist skill. Second bathrooms, second phones, and second TV sets were common by the late 1950s, and within another decade people aspired to thirds. Those who kept the twelve-inch TV when they got the twenty-one-inch had to decide what to do with it when they upgraded again to color TV. Garage sales— along with bigger houses and mini-storage facilities—took care of such things and freed up space for more consumption. They created a secondhand market in Crock-Pots and electric yogurt makers, items not worth advertising in newspapers or selling by themselves.[31]

The very first residential sales were called rummage sales, but after 1967 people made a verbal distinction between rummage sales for charity and garage or yard sales for profit. Rummage sales brought their organizers together in service to the common good, but as more women worked for pay, few had both the time and the administrative skills to manage the considerable planning that a large charitable sale demanded. Both kinds of sales provided opportunities to meet neighbors, to pass time without the stigma of idleness, and to shop without spending much money. While garage sales were not charity events, they gave people—mostly women—opportunities to show their charitable sides. Buyers picked up bargains for their friends, sellers lowered prices for customers who seemed to need it. Like rummage sales, garage sales were also community-making institutions, social arenas as well as markets for objects.[32]

Profit-making sales did not obliterate the practice of donating discards to charitable causes, which was considerably less trouble. People continued to give things to charities, just as they continued to throw some things out and save others for relatives. Holding a garage sale was a new option, an additional sorting category. "You sell things you don't really want, but someone else might want," explained the head-waiter at an upstate New York restaurant who had just held his first sale. "Good stuff, you don't just sell trash or junk." As at the charitable rummage sales, Goodwill and the Salvation Army got the discards from garage sales, the things that did not qualify or did not sell.[33]

Garage sales were not charity, but they were not purely business, either. People held them for many reasons: to make money, to host a quasi-social event, and to ensure that their aunt's bedspread or their college books remained in good hands. Many women held sales as a result of the sorting that came with a major housecleaning. The head-waiter described himself as part of a "yard sale culture," required to give one because he had attended so many. "It's like, you go to dinner parties and you have to give one in return," he explained.[34]

Selling things they had gotten some use out of or things they had bought but never used, garage sale operators priced merchandise according not to rationalized concepts of profit and loss so much as to ideas about a fair price, ideas that might change with the customer. "You can sell it cheap and still feel good about it," explained the headwaiter, "if you realize that you've owned this thing for four, five years, used it for four, five years, you've gotten something out of it and you can sell it for half, a quarter of what you paid for it and still feel good."[35]

Garage sales were part of the "informal economy" of under-the-table business, economic activity that never showed up on the books and on which nobody paid taxes. While some people sought only bargains or extra cash, many during the early 1970s used radical rhetoric and the ideas of the counterculture to describe garage sales in the language of community, social justice, and challenge to the capitalist system. "Garage sales are almost a lifestyle," one young man in his twenties told sociologists, "like sending a message to makers of junk food by not buying any of it." The headwaiter called it "people to people, getting people in the community to come take things of yours that they can use, and to give you *some* money for it, and everyone feels happy about it and you cut out Woolworth's."[36]

Mainstreaming Recycling

Like the origins of garage sales, those of contemporary recycling lie partly in the counterculture of the late 1960s and early 1970s. In its earliest manifestations, recycling was not the province of municipalities and big waste companies but an activity of counterculture environmentalists. Hippie activists organized voluntary recycling centers to which individuals brought their glass and paper. These centers were not small businesses so much as offshoots of social and cultural movements.

Recycling was linked to a counterculture ethos that went well beyond Packard's critique of consumer society and the cult of the new. The ideas of the counterculture encouraged living free of conventional employment, and as cheaply as possible: scrounging for free food from the supermarket trash bin or finding free furniture in the alley. Young people celebrated the old-fashioned as subversive. They baked their own bread and grew vegetable gardens. Many learned handwork skills: sewing, carpentry, potting, and weaving. They remade clothing, fashioning bell bottoms from straight-legged blue jeans purchased at thrift stores or picked up at "free stores," where people traded clothes they were not using. Some went "back to the land," reviving such nineteenth-century activities as making soap from wood-ash lye; many others read about doing these things in Alicia Bay Laurel's *Living on the Earth* or in *The Whole Earth Catalog*.[37]

City hippies created collectively run alternative businesses like food co-ops and recycling centers. About three thousand voluntary recycling centers were organized during the months before and after Earth Day, April 22, 1970. People brought their bottles, cans, and newspapers, and the collectives sold the materials to the few companies that would buy them—initially only Reynolds Aluminum and Owens-Illinois; these two container manufacturers had begun buying aluminum in 1967 and glass in 1968, thus creating markets and making recycling a reality. Activists pressured other corporations and municipalities to support recycling. On some level, everybody who recycled was an activist: recycling signified seriousness about the environment because it required commitment to sort materials at home and effort to take them to the recycling center.[38]

But the voluntary recycling programs of the early 1970s could not handle the typical cycles of the waste trade: in general, when prices are high, more bottles and cans are collected; when the resulting big supplies bring prices down, collecting declines, which raises the price and starts the cycle again. Like any other businesses their size, the recyclers were vulnerable to collapse during the inevitable downswings, when markets were glutted, prices were low, and they might not be able to sell materials at all. They were especially susceptible because recyclables kept pouring in, from donors who cared not about price, but about saving the earth.

Along with junkyards, collection companies, and other small waste businesses, the voluntary programs could not compete with the efficiencies and the economies of scale achieved by the large companies that took over the waste business. By the late 1980s, municipal solid-waste hauling—once done by ten to twelve thousand independent companies—was dominated by four big firms. These were integrated businesses, handling all aspects of trash with expensive technology. The big firms were in a position to take advantage both of environmental regulations that could not be obeyed without up-to-date equipment and of Reagan-era calls for privatization. They operated landfills, recycling plants, and high-tech incinerators.[39]

As the waste industry centralized, recycling developed into a mainstream value, as well as a viable option for handling municipal trash. Environmental activists prodded, and in some cases went to work for, the sanitary engineers and politicians who oversaw municipal trash collection, the federal Environmental Protection Agency, and businesses whose managers were sensitive to environmental issues. Community political activists demanded recycling and protested the siting of incinerators and landfills. Their successes were impressive. Whereas only two cities operated municipal recycling programs in 1970, more than two hundred did in 1982.[40]

By the late 1980s, public officials and representatives of industry generally agreed that some recycling was a good idea, as part of a strategy that combined waste reduction, recycling, incineration, and landfilling. Local infrastructures were developed in many municipalities in support of recycling, assuring the futures of recycling programs even once federal and state support was withdrawn in the budget-cutting climate of the mid-1990s. Recycling goals were firmly instituted not only as matters of policy but as bureaucratic realities. Thus, the Chicago Board of Trade, the agency that handled the markets for agricultural futures, developed a new system for marketing waste materials. Working with the EPA and the National Recycling Coalition, the board established a Recyclables Exchange to act as a marketplace, post public prices, and establish procedures for resolving disputes and verifying the quality of merchandise. In 1999, the exchange handled primarily tires, plastic, glass, and paper.[41]

Indeed, as critics complained, recycling had been elevated to the status of motherhood and apple pie. It involved participants on many levels—manufacturing corporations, environmentalists, government agencies, the waste industry, coalitions of these groups, and perhaps above all, the many children who learned about it in school and harangued their parents to help "save the earth." Recycling had become a fact of life, a mainstream activity, no longer the enterprise of hippies and radicals. For those who could put their separated boxes and bottles out with the trash, it had become a kind of throwing-away—like Goodwill, a means to get rid of things with a clean conscience. Across the country, recycling advocates could point to the success of both mandatory and voluntary programs. The EPA reported on the twenty-fifth anniversary of Earth Day in 1995 that the United States was on its way to the 25 percent goal the agency had set in the late 1970s: domestic-waste recovery had increased from 7.1 percent by weight in 1970 to 21.7 percent in 1993.[42]

The new recycling, however, was in no way a reinstatement of the nineteenth-century recycling system run by Morillo Noyes and other tin manufacturers. Noyes's peddlers engaged in two-way relationships, paying for rags and old rubber with cash and credit. Late-twentieth-century households just put the stuff out on the curb, expecting nothing tangible back. What the new systems recalled was the "primary separation" plans of early-twentieth-century cities. Bottles, cans, and newspaper were the new sorting categories, instead of ashes, paper, and food wastes. In both cases, people put refuse into the municipal waste stream with the belief and expectation that the material would be reused. In both cases, municipalities made money from selling the wastes—or, if the markets were bad, they absorbed the costs.

As political environmentalism made recycling a reality, Americans became conscious of reuse and waste reduction in everyday life. The how-to lore of the counterculture contained instructions for making things at home that were generally made in factories and for reusing industrially produced wastes: cable spools became coffee tables, and bottles could be sawed in half to make drinking glasses. Over the next decades there was a steady stream of articles and books. Some followed the line of the bestselling *50 Simple Things You Can Do to Save the Earth* (1989), which asserted that individual daily acts—planting trees, reducing junk mail, or buying energy-efficient lightbulbs—would add up to a significant environmental effect. Environmentalist critics of this approach complained that the sum of such individual acts was too inconsequential to counteract the damage caused by industrial pollution. But people bought *50 Simple Things* and its many imitators, and they went to the trouble of sorting their bottles and cans, because they wanted to contribute to environmental solutions. They were not exactly taking stands in opposition to the consumer culture by replacing their showerheads with low-flow chlorine filters or purchasing containers for sorting and storing recyclables. But by asserting that their personal consumption habits had significance beyond their individual lives and by suggesting that the future of the planet might take precedence over personal convenience, they echoed both the sixties counterculture and the women of the turn-of-the-century municipal housekeeping movement.[43]

Bricolage as Art

In the late 1950s and early 1960s, magazines from time to time advised adventuresome eccentrics and bargain hunters of all classes to go junking. "Bargain Buys from the Salvation Army?" asked *Good Housekeeping,* explaining how to find the Army's stores and what kinds of merchandise to expect at what kinds of prices. *American Home* staffers went to a country auction, lamenting that they were decades too late to make a "killing" but assembling a roomful of attractive furniture and folk art. *House Beautiful* described homeowners who found "beauty in the junkyard," decorating houses with scavenged barn wood, lumber salvaged from crates, and old windows. The designs could not be copied directly, because they were dependent on found materials and devised for individual houses. Instead of giving how-to instructions, the article offered inspiration for "proving your mettle and refusing to bow to the precept that what is good is inevitably expensive."[44]

But few readers really had the touch. In a consumer culture, it took a special eye to see the possibilities in the junkyard and the Salvation Army store, and those who reused junk in clever and innovative ways were considered artists. The people who continued to practice the once-commonplace habits of collecting materials to use in doing handwork were usually described as eccentrics or folk artists if they were not "real" artists making work for galleries and museums.

Bricolage had become part of the history of Western art as it was receding from everyday experience at the beginning of the century. The idea of using the industrially produced refuse of daily life as art materials is usually traced to Pablo Picasso and Georges Braque, who created their first collages—combining painted images with wallpaper, newspaper, and sheet music—in 1910. A few years later, Marcel Duchamp's "ready-mades" and kinetic sculptures extended the concept into three dimensions. Over the following decades, junk became art in works as diverse as Kurt Schwitters's constructions of old lace, foil, and canceled train tickets, Robert Rauschenberg's pioneering trash sculptures, Joseph Cornell's boxes, and John Chamberlain's welded sculptures of automobile parts.[45]

As many women artists pointed out during the 1970s, the founders of cubism may have brought collage into the museum, but Victorian women had used it to make valentines and scrapbooks decades earlier. Quilting, the women suggested, was a women's art form. Besides organizing the first museum exhibitions of quilts, women artists honored quilting and quilters in their own artwork. Among others, Miriam Schapiro, Betye Saar, and Faith Ringgold have made assemblages using artifacts from women's work culture.[46]

Some artists employed found materials to make statements specifically about the environment and about the connections between trash and consumerism. Jac Leirner, a Brazilian artist, used airplane boarding passes and plastic shopping bags from museum shops around the world. "Can Man," a New York performance artist named Gene Pool, rode up to public places on his unicycle, wearing a suit made of five hundred aluminum cans. Mierle Laderman Ukeles, the unsalaried artist-in-residence of New York's Department of Sanitation, constructed *Ceremonial Arch Honoring Service Workers in the New Service Economy* from the castoffs of the city's public service agencies, including gauges from the Fresh Kills landfill, mailbags, police walkie-talkies, street-cleaning brushes, and hundreds of used gloves. Trash was Ukeles's topic as well as her medium; her other pieces included *Touch Sanitation* (1979–80), an eleven-month performance in which she shook hands with all eighty-five hundred of the city's sanitation workers, and *The Social Mirror* (1983), a sanitation truck resurfaced in mirrors.[47]

To describe art in museums as bricolage is to follow women's art— and much of the art of Hispanics, African Americans, and other people of color—in challenging the dividing lines between art and craft and between folk art and high art. Critics generally discuss Schapiro and Ringgold, and certainly Schwitters and Cornell, as if these artists were creating art, not making do. The issues they address in their work are described as formal, art-historical, and, in the case of the women, political. But in talking about their work, artists describe the essence of bricolage, the dialogue between the materials available and the artist's imagination. "I had a lot of stuff around," remembered Edward

Kienholz, a California artist who constructed elaborate environments from found materials. "I'd go through trash cans and back alleys and junk stores and just keep collecting lots and lots of stuff. And depending how I felt any particular day, I'd take a little of this and a little of that, and I'd screw around with it until it was something that satisfied me."[48]

The lines between art and craft dissolved further during the 1980s and 1990s, in an art market hungry for affordable objects. Books and magazines hailed "grassroots" artists who had for years been using waste materials to transform their property into folk art environments: in California, Emanuele ("Litto") Damonte's hubcap ranch, Simon Rodia's Watts Towers, and Tressa Prisbrey's Bottle Village, and, in Wisconsin, the Dickeyville Grotto and Fred Smith's sculptures at the Rock Garden Tavern. Museums displayed utilitarian and ornamental objects made from the detritus of industrial culture by self-taught "folk artists" or "vernacular artists." Art critics hailed "outsider art" by untrained artists, describing it as a critique of the domination of commodity culture, revealing "aspects of the world previously hidden by the barriers of class."[49]

A 1996 exhibition at the Museum of International Folk Art in Santa Fe, *Recycled, Re-Seen: Folk Art from the Global Scrap Heap*, specifically celebrated the use of waste materials in objects like kerosene lanterns fashioned from cans or a doll-sized hot-air balloon made from a macramé-wrapped lightbulb. This was small-scale handwork, constructed from industrially produced materials discarded by consumers. It was for sale by its makers on the streets of poor countries all over the world. While few of the artists were motivated to recycle by environmental awareness, many of them communicated an ironic understanding of consumer culture in the ways they transformed objects. Art made of waste materials raises central questions about how we live—and how we should live—in the material world. It comments on industrial culture and on the meaning of high culture. It reminds us that trash has always been a product of sorting and that what counts as trash has always depended on who was counting.[50]

People who could not afford to buy most work displayed in museums could buy folk art and other original craft objects, examples of hand-work that challenged the dominance of the mass-produced. Most of these articles, and others like them, could be found in SoHo and Berkeley boutiques as well as in museum shops. *Metropolitan Home* declared reuse and recycling "the wave of the present" in 1997, pictur-ing bowls made from materials including dryer lint, long-playing records, and old bottles, at prices ranging from ten to a thousand dollars. Old quilts, hooked rugs, and other folk art objects became valuable collectibles. Hooked rugs, one New Jersey collector told the *New York Times,* are "more luxurious than Orientals and they have a throw-away chic."[51]

The Way We Live Now

Recycling has expanded since the 1970s, but so has trash—and at a faster rate. During the same twenty-three years (1970–93) that recy-cling programs increased domestic-waste recovery from 7 percent to nearly 22 percent, solid-waste production in the United States increased from 3.2 pounds per person per day to 4.4 pounds per person per day. Put another way, after recycling, the trash that had to be dumped or burned increased from 3 pounds to 3.4 pounds per person per day.[52]

The most devoted recyclers buy more food in disposable containers than ever before; the most dutiful reusers of plastic containers cannot find uses for all the ones that come their way. Americans take the word of companies that make razors, batteries, toothbrushes, and processed food, throwing away the old one when the manufacturer says it's time to buy again. Without really meaning to thumb our noses at starving children overseas, we waste food and countenance its waste. We are so accustomed to drinks' coming in disposable bottles and paper cups that it's hard to imagine how people managed to avoid dehydration in the old days. The "paperless office" never materialized: the computer has generated more communication, and much of it gets printed out. And as we keep buying new computers and not knowing what to do with the old ones, planned obsolescence has come to seem like a fact of life, not a historical development.[53]

Although few people still celebrate disposing for its own sake, our consumer culture continues to thrive on taking in natural resources and excreting refuse, in what industrial ecologists describe as an open system, where waste does not get used. Medical waste washes up on the beach. Urban trash is shipped ever greater distances. The refuse of the wealthy endangers the living spaces of the poor, in the United States and all over the world. And consumer trash is only part of the refuse problem, which in itself probably creates less damage to the global environment than automobile emissions, air-conditioning, and the production of consumer goods. The population of the world continues to multiply, and so does the proportion adopting Western lifestyles and patterns of economic growth. It seems that anything we might do is too little, too late.

A harbinger of things to come, the garbage barge *Mobro* roamed Atlantic waterways for two months in 1987, searching for a dumping place and being rejected by five states and three foreign countries. There were dire projections that the United States would soon run out of landfill space. In response, the big waste companies raised tipping fees and built immense landfills. Observers of trash eventually declared the problem solved; in 1993, even the editor of the short-lived magazine *Garbage* declared that trash did not constitute an environmental crisis. But the life expectancies of the new landfills were measured in decades—hardly a long-term view from the standpoint of the planet—and soon enough, trash was back in the news.[54]

As so often in the past, New York City led the way, thanks to its size and its concentrated population. In December 1998, its enormous Fresh Kills landfill nearly full, New York began making arrangements to ship refuse elsewhere. A plan to send the city's residential trash to New Jersey met protest from officials there; a month later, a contract to ship it to Virginia provoked a challenge from that state's governor. New York's mayor declared that people from other states should accept the trash because the city provided cultural benefits for tourists from all over America, a statement that drew even more complaints. But the Virginians who visited Manhattan were not the ones living near the landfills that took New York's trash. The population of Charles

City County, where Waste Management Inc. of Houston operated a 934-acre landfill, was among the poorest in Virginia, nearly two-thirds African American. Like poor people elsewhere, they did it for the money: the landfill brought in revenue to build schools and cut property taxes.[55]

The prospects are not encouraging. Powerful institutions play for high stakes in such debates. Garage sales flourish but everybody has more stuff; bigger houses, mini-storage, and overflowing trash cans go together. People of the developed economies show no signs of giving up their status objects and handy products, nor will those from less developed ones give up their desire for the popular consumer goods of the twentieth century. Most people have been glad to jettison the habits of making do, which may have fostered ingenuity but took time and effort. "Today, we feel we have a natural right to new objects," writes Gilles Lipovetsky; "we know nothing but the ethic of consumption." Environmental warnings are opposed less by rational disagreement or scientific argument than by recklessness: they may be true (the reasoning goes), but who wants to hear them and how much difference can one person make, anyhow—we might as well do what's easy, what makes us happy. The moon is littered with astronauts' castoffs, while tens of thousands of pieces of debris orbit the earth—spent rocket boosters, dead satellites, garbage from manned space missions, and tiny but fast-moving bits of metal and chips of paint. Those of us not responsible for safeguarding the operational spacecraft endangered by this orbiting trash grimace at the very idea of it, but then we shrug.[56]

There are some promising signs. Recycling and composting programs have come to be recognized as viable options; such programs contributed to the mix of effective approaches that proved the Cassandras wrong—at least in the short term—in the wake of the *Mobro*. Activists have pressured both government agencies and corporations to create recycling programs and to reduce waste at the source, in the service of global, regional, and local environments. Some businesses have responded only under pressure; others have cooperated or created their own initiatives, usually persuaded by environmentally concerned managers in their own ranks. Green research and development, a vocal minority insist, is good business.[57]

The success of such programs suggests that many at the very heart of consumer culture—Americans and Western Europeans—are willing to give up some level of personal convenience, and a few businesses may even be willing to risk profits, in order to foster solutions to environmental problems or to avoid contributing to them. After decades of assuming that public policy and corporate profit making would send us always in the direction of saving time and trouble, some people and enterprises have begun to promote practices that require more of both. Recycling has been successful, and not because of market incentives.[58]

Sorting trash for recycling—which people used to do for money—has become a moral act, a symbol of care about the environment. To call it a symbol is not to diminish its significance. Recycling and reuse—however limited their contributions to long-term environmental solutions—remind us of the threads that bind our individual households to the planet and the activities of our daily lives to its future. That awareness is new to the late twentieth century, sustained by the globalization of economic life, and it provides a source of hope as well as a basis for fear. Americans and Western Europeans have responded to environmental problems by returning to reuse and recycling, sometimes in high-tech versions. If we can go further, taking steps to reduce the production of waste and pollution, profligacy may one day be understood as a stage of development. In the United States, it emerged early in the twentieth century as the prevalent version of consumer culture; maybe we will be able to say that it began to decline in the 1970s and possibly even that it proved to be avoidable in developing countries. We are not likely to revive the stewardship of objects and materials, formed in a bygone culture of handwork. But perhaps new ideas of morality, utility, common sense, and the value of labor—based on the stewardship of the earth and of natural resources—can replace it.

Notes

TOWARD A HISTORY OF TRASHMAKING

1. Lars Eighner, *Travels with Lizbeth* (New York: St. Martin's, 1993), pp. 118–19.
2. Mary Douglas, *Purity and Danger: An Analysis of Concepts of Pollution and Taboo* (London: Routledge & Kegan Paul, 1966), pp. 2, 35–36.
3. Mrs. [Lydia Maria] Child, *The American Frugal Housewife*, 16th ed., enlarged and corrected (Boston: Carter, Hendee, 1835), p. 8; Charles Dawson Shanley, "The Small Arabs of New York," *Atlantic Monthly,* Mar. 1869, p. 284; Thomas Lambert, *Bone Products and Manures: A Treatise on the Manufacture of Fat, Glue, Animal Charcoal, Size, Gelatin, and Manures* (New York: D. Van Nostrand, 1925), p. 3; Eighner, *Travels with Lizbeth,* pp. 112–13.
4. Douglas, *Purity and Danger,* pp. 114–28; Michael Thompson, *Rubbish Theory: The Creation and Destruction of Value* (Oxford: Oxford University Press, 1979), p. 92.
5. Kevin Lynch, with contributions by Michael Southworth, *Wasting Away: An Exploration of Waste—What It Is, How It Happens, Why We Fear It, How to Do It Well* (San Francisco: Sierra Club, 1990), pp. 25, 45; see also Park Benjamin, *Wrinkles and Recipes Compiled from the* Scientific American (New York: H. N. Munn, 1875), p. 236.
6. Josiah Quincy, "An Address Delivered before the Massachusetts Agricultural Society at the Brighton Cattle Show, October 12, 1819," and Delia Ellsworth

Taintor (1818–89), quoted in Caroline Fuller Sloat, "Dishwashing and the Domestic Landscape: Reform Begins at Home," paper delivered at Winterthur Conference on the American Home, Oct. 29–31, 1992, pp. 2–3. See also Jack Larkin, "From 'Country Mediocrity' to 'Rural Improvement': Transforming the Slovenly Countryside in Central Massachusetts, 1775–1840," *Everyday Life in the Early Republic,* ed. Catherine E. Hutchins (Winterthur, DE: H. F. du Pont Winterthur Museum, 1994).

7. Barrie M. Ratcliffe, "Perceptions and Realities of the Urban Margin: The Rag Pickers of Paris in the First Half of the Nineteenth Century," *Canadian Journal of History* 27 (Aug. 1992), pp. 198, 205. On swill children, see Charles Loring Brace, *The Dangerous Classes of New York, and Twenty Years' Work among Them* (New York: Wynkoop & Hallenbeck, 1872), p. 152, and Judith Walzer Leavitt, "The Wasteland: Garbage and Sanitary Reform in the Nineteenth-Century American City," *Journal of the History of Medicine and Allied Sciences* 35 (Oct. 1980), pp. 431–52.

8. Lynch, *Wasting Away,* pp. 31–32.

9. Sidney Mintz, "Poverty and Creativity in the Caribbean," *Pauvreté et Développement dans les Pays Tropicaux: Hommage à Guy Lasserre,* ed. Singaravelou (Paris: Centre d'études de geographie tropicale, CNRS, 1989), pp. 391–92. See also Mintz, "Men, Women, and Trade," *Comparative Studies in Society and History* 13 (July 1971), 249–50.

10. Charles Godfrey Leland, *A Manual of Mending and Repairing, with Diagrams* (New York: Dodd, Mead, 1896), p. xxi. On repair as an extension of fabrication, see Douglas Harper, *Working Knowledge: Skill and Community in a Small Shop* (Chicago: University of Chicago Press, 1987), pp. 19, 21; on the separation of conception and production, see Harry Braverman, *Labor and Monopoly Capital: The Degradation of Work in the Twentieth Century* (New York: Monthly Review, 1974).

11. George Sturt, *The Wheelwright's Shop* (Cambridge: University Press, 1923), pp. 24, 20.

12. Claude Lévi-Strauss, *The Savage Mind* (Chicago: University of Chicago Press, 1966), pp. 17–18, 33.

13. See Susan Strasser, *Satisfaction Guaranteed: The Making of the American Mass Market* (New York: Pantheon, 1989).

14. T. E. Graedel, B. R. Allenby, and P. B. Linhart, "Implementing Industrial Ecology," *IEEE Technology and Society Magazine,* Spring 1993, p. 19.

15. Robert U. Ayres, "Industrial Metabolism: Theory and Policy," *The Greening of Industrial Ecosystems,* ed. Braden R. Allenby and Deanna J. Richards (Washington: National Academy of Engineering, 1994), p. 25.

16. Allenby and Richards, *Greening,* p. v; Christine Meisner Rosen, "Industrial Ecology and the Greening of Business History," *Business and Economic History* 26 (Fall 1997), p. 123.

17. Christine Frederick, *Selling Mrs. Consumer* (New York: Business Bourse, 1929), pp. 246, 250–51. On Frederick and progressive obsolescence, see also Roland

Marchand, *Advertising the American Dream: Making Way for Modernity* (Berkeley: University of California Press, 1985), pp. 156–60, and below, ch. 4.

18. On byproducts, see "joint production" in *The New Palgrave: A Dictionary of Economics,* ed. John Eatwell, Murray Milgate, and Peter Newman (London: Macmillan, 1987), vol. 2, pp. 1028–30. On secondhand goods, see Tibor Scitovsky, "Towards a Theory of Second-Hand Markets," *Kyklos* 47 (1994), pp. 33–52; Daniel K. Benjamin and Roger C. Kormendi, "The Interrelationship between Markets for New and Used Durable Goods," *Journal of Law and Economics* 17 (Oct. 1974), pp. 381–401; H. Laurence Miller, Jr., "A Note on Fox's Theory of Second-Hand Markets," *Economica,* n.s. 27 (Aug. 1960), 249–52; Arthur H. Fox, "A Theory of Second-Hand Markets," *Economica,* n.s. 24 (May 1957), pp. 99–115; H. Laurence Miller, Jr., "On Killing Off the Market for Used Textbooks and the Relationship between Markets for New and Second-hand Goods," *Journal of Political Economy* 82 (May/June 1974), pp. 612–19.

19. Irving Wohlfarth, "Et Cetera? The Historian as Chiffonnier," *New German Critique* 39 (1986), p. 151; Walter Benjamin, *Charles Baudelaire: A Lyric Poet in the Era of High Capitalism,* trans. Harry Zohn (London: Verso, 1973), pp. 19–20; Ratcliffe, "Perceptions and Realities," p. 205. See also Jerrold Seigel, *Bohemian Paris: Culture, Politics, and the Boundaries of Bourgeois Life, 1830–1930* (New York: Viking, 1986), pp. 140–42.

CHAPTER ONE: THE STEWARDSHIP OF OBJECTS

1. James Deetz, *Flowerdew Hundred: The Archaeology of a Virginia Plantation, 1619–1864* (Charlottesville: University Press of Virginia, 1993), p. 30.

2. Mrs. [Lydia Maria] Child, *The American Frugal Housewife,* 16th ed., enlarged and corrected (Boston: Carter, Hendee, 1835), p. 19. On coal ashes, see Park Benjamin, *Wrinkles and Recipes, Compiled from the* Scientific American (New York: H. N. Munn [1875]), p. 206; Catharine E. Beecher, *A Treatise on Domestic Economy* (New York: Marsh, Capen, Lyon, and Webb, 1841), pp. 302, 373; Mrs. Julia McNair Wright, *The Complete Home: An Encyclopaedia of Domestic Life and Affairs* (Philadelphia: J. C. McCurdy, 1879), p. 559. On corn-cobs, see Benjamin, *Wrinkles and Recipes,* p. 206; on husks, see George E. Blakelee, *Blakelee's Industrial Cyclopedia: How to Make and How to Mend* (New York: Fords, Howard & Hulbert, 1884), p. 548. On soap suds, see Child, *American Frugal Housewife,* p. 13. On tea leaves for sweeping, see Beecher, *Treatise,* pp. 341, 362; see also [Robert Kemp Philp], *The Family Save-All: A System of Secondary Cookery* (London: Houlston & Wright; Philadelphia: J. B. Lippincott, 1869), p. 320. On damp paper, see Anna Barrows, "Waste Paper: What to Do With It That It May Not Be Wasted," *Good Housekeeping,* Sept. 19, 1885, p. 12.

3. Wright, *Complete Home,* p. 82.

4. Wright, *Complete Home,* pp. 74, 78, 80. On American extravagance, see also F. E. Fryatt, "The New York Cooking School," *Harper's,* Dec. 1879, p. 22.

5. Christine Terhune Herrick, "The Wastes of the Household: Watching and Saving the 'Left-Overs,' " *Good Housekeeping*, May 2, 1885, p. 16.

6. Wright, *Complete Home*, p. 564; Catharine E. Beecher and Harriet Beecher Stowe, *The American Woman's Home; or, Principles of Domestic Science* (New York: J. B. Ford, 1869), pp. 358–59; Beecher, *Treatise on Domestic Economy*, p. 384; Christine Terhune Herrick, *Housekeeping Made Easy* (New York: Harper, 1888), p. 153. See also Jay Mechling, "Advice to Historians on Advice to Mothers," *Journal of Social History* 9 (Fall 1975), p. 46.

7. Beecher, *Treatise on Domestic Economy*, p. 373; Blakelee, *Industrial Cyclopedia*, pp. 617–18; Child, *American Frugal Housewife*, p. 19; Wright, *Complete Home*, pp. 84–85, 559; Benjamin, *Wrinkles and Recipes*, p. 224; Almon C. Varney, *Our Homes and Their Adornments; or, How to Build, Finish, Furnish, and Adorn a Home* (Detroit: J. C. Chilton, 1883), p. 406; Philp, *Family Save-All*, p. 271.

8. Benjamin, *Wrinkles and Recipes*, pp. 225, 236; Beecher and Stowe, *American Woman's Home*, pp. 350–51.

9. Child, *American Frugal Housewife*, pp. 9, 11; Benjamin, *Wrinkles and Recipes*, pp. 250, 229; Wright, *Complete Home*, p. 556; Beecher, *Treatise on Domestic Economy*, p. 373; Blakelee, *Industrial Cyclopedia*, pp. 622–23, 625.

10. Carolyn L. Karcher, *The First Woman in the Republic: A Cultural Biography of Lydia Maria Child* (Durham: Duke University Press, 1994), p. 129; Herrick, "Wastes of the Household," p. 16; Beecher, *Treatise on Domestic Economy*, pp. 175–86; Beecher and Stowe, *American Woman's Home*, pp. 215, 251–54.

11. Katherine C. Grier, *Culture and Comfort: People, Parlors, and Upholstery, 1850–1930* (Rochester, NY: Strong Museum, 1988), p. 274.

12. For a discussion of the relation between economic processes of waste and natural ones, see Kevin Lynch, with contributions by Michael Southworth, *Wasting Away: An Exploration of Waste—What It Is, How It Happens, Why We Fear It, How to Do It Well* (San Francisco: Sierra Club, 1990).

13. Willa Cather, "A Wagner Matinee," *The Troll Garden*, 1905 (New York: New American Library, 1984), p. 115; Jack Larkin, "From 'Country Mediocrity' to 'Rural Improvement': Transforming the Slovenly Countryside in Central Massachusetts, 1775-1840," *Everyday Life in the Early Republic*, ed. Catherine E. Hutchins (Winterthur, DE: H. F. du Pont Winterthur Museum, 1994); Caroline Fuller Sloat, "Dishwashing and the Domestic Landscape: Reform Begins at Home," paper delivered at Winterthur Conference on the American Home, Oct. 29–31, 1992; Charles S. Templer, "The Swill Barrel," *Timeline*, Aug.–Sept. 1991, pp. 53–54. On horse pollution, see Joel A. Tarr, "Urban Pollution—Many Long Years Ago," *American Heritage*, Oct. 1971, pp. 65–69, 106.

14. See John Duffy, *The Sanitarians: A History of American Public Health* (Urbana: University of Illinois Press, 1990), pp. 71, 86–87; Susan Strasser, *Never Done: A History of American Housework* (New York: Pantheon, 1982), p. 16.

15. Duffy, *Sanitarians*, pp. 87, 146; Judith Walzer Leavitt, "The Wasteland: Garbage and Sanitary Reform in the Nineteenth-Century American City," *Journal of the History of Medicine and Allied Sciences* 35 (Oct. 1980), pp. 431–52;

Charles Loring Brace, *The Dangerous Classes of New York, and Twenty Years' Work among Them* (New York: Wynkoop & Hallenbeck, 1872), p. 152; Strasser, *Never Done*, p. 28.

16. Jane C. Nylander, *Our Own Snug Fireside: Images of the New England Home, 1760–1860* (New Haven: Yale University Press, 1994), pp. 109–11; Ella Shannon Bowles, *Homespun Handicrafts* (New York: Benjamin Blom, 1972), p. 239; Strasser, *Never Done*, p. 58; Alice Morse Earle, *Home Life in Colonial Days* (New York: Macmillan, 1898), pp. 35–38; Julia Cherry Spruill, *Women's Life and Work in the Southern Colonies* (New York: Norton, 1972), p. 110.

17. Beecher, *Treatise on Domestic Economy*, pp. 303, 306; Beecher and Stowe, *American Woman's Home*, pp. 363, 365.

18. Beecher, *Treatise on Domestic Economy*, p. 318; Blakelee, *Industrial Cyclopedia*, p. 603. See also Nylander, *Our Own Snug Fireside*, pp. 135–37.

19. Child, *American Frugal Housewife*, p. 22; Richard L. Bushman and Claudia L. Bushman, "The Early History of Cleanliness in America," *Journal of American History* 74 (Mar. 1988), p. 1234.

20. Bushman and Bushman, "Early History of Cleanliness," p. 1236.

21. Benjamin, *Wrinkles and Recipes*, p. 249; Wright, *Complete Home*, p. 64; William Paul Gerhard, *The Disposal of Household Wastes* (New York: D. Van Nostrand, 1890), p. 21.

22. Child, *American Frugal Housewife*, p. 17; Beecher, *Treatise on Domestic Economy*, p. 368; Beecher and Stowe, *American Woman's Home*, p. 372; see also Benjamin, *Wrinkles and Recipes*, p. 226.

23. Child, *American Frugal Housewife*, pp. 57, 73, 114; Karcher, *First Woman in the Republic*, p. 132.

24. See Strasser, *Never Done*, pp. 19–22; [Catharine E. Beecher], *Miss Beecher's Domestic Receipt Book, Designed as a Supplement to Her* Treatise on Domestic Economy (New York: Harper, 1846), p. 267; Wright, *Complete Home*, p. 83.

25. Wright, *Complete Home*, pp. 82–83; Herrick, *Housekeeping Made Easy*, p. 272.

26. Herrick, *Housekeeping Made Easy*, p. 206; Beecher and Stowe, *American Woman's Home*, p. 184.

27. Beecher and Stowe, *American Woman's Home*, pp. 184–85.

28. Wright, *Complete Home*, pp. 66–68, 161.

29. Philp, *Family Save-All*, p. 1.

30. Herrick, *Housekeeping Made Easy*, pp. 290, 206; Herrick, "Wastes of the Household," p. 16.

31. Benjamin, *Wrinkles and Recipes*, p. 230; Herrick, "Wastes of the Household," p. 16; Herrick, *Housekeeping Made Easy*, p. 203.

32. Herrick, *Housekeeping Made Easy*, pp. 294–95.

33. Tera Hunter, *To 'Joy My Freedom: Southern Black Women's Lives and Labors after the Civil War* (Cambridge: Harvard University Press, 1997), pp. 60–61, 132, 225–27, 259n58.

34. Louisa May Alcott, *Little Women*, 1868 (Harmondsworth, Eng.: Penguin, 1953), p. 34; Herrick, *Housekeeping Made Easy*, p. 205.

35. Gerhard, *Disposal of Household Wastes,* pp. 34–35. On burning food garbage, see also Benjamin, *Wrinkles and Recipes,* p. 236.

36. George G. Foster, *New York by Gas-Light and Other Urban Sketches,* 1850, ed. Stuart M. Blumin (Berkeley: University of California Press, 1990), p. 228.

37. See Amy Boyce Osaki, "A 'Truly Feminine Employment': Sewing and the Early Nineteenth-Century Woman," *Winterthur Portfolio* 23 (Winter 1988), pp. 225–41, esp. pp. 227, 230; quotation on p. 238.

38. Gladys-Marie Fry, *Stitched from the Soul: Slave Quilts from the Ante-Bellum South* (New York: Dutton Studio, 1990), p. 17, 27, 31; Elizabeth Fox-Genovese, *Within the Plantation Household: Black and White Women of the Old South* (Chapel Hill: University of North Carolina Press, 1988), p. 120. See also Gloria Seaman Allen, "Quiltmaking on Chesapeake Plantations," *On the Cutting Edge: Textile Collectors, Collections, and Traditions,* ed. Jeannette Lasansky (Lewisburg, PA: Union County Historical Society Oral Traditions Project, 1994), pp. 60, 61; Eugene D. Genovese, *Roll, Jordan, Roll: The World the Slaves Made* (New York: Vintage, 1974), p. 551.

39. Beecher, *Treatise,* p. 181; Herrick, *Housekeeping Made Easy,* pp. 147–54, 276. See also Strasser, *Never Done,* p. 131; Harvey Green, *The Light of the Home: An Intimate View of the Lives of Women in Victorian America* (New York: Pantheon, 1983), pp. 80–81. On darning, see Eliza Farrar, *The Young Lady's Friend* (New York: Samuel S. & William Wood, 1838), pp. 124–26.

40. Alcott, *Little Women,* p. 55; Beecher, *Treatise on Domestic Economy,* pp. 372–73; Beecher and Stowe, *American Woman's Home,* p. 352.

41. Herrick, *Housekeeping Made Easy,* pp. 151–52.

42. Fry, *Stitched from the Soul,* p. 82; Shane White and Graham White, "Every Grain Is Standing for Itself: African-American Style in the 19th and 20th Centuries," *Australian Cultural History* (Sydney) 13 (1994), pp. 111–28; Terry Thompson and Barbara Brackman, "Fabric and Conversation Prints," *Kansas Quilts and Quilters,* ed. Barbara Brackman et al. (Lawrence: University Press of Kansas, 1993), p. 97.

43. "How to Mend Stockings," *Good Housekeeping,* Sept. 19, 1885, p. 19; Wright, *Complete Home,* pp. 565, 563.

44. Child, *American Frugal Housewife,* p. 19; Farrar, *Young Lady's Friend,* p. 126; Wright, *Complete Home,* p. 563; see also Herrick, *Housekeeping Made Easy,* p. 148.

45. Beecher, *Treatise on Domestic Economy,* p. 176n; Herrick, *Housekeeping Made Easy,* pp. 149–50.

46. Claudia B. Kidwell and Margaret C. Christman, *Suiting Everyone: The Democratization of Clothing in America* (Washington: Smithsonian Institution Press, 1974), p. 79.

47. Nancy Page Fernandez, "Innovations for Home Dressmaking and the Popularization of Stylish Dress," *Journal of American Culture* 17 (Fall 1994), pp. 27–28. See also *Delineator,* April 1886, pp. 320–21.

48. I am grateful to Nancy Page Fernandez for sharing her notes on these dresses with me.

49. Beecher, *Treatise on Domestic Economy,* p. 384; Beecher and Stowe, *American Woman's Home,* pp. 358–59.

50. Beecher, *Treatise on Domestic Economy,* p. 383; Beecher and Stowe, *American Woman's Home,* p. 358; Wright, *Complete Home,* pp. 564–65. On planning for remaking, see Mrs. H. W. Beecher, "Fashion, or Economy?" *All Around the House; or, How to Make Homes Happy* (New York: D. Appleton, 1879), p. 41.

51. Green, *Light of the Home,* p. 80; Alcott, *Little Women,* pp. 122–24.

52. Miriam DeCosta-Willis, ed., *The Memphis Diary of Ida B. Wells* (Boston; Beacon, 1995), p. 117; Edith Wharton, *The Age of Innocence,* 1920 (New York: Scribner's, 1970), p. 194.

53. Catherine Broughton, *Suggestions for Dressmakers* (New York: Morse-Broughton, 1896), pp. 77, 81; Wendy Gamber, *The Female Economy: The Millinery and Dressmaking Trades, 1860–1930* (Urbana: University of Illinois Press, 1997), p. 115.

54. Child, *American Frugal Housewife,* p. 39; Helen N. Packard, "Making Clothes for the Boys," *Good Housekeeping,* Sept. 5, 1885, p. 17.

55. Wright, *Complete Home,* pp. 65–66.

56. Child, *American Frugal Housewife,* p. 39; Candace Wheeler, *How to Make Rugs* (New York: Doubleday, Page, 1902), p. 22; Blakelee, *Industrial Cyclopedia,* pp. 581–82, 592–601; Benjamin, *Wrinkles and Recipes,* p. 230; Varney, *Our Homes,* pp. 360–71; Beecher, *Treatise on Domestic Economy,* pp. 327–37 (quotation on p. 328). See also, among others, Blakelee, *Industrial Cyclopedia,* pp. 575ff.; Varney, *Our Homes,* pp. 371–74, 398–403.

57. Child, *American Frugal Housewife,* p. 12.

58. Wright, *Complete Home,* p. 564; Linnie C. Morse, "The Philosophy of Dish-Towels," *Good Housekeeping,* Oct. 17, 1885, p. 14; Herrick, *Housekeeping Made Easy,* p. 154.

59. New-York Clothing Society for the Relief of the Industrious Poor, *Ninth Annual Report and Constitution* (New York: John S. Taylor, 1838), pp. 10, 13–14; Packard, "Making Clothes for the Boys," p. 17; "Old-Clothes Sensations," *Atlantic,* July 1915, p. 140. On clothing philanthropy in Britain, see Madeleine Ginsburg, "Rags to Riches: The Second-Hand Clothes Trade, 1700–1978," *Costume: The Journal of the Costume Society* 14 (1980), pp. 128–29.

60. Genovese, *Roll, Jordan, Roll,* pp. 556–57. On runaways' clothing, see Patricia Campbell Warner and Debra Parker, "Slave Clothing and Textiles in North Carolina, 1775–1835," *African American Dress and Adornment: A Cultural Perspective,* ed. Barbara M. Starke, Lillian O. Holloman, and Barbara K. Nordquist (Dubuque, IA: Kendall/Hunt, 1990), p. 89. On castoffs and Northern servants, see Faye E. Dudden, *Serving Women: Household Service in Nineteenth-Century America* (Middletown, CT: Wesleyan University Press, 1983), pp. 120–21.

61. Virginia Writers' Project, Work Projects Administration, *The Negro in Virginia* (New York: Hastings House, 1940), p. 72. For a discussion of the veracity of this book and its use of language, see Charles L. Perdue, Jr. et al., eds., *Weevils in the Wheat: Interviews with Virginia Ex-Slaves* (Charlottesville: University Press of Virginia, 1976), pp. xi, xlv. For more on slaves' clothing, see Perdue, *Weevils*, 71, 79, 80–82, 103, 107, 140–41, 229, 266, 294–95, 309, 315–16, 322, 333.

62. Louis Hughes, *Thirty Years a Slave: From Bondage to Freedom* (New York: Negro Universities Press, 1969), p. 42. Aunt Sally quoted in Barbara M. Starke, "Nineteenth-Century African-American Dress," *Dress in American Culture,* ed. Patricia A. Cunningham and Susan Voso Lab (Bowling Green, OH: Bowling Green State University Popular Press, 1993), pp. 73–74; also quoted in Barbara M. Starke, "Slave Narratives: Accounts of What They Wore," *African American Dress and Adornment,* p. 75. For other examples of servants receiving masters' clothes for special occasions, see Lydia Jean Wares, "Dress of the African-American Woman in Slavery and in Freedom: 1500–1935," Ph.D. dissertation, Purdue University, 1981, pp. 150, 169.

63. Ginsburg, "Rags to Riches," pp. 121–22; Donald Woodward, " 'Swords into Ploughshares': Recycling in Pre-industrial England," *Economic History Review,* 2nd ser. 38 (May 1985), pp. 178–79; Beverly Lemire, "Consumerism in Pre-industrial and Early Industrial England: The Trade in Secondhand Clothes," *Journal of British Studies* 27 (Jan. 1988), pp. 1–24.

64. Foster, *New York by Gas-Light,* p. 127; Frederick Law Olmsted, *The Cotton Kingdom: A Traveller's Observations on Cotton and Slavery in the American Slave States,* ed. Arthur M. Schlesinger (New York: Knopf, 1953), pp. 37, 451. See also Daniel J. Boorstin, *The Americans: The Democratic Experience* (New York: Vintage, 1973), pp. 97–98.

65. Mary Boykin Chesnut, *A Diary from Dixie,* ed. Ben Ames Williams (Boston: Houghton Mifflin, 1961), pp. 395, 434.

66. Alan G. Keyser, "All In and All Done? The Pennsylvania Vendue," Lasansky, *On the Cutting Edge,* pp. 43–47; Allen, "Quiltmaking on Chesapeake Plantations," Lasansky, *On the Cutting Edge,* p. 65; "The Public Sale 60 Years Ago," *Pennsylvania Folklife,* Summer 1969, p. 50; C. M. Bomberger, "Vendues," *Pennsylvania Dutchman,* July 1950, p. 7; "Vendue–Dutch Style," *Pennsylvania Dutchman,* Jan. 15, 1952, p. 7. On broadsides advertising estate sales, see Florence M. Jumonville, "The Wastebasket and the Grave: Funeralia in the South," *Southern Quarterly* 31 (Winter 1993), p. 112.

67. Quoted in Strasser, *Never Done,* p. 131.

68. Green, *Light of the Home,* p. 100.

69. Quoted in Bowles, *Homespun Handicrafts,* pp. 200–01. On quilts as income and fund-raisers, see Barbara Brackman, *Clues in the Calico: A Guide to Identifying and Dating Antique Quilts* (McLean, VA: EPM, 1989), pp. 18–19; for Harriet Powers, see Fry, *Stitched from the Soul,* p. 86.

70. Jeannette Lasansky, "Myth and Reality in Craft Tradition: Were Blacksmiths Really Muscle-Bound? Were Basketmakers Gypsies? Were Thirteen Quilts in

the Dowry Chests?" *On the Cutting Edge,* pp. 109–19; Brackman, *Clues in the Calico,* pp. 15–16. On colonial quilts, see Roderick Kiracofe, *The American Quilt: A History of Cloth and Comfort, 1750–1950* (New York: Clarkson Potter, 1993), pp. 58–59; Brackman, *Clues in the Calico,* p. 13.

71. Nancy Grey Osterud, *Bonds of Community: The Lives of Farm Women in Nineteenth-Century New York* (Ithaca: Cornell University Press, 1991, pp. 191–92; see also pp. 231–32; "Prelude: The Papers of Mary Ellison," Brackman, *Kansas Quilts,* p. 5. See also Nylander, *Our Own Snug Fireside,* pp. 228ff., and Lasansky, "Myth and Reality," p. 113. For a discussion of quilting parties in a theoretical framework, see Karen V. Hansen, *A Very Social Time: Crafting Community in Antebellum New England* (Berkeley: University of California Press, 1994, pp. 106ff. and passim.

72. Lasansky, "Myth and Reality," p. 115. On slave quilts, see John Michael Vlach, *The Afro-American Tradition in Decorative Arts* (Cleveland: Cleveland Museum of Art, 1978), pp. 44–75; William Ferris, ed., *Afro-American Folk Art and Crafts* (Boston: G. K. Hall, 1983), pp. 67–110.

73. Allen, "Quiltmaking on Chesapeake Plantations," p. 63.

74. Lasansky, "Myth and Reality," p. 115; Fry, *Stitched from the Soul,* pp. 46–47; Gladys-Marie Fry, "Slave Quilting on Ante-Bellum Plantations," *Something to Keep You Warm,* ed. Roland Freeman (Jackson: Mississippi Department of Archives and History, 1981), p. 4.

75. "Annette," "The Patchwork Quilt," *The Lowell Offering: Writings by New England Mill Women (1840–1845),* ed. Benita Eisler (New York: Harper Colophon, 1977), p. 153.

76. Miss C. M. Sedgwick, "The Patch-Work Quilt," *Columbian Magazine,* Mar. 1846, pp. 123–26 (quotation on p. 125).

77. "Mary's Patchwork," *H. Trusta's Talk and Tales for Children,* reprinted in *Home Memories; or, Social Half-Hours with the Household,* ed. Mrs. Mary G. Clarke (Philadelphia: J. C. McCurdy, 1881), pp. 300–03; Lucy Larcom, *A New England Girlhood: Outlined from Memory,* new ed. (Boston: Houghton Mifflin, 1924), pp. 122–24; S. Annie Frost [Shields], *The Ladies' Guide to Needle Work, Embroidery, Etc., Being a Complete Guide to All Kinds of Ladies' Fancy Work* (New York: Henry T. Williams, 1877), p. 128. On the "stint" as a teaching method for needlework, see Elaine Hedges, *Hearts and Hands: The Influence of Women & Quilts on American Society* (San Francisco: Quilt Digest Press, 1987), p. 18. On children's quilt projects, see Virginia Gunn, "Template Quilt Construction and Its Offshoots," *Pieced By Mother: Symposium Papers,* ed. Jeannette Lasansky et al. (Lewisburg, PA: Union County Historical Society Oral Traditions Project, 1988), p. 70; *The Lady's Book,* Jan. 1835, p. 41, quoted in Patsy Orlofsky and Myron Orlofsky, *Quilts in America* (New York: Abbeville, 1992), pp. 76–77. On rag dolls, see Miriam Formanek-Brunell, *Made to Play House: Dolls and the Commercialization of American Girlhood, 1830–1930* (New Haven: Yale University Press, 1993), pp. 11, 14, 24.

78. Florence Hartley, *The Ladies' Hand Book of Fancy and Ornamental Work*

(Philadelphia: G. G. Evans, 1859), p. 189; Mrs. [Matilda Marian Chesney] Pullan, *The Lady's Manual of Fancy Work* ... (New York: Dick & Fitzgerald, 1859), p. 95. Most of Hartley's section on patchwork is reprinted from Ellen Lindsay, "Patchwork," *Godey's Lady's Book*, Feb. 1857, pp. 166–67. On gaslight, see Strasser, *Never Done*, pp. 68ff.

79. Pullan, *Lady's Manual of Fancy Work*, p. 95; "Patch-Work," *Peterson's Magazine*, June 1877, p. 448. On fancywork, see Nancy Dunlap Bercaw, "Solid Objects/Mutable Meanings: Fancywork and the Construction of Bourgeois Culture, 1840–1880," *Winterthur Portfolio* 26 (Winter, 1991), pp. 231–47.

80. Jeannette Lasansky, *Pieced by Mother: Over 100 Years of Quiltmaking Traditions* (Lewisburg, PA: Union County Historical Society Oral Traditions Project, 1987), p. 85; Dulcie Weir, "The Career of a Crazy Quilt, *Godey's Lady's Book and Magazine*, July 1884, pp. 77–82, reproduced in Jeannette Lasansky, *In the Heart of Pennsylvania: 19th & 20th Century Quiltmaking Traditions* (Lewisburg, PA: Union County Historical Society Oral Traditions Project, 1985), pp. 80–88.

81. Wright, *Complete Home*, p. 564; Blakelee, *Industrial Cyclopedia*, pp. 572–74.

82. For such sentimentality, see Bowles, *Homespun Handicrafts*, pp. 184, 189.

83. "Prelude: The Papers of Mary Ellison," Brackman, *Kansas Quilts*, pp. 5, 7; Henry T. Williams and Mrs. C. S. Jones, *Beautiful Homes; or, Hints in House Furnishing*, Williams' Household Series vol 4 (New York: Henry T. Williams, 1878), p. 302; Wares, "Dress of the African-American Woman," p. 176.

84. Blakelee, *Industrial Cyclopedia*, p. 537; Ella Shannon Bowles, *Handmade Rugs* (Garden City, NY: Garden City Publishing, 1937), p. 70; Bowles, *Homespun Handicrafts*, p. 200; Janet Meany and Paula Pfaff, *Rag Rug Handbook* (St. Paul: Dos Tejedoras Fiber Arts Publications, 1988), p. 95.

85. Blakelee, *Industrial Cyclopedia*, p. 537; Bonnie J. Krause and Cynthia R. Houston, "Bits and Pieces: The Southern Illinois Tradition in Rag Rugs," *Mid-America Folklore* 21 (Spring 1993), p. 20; for a later period, see p. 23.

86. Laurel Thatcher Ulrich, *A Midwife's Tale: The Life of Martha Ballard, Based on Her Diary, 1785–1812* (New York: Vintage, 1990), pp. 131, 161, 387–88n; Rodris Roth, "Floor Coverings in 18th-Century America," *Contributions from the Museum of History and Technology*, Paper 59 (Washington: Smithsonian, 1967), p. 46; Williams and Jones, *Beautiful Homes*, p. 302.

87. See Wheeler, *How to Make Rugs*, passim; see also Geraldine Johnson, *Weaving Rag Rugs: A Women's Craft in Western Maryland* (Knoxville: University of Tennessee, 1985), p. 139.

88. Grier, *Culture and Comfort*, p. 284; Blakelee, *Industrial Cyclopedia*, p. 535; Varney, *Our Homes*, pp. 260–61.

89. Child, *American Frugal Housewife*, p. 13; Blakelee, *Industrial Cyclopedia*, p. 567; Williams and Jones, *Beautiful Homes*, pp. 302–04.

90. Bowles, *Homespun Handicrafts*, p. 200; Virginia Churchill Bath, *Needlework in America: History, Designs, and Techniques* (New York: Viking, 1979), p. 285; Wheeler, *How to Make Rugs*, passim; Johnson, *Weaving Rag Rugs*, p. 139.

91. Bowles, *Handmade Rugs,* p. 70; Bowles, *Homespun Handicrafts,* pp. 198, 200; Blakelee, *Industrial Cyclopedia,* pp. 567–68, 638; Margaret Vincent, *The Ladies' Work Table: Domestic Needlework in Nineteenth-Century America* (Allentown, PA: Allentown Art Museum, 1988), pp. 108–10; Bath, *Needlework in America,* pp. 293–94.

92. Blakelee, *Industrial Cyclopedia,* p. 566; for coffee-sack rugs, see also Varney, *Our Homes,* p. 353.

93. Joel Kopp and Kate Kopp, *American Hooked and Sewn Rugs: Folk Art Underfoot* (New York: E. P. Dutton, 1975), pp. 87–90.

94. Grier, *Culture and Comfort,* pp. 263–64.

95. Blakelee, *Industrial Cyclopedia,* pp. 520–22; Henry W. Cleaveland, William Backus, and Samuel D. Backus, *The Requirements of American Village Homes* (New York: D. Appleton, 1856), p. 133; A. J. Downing, *The Architecture of Country Houses* (New York: D. Appleton, 1850), p. 414; Beecher and Stowe, *American Woman's Home,* p. 89.

96. "Elegant Home-Made Furniture: For Home Comfort and Enjoyment," *Good Housekeeping,* Oct. 31, 1885, p. 17; Wright, *Complete Home,* pp. 157–58.

97. Beecher and Stowe, *American Woman's Home,* p. 89; Blakelee, *Industrial Cyclopedia,* pp. 516ff., 519, 9; see also p. 541.

98. Blakelee, *Industrial Cyclopedia,* p. 550; Grier, *Culture and Comfort,* p. 271.

99. Williams and Jones, *Beautiful Homes,* p. 99.

100. Grier, *Culture and Comfort,* p. 273.

101. Jane Busch, "Second Time Around: A Look at Bottle Reuse," *Historical Archaeology* 21 (1987), pp. 67–80; Jane Busch, "The Throwaway Ethic in America," Ph.D. dissertation, University of Pennsylvania, 1983, p. 188; Child, *American Frugal Housewife,* pp. 10, 14; Kitchen-Garden Association, *Household Economy: A Manual for Use in Schools* (New York: Ivison, Blakeman, Taylor, 1882), p. 132; *Gould's Directory for Saint Louis,* 1891, p. 1561; 1906, p. 1993; "Old Bottles and Corks," *National Bottler's Gazette,* Oct. 1882, p. 19; Morse, "Philosophy of Dish-Towels," p. 14.

102. Beecher, *Treatise on Domestic Economy,* p. 360; Varney, *Our Homes,* p. 352; Kitchen-Garden Association, *Household Economy,* p. 98.

CHAPTER TWO: ANY RAGS, ANY BONES

1. Morillo Noyes manuscripts, box 5, no. 778/1859–1877/N956, Baker Library, Harvard Business School (hereafter "Noyes mss.").

2. Judith A. McGaw, *Most Wonderful Machine: Mechanization and Social Change in Berkshire Paper Making, 1801–1885* (Princeton: Princeton University Press, 1987), p. 29.

3. C. C. Reynolds to Morillo Noyes, June 27, 1883, box 5; memorandum book 4/25/59–6/28/59, pp. 33, 76; memorandum book 4/11/77–6/25/77, pp. 1–2, 61, all in Noyes mss.

4. Memorandum book 4/11/77–6/25/77, pp. 77, 83–84, 90, Noyes mss.

5. Alan Taylor, "Unnatural Inequalities: Social and Environmental Histories," *Environmental History* 1 (Oct. 1996), pp. 13–14; Richard L. Bushman and Claudia L. Bushman, "The Early History of Cleanliness in America," *Journal of American History* 74 (Mar. 1988), p. 1234. See also Beverly Lemire, "Consumerism in Preindustrial and Early Industrial England: The Trade in Second-hand Clothes," *Journal of British Studies* 27 (Jan. 1988), p. 9.

6. Frederick Law Olmsted, *A Journey in the Back Country,* 1860 (New York: Burt Franklin, 1970), pp. 33–34.

7. David Jaffee, "Peddlers of Progress and the Transformation of the Rural North, 1760–1860," *Journal of American History* 78 (Sept. 1991), p. 535; Jackson Lears, "Beyond Veblen: Rethinking Consumer Culture in America," *Consuming Visions: Accumulation and Display of Goods in America, 1880–1920,* ed. Simon J. Bronner (New York: W. W. Norton, 1989), p. 78.

8. Robert Friedel, "Tinplate and the Nineteenth Century American Experience," ts., Nov. 1994, p. 5; courtesy of the author.

9. Fred Mitchell Jones, *Middlemen in the Domestic Trade of the United States, 1800–1860* (New York: Johnson Reprint, 1968), p. 61; William G. Lathrop, *The Brass Industry in the United States* (Mount Carmel, CT: William G. Lathrop, 1926), p. 29; S. M. Hunt, "Old Days in the Rag Trade," *Paper Trade Journal,* May 23, 1912, p. 54; Richardson Wright, *Hawkers and Walkers in Early America* (New York: Frederick Ungar, 1927), p. 74.

10. R. Malcolm Keir, "The Unappreciated Tin Peddler," *Annals of the American Academy of Political and Social Science* 46 (1913), p. 185; R. Malcolm Keir, "The Tin Peddler," *Journal of Political Economy* 21 (1913), p. 256; box 5, memoranda, Noyes mss.

11. Margaret Coffin, *American Country Tinware, 1700–1900* (Camden: Thomas Nelson, 1968), pp. 97, 173–74, 176, 178.

12. Quoted in Jeannette Lasansky, *To Cut, Piece, & Solder: The Work of the Rural Pennsylvania Tinsmith, 1778–1908* (Lewisburg, PA: Union County Historical Society Oral Traditions Project, 1982), pp. 14–15.

13. See Hasia R. Diner, *A Time for Gathering: The Second Migration, 1820–1880* (Baltimore: Johns Hopkins University Press, 1992), pp. 66ff.; Lee M. Friedman, "The Problems of Nineteenth Century American Jewish Peddlers," *Publications of the American Jewish Historical Society,* 44 (Sept. 1954), pp. 1–7; Rudolf Glanz, "Notes on Early Jewish Peddling in America," *Studies in Judaica Americana* (New York: Ktav, 1970), pp. 112ff. For a discussion of the image of the Jewish peddler, see Lears, "Beyond Veblen," pp. 79–80. On Jewish rag dealers, see S. M. Hunt, "Old Days in the Rag Trade," *Paper Trade Journal,* June 27, 1912, p. 46.

14. Lasansky, *To Cut,* pp. 14–15. See also Jackson Lears, *Fables of Abundance: A Cultural History of Advertising in America* (New York: Basic, 1994), pp. 64ff.; Lewis Hyde, *Trickster Makes This World: Mischief, Myth, and Art* (New York: Farrar, Straus & Giroux, 1998).

15. Joseph T. Rainer, "The 'Sharper' Image': Yankee Peddlers, Southern Con-

sumers, and the Market Revolution," *Business and Economic History* 26 (Fall 1997), pp. 37–40.

16. Lasansky, *To Cut*, p. 13; Lears, *Fables of Abundance*, p. 72.

17. Laura Ingalls Wilder, *Farmer Boy*, 1933 (New York: Harper, 1953), pp. 138–39. For a similar description of the rag and tinware barter process, see Helen Marshall North, "The Tin-Peddler's Cart," *New England Magazine*, Aug. 1899, pp. 712–13.

18. Laurel Thatcher Ulrich, *A Midwife's Tale: The Life of Martha Ballard, Based on Her Diary, 1785–1812* (New York: Vintage, 1990), pp. 84, 197; Viviana A. Zelizer, *The Social Meaning of Money: Pin Money, Paychecks, Poor Relief, and Other Currencies* (New York: Basic, 1994), pp. 41–42, 62–67.

19. Louisa May Alcott, *Little Women*, 1868 (Harmondsworth, Eng.: Penguin, 1953), p. 98.

20. Harvey A. Wooster, "A Forgotten Factor in American Industrial History," *American Economic Review* 16 (Mar. 1926), pp. 17–18; Jaffee, "Peddlers of Progress," pp. 511–35; William J. Gilmore, "Peddlers and the Dissemination of Printed Material in Northern New England, 1780–1840," *Itinerancy in New England and New York*, ed. Peter Benes, Dublin Seminar for New England Folklife Annual Proceedings, 1984 (Boston: Boston University, 1986), pp. 81–82; Lears, *Fables of Abundance*, pp. 79–80.

21. Maxwell Whiteman, "Notions, Dry Goods, and Clothing: An Introduction to the Study of the Cincinnati Peddler," *Jewish Quarterly Review* 53 (1963), pp. 310–17; Rainer, " 'Sharper Image,' " pp. 32–33; Diner, *Time for Gathering*, pp. 69–70; Wilder, *Farmer Boy*, p. 136; Memorandum book May 31, 1859, p. 33, Noyes mss. See also Priscilla Carrington Kline, "New Light on the Yankee Peddler," *New England Quarterly* 12 (Mar. 1939), p. 88; Coffin, *American Country Tinware*, p. 173.

22. McGaw, *Most Wonderful Machine*, p. 40.

23. McGaw, *Most Wonderful Machine*, p. 67; David C. Smith, *History of Papermaking in the United States (1691–1969)* (New York: Lockwood, 1970), p. 69.

24. Lyman Horace Weeks, *A History of Paper-Manufacturing in the United States, 1690–1916* (New York: Lockwood Trade Journal, 1916), pp. 67, 218.

25. Weeks, *History of Paper-Manufacturing*, pp. 66–67, 115.

26. Weeks, *History of Paper-Manufacturing*, p. 64; Joel Munsell, *Chronology of the Origin and Progress of Paper and Paper-Making*, 5th ed. (Albany: J. Munsell, 1876), pp. 57–58.

27. Weeks, *History of Paper-Manufacturing*, pp. 61, 65–66.

28. Weeks, *History of Paper-Manufacturing*, pp. 65, 28, 61–62.

29. Weeks, *History of Paper-Manufacturing*, pp. 62–64; see also Massachusetts General Court, "In the House of Representatives, February 16, 1776" (Salem: E. Russell, 1776), broadside; McGaw, *Most Wonderful Machine*, p. 28.

30. Weeks, *History of Paper-Manufacturing*, pp. 67, 114; McGaw, *Most Wonderful Machine*, pp. 27–28.

31. McGaw, *Most Wonderful Machine*, pp. 191–92; Smith, *History of Papermaking*,

p. 107; Norman B. Wilkinson, *Papermaking in America* (Greenville, DE: Hagley Museum, 1975), p. 44; "Parliamentary Reports on the Rag Trade of Foreign Countries," *Practical Magazine,* n.s. 6, vol. 5, 1875, p. 221.

32. McGaw, *Most Wonderful Machine,* pp. 66–67; Munsell, *Chronology,* p. 168.

33. McGaw, *Most Wonderful Machine,* pp. 40, 192; G. Austin, "Rags," *Atlantic Monthly,* Mar. 1867, pp. 365–66. On mummies, see also Smith, *History of Papermaking,* p. 145n19, and Munsell, *Chronology,* pp. 149, 198, for references to at least four accounts of the practice.

34. McGaw, *Most Wonderful Machine,* p. 50; Hermann Burrows, *A History of the Rag Trade* (London: Maclaren, 1956), p. 24.

35. Hunt, "Old Days," May 23, 1912, p. 54; McGaw, *Most Wonderful Machine,* p. 193; see also Austin, "Rags," p. 365.

36. McGaw, *Most Wonderful Machine,* p. 40; Austin, "Rags," p. 365; Herman Melville, "The Tartarus of Maids," *"The Apple-Tree Table" and Other Sketches* (Princeton: Princeton University Press, 1922), pp. 197–98. "The Tartarus of Maids" was originally published in *Putnam's* during the 1850s.

37. Austin, "Rags," p. 365; McGaw, *Most Wonderful Machine,* pp. 113, 182.

38. Melville, "Tartarus of Maids," p. 198; Austin, "Rags," p. 365; S. M. Hunt, "Old Days in the Rag Trade," *Paper Trade Journal,* July 11, 1912, p. 60; see also McGaw, *Most Wonderful Machine,* p. 344; Smith, *History of Papermaking,* p. 143n6.

39. Wilkinson, *Papermaking in America,* p. 12; McGaw, *Most Wonderful Machine,* pp. 41, 195.

40. Theodore Steinberg, *Nature Incorporated: Industrialization and the Waters of New England* (Cambridge: Cambridge University Press, 1991), pp. 208–09; Wilkinson, *Papermaking in America,* p. 13; McGaw, *Most Wonderful Machine,* pp. 41, 109, 208; Richard G. Wilkinson, "The English Industrial Revolution," *The Ends of the Earth: Perspectives on Modern Environmental History,* ed. Donald Worster (Cambridge: Cambridge University Press, 1988), pp. 95–96; Austin, "Rags," p. 366.

41. McGaw, *Most Wonderful Machine,* p. 196; Weeks, *History of Paper-Manufacturing,* p. 216; Smith, *History of Papermaking,* pp. 129–30.

42. Hunt, "Old Days," May 23, 1912, p. 54; McGaw, *Most Wonderful Machine,* pp. 196–199.

43. Anna Barrows, "Waste Paper: What to Do with It That It May Not Be Wasted," *Good Housekeeping,* Sept. 19, 1885, p. 12.

44. Lydia Maria Child, *The American Frugal Housewife,* 16th ed., enlarged and corrected (Boston: Carter, Hendee, 1835), p. 16.

45. Barter list, 1854, box 5; Memorandum book June 6, 1859, pp. 54–55, Noyes mss.; Munsell, *Chronology,* p. 155. See also James Strachan, *The Recovery and Re-manufacture of Waste-Paper* (Aberdeen, Scot.: Albany, 1918), pp. 4–5.

46. S. M. Hunt, "Old Days in the Rag Trade," *Paper Trade Journal,* May 9, 1912, p. 46; Smith, *History of Papermaking,* p. 126; Munsell, *Chronology,* p. 191; McGaw, *Most Wonderful Machine,* p. 193.

47. Hunt, "Old Days," June 27, 1912, p. 46; Holyoke Machine Company, *Rag Cutters and Rag Dusters* (Holyoke, MA: Holyoke Machine, 1894), pp. 3–10.

48. Austin, "Rags," p. 366; Madeleine Ginsburg, "Rags to Riches: The Second-Hand Clothes Trade, 1700–1978," *Costume: The Journal of the Costume Society* 14 (1980), p. 128.

49. U.S. Tariff Commission, *Rag Rugs* (Washington: GPO, 1928), pp. 4–5; William Howard Shaw, *Value of Commodity Output since 1869* (New York: National Bureau of Economic Research, 1947), p. 119.

50. Samuel Jubb, *The History of the Shoddy-Trade: Its Rise, Progress, and Present Position* (London: Houlston and Wright, 1860), pp. 17, 19, 25–26; Burrows, *History of the Rag Trade*, p. 30; J. H. Clapham, *An Economic History of Modern Britain: Free Trade and Steel, 1850–1886* (Cambridge: Cambridge University Press, 1932), p. 38.

51. Jubb, *History of the Shoddy-Trade*, pp. 23–24.

52. Hunt, "Old Days," May 9, 1912, p. 46; Gary L. Bunker and John Appel, " 'Shoddy,' Anti-Semitism, and the Civil War," *American Jewish History* 82 (1994), pp. 43–71.

53. Helen N. Packard, "Making Clothes for the Boys," *Good Housekeeping*, Sept. 5, 1885, p. 17; Philip Scranton, *Figured Tapestry: Production, Markets, and Power in Philadelphia Textiles, 1885–1941* (Cambridge: Cambridge University Press, 1989), p. 140.

54. Scranton, *Figured Tapestry*, p. 308; U.S. Federal Trade Commission, *Report on the Woolen Rag Trade, June 30, 1919* (Washington: GPO, 1920), pp. 3–4, 17; U.S. Department of Commerce, Bureau of the Census, *Census of Manufactures 1937: Waste and Related Products* (Washington: GPO, 1939), pp. 30–31.

55. Barbara Beving Long, "Phase III Historical Documentation Study: The Moritz & Bertha Bergstein House, Shoddy Mill & Waste Materials Yard, St. Croix River Crossing Project," Minnesota Department of Transportation SHPO 94-1390.

56. Carolyn Merchant, *The Death of Nature: Women, Ecology, and the Scientific Revolution* (San Francisco: Harper & Row, 1980), pp. 29–41; Billy G. Smith, *The 'Lower Sort': Philadelphia's Laboring People, 1750–1800* (Ithaca: Cornell University Press, 1990), p. 162.

57. Donald Woodward, " 'Swords into Ploughshares': Recycling in Pre-industrial England," *Economic History Review,* 2nd ser., 38 (May 1985), p. 183. On lead in makeup, see Kathy Peiss, *Hope in a Jar: The Making of America's Beauty Culture* (New York: Metropolitan, 1998), pp. 10, 21.

58. Woodward, " 'Swords into Ploughshares,' " p. 184; Charles F. Montgomery, *A History of American Pewter* (New York: E. P. Dutton, 1978), pp. 10, 21.

59. See Joseph J. Schroeder, Jr., ed., *Sears, Roebuck & Co. 1908 Catalogue No. 117* (Chicago: Follett, 1969), pp. 340, 343; "Metals," *Waste Trade Journal*, Nov. 9, 1912, pp. 9–10.

60. Lathrop, *Brass Industry*, pp. 37ff., 77ff.

61. Woodward, " 'Swords into Ploughshares,' " pp. 185–86; *The Blacksmith in Eighteenth-Century Williamsburg*, Williamsburg Craft Series (Williamsburg: Colonial Williamsburg, 1971), pp. 14–16; Peter Temin, *Iron and Steel in Nineteenth-Century America: An Economic Inquiry* (Cambridge: MIT Press, 1964), pp. 13–14.

62. Temin, *Iron and Steel*, pp. 13ff., 27, 49, 145–47. On iron and steel rails, see also Harold C. Livesay, *Andrew Carnegie and the Rise of Big Business* (Boston: Little, Brown, 1975), pp. 78–81.

63. Charles Loring Brace, *The Dangerous Classes of New York, and Twenty Years' Work among Them* (New York: Wynkoop & Hallenbeck, 1872), pp. 152–53; "Scrap Iron Market," *Waste Trade Journal,* Nov. 9, 1912, pp. 6–7; "Metals," pp. 9–10.

64. Charles Dawson Shanley, "The Small Arabs of New York," *Atlantic Monthly,* Mar. 1869, p. 284; Harry H. Grigg and George E. Haynes, *Junk Dealing and Juvenile Delinquency*, text by Albert E. Webster (Chicago: Juvenile Protective Association, [1919?], pp. 8–10, 40–41; Betty Smith, *A Tree Grows in Brooklyn* (New York: Harper, 1947), pp. 4–5.

65. Thomas Webster, *An Encyclopaedia of Domestic Economy* (London: Longman, Brown, Green, and Longmans, 1847), p. 196.

66. U.S. Environmental Protection Agency, "History of the Reclaimed Rubber Industry," *Waste Rubber and Its Reuse: 1968*, part 2 of *Rubber Reuse and Solid Waste Management* (Washington: EPA, 1971), pp. 48–49; Howard Wolf, *The Story of Scrap Rubber* (Akron: A. Schulman, 1943), pp. 19–33.

67. Thomas Lambert, *Bone Products and Manures,* 3rd ed. (London: Scott, Greenwood, 1925) pp. 35–37.

68. Lambert, *Bone Products*, p. 3.

69. Richard A. Wines, *Fertilizer in America: From Waste Recycling to Resource Exploitation* (Philadelphia: Temple University Press, 1985), pp. 6–7, 23.

70. Wines, *Fertilizer in America*, pp. 13–14, 24.

71. John George Glover and William Bouck Cornell, eds., *The Development of American Industries: Their Economic Significance* (New York: Prentice-Hall, 1936), p. 278; Wines, *Fertilizer in America*, p. 100.

72. Lambert, *Bone Products*, p. 2; LeRoy Barnett, "The Buffalo Bone Commerce on the Northern Plains," *North Dakota History* 39 (Winter 1972), pp. 23–42.

73. William Chaffee to Henry Greene, Nov. 22, 1883, box 5, Letters, Noyes mss.

74. Philip Flower, quoted in Friedel, "Tinplate," p. 27.

75. Boris Emmet and John E. Jeuck, *Catalogues and Counters: A History of Sears, Roebuck and Company* (Chicago: University of Chicago Press, 1950), pp. 19–20; Ralph M. Hower, *History of Macy's of New York, 1858–1919: Chapters in the Evolution of the Department Store* (Cambridge: Harvard University Press, 1943), pp. 105–06.

76. Artemas Ward, *The Grocers' Hand-Book and Directory for 1883* (Philadelphia: Philadelphia Grocer, 1882), p. 22; Susan Strasser, *Satisfaction Guaran-*

teed: *The Making of the American Mass Market* (New York: Pantheon, 1989), pp. 69–73.

77. Robert W. Twyman, *History of Marshall Field and Co., 1852–1906* (Philadelphia: University of Pennsylvania Press, 1954), p. 98. On wholesalers, see Strasser, *Satisfaction Guaranteed,* pp. 58–88; Glenn Porter and Harold C. Livesay, *Merchants and Manufacturers: Studies in the Changing Structure of Nineteenth-Century Marketing* (Baltimore: Johns Hopkins Press, 1971), pp. 214–31; Alfred D. Chandler, Jr., *The Visible Hand: The Managerial Revolution in American Business* (Cambridge: Harvard University Press, 1977), pp. 215–24, 236–37.

78. See Hunt, "Old Days," July 11, 1912, p. 60.

CHAPTER THREE: TRASH AND REUSE TRANSFORMED

1. Editorial Board of the University Society, *Save and Have, a Book of 'Saving Graces' for American Homes* (New York: University Society, 1919), pp. 105, 108, 121.

2. *Harper's Household Handbook: A Guide to Easy Ways of Doing Woman's Work* (New York: Harper, 1913), p. 108; Emily Holt, *The Complete Housekeeper* (Garden City: Doubleday, Page, 1917), pp. 40–41, 380, 382; Mrs. Julia McNair Wright, *The Complete Home: An Encyclopaedia of Domestic Life and Affairs* (Philadelphia: J. C. McCurdy, 1879), pp. 56–57.

3. S. Maria Elliott, *Household Hygiene* (Chicago: American School of Home Economics, 1907), pp. 115–16 (part of a "complete home study course," the Library of Home Economics, with volumes by Ellen Richards, Mary Hinman Abel, Isabel Bevier, and Anna Barrows, among other distinguished home economists); Helen Kinne and Anna M. Cooley, *Shelter and Clothing: A Textbook of the Household Arts* (New York: Macmillan, 1913), pp. 327–31. On home economics, see Susan Strasser, *Never Done: A History of American Housework* (New York: Pantheon, 1982), pp. 202–13; Carolyn Goldstein, "Mediating Consumption: Home Economics and American Consumers, 1900–1940," Ph.D. dissertation, University of Delaware, 1994.

4. Rocco Corresca, "The Biography of a Bootblack," *Independent,* Dec. 4, 1902, p. 2865.

5. S. M. Hunt, "Old Days in the Rag Trade," *Paper Trade Journal,* July 11, 1912, p. 60.

6. Robert A. Slayton, *Back of the Yards: The Making of a Local Democracy* (Chicago: University of Chicago Press, 1986), p. 28; David Nasaw, *Children of the City: At Work and at Play* (Garden City, NY: Anchor, 1985), p. 88; Harry H. Grigg and George E. Haynes, *Junk Dealing and Juvenile Delinquency,* text by Albert E. Webster (Chicago: Juvenile Protective Association, [1919?]; Benjamin R. Andrews, *Economics of the Household: Its Administration and Finance* (New York: Macmillan, 1923), pp. 421–22.

7. Henry Mayhew, *London Labour and the London Poor: A Cyclopaedia of the Condition and Earnings of Those That Will Work, Those That Cannot Work, and Those That Will Not Work*, 4 vols., 1861–62 (New York: Dover, 1968); George G. Foster, *New York by Gas-Light and Other Urban Sketches*, 1850, ed. Stuart M. Blumin (Berkeley: University of California Press, 1990), p. 189; Charles Loring Brace, *The Dangerous Classes of New York, and Twenty Years' Work among Them* (New York: Wynkoop & Hallenbeck, 1872), pp. 152–53; Frank Norris, *McTeague: A Story of San Francisco*, 1899 (New York: Penguin, 1982), p. 81.

8. Lyman Horace Weeks, *A History of Paper-Manufacturing in the United States, 1690–1916* (New York: Lockwood Trade Journal, 1916), p. 68n; Charles Dawson Shanley, "The Small Arabs of New York," *Atlantic Monthly*, Mar. 1869, p. 284.

9. Christine Stansell, *City of Women: Sex and Class in New York, 1789–1860* (Urbana: University of Illinois Press, 1987), pp. 50–51, 144n, 205; Jeanne Boydston, *Home and Work: Housework, Wages, and the Ideology of Labor in the Early Republic* (New York: Oxford University Press, 1990), p. 91.

10. James D. McCabe, *New York by Sunlight and Gaslight* (Philadelphia; Douglass Brothers, 1882), pp. 584–85; Jacob August Riis, *The Children of the Poor* (New York: Johnson Reprint, 1970), p. 27. On scow trimming, see Martin V. Melosi, *Garbage in the Cities: Refuse, Reform, and the Environment, 1880–1980* (Chicago: Dorsey, 1981), pp. 71–72.

11. *Waste Trade Journal, Waste Trade Specifications, Compliments of the Waste Trade Journal* (New York: Atlas, n.d.), passim.

12. National Association of Waste Material Dealers, *Fifteenth Anniversary Blue Book, 1913–1928* (New York: National Association of Waste Material Dealers, 1928), pp. 9, 17–19, 47–49; *Waste Trade Journal, Waste Trade Specifications, 1917* (New York: Atlas, 1917), pp. 13–14.

13. Carl Bridenbaugh, *Cities in the Wilderness: Urban Life in America, 1625–1742* (New York: Capricorn, 1964), p. 18; "One Alley's Trash Is a Treasure to Archaeologists at Mall Dig," *Washington Post*, Nov. 9, 1994, p. C1.

14. John Duffy, *The Sanitarians: A History of American Public Health* (Urbana: University of Illinois Press, 1990), pp. 69, 86; Judith Walzer Leavitt, *The Healthiest City: Milwaukee and the Politics of Health Reform* (Princeton: Princeton University Press, 1982), p. 123.

15. Melosi, *Garbage in the Cities*, pp. 20–21; Leavitt, *Healthiest City*, p. 4.

16. Leavitt, *Healthiest City*, pp. 4, 125–26; "Disposal of Refuse in American Cities," *Scientific American*, Aug. 29, 1891, p. 136 (reprint of article originally published in *Sanitary News*).

17. "Disposal of Refuse in American Cities," p. 136.

18. Daniel Eli Burnstein, "Progressivism and Urban Crisis: The New York City Garbage Workers' Strike of 1907," *Journal of Urban History* 16 (Aug. 1990), p. 400; Civic Improvement League of Saint Louis, Public Sanitation Committee, *Disposal of Municipal Waste*, St. Louis, 1906, p. 2. See also David

Ward, *Poverty, Ethnicity, and the American City, 1840–1925: Changing Conceptions of the Slum and the Ghetto* (Cambridge: Cambridge University Press, 1989), p. 31; Elizabeth Fee and Steven H. Corey, *Garbage! The History and Politics of Trash in New York City* (New York: New York Public Library, 1994), p. 24.

19. Suellen Hoy, *Chasing Dirt: The American Pursuit of Cleanliness* (New York: Oxford University Press, 1995), pp. 74–75, 81. See also Melosi, *Garbage in the Cities,* pp. 35–36, 122ff.; Suellen Hoy, " 'Municipal Housekeeping': The Role of Women in Improving Urban Sanitation Practices, 1880–1917," *Pollution and Reform in American Cities, 1870–1930,* ed. Martin V. Melosi (Austin: University of Texas Press, 1980), pp. 173–98.

20. Jane Addams, *Twenty Years at Hull-House,* introd. and notes by James Hurt (Urbana: University of Illinois Press, 1990), pp. 164–67.

21. Helen Campbell, *Household Economics: A Course of Lectures in the School of Economics of the University of Wisconsin* (New York; G. P. Putnam's, 1896), pp. 200–02, 205–06; Kinne and Cooley, *Shelter and Clothing,* p. 48.

22. Quoted in Daniel Thoreau Sicular, "Currents in the Waste Stream: A History of Refuse Management and Resource Recovery in America, M.A. thesis, Department of Geography, University of California, Berkeley, 1984, pp. 39–40.

23. Gwendolyn Wright, *Building the Dream: A Social History of Housing in America* (New York: Pantheon, 1981), p. 173.

24. Burnstein, "Progressivism and Urban Crisis," p. 387; H. de B. Parsons, *The Disposal of Municipal Refuse* (New York: John Wiley, 1906), p. 27; Civic Improvement League of Saint Louis, *Disposal of Municipal Waste,* p. 5.

25. John McGaw Woodbury, "The Wastes of a Great City," *Scribner's Magazine,* Oct. 1903, p. 396; George E. Waring, Jr., "The Disposal of a City's Waste," *North American Review,* July 1895, p. 55; Melosi, *Garbage in the Cities,* pp. 24–25. See also Joel A. Tarr, "Urban Pollution—Many Long Years Ago," *American Heritage,* Oct. 1971, pp. 65–69, 106.

26. Rudolph Hering and Samuel A. Greeley, *Collection and Disposal of Municipal Refuse* (New York: McGraw-Hill, 1921), p. 37; Melosi, *Garbage in the Cities,* p. 160.

27. For a similar argument about how New York's size and density influenced the national debate about housing conditions, see Ward, *Poverty,* pp. 61, 79.

28. E. R. Conant, "Refuse Disposal in Southern Cities with Particular Reference to Savannah, Ga., and Its New Incinerator," *American Journal of Public Health 5* (Sept. 1915), p. 905; "Disposal of Refuse in American Cities," p. 136.

29. Leavitt, *Healthiest City,* pp. 124, 135; Woodbury, "Wastes of a Great City," p. 399.

30. Conant, "Refuse Disposal in Southern Cities," p. 904; Melosi, *Garbage in the Cities,* p. 167.

31. Waring, "Disposal of a City's Waste," p. 54; Leavitt, *Healthiest City,* p. 129; Melosi, *Garbage in the Cities,* pp. 165–66.

32. Melosi, *Garbage in the Cities,* pp. 168–69; Sicular, "Currents in the Waste

Stream," p. 61; "Cremating Garbage," *American Architect and Building News,* Mar. 11, 1893, p. 155; Woodbury, "Wastes of a Great City," p. 396.

33. Helen Campbell, "As to Ashes and Rubbish," *American Kitchen Magazine* 12 (Aug. 1900), pp. 174–76.

34. Woodbury, "Wastes of a Great City," pp. 388–90, 395.

35. Sicular, "Currents in the Waste Stream," p. 76; Melosi, *Garbage in the Cities,* p. 157. On civic groups, see Melosi, *Garbage in the Cities,* pp. 105–06.

36. U.S. Food Administration, *Garbage Utilization: With Particular Reference to Utilization by Feeding* (Washington: GPO, 1918), pp. 8, 12; Melosi, *Garbage in the Cities,* p. 170; Hering and Greeley, *Collection and Disposal,* pp. 41, 258; U.S. Department of Agriculture, *Feeding Garbage to Hogs,* Farmers' Bulletin 1133, Aug. 1920.

37. Food Administration, *Garbage Utilization,* p. 11; see also Department of Agriculture, *Feeding Garbage to Hogs,* p. 6.

38. Waring, "Disposal of a City's Waste," p. 50; Woodbury, "Wastes of a Great City," p. 400; Parsons, *Disposal of Municipal Refuse,* p. 23.

39. Parsons, *Disposal of Municipal Refuse,* pp. 22–23; Campbell, "As to Ashes and Rubbish," p. 175; Waring, "Disposal of a City's Waste," p. 50.

40. *Metal Worker* article reprinted in *American Architect and Building News,* June 7, 1884, p. 274; Hering and Greeley, *Collection and Disposal,* pp. 302–07; Woodbury, "Wastes of a Great City," p. 400.

41. "The Destruction of House Refuse," *American Architect and Building News,* Apr. 23, 1887, pp. 197–99.

42. W. F. Morse, "Disposal of Waste at the World's Columbian Exposition," *Science,* Dec. 8, 1893, pp. 316–17. On Morse's work for Engle, see Melosi, *Garbage in the Cities,* p. 173.

43. "Cremating Garbage," *American Architect and Building News,* Mar. 11, 1893, pp. 155–56.

44. Leavitt, *Healthiest City,* pp. 129, 154.

45. Woodbury, "Wastes of a Great City," p. 400; "Destruction of House Refuse," pp. 197–99.

46. [Bruno Terne], "The Utilization of Garbage," *American Architect and Building News,* Sept. 23, 1893, pp. 185–86.

47. See Irwin S. Osburn, "Disposal of Garbage by the Reduction Method," *American Journal of Public Health* 2 (Dec. 1912), pp. 937–42.

48. On meatpackers' byproducts, see William Cronon, *Nature's Metropolis: Chicago and the Great West* (New York: W. W. Norton, 1991), pp. 250–54. On byproduct chemistry more generally, see David C. Mowery and Nathan Rosenberg, *Technology and the Pursuit of Economic Growth* (Cambridge: Cambridge University Press, 1989), pp. 54–57. See also P. L. Simmonds, *Waste Products and Undeveloped Substances: A Synopsis of Progress Made in Their Economic Utilisation during the Last Quarter of a Century at Home and Abroad,* 3rd ed. (London: Hardwicke and Bogue, 1876); Theodor Koller, *The Utilization of Waste Products: A Treatise on the Rational Utilization, Recovery, and Treat-*

ment of Waste Products of All Kinds, 2nd rev. and enl. English ed. (London: Scott, Greenwood, 1915); Henry J. Spooner, *Wealth from Waste: Elimination of Waste a World Problem* (London: G. Routledge, 1918); Frederick A. Talbot, *Millions from Waste* (Philadelphia: J. B. Lippincott; London: T. F. Unwin, 1920); Arturo Bruttini, *Uses of Waste Material: The Collection of Waste Materials and Their Uses for Human and Animal Food, in Fertilisers, and in Certain Industries, 1914–1922* (London: P. S. King, 1923).

49. Leavitt, *Healthiest City*, p. 132.

50. Sicular, "Currents in the Waste Stream," p. 52; Parsons, *Disposal of Municipal Refuse*, p. 95.

51. Martin V. Melosi, "Sanitary Services and Decision Making in Houston, 1876–1945," *Journal of Urban History* 20 (May 1994), pp. 385, 395.

52. Melosi, *Garbage in the Cities*, pp. 161–62; Hering and Greeley, *Collection and Disposal*, p. 38.

53. Parsons, *Disposal of Municipal Refuse*, p. 6.

54. Woodbury, "Wastes of a Great City," p. 390.

55. Woodbury, "Wastes of a Great City," p. 398.

56. Jacob A. Riis, *How the Other Half Lives: Studies among the Tenements of New York*, ed. Sam Bass Warner (Cambridge: Belknap Press of Harvard University Press, 1970), p. 46.

57. Nasaw, *Children of the City*, p. 98; Ward, *Poverty*, pp. 17–18, 33–34, 77.

58. Leavitt, *Healthiest City*, p. 127.

59. Waring, "Disposal of a City's Waste," pp. 51, 54. See also Sicular, "Currents in the Waste Stream," pp. 33–34.

60. *The Salvation Army in the United States* (New York, 1899), reprinted in Frederick Booth-Tucker, *The Salvation Army in America: Selected Reports, 1899–1903* (New York: Arno, 1972), n.p. See also Madeleine Ginsburg, "Rags to Riches: The Second-Hand Clothes Trade, 1700–1978," *Costume: The Journal of the Costume Society* 14 (1980), p. 130.

61. Lyman Abbott, "The Personal Problem of Charity," *Forum* 16 (Feb. 1894), pp. 666–69.

62. C. K. Jenness, *The Charities of San Francisco: A Directory* (San Francisco: Book Room Print, for the Department of Economics and Social Science, Stanford University, 1894), pp. 17–20, 49.

63. Aaron Ignatius Abell, *The Urban Impact on American Protestantism, 1865–1900* (Hamden, CT: Archon, 1962), p. 119.

64. E. H. McKinley, *Somebody's Brother: A History of the Salvation Army Men's Social Service Department, 1891–1985* (Lewiston, PA: Edwin Mellen, 1986), p. 42; Edward H. McKinley, *Marching to Glory: The History of the Salvation Army in the United States of America, 1880–1980* (San Francisco: Harper & Row, 1980), p. 57; Commander Booth-Tucker, *The Social Relief Work of the Salvation Army in the United States*, Monographs on American Social Economics 20, ed. Herbert B. Adams (New York: League for Social Service, 1900), reprinted in Booth-Tucker, *The Salvation Army in*

America, p. 23; Herbert A. Wisbey, Jr., *Soldiers without Swords: A History of the Salvation Army in the United States* (New York: Macmillan, 1956), p. 103. See also "Odds-and-Ends Charity," *Harper's Weekly*, Dec. 2, 1899, p. 1220.

65. Edwin Gifford Lamb, "The Social Work of the Salvation Army," Ph.D. dissertation, Columbia University, 1909, p. 17.

66. Lamb, "Social Work," pp. 10–11, 25–26.

67. Wisbey, *Soldiers without Swords*, pp. 102–3. On Charity Organization Societies, see Michael B. Katz, *In the Shadow of the Poorhouse: A Social History of Welfare in America* (New York: Basic, 1986), pp. 66–84; Roy Lubove, *The Professional Altruist: The Emergence of Social Work as a Career, 1880–1930* (Cambridge: Harvard University Press, 1965), pp. 1–21.

68. Commander Booth-Tucker, *Light in Darkness, Being an Account of the Salvation Army in the United States* (New York: Salvation Army, 1902), n.p.; *Love's Labor Not Lost, Being the Annual Report of the Salvation Army for Boston and the New England States in the Eighteenth Year of Its Work* (Boston: Salvation Army, 1903), p. 8.

69. Lamb, "Social Work," pp. 41, 48, 62

70. Booth-Tucker, *Social Relief Work*, p. 23; McKinley, *Somebody's Brother*, p. 87.

71. Robert Sandall, *The History of the Salvation Army, Vol. III: 1883–1953* (London: Thomas Nelson, 1955), p. 128.

72. "Odds-and-Ends Charity," p. 1220; Lamb, "Social Work," p. 18.

73. John Fulton Lewis, *Goodwill: For the Love of People* (Washington: Goodwill Industries of America, 1977), p. 90.

74. Earl Christmas, *The House of Goodwill: A Story of Morgan Memorial* (Boston: Morgan Memorial, 1924), p. 158.

75. Christmas, *House of Goodwill*, pp. 45–46, 154–55; Horace Warren Kimbrell, *This Is Goodwill Industries* (New York: Newcomen Society in North America, 1962), pp. 13–16; Lewis, *Goodwill*, pp. 64–66; Ralph Welles Keeler, "Men and Goods Repaired," *World Outlook*, May 1919, pp. 18–19.

76. Betty Harris, *With Courage Adequate ... With Dignity Intact: The Story of Goodwill Industries of Southern California* (Los Angeles: Goodwill Industries of Southern California, 1971), pp. 14–15, 17, 19–21, 27–29; Christmas, *House of Goodwill*, p. 152.

77. Harris, *With Courage Adequate*, pp. 34–35; Christmas, *House of Goodwill*, pp. 58–60, 63–64, 68–70, 75, 88; *The Goodwill Industries: A Manual* (Boston: Morgan Memorial Goodwill, 1935), p. 5.

78. Daniel T. McColgan, *A Century of Charity: The First One Hundred Years of the Society of St. Vincent de Paul in the United States* (Milwaukee: Bruce, 1951), vol. 1, p. 53; vol. 2, pp. 18–19, 435–36.

79. McColgan, *Century of Charity*, vol. 2, pp. 187–88; Albert Paul Schimberg, *Humble Harvest: The Society of St. Vincent de Paul in the Milwaukee Archdiocese, 1849–1949* (Milwaukee: Bruce, 1949), pp. 54, 102.

80. McColgan, *Century of Charity*, vol. 2, p. 7.

81. Lamb, "Social Work," p. 11; T. H. Huxley, *Social Diseases and Worse Remedies: Letters to the "Times" on Mr. Booth's Scheme, with a Preface and (Reprinted) Introductory Essay* (London: Macmillan, 1891), pp. 7, 10–11; Bernard Bosanquet, *'In Darkest England' on the Wrong Track* (London: Swan Sonnenschein, 1891); Henry Mayers Hyndman, *General Booth's Book Refuted* (London: Justice Printery, 1890); C. S. Loch, *An Examination of "General" Booth's Social Scheme, Adopted by the Council of the London Charity Organisation Society* (London: Swan Sonnenschein, 1890). Loch's and Bosanquet's critiques were reprinted, along with that of the Reverend Canon Philip Dwyer, in C. S. Loch, *Criticisms of "General" Booth's Social Scheme, from Three Different Points of View* (London: Swan Sonnenschein, 1891).

82. John Manson, *The Salvation Army and the Public: A Religious, Social, and Financial Study* (London: George Routledge; New York: E. P. Dutton, 1906), p. vi.

83. Lamb, "Social Work," pp. 26–36, 132–39.

84. Lamb, "Social Work," pp. 34–35, 132; Hunt, "Old Days," p. 60.

85. Robert H. Bremner, *The Discovery of Poverty in the United States*, 1956 (New Brunswick: Transaction, 1992) pp. 29, 124; Abell, *Urban Impact*, p. 122; *Love's Labors Not Lost*, pp. 22, 28; "From Our Friends," *Servants of the Poor; or, Solving Social Problems* (Boston: Salvation Army, 1902), n.p.; Michigan Historical Records Survey Project, Works Projects Administration, "Inventory of the Church Archives of Michigan: Salvation Army in Michigan," Apr. 1942, pp. 7–8.

86. Lewis, *Goodwill*, pp. 116, 119–20; Christmas, *House of Goodwill*, pp. 47–50.

87. Hering and Greeley, *Collection and Disposal*, pp. 39–41; Sicular, "Currents in the Waste Stream," p. 74–5.

88. Grosvenor B. Clarkson, *Industrial America in the World War: The Strategy behind the Line* (Boston: Houghton Mifflin, 1923), pp. 209–31; Benedict Crowell and Robert Forrest Wilson, *The Giant Hand: Our Mobilization and Control of Industry and Natural Resources, 1917–1918* (New Haven: Yale University Press, 1921), pp. 64–70; Bernard M. Baruch, *American Industry in the War*, 1921 (New York: Prentice-Hall, 1941), pp. 62–72. See also Robert D. Cuff, *The War Industries Board: Business-Government Relations during World War I* (Baltimore: Johns Hopkins University Press, 1973), pp. 216, 234–35; Andrews, *Economics of the Household*, p. 382.

89. U.S. Department of Agriculture, *Food Thrift Series* (Washington: GPO, 1917), no. 4, p. 1.

90. U.S. Committee on Public Information, "Win the War by Giving Your Own Daily Service," *National Service Handbook* (Washington: GPO, 1917), pp. 84–85; William J. Breen, *Uncle Sam at Home: Civilian Mobilization, Wartime Federalism, and the Council of National Defense, 1917–1919* (Westport, CT: Greenwood, 1984), pp. 122–23; David M. Kennedy, *Over Here: The First World War and American Society* (New York: Oxford University Press, 1980), p. 118; Alfred E. Cornebise, *War as Advertised: The Four Minute Men*

and America's Crusade, 1917–1918 (Philadelphia: American Philosophical Society, 1984), pp. 87–99.

91. Department of Agriculture, *Food Thrift Series*, no. 1, pp. 2, 4; no. 2, p. 1; no. 3, pp. 1, 4–6; no. 5, p. 6.

92. Alice Gitchell Kirk, *Practical Food Economy* (Boston: Little, Brown, 1917), pp. 78–79; Holt, *Complete Housekeeper*, pp. 167, 184ff.

93. Department of Agriculture, *Food Thrift Series*, no. 4, p. 1. See also Andrews, *Economics of the Household*, pp. 419–20.

94. U.S. Department of Commerce, Waste-Reclamation Service, *Waste Reclamation: Organization, Functions, and Objects of the National and Local Service* (Washington: GPO, 1919).

95. Andrews, *Economics of the Household*, p. 279; Rex Stuart, "Billions in Junk!" *American Magazine*, June 1923, pp. 62, 179.

96. Agnes L. Palmer, *Twenty-Two: The Time between 1904–1926: Reviewing the Progress of the Salvation Army in the United States under the Leadership of Commander Evangeline Booth* (New York: Salvation Army, 1926), pp. 67–68.

97. Lamb, "Social Work," p. 19; Sandall, *History of the Salvation Army*, p. 128; McKinley, *Somebody's Brother*, p. 88; Edward H. McKinley, "Brass Bands and God's Work: One Hundred Years of the Salvation Army in Georgia and Atlanta," *Atlanta History* 34 (Winter 1990–91), p. 14. On employers selling castoffs to servants, see Tera Hunter, *To 'Joy My Freedom: Southern Black Women's Lives and Labors after the Civil War* (Cambridge: Harvard University Press, 1997), p. 106.

98. Christmas, *House of Goodwill*, pp. 47–50, 149–51; Harris, *With Courage Adequate*, pp. 19–21, 27–30.

99. Christmas, *House of Goodwill*, p. 86; Lewis, *Goodwill*, pp. 117, 120, 124; Harris, *With Courage Adequate*, pp. 29–30.

100. Lewis, *Goodwill*, p. 124.

101. McColgan, *Century of Charity*, vol. 2, p. 195; Schimberg, *Humble Harvest*, pp. 103–04.

102. Lewis, *Goodwill*, p. 116; Andrews, *Economics of the Household*, pp. 418–19, 421. On Andrews, see Goldstein, "Mediating Consumption," p. 49.

103. Andrews, *Economics of the Household*, p. 420.

CHAPTER FOUR:
HAVING AND DISPOSING IN THE NEW CONSUMER CULTURE

1. R. W. Johnson to Lillian Gilbreth, Sept. 29, 1926; Lillian Gilbreth to R. W. Johnson, Sept. 30, 1926; "Report of Gilbreth, Inc.," p. 14, Gilbreth Collection, Special Collections, Purdue University Library. For an introduction to the study, and brief excerpts, see Vern L. Bullough, "Merchandising the Sanitary Napkin: Lillian Gilbreth's 1927 Survey," *Signs* 10 (Spring 1985), pp. 615–27.

2. See Ruth Schwartz Cowan, "Lillian Evelyn Moller Gilbreth," *Notable American*

Women, the Modern Period (Cambridge: Harvard University Press, 1980), pp. 271–72.

3. Joan Jacobs Brumberg, " 'Something Happens to Girls': Menarche and the Emergence of the Modern American Hygienic Imperative," *Journal of the History of Sexuality* 4 (1993), pp. 112–14.

4. Fred E. H. Schroeder, "Feminine Hygiene, Fashion, and the Emancipation of American Women," *American Studies* 17 (Fall 1976), p. 107; Anne M. Spurgeon, "Marketing the Unmentionable: Wallace Meyer and the Introduction of Kotex," *Maryland Historian* 19 (Spring/Summer 1988), p. 17; "Cellucotton," *Fortune,* Nov. 1937, p. 196. Spurgeon offers the best account of the Kotex introduction.

5. Spurgeon, "Marketing the Unmentionable," pp. 20, 22, 26–29; John Gunther, *Taken at the Flood: The Story of Albert D. Lasker* (New York: Harper, 1960), p. 154.

6. *Ladies' Home Journal,* Nov. 1927, p. 79, reproduced in Roland Marchand, *Advertising the American Dream: Making Way for Modernity, 1920–1940* (Berkeley: University of California Press, 1985), p. 23; "Is Advertising Read?" Lord & Thomas and Logan advertisement, *Printers' Ink,* Apr. 21, 1927, pp. 74–75.

7. "Report of Gilbreth, Inc.," pp. 15, 16, 65.

8. "Report of Gilbreth, Inc.," pp. 13, 18, 90.

9. "Report of Gilbreth, Inc.," pp. 29, 33, 60, 65; [Mrs.] V. V. Davidson to Johnson & Johnson, Oct. 12, 1926, Gilbreth Collection, Special Collections, Purdue University Library.

10. "Report of Gilbreth, Inc.," pp. 13, 18, 24, 90; R. W. Johnson to Lillian Gilbreth, Sept. 29, 1926.

11. "Report of Gilbreth, Inc.," p. 7; Schroeder, "Feminine Hygiene," p. 108.

12. Kotex advertisements, *Ladies' Home Journal,* Apr. 1927, p. 96; Oct. 1927, p. 86; Nov. 1927, p. 79. The November ad is reproduced in Marchand, *Advertising the American Dream,* p. 23. See also Kotex advertisements, *Ladies' Home Journal,* Jan. 1923, p. 104; May 1923, p. 153.

13. [Mrs.] V. V. Davidson to Johnson & Johnson, Oct. 12, 1926; "Comments on Diaper Pad Report," n.p. [p. 2], Gilbreth Collection, Special Collections, Purdue University Library.

14. "Report of Gilbreth, Inc.," pp. 63–64.

15. "Report of Gilbreth, Inc.," pp. 20–21.

16. "Report of Gilbreth, Inc.," pp. 35, 44, 64, 132.

17. "Sanitary Napkins," *Consumers' Union Reports,* June 1937, p. 22.

18. Marchand, *Advertising the American Dream,* pp. 1–2, 20–22; *Good Housekeeping,* May 1922, p. 103 (quoted in Spurgeon, "Marketing the Unmentionable," p. 22); Kotex advertisements, *Good Housekeeping,* Dec. 1922, p. 206; and *Ladies' Home Journal,* Jan. 1923, p. 104; Spurgeon, "Marketing the Unmentionable," p. 28.

19. Spurgeon, "Marketing the Unmentionable," p. 25.

20. Brumberg, " 'Something Happens to Girls,' " p. 104; Marchand, *Advertising the American Dream*, pp. 56, 196–97.

21. President's Conference on Unemployment, Committee on Recent Economic Changes, *Recent Economic Changes in the United States*, vol. 1 (New York: McGraw-Hill, 1929), pp. 97, 126; *Historical Statistics of the United States, Colonial Times to 1970*, (Washington: GPO, 1975), p. 8.

22. Robert S. Lynd and Helen Merrell Lynd, *Middletown: A Study in Modern American Culture* (New York: Harcourt, Brace & World, 1929), p. 83; see also p. 232.

23. See Susan Strasser, *Satisfaction Guaranteed: The Making of the American Mass Market* (New York: Pantheon, 1989), pp. 213, 189, 184, 195.

24. Reproduced in Strasser, *Satisfaction Guaranteed*, pp. 33–34.

25. James T. Rock, "Cans in the Countryside," *Historical Archaeology* 18 (1984), p. 110; "Paterson Pioneer" Parchment Paper, in Paper Products, box 1, Warshaw Collection of Business Americana, Archives Center, National Museum of American History, Smithsonian Institution (hereafter WCBA).

26 Mary Neth, *Preserving the Family Farm: Women, Community, and the Foundations of Agribusiness in the Midwest, 1900–1940* (Baltimore: Johns Hopkins University Press, 1995), p. 200.

27. "Report of Gilbreth, Inc.," pp. 13, 130.

28. Richard L. Bushman and Claudia L. Bushman, "The Early History of Cleanliness in America," *Journal of American History* 74 (Mar. 1988), pp. 1225–26, 1228; Maureen Ogle, *All the Modern Conveniences: American Household Plumbing, 1840–1890* (Baltimore: Johns Hopkins University Press, 1996), p. 3; Andrew McClary, "Germs Are Everywhere: The Germ Threat as Seen in Magazine Articles, 1890–1920," *Journal of American Culture* 3 (Spring 1980), p. 34; Nancy Tomes, *The Gospel of Germs: Men, Women, and the Microbe in American Life* (Cambridge: Harvard University Press, 1998), passim.

29. Brumberg, " 'Something Happens to Girls,' " p. 113; Bushman and Bushman, "Early History of Cleanliness"; Suellen Hoy, *Chasing Dirt: The American Pursuit of Cleanliness* (New York: Oxford University Press, 1995); Stanley Lebergott, *Pursuing Happiness: American Consumers in the Twentieth Century* (Princeton: Princeton University Press, 1993), p. 149; Jacqueline S. Wilkie, "Submerged Sensuality: Technology and Perceptions of Bathing," *Journal of Social History* 19 (Summer 1986), p. 654.

30. Joel Munsell, *Chronology of the Origin and Progress of Paper and Paper-Making*, 5th ed. (Albany: J. Munsell, 1876), p. 203.

31. Munsell, *Chronology*, p. 223; "Japanese Paper Ware Manufactured by Jennings Brothers," Paper Products, box 1, WCBA.

32. Munsell, *Chronology*, p. 171; G. Austin, "Rags," *Atlantic Monthly*, Mar. 1867, p. 370; Jane Celia Busch, "The Throwaway Ethic in America," Ph.D. dissertation, University of Pennsylvania, 1983, p. 83. On detachable collars, see Carole Turbin, *Working Women of Collar City: Gender, Class, and Community in Troy, New York, 1864–66* (Urbana: University of Illinois Press, 1992), pp. 19–29.

33. Eleanor Arnold, ed., *Voices of American Homemakers* (Bloomington: Indiana University Press, 1985), pp. 195–96.

34. Marchand, *Advertising the American Dream*, p. 102; A. P. W. Paper Co. materials, Paper Products, box 1, WCBA.

35. George C. Mather & Co. to Fonda, Johnstown & Gloversville Railroad, July 17, 1903, Paper Products, box 1, WCBA; Manahan's Japanese Tar Sanitary Toilet Paper, Paper Products, box 1, WCBA.

36. Amendment to Interstate Quarantine Regulations, Paper Products, box 2, Drinking Cups folder, WCBA.

37. Letters, Stone & Forsyth to Fonda, Gloversville and Johnstown RR Co. Purchasing Department, Mar. 18, May 14, and Nov. 30, 1912, Paper Products, box 1, WCBA; Individual Drinking Cup Co. to W. H. Collins, Aug. 13, 1914, Paper Products, box 2, Paper Drinking Cups folder, WCBA; Busch, "Throwaway Ethic," p. 92.

38. "Sounding the Knell of Common Drinking Cup," *Survey,* Dec. 31, 1910, p. 508; "Public Drinking Water and Health," *Independent,* May 22, 1913; see also McClary, "Germs Are Everywhere," p. 37.

39. "Sounding the Knell," p. 508; Busch, "Throwaway Ethic," pp. 93–94.

40. "Stone's Patent Paper Julep Straws," *National Bottler's Gazette,* Apr. 5, 1895, p. 29; *National Bottler's Gazette,* June 5, 1895, p. 67; "Handling Drinking Straws," *National Bottler's Gazette,* Feb. 5, 1918, p. 89.

41. Busch, "Throwaway Ethic," pp. 96–97; Hygienic Paper Towel, Paper Products, box 1, WCBA. In 1929, about 52,000 tons of paper towels were produced every year; ten years earlier, the figure was a little over 19,000 tons of towels and napkins combined. See Busch, "Throwaway Ethic," p. 99.

42. Christine Frederick, *Household Engineering: Scientific Management in the Home* (Chicago: American School of Home Economics, 1920), p. 142; Vincent Vinikas, *Soft Soap, Hard Sell: American Hygiene in an Age of Advertisement* (Ames: Iowa State University Press, 1992), p. 94.

43. McClary, "Germs Are Everywhere," p. 36.

44. Kleenex advertisements, *Ladies' Home Journal,* Aug. 1927, p. 84; Feb. 1932, p. 112. See also *Good Housekeeping* and *Parents'* advertisements cited in Busch, "Throwaway Ethic," p. 155n176.

45. Busch, "Throwaway Ethic," p. 107.

46. Busch, "Throwaway Ethic," p. 84; Dennison advertisement, *Country Life in America,* Sept. 1, 1911, p. 21; Frederick, *Household Engineering,* p. 143.

47. Busch, "Throwaway Ethic," p. 87; Frederick, *Household Engineering,* pp. 142–43.

48. See Susan Strasser, *Never Done: A History of American Housework* (New York: Pantheon, 1982), pp. 214–19.

49. Lillian M. Gilbreth, *The Home-Maker and Her Job* (New York: D. Appleton, 1927), p. vii.

50. Thomas F. Tierney, *The Value of Convenience: A Genealogy of Technical Culture* (Albany: State University of New York Press, 1993), pp. 6, 30, 36.

51. Hotpoint advertisement, *Ladies' Home Journal,* May 1923, p. 138; other advertisements reproduced in Marchand, *Advertising the American Dream,* pp. 57, 58, 143.

52. Marchand, *Advertising the American Dream,* pp. 117–19.

53. Fels-Naptha advertisement, *Ladies' Home Journal,* Nov. 1927, p. 47; Procter & Gamble advertisement from *Good Housekeeping,* Oct. 1916, p. 11, reproduced in Marchand, *Advertising the American Dream,* p. 10. See also, among many others, Hotpoint advertisement, *Ladies' Home Journal,* May 1923, p. 138.

54. William Leach, *Land of Desire: Merchants, Power, and the Rise of a New American Culture* (New York: Pantheon, 1993), pp. 112, 139ff., 149; Delco-Light advertisement, *Good Housekeeping,* July 1925, p. 132.

55. General Electric advertisement, *Good Housekeeping,* Oct. 1925, p. 227; Armstrong advertisement, *Good Housekeeping,* July 1925, p. 105.

56. Lynd and Lynd, *Middletown,* p. 175; Chipso advertisement, *Good Housekeeping,* Sept. 1925, pp. 118–19; LaFrance advertisement, *Good Housekeeping,* July 1925, p. 130.

57. Wilcolator advertisement, *Good Housekeeping,* Sept. 1925, p. 150; Vacuette advertisement, *Good Housekeeping,* July 1925, p. 164.

58. Shredded Wheat advertisement, *Good Housekeeping,* Aug. 1925, p. 108; Hoover advertisement, *Good Housekeeping,* Aug. 1925, p. 101.

59. Gilles Lipovetsky, *The Empire of Fashion: Dressing Modern Democracy,* trans. Catherine Porter (Princeton: Princeton University Press, 1994), pp. 5, 134–35. "The Empire of the Ephemeral" is a literal translation of Lipovetsky's title.

60. See Strasser, *Satisfaction Guaranteed,* ch. 5.

61. Roland Barthes, *The Fashion System,* trans. Matthew Ward and Richard Howard (New York: Hill and Wang, 1983), pp. 297–98; Lipovetsky, *Empire of Fashion,* p. 80.

62. Two-thirds of the working-class women whom the Lynds interviewed in Muncie in 1924 spent less than six hours a week sewing and mending; half the business-class women spent less than two hours. The head of the fabric department of Muncie's largest department store testified that demand for yard goods was "only a fraction of that in 1890" (*Middletown,* p. 165). On fashion plates, see Nancy Page Fernandez, "Innovations for Home Dressmaking and the Popularization of Stylish Dress," *Journal of American Culture* 17 (Fall 1994), pp. 27–28; Margaret Walsh, "The Democratization of Fashion: The Emergence of the Women's Dress Pattern Industry," *Journal of American History* 66 (1979), p. 301.

63. Mrs. H. C. Gardner, "Fashion," *Ladies' Repository,* May 1967, p. 263; Benjamin R. Andrews, *Economics of the Household: Its Administration and Finance* (New York: Macmillan, 1923), p. 384; Hazel Kyrk, *A Theory of Consumption* (Boston: Houghton Mifflin, 1923), p. 267.

64. Marchand, *Advertising the American Dream,* pp. 122, 123.

65. Ads reproduced in Marchand, *Advertising the American Dream,* pp. 125, 123.

66. Kodak advertisement reproduced in Marchand, *Advertising the American*

Dream, p. 134; Christine Frederick, *Selling Mrs. Consumer* (New York: Business Bourse, 1929), pp. 250–51.

67. Edward Alsworth Ross, *Social Psychology: An Outline and Source Book* (New York: Macmillan, 1908), p. 94.

68. Susan Smulyan, *Selling Radio: The Commercialization of American Broadcasting, 1920–1934* (Washington: Smithsonian Institution, 1994), p. 20; Frederick, *Selling Mrs. Consumer,* p. 253; see also Susan J. Douglas, *Inventing American Broadcasting, 1899–1922* (Baltimore: Johns Hopkins University Press, 1987), p. 303.

69. Richard Tedlow, *New and Improved: The Story of Mass Marketing in America* (New York: Basic, 1990), pp. 167–68. See also Jeffrey L. Meikle, *Twentieth Century Limited: Industrial Design in America, 1925–1939* (Philadelphia: Temple University Press, 1979), pp. 12–13. For a contemporary telling of the story, see Merryle Stanley Rukeyser, "General Motors and Ford: A Race for Leadership," *American Review of Reviews,* Oct. 1927, pp. 372–79.

70. Marchand, *Advertising the American Dream,* p. 156; Lipovetsky, *Empire of Fashion,* p. 80; "Announcing a Special Showing of Ford Cars" and "Complete Showing of Ford Cars," N. W. Ayer Collection, box 331, book 564, Archives Center, National Museum of American History, Smithsonian Institution.

71. Ford quoted in Marchand, *Advertising the American Dream,* p. 158; N. W. Ayer Collection, box 330, book 561. See also "Put your model T Ford in shape for *thousands of miles of additional service*" and "Years of Service in Model T Fords."

72. Tedlow, *New and Improved,* pp. 156, 163, 168; President's Conference on Unemployment, *Recent Economic Changes,* p. 61; Walter Davenport, "Old Cars for New," *Collier's,* Jan. 12, 1929, p. 8.

73. Philco advertisement, *Good Housekeeping,* Aug. 1934, p. 5; Meikle, *Twentieth Century Limited,* pp. 104–06; Kotex advertisement, *Good Housekeeping,* Aug. 1934, p. 150.

74. "Are Used Sets Like Used Cars?" *Radio Broadcast,* Oct. 1929, p. 321; see the following articles in *Electrical Merchandising:* "We Can't Afford to Junk Trade-Ins," July 1928, pp. 60–61, 84; "Do Trade-Ins Work?" Mar. 1936, pp. 31–32; "We're in the Junk Business," Oct. 1937, pp. 2–3, 29; "The Rising Tide of Trade-Ins," Dec. 1937, p. 23. "Trade-Ins Again," Feb. 1938, p. 100; Sam Farnsworth, "Trade-In-Tragedy," Mar. 1938, pp. 22, 89.

75. Leach, *Land of Desire,* pp. 4–5.

76. Frederick, *Selling Mrs. Consumer,* pp. 253–54.

77. Frederick, *Selling Mrs. Consumer,* p. 246. On progressive obsolescence and the Fredericks, see Marchand, *Advertising the American Dream,* pp. 156–60.

78. Frederick, *Selling Mrs. Consumer,* pp. 246–47, 251.

79. Frederick, *Selling Mrs. Consumer,* pp. 249–50.

80. J. George Frederick, ed., *A Philosophy of Production: A Symposium* (New York: Business Bourse, 1930), pp. 156, 227.

81. Quoted in David M. Tucker, *The Decline of Thrift in America: Our Cultural*

Shift from Saving to Spending (New York: Praeger, 1991), p. 116. See, among many examples of thrift literature, American Society for Thrift, *The Thrift Propaganda in America* (n.p. [1915?]); Arthur Henry Chamberlain, *Thrift Education: Course of Study Outline for Use in Years One to Eight Inclusive* (New York: American Society for Thrift, 1928); Philadelphia Chamber of Commerce Educational Committee, *Thrift: A Short Text Book for Elementary Schools of Philadelphia* (Philadelphia: Chamber of Commerce, 1917); Mary Lillian Patterson, *How to Teach Thrift: A Manual for Teachers and Parents (To Be Used in Opening or Closing Exercises with Children between the Fourth and Tenth Grades)* (Oklahoma City: Harlow Publishing, 1927). See also Tucker, *Decline of Thrift,* esp. p. 69; for a typical standardization discussion, see Warren C. Waite, *Economics of Consumption* (New York: McGraw-Hill, 1928), pp. 73–74.

CHAPTER FIVE: MAKING DO AND BUYING NEW IN HARD TIMES

1. Richardson Wright, "The Decay of Tinkers Recalls Olden Days of Repairing," *House & Garden,* Aug. 1930, p. 48.

2. Robert S. Lynd, *Middletown in Transition: A Study in Cultural Conflicts* (New York: Harcourt, Brace, 1937), p. 17.

3. Jeffrey L. Meikle, *Twentieth Century Limited: Industrial Design in America, 1925–1939* (Philadelphia: Temple University Press, 1979), p. 68.

4. Kotex advertisement, *Good Housekeeping,* Aug. 1934, p. 150; Bon Ami advertisement, *Cosmopolitan,* Mar. 1932, inside front cover; see also Bon Ami ad, *Good Housekeeping,* July 1934, p. 157.

5. "The Package as Merchandiser," *Fortune,* May 1931, pp. 76–81; "New Hosiery Pack Tripled First Day's Sales," *Packaging Digest,* June 10, 1934, p. 3; "700 Percent Sales Increase Followed Repackaging Plans," *Packaging Digest,* Nov. 10, 1934, p. 2.

6. Earnest Elmo Calkins, "What Consumer Engineering Really Is," introd., *Consumer Engineering: A New Technique for Prosperity,* by Roy Sheldon and Egmont Arens (New York: Harper, 1932), pp. 1–2, 7; Aldous Huxley, *Brave New World,* 1932 (New York: Harper Perennial, 1946), pp. 32–33.

7. Sheldon and Arens, *Consumer Engineering,* pp. 55–56, 61; see also Meikle, *Twentieth Century Limited,* pp. 71ff.

8. Calculated from *Historical Statistics of the United States, Colonial Times to 1970* (Washington: GPO, 1975), p. 843; Roland S. Vaile, *Research Memorandum on Social Aspects of Consumption in the Depression* (New York: Social Science Research Council, 1937), p. 18; Lynd, *Middletown in Transition,* p. 11.

9. Vaile, *Research Memorandum,* p. 19.

10. Eleanor P. Rand, "An Old-Fashioned Kitchen Replanned," *House Beautiful,* Aug. 1930, pp. 152–53; Robert Friedel, "Scarcity and Promise: Materials and American Domestic Culture during World War II," *World War II and the American Dream: How Wartime Building Changed a Nation,* ed. Donald

Albrecht (Washington, DC: National Building Museum; Cambridge: MIT Press, 1995), p. 47; Carolyn M. Goldstein, *Do It Yourself: Home Improvement in 20th-Century America* (Washington: National Building Museum, 1998) pp. 19–21.

11. Mary Margaret McBride, "Spruce Up, America!" *Good Housekeeping,* July 1934, pp. 44–45, 153–56; "Now Is the Time to Modernize—Good Housekeeping Studio Offers $1000 in Cash Awards," *Good Housekeeping,* Aug. 1934, p. 52; Kenneth T. Jackson, *Crabgrass Frontier: The Suburbanization of the United States* (Oxford: Oxford University Press, 1985), p. 206; Goldstein, *Do It Yourself,* p. 26.

12. Mary Neth, *Preserving the Family Farm: Women, Community, and the Foundations of Agribusiness in the Midwest, 1900–1940* (Baltimore: Johns Hopkins University Press, 1995), pp. 203–04.

13. Vincent Vinikas, *Soft Soap, Hard Sell: American Hygiene in an Age of Advertisement* (Ames: Iowa State University Press, 1992), p. 94; R. O. Eastman, Inc., *Zanesville and 36 Other American Communities: A Study of Markets and of the Telephone as a Market Index* (New York: Literary Digest, 1927), p. 108; Meikle, *Twentieth Century Limited,* p. 97.

14. R. O. Eastman, *Zanesville,* p. 108; Vinikas, *Soft Soap, Hard Sell,* p. 94; General Electric advertisement, *House Beautiful,* Aug. 1930, between pp. 101–02.

15. General Electric advertisement, *Cosmopolitan,* Mar. 1932, p. 5; Katherine Fisher, "Breezy Notes on August Housekeeping," *Good Housekeeping,* Aug. 1934, p. 133; Norge advertisement, *Good Housekeeping,* July 1934, p. 127.

16. Alice Bradley, *Electric Refrigerator Menus and Recipes: Recipes Prepared Especially for the General Electric Refrigerator* (Cleveland: General Electric, 1929), pp. 11, 36; Frigidaire Corporation, "Left-Overs," *Frigidaire Recipes* (Dayton: Frigidaire, 1928), pp. 55–62.

17. *Your Frigidaire: Recipes and Other Helpful Information* (Dayton: Frigidaire, 1934), p. 13.

18. *Your Frigidaire,* pp. 14–15; see also Montgomery Ward, *Cold Cooking* (n.p.: Montgomery Ward, 1942), which was based on the Frigidaire book.

19. Paul Hendrickson, *Looking for the Light: The Hidden Life and Art of Marion Post Wolcott* (New York: Knopf, 1992), p. 101.

20. Neth, *Preserving the Family Farm,* p. 32; Roderick Kiracofe, *The American Quilt: A History of Cloth and Comfort, 1750–1950* (New York: Clarkson Potter, 1993), p. 233; Pat Nickols, "Feed, Flour, Tobacco, and Other Sacks: Their Use in the 20th Century," *On the Cutting Edge: Textile Collectors, Collections, and Traditions,* ed. Jeannette Lasansky (Lewisburg, PA: Union County Historical Society Oral Traditions Project, 1994), pp. 97–98; Anna Lue Cook, *Identification and Value Guide to Textile Bags* (Florence, AL: Books Americana, 1990), pp. 149–50.

21. William T. Laing, " 'You Sold Chemises, Not Flour!' " *Printers' Ink,* Aug. 10, 1933, pp. 64–67; Ralph Crothers, "Salesman's Wife Helps Produce Advertising Idea," *Printers' Ink,* June 29, 1933, pp. 27–28.

22. Cook, *Identification and Value Guide,* p. 12; Kiracofe, *American Quilt,* p. 233.

23. Cook, *Identification and Value Guide,* pp. 9–11; Eleanor Arnold, ed., *Voices of American Homemakers* (Bloomington: Indiana University Press, 1985), p. 154.

24. C. B. Larrabee, "Go Slowly with the Dual-Use Package," *Printers' Ink,* Dec. 22, 1932, p. 56.

25. H. W. Marks, "How to Squeeze Extra Profits Out of the Package," *Printers' Ink Monthly,* Dec. 1932, p. 27; "Borden's New Jar for Malted Milk Has Shelf Reuse," *Packaging Digest,* Sept. 10, 1934, pp. 1, 11; "From Boudoir to Banquet," *Modern Packaging,* Nov. 1934, p. 78; "Revision and Innovation," *Modern Packaging,* Dec. 1934, pp. 27–31; "Smartness Combined with Triple Duty," *Modern Packaging,* Dec. 1934, p. 56.

26. "Packages with a Second Use Have Added Sales Value," *Printers' Ink,* Feb. 16, 1933, p. 40; Larrabee, "Go Slowly," p. 56; Lillian Gilbreth, "Report of Gilbreth, Inc.," pp. 46–47, Gilbreth Collection, Special Collections, Purdue University Library.

27. Arnold, *Voices of American Homemakers,* pp. 154–55; Rita J. Adrosko, "The Fashion's in the Bag: Recycling Feed, Flour, and Sugar Sacks during the Middle Decades of the 20th Century," paper delivered at the symposium "Textiles in Daily Life," sponsored by the Textile Society of America, Seattle, Sept. 24–26, 1992.

28. Gertrude Allen, "Feed Bags De Luxe," reprinted in *Reader's Digest,* Mar. 1942, p. 111; Nickols, "Feed, Flour, Tobacco," pp. 97–98; Cook, *Identification and Value Guide,* p. 201; Arnold, *Voices of American Homemakers,* p. 154.

29. Reproduced in Maerikay Waldvogel, "Quilt Design Explosion of the Great Depression," Lasansky, *On the Cutting Edge,* p. 92.

30. Boris Emmet and John E. Jeuck, *Catalogues and Counters: A History of Sears, Roebuck and Company* (Chicago: University of Chicago Press, 1950), p. 629; Jeannette Lasansky, "The Colonial Revival and Quilts, 1864–1976," *Pieced by Mother: Symposium Papers,* ed. Lasansky (Lewisburg, PA: Union County Historical Society Oral Traditions Project, 1988), pp. 97–106.

31. Karal Ann Marling, "From the Quilt to the Neocolonial Photograph: The Arts of the Home in an Age of Transition," *The Arts and the American Home, 1890–1930,* ed. Jessica H. Foy and Karal Ann Marling (Knoxville: University of Tennessee Press, 1994), pp. 2, 9; Waldvogel, "Quilt Design Explosion," p. 85; Lasansky, "Colonial Revival and Quilts," p. 97.

32. Barbara Brackman, *Clues in the Calico: A Guide to Identifying and Dating Antique Quilts* (McLean, VA: EPM, 1989), p. 32.

33. Barbara Brackman, "Rocky Road to Kansas," *Kansas Quilts and Quilters,* ed. Brackman et al. (Lawrence: University Press of Kansas, 1993), p. 46; Waldvogel, "Quilt Design Explosion," p. 91.

34. Brackman, *Clues in the Calico,* 30–31; Patsy Orlofsky and Myron Orlofsky, *Quilts in America* (New York: Abbeville, 1992), p. 80; Brackman, "Rocky Road," p. 43.

35. Jeannette Lasansky, *In the Heart of Pennsylvania: 19th & 20th Century Quilt-*

making Traditions (Lewisburg, PA: Union County Historical Society Oral Traditions Project, 1985), p. 95; Brackman, *Clues in the Calico*, p. 32; Orlofsky and Orlofsky, *Quilts in America*, p. 80.

36. Lasansky, *In the Heart*, p. 95; Orlofsky and Orlofsky, *Quilts in America*, p. 82. On the working conditions of the women who did the quilting, see Jane S. Becker, *Selling Tradition: Appalachia and the Construction of an American Folk, 1930–1940* (Chapel Hill: University of North Carolina Press, 1998), pp. 143–44.

37. Orlofsky and Orlofsky, *Quilts in America*, p. 80; Brackman, *Clues in the Calico*, p. 33.

38. Steven M. Gelber, "A Job You Can't Lose: Work and Hobbies in the Great Depression," *Journal of Social History* 24 (Summer 1991), p. 742.

39. Steven M. Gelber, "Do-It-Yourself: Constructing, Repairing, and Maintaining Domestic Masculinity," *American Quarterly* 49 (Mar. 1997), p. 87. See also Goldstein, *Do It Yourself*.

40. Joseph J. Corn, "The Birth of a How-to-Do-It Culture: *Popular Mechanics* and American Life, 1900–1950," lecture delivered at Princeton University, Mar. 23, 1993, pp. 21–22.

41. Arthur W. Wilson, "Home Hobbyists Offer a Market," *Printers' Ink*, May 4, 1933, p. 73; Gelber, "Job You Can't Lose," p. 744.

42. Waldvogel, "Quilt Design Explosion," p. 92; Katherine Jellison, *Entitled to Power: Farm Women and Technology, 1913–1963* (Chapel Hill: University of North Carolina Press, 1993), p. 16; Carolyn M. Goldstein, "Mediating Consumption: Home Economics and American Consumers, 1900–1940," Ph.D. dissertation, University of Delaware, 1994, pp. 36–38.

43. Marjorie Patten, *The Arts Workshop of Rural America: A Study of the Rural Arts Program of the Agricultural Extension Service* (New York: Columbia University Press, 1937), pp. 170, 172; Kathleen R. Babbitt, "The Productive Farm Woman and the Extension Home Economist in New York State, 1920–1940," *Agricultural History* 67 (Spring 1993), pp. 91, 97.

44. Patten, *Arts Workshop*, pp. 10–12, 160–62; Geraldine Niva Johnson, *Weaving Rag Rugs: A Women's Craft in Western Maryland* (Knoxville: University of Tennessee Press, 1985), p. 138; Orlofsky and Orlofsky, *Quilts in America*, p. 82.

45. Arnold, *Voices of American Homemakers*, p. 153.

46. Janet B. Wattles, " 'Jobs from Junk—Wages from Waste,' " *Scientific American*, Feb. 1932, pp. 84–85.

47. "Notices of Importance to Our Contributors," *Goodwill*, Morgan Memorial ed., June-July-Aug. 1939, p. 3.

48. "Will You Help Us—*Now?*" *Goodwill*, Morgan Memorial ed., Sept.-Oct.-Nov. 1939, p. 1; "Our Business Is FINDING JOBS," *Goodwill*, Morgan Memorial ed., Dec. 1939, Jan.-Feb. 1940, p. 1.

49. *The Goodwill Industries: A Manual* (Boston: Morgan Memorial Goodwill, 1935), p. 20. Emphasis added.

50. Edward H. McKinley, *Marching to Glory: The History of the Salvation Army in*

the United States of America, 1880–1980 (San Francisco: Harper & Row, 1980), p. 161; Edward H. McKinley, *Somebody's Brother: A History of the Salvation Army Men's Social Service Department, 1891–1985* (Lewiston, NY: Edwin Mellen, 1986), pp. 105–06; *Goodwill Manual*, pp. 21–22.

51. *Goodwill Manual*, p. 60.

52. " 'Hijacking' and 'Kidnapping,' " *Goodwill*, Morgan Memorial ed., Sept.-Oct.-Nov. 1939, p. 4; "Will You Help Us—*Now?*" p. 1.

53. *Goodwill Manual*, pp. 53, 57–59, 62.

54. "An Urgent 'Open Letter,' " *Goodwill*, Morgan Memorial ed., Mar.-Apr.-May 1940, p. 1; "You Can Help Us Keep These and Hundreds of Others at WORK!!" *Goodwill*, Morgan Memorial ed., Sept.-Oct.-Nov. 1940, p. 1; "An EMERGENCY EXITS at Morgan Memorial," *Goodwill*, Morgan Memorial ed., Dec. 1940, Jan.-Feb. 1941, p. 1; "DURING SPRING HOUSE-CLEANING TIME," *Goodwill*, Morgan Memorial ed., Mar.-Apr.-May 1941, p. 1;

55. "Collection Note," *Goodwill*, June-Aug. 1941, p. 4; John Fulton Lewis, *Goodwill: For the Love of People* (Washington: Goodwill Industries of America, 1977), pp. 250–51, 255.

CHAPTER SIX: USE IT UP! WEAR IT OUT! GET IN THE SCRAP!

1. Paul Fridlund, *Two Fronts: A Small Town at War* (Fairfield, WA: Ye Galleon, 1984), pp. 76–77.

2. Fridlund, *Two Fronts*, pp. 78–79.

3. U.S. War Production Board, Conservation and Salvage Division, *Utah Minute Women, World War II, 1942–1945* ([Salt Lake City?]: War Production Board, [1945]), pp. 24, 31, 33.

4. Perry R. Duis, "No Time for Privacy: World War II and Chicago's Families," *The War in American Culture: Society and Consciousness during World War II*, ed. Lewis A. Erenberg and Susan E. Hirsch (Chicago: University of Chicago Press, 1996), p. 2; Marc Scott Miller, *The Irony of Victory: World War II and Lowell, Massachusetts* (Urbana: University of Illinois Press, 1988), p. 146; Robert Friedel, "Scarcity and Promise: Materials and American Domestic Culture during World War II," *World War II and the American Dream: How Wartime Building Changed a Nation*, ed. Donald Albrecht (Washington: National Building Museum; Cambridge: MIT Press, 1995), pp. 74–75; Amy Bentley, *Eating for Victory: Food Rationing and the Politics of Domesticity* (Urbana: University of Illinois Press, 1998).

5. Robert B. Westbrook, "Fighting for the American Family: Private Interests and Political Obligation in World War II," *The Power of Culture: Critical Essays in American History*, ed. Richard Wightman Fox and T. J. Jackson Lears (Chicago: University of Chicago Press, 1993), p. 204; Lawrence R. Samuel, *Pledging Allegiance: American Identity and the Bond Drive of World War II* (Washington: Smithsonian Institution, 1997), p. 50; Meg Jacobs, " 'How about Some Meat?' The Office of Price Administration, Consumption Politics, and State Building

from the Bottom Up, 1941–1946," *Journal of American History* 84 (Dec. 1997), p. 920.

6. Jane Seaver, "What You Can Do for Your Country: Salvage for Victory," *Scholastic*, Jan. 19–24, 1942, p. 8; "Save! Save! Save!" *Scholastic*, Mar. 2–7, 1942, p. 8; poster reproduced in *Produce and Conserve, Share and Play Square: The Grocer and the Consumer on the Home-Front Battlefield during World War II*, ed. Barbara McLean Ward (Hanover: University Press of New England, 1993), p. 104.

7. Pearl S. Buck, "Don't Throw Away the Best Part," *Collier's*, Aug. 1, 1942, pp. 11ff.; "On the Home Front," *Real Story*, June 1943, p. 8; "Clothes Salvage Course," *Real Story*, June 1943, p. 10; "Amazing New Invention Automatically Re-Knits Hosiery," *Real Story*, June 1943, p. 63.

8. Carey L. Draeger, " 'Use It All; Wear It Out; Make It Do; or Go Without!' " *Michigan History*, Sept./Oct. 1994, p. 46; "Big Returns from Little Pieces," *American Home*, Aug. 1942, pp. 38–39; "A Flock of Ways to Save!" *American Home*, Apr. 1942, pp. 18–19; Julian J. Proskauer, *ABC of Victory Gardens* (New York: H. Bedford, 1943), p. 16; *The Authentic Guide to Victory Gardens* (New York: Authentic, 1943), p. 38; James H. Burdett, *Victory Garden Manual* (Chicago: Ziff-Davis, 1943), pp. 45–46.

9. Friedel, "Scarcity and Promise," pp. 74–75.

10. Alan Brinkley, *The End of Reform: New Deal Liberalism in Recession and War* (New York: Knopf, 1995), pp. 146–48, 177–82.

11. I. L. Smith, "We Never Threw Anything Away," *Atlantic Monthly*, Feb. 1941, pp. 235–36; Corey Ford, "I Married All Three . . ." *Better Homes and Gardens*, Sept. 1941, pp. 80–82.

12. Alcoa advertisement, *Modern Packaging*, May 1941, p. 69; "Aluminum Emergency," *Business Week*, May 31, 1941, p. 15; "U.S. Defense Program and the U.S. Packager," *Modern Packaging*, May 1941, p. 38; "Plastics in Packaging," *Modern Packaging*, May 1941, pp. 67–70; *Modern Packaging*, May 1941, pp. 46–47.

13. "OPM Asks Sacrifices as a Shortage of Aluminum Wakes Nation to Crisis," *Life*, June 16, 1941, p. 23.

14. "Something to Do," *Time*, Aug. 4, 1941, p. 31; *New York Times*, July 28, 1941, p. 16; "End to Prodigality," *Time*, July 28, 1941, p. 63; "Shortages," *Life*, Aug. 4, 1941, p. 19.

15. "Get the Junk Man," *Time*, Sept. 8, 1941, p. 63; "Washington Bulletin," *Business Week*, Jan. 17, 1942, p. 8; *New York Times*, Oct. 11, 1941, p. 22; *New York Times*, Oct. 28, 1941, p. 41; Helen G. Thompson, "Pans into Planes," *Woman's Home Companion*, Nov. 1941, pp. 120; "Scrap Scramble," *Business Week*, Feb. 14, 1942, p. 18.

16. *The Appleton Plan for the Recovery of Waste Paper*, Appleton, WI, 1941, pp. 13–16.

17. "Live on Less and Like It," *House Beautiful*, Dec. 1941, pp. 64–65, 104–05.

18. Brinkley, *End of Reform*, pp. 182–92.

19. "War Business Checklist," *Business Week,* Jan. 17, 1942, p. 38; Friedel, "Scarcity and Promise," pp. 49–50; Barbara McLean Ward, "A Fair Share at a Fair Price: Rationing, Resource Management, and Price Controls during World War II," *Produce and Conserve,* pp. 93–94.

20. Ward, "A Fair Share," pp. 92–93. Pebeco container in collection of the author. For other examples of wartime packaging, see "Selected Catalogue" in Ward, *Produce and Conserve,* pp. 171–237.

21. "Important!" *American City,* May 1945, p. 89; David C. Smith, *History of Papermaking in the United States, 1691–1969* (New York: Lockwood, 1970), ch. 14; WPB, *Utah Minute Women,* pp. 27–28.

22. "Materials for Victory" and "Concerning Waste Paper," *Goodwill,* June-July-Aug. 1942, p. 3; "Scrap Scramble," pp. 17–18.

23. "Better Things Are Needed Now!" *Goodwill,* Mar.-Apr.-May 1942, p. 1; John Fulton Lewis, *Goodwill: For the Love of People* (Washington: Goodwill Industries of America, 1977) p. 254.

24. "Scrap-Happy," *Business Week,* Feb. 28, 1942, pp. 14–15.

25. "Scrap Scramble," p. 18; "*Life* Goes to a Scrap Party," *Life,* Apr. 13, 1942, pp. 102–05.

26. "Radio Appeal on the Scrap Rubber Campaign, June 12, 1942," *Humanity on the Defensive,* 1942 vol. of *The Public Papers and Addresses of Franklin D. Roosevelt,* ed. Samuel I. Rosenman (New York: Harper, 1950), pp. 271–73.

27. Howard Wolf, *The Story of Scrap Rubber* (Akron: A. Schulman, 1943), pp. 56–60; Betty Burnett, *St. Louis at War: The Story of a City, 1941–1945* (St. Louis: Patrice, 1987), p. 34.

28. "Washington Bulletin," *Business Week,* June 13, 1942, p. 5.

29. American Industries Salvage Committee, *Scrap and How to Collect It,* Sept. 1942, p. 18; "Collecting Scrap Aids the War," *American City,* May 1945, p. 89; "Municipal Scrap Collections Can Help Win the War," *American City,* July 1942, p. 35; "Some Fundamentals on Scrap Collection," *American City,* Aug. 1942, p. 41.

30. "The Salvage Program a Municipal Obligation," *American City,* Nov. 1942, pp. 55–56; Kathleen White Miles ed., *Henry County People in World War II: A Scrapbook of Articles Which Appeared during the War Years in the* Clinton Eye *and the* Henry County Democrat (Clinton, MO: *Clinton Daily Democrat,* 1972), pp. 156–57.

31. Harold J. Ruttenberg, "What the Scrap Campaign Needs," *New Republic,* Oct. 4, 1942, p. 401; Young & Rubicam, Inc., Market Research Department, *A Study of Salvageable Goods Available in American Domiciles,* Aug. 1942.

32. Ruttenberg, "What the Scrap Campaign Needs," pp. 401–02.

33. U.S. War Production Board Salvage Division and U.S. Office of Education, *Your School Can Salvage for Victory* (Washington: GPO, 1943), p. 3; "Scrap Scramble," p. 18; "The WPB Answers Salvage Questions," *Effective Plant Salvage Programs,* ed. L. C. Morrow et al. (New York: American Management Association, 1942), p. 29; Young & Rubicam, *Study of Salvageable Goods.*

34. War Production Board, *Your School Can Salvage,* p. 3.

35. Perry R. Duis, "Symbolic Unity and the Neighborhood: Chicago during World War II," *Journal of Urban History* 21 (Jan. 1995), p. 187; Caroline F. Ware, *The Consumer Goes to War: A Guide to Victory on the Home Front* (New York: Funk & Wagnalls, 1942), pp. 180–81.

36. Duis, "Symbolic Unity," 195–96.

37. Duis, "No Time," pp. 17–45; Duis, "Symbolic Unity," p. 188; Miles, *Henry County People,* pp. 156–57; Young & Rubicam, *Study of Salvageable Goods;* Young & Rubicam, Inc., Market Research Department, *Statistical Appendix for the Study of Salvageable Goods Available in American Domiciles,* Aug. 1942, pp. 74–75.

38. Burnett, *St. Louis at War,* p. 34.

39. "Scrap Scramble," p. 20; "Harvesting Scrap," *Business Week,* Feb. 21, 1942, p. 28.

40. Farm Equipment Institute, *National Scrap Harvest Handbook for Workers* (Chicago: Farm Equipment Institute, 1942), pp. 1–2.

41. Farm Equipment Institute, *National Scrap Harvest Handbook,* pp. 6, 9.

42. "Big Push on Scrap," *Business Week,* June 27, 1942, p. 20; "Scrap Scramble," p. 18.

43. Frank W. Fox, *Madison Avenue Goes to War: The Strange Military Career of American Advertising, 1941–45* (Provo: Brigham Young University Press, 1975), pp. 49–51; Mark H. Leff, "The Politics of Sacrifice on the American Home Front in World War II," *Journal of American History* (Mar. 1991), p. 1298.

44. Ruttenberg, "What the Scrap Campaign Needs," p. 401.

45. Fridlund, *Two Fronts,* p. 76; "Scrap-Happy," pp. 14-15.

46. "Seek Idle Metal," *Business Week,* Jan. 31, 1942, p. 18; "Scrap Scramble," p. 20; "A Scrap of Evidence," *Business Week,* Feb. 14, 1942, p. 17; "Junk Hoard," *Business Week,* June 13, 1942, p. 18.

47. "Scrap Scramble," pp. 17–18; American Industries Salvage Committee, *Scrap and How to Collect It,* p. 22; Warren Hall, "You Can Do Business with Your Junkman," *Saturday Evening Post,* June 27, 1942, pp. 29–30.

48. Karen Anderson, *Wartime Women: Sex Roles, Family Relations, and the Status of Women during World War II* (Westport, CT: Greenwood, 1981), pp. 86–87.

49. War Production Board, *Utah Minute Women,* pp. 14, 18–20, 31, 50.

50. "The Salvage Program a Municipal Obligation," *American City,* Nov. 1942, p. 56; Susan M. Hartmann, *The Home Front and Beyond: American Women in the 1940s* (Boston: Twayne, 1982), pp. 82–84; Samuel, *Pledging Allegiance,* pp. 20–21; Anderson, *Wartime Women,* p. 89; Jacobs, "Office of Price Administration," pp. 923–24; Robert B. Westbrook, " 'I Want a Girl, Just Like the Girl That Married Harry James': American Women and the Problem of Political Obligation in World War II," *American Quarterly* 42 (Dec. 1990), pp. 587–615.

51. D'Ann Campbell, *Women at War with America: Private Lives in a Patriotic Era*

(Cambridge: Harvard University Press, 1984), pp. 172–74; Hartmann, *Home Front and Beyond*, pp. 82–84; Anderson, *Wartime Women*, p. 88.

52. Anderson, *Wartime Women*, p. 88; American Fat Salvage Committee, *Used Household Fat Salvage Facts*, pp. 6–7.

53. Mary Drake McFeely, "The War in the Kitchen," Ward, *Produce and Conserve*, p. 107; conversation with Alexander Strasser, June 14, 1997.

54. "New Salvage Drive for Fats," *Business Week*, June 27, 1942, p. 8; War Production Board, *Utah Minute Women*, p. 23; "For Women Dodger Fans," *New York Times*, July 8, 1943, quoted in "Metropolitan Diary," *New York Times*, June 3, 1992, p. C2.

55. American Fat Salvage Committee, Inc., *Used Household Fat Salvage Facts* (New York: American Fat Salvage Committee, 1944), pp. 9–14.

56. American Fat Salvage Committee, *Used Household Fat Salvage Facts*, pp. 7, 2; War Production Board, *Your School Can Salvage*, p. 5.

57. Young & Rubicam, *Study of Salvageable Goods*, n.p.; American Fat Salvage Committee, *Used Household Fat Salvage Facts*, p. 1.

58. Anderson, *Wartime Women*, p. 88.

59. Anderson, *Wartime Women*, pp. 92–93; William M. Tuttle, Jr., *"Daddy's Gone to War": The Second World War in the Lives of America's Children* (New York: Oxford University Press, 1993), pp. 112–19, 121–22; Samuel, *Pledging Allegiance*, pp. 18, 36–37.

60. Seaver, "What You Can Do," p. 8; "Save! Save! Save!" p. 8; Robert William Kirk, "Getting in the Scrap: The Mobilization of American Children in World War II," *Journal of Popular Culture* 29 (Summer 1995), pp. 224, 228.

61. U.S. War Production Board, Conservation Division, *Get in the Scrap* (Washington: 1942), pp. 5–6; "What You Can Do for Your Country: Get in the Scrap!" *Scholastic*, Sept. 28–Oct. 3, 1942, p. 13.

62. War Production Board, *Get in the Scrap*, pp. 7, 11.

63. War Production Board, *Your School Can Salvage*, pp. 2, 9, 11.

64. "Editorial: 36,000,000 x ?" *Scholastic*, Oct. 5–10, 1942, p. 39.

65. Kirk, "Getting in the Scrap," p. 223; Duis, "Symbolic Unity," p. 189; Samuel, *Pledging Allegiance*, p. 72; War Production Board, *Get in the Scrap*, p. 13; James Ward Lee et al., eds., *1941: Texas Goes to War* (Denton: University of North Texas Press, 1991), p. 84; Tuttle, *"Daddy's Gone to War,"* p. 124.

66. Tuttle, *"Daddy's Gone to War,"* pp. 112, 120; Kirk, "Getting in the Scrap," pp. 224, 228.

67. Donald M. Nelson, *Arsenal of Democracy: The Story of American War Production* (New York: Harcourt, Brace, 1946), p. 304; Duis, "No Time," pp. 33–34.

68. United States, Great Britain, and Canada, Combined Production and Resources Board, Combined Committee on Nonfood Consumption Levels, *The Impact of the War on Civilian Consumption in the United Kingdom, the United States, and Canada* (Washington: GPO, 1945), pp. 1–3, 21, 24; John W. Jeffries, *Wartime America: The World War II Home Front* (Chicago: Ivan R.

Dee, 1996), p. 188; John Morton Blum, *V Was for Victory: Politics and American Culture during World War II* (New York: Harcourt Brace Jovanovich, 1976), p. 98.

69. Friedel, "Scarcity and Promise," p. 75; Leff, "Politics of Sacrifice," p. 1307; Roland Marchand, "Suspended in Time: Mom-and-Pop Groceries, Chain Stores, and National Advertising during the World War II Interlude," Ward, *Produce and Conserve*, pp. 117–39; Kotex advertisement, *True Story*, Sept. 1942, p. 54.

70. Fox, *Madison Avenue Goes to War*, p. 40.

71. Samuel, *Pledging Allegiance*, American Industries Salvage Committee, *Scrap and How to Collect It*, pp. 10–11; "What You Can Do for Your Country: On Your Metal!" *Scholastic*, Oct. 5–10, 1942, p. 12; Kotex advertisement, *True Story*, Sept. 1942, p. 54.

72. American Industries Salvage Committee, *Scrap and How to Collect It*, p. 24; Nelson, *Arsenal of Democracy*, pp. 352–53.

CHAPTER SEVEN: GOOD RIDDANCE

1. Color Scents advertisement, *Metropolitan Home*, Mar./Apr. 1994, p. 140.

2. Jane Celia Busch, "The Throwaway Ethic in America," Ph.D. dissertation, University of Pennsylvania, 1983, pp. 83ff.; Reynolds Wrap advertisement, *Woman's Day*, May 1952, p. 6; Janet McCorkindale, "Paper Products Speed Your Housework," *Better Homes and Gardens*, Apr. 1950, pp. 127–31; Pamela M. W. Anderson, "The Hope Chest," *Good Housekeeping*, June 1950, pp. 26–27; Bernice Strawn, "How to Stretch a Refrigerator," *Woman's Home Companion*, Dec. 1950, pp. 86–87; "Time-Saving Throwaways," *Woman's Home Companion*, Feb. 1951; pp. 152, 154; "Do You Make the Most of Aluminum Foil?" *Better Homes and Gardens*, Apr. 1954, pp. 170–72; "How Did We Ever Get Along without Aluminum Foil?" *Good Housekeeping*, June 1957, p. 48; "Time Saving Ideas with Aluminum Foil," *Sunset*, Oct. 1957, pp. 162–67; Virginia Heffington, "Food Is Money—Store It Right," *Better Homes and Gardens*, Oct. 1961, pp. 92, 94, 96; Marjorie Griffin Groll, "Aluminum Foil—A New Kitchen Timesaver," *Household*, Nov. 1950, pp. 28, 30–31; Marjorie Griffin Groll, "More Uses for Aluminum Foil," *Household*, Feb. 1951, pp. 36–37, 77; Eleanor Lynch, *Reynolds Wrap Creative Cooking with Aluminum Foil* (New York: Benjamin, 1967); ScotTowels advertisement, *Good Housekeeping*, Apr. 1951, p. 128. On strategies for increasing consumption through marketing, see Susan Strasser, *Satisfaction Guaranteed: The Making of the American Mass Market* (New York: Pantheon, 1989), pp. 129–33; on the photographic format, see Karal Ann Marling, *As Seen on TV: The Visual Culture of Everyday Life in the 1950s* (Cambridge: Harvard University Press, 1994), pp. 202–06, 214–17.

3. Dorothy B. Marsh, "The Institute Reports on Quick-Frozen Foods," *Good Housekeeping*, May 1946, p. 89; Marling, *As Seen on TV*, p. 233; "Packaging

with the Stress on Design," *Business Week,* Aug. 2, 1958, p. 54; Leonard M. Guss, *Packaging Is Marketing* (New York: American Management Association, 1967).

4. "Cake Mixes," *Consumer Reports,* Sept. 1953, pp. 385–87; "Boom in Frozen Dinners," *Consumer Reports,* Jan. 1959, p. 16.

5. "You Have 1001 Servants in Your Kitchen," p. 74; "Is Your Grandmother Standing between You and Today's Freedom?" pp. 78–79, both in "The Daily Arts of Good Living," *House Beautiful,* Mar. 1951, pp. 70–91; "America's Amazing New Easy Foods," *Look,* Jan. 6, 1959, p. 65.

6. John A. Kouwenhoven, "Waste Not, Have Not: A Clue to American Prosperity," *Harper's,* Mar. 1959, pp. 74, 75; Elaine Tyler May, *Homeward Bound: American Families in the Cold War Era* (New York: Basic, 1988), p. 17; Marling, *As Seen on TV,* pp. 242–83; Robert H. Haddow, *Pavilions of Plenty: Exhibiting American Culture Abroad in the 1950s* (Washington: Smithsonian, 1997).

7. "Time-Saving Throwaways," pp. 153–55.

8. "Those Wonderful Throwaways," *Look,* Jan. 26, 1954, pp. 73–74; Busch, "Throwaway Ethic," p. 340; Vera D. Hahn, "Everything's Paper but the Doll," *American Home,* Summer 1967, pp. 66–67.

9. See Michiel Schwarz and Michael Thompson, *Divided We Stand: Redefining Politics, Technology, and Social Choice* (Philadelphia: University of Pennsylvania Press, 1990).

10. Kenneth L. Bowman, "We Buried Our Complaints with the Refuse," *American City,* June 1956, pp. 150–52; Edward J. Booth, "Buried 25 Years and Still Legible," *American City,* July 1965, p. 26; Leo Weaver, "The Sanitary Landfill," *American City,* March 1956, pp. 122–24; Leo Weaver, "The Sanitary Landfill, Part II: Selection of Site," *American City,* April 1956, pp. 132–34, 169–70; Leo Weaver, "The Sanitary Landfill, Part III: Method and Operation," *American City,* May 1956, pp. 134–36, 167–70; William Rathje and Cullen Murphy, *Rubbish! The Archaeology of Garbage* (New York: HarperCollins, 1992); Martin V. Melosi, "Sanitary Services and Decision Making in Houston, 1876–1945," *Journal of Urban History* 20 (May 1994), pp. 386, 395; Andrew Hurley, *Environmental Inequalities: Class, Race, and Industrial Pollution in Gary, Indiana, 1945–1980* (Chapel Hill: University of North Carolina Press, 1995).

11. Suellen Hoy, "The Garbage Disposer, the Public Health, and the Good Life," *Technology and Choice: Readings from Technology and Culture,* ed. Marcel C. LaFollette and Jeffrey K. Stine (Chicago, 1991), esp. pp. 149–58; "What You Need to Know about Garbage Disposers," *House Beautiful,* Feb. 1949, pp. 84–85, 140–41; Frances Meyer, "What a Waste Disposer Can Mean to You," *Better Homes and Gardens,* Aug. 1949, pp. 93–95, 117; Sylvia Wright, "No More Garbage in this Town," *McCall's,* Aug. 1950, pp. 86, 91.

12. "Disposers and Incinerators," *Electrical Merchandising,* Jan. 1959, p. 88; "Meet Mrs. America: She's the Key to Your Market Break-Through in Dis-

posers," *Domestic Engineering*, July 1963, pp. 64–67; Susan Strasser, " 'The Convenience Is out of This World': The Garbage Disposer and American Consumer Culture," *Getting and Spending: European and American Consumer Societies in the Twentieth Century*, ed. Susan Strasser, Charles McGovern, and Matthias Judt (Cambridge: Cambridge University Press, 1998), pp. 263–80.

13. "The Kitchen Appliance with the 1-2 Punch," *Domestic Engineering*, Oct. 1954.

14. "What You Need to Know, . . ." p. 84; "Getting Down, . . ." p. 31.

15. "Trash Compactors," *Consumer Reports*, June 1973, p. 395; Sheldon M. Gallager, "Handy New Compactors Put the Squeeze on Trash," *Popular Mechanics*, June 1972, pp. 118–21; R. S. Hedin, "Homebuilt Masher Puts the Squeeze on Trash," *Popular Mechanics*, Nov. 1972, pp. 162–65. See also Jeanne M. Bauer, "Good Riddance," *American Home*, June 1974, pp. 15–16; "Kitchen Machines to Squash Your Trash," *Changing Times*, Sept. 1971, p. 11.

16. KitchenAid press release, Benton Harbor, MI, Aug. 28, 1997, http://kitchenaid. com/pressroom-major/PR07.shtml; "History of the Trash Compactor," http://www2.whirlpool.com/html/homelife/cookin/cooktrsh5.htm; Pat Ragin, "Lowering Waste Disposal Costs," *Journal of Property Management* 58 (March-April 1993) pp. 26–28; "Nuclear Leftovers: Waste Not, Want Not," *Science News*, Mar. 20, 1993, p. 186; Mike Yuen, "Take Out Trash? Not on Columbia," *Houston Post*, Dec. 4, 1990, p. A26:2.

17. James Bolger, "Refrigerator Selling Is a Replacement Business," *Electrical Merchandising*, Jan. 1950, pp. 74–75; "New Worlds for the Trade-In," *Business Week*, Mar. 19, 1955, pp. 70–78 (quotation on p. 72).

18. "Frigidaire One/Ten Plan," *Electrical Merchandising*, May 1956, p. 204; Daniel Horowitz, *Vance Packard and American Social Criticism* (Chapel Hill: University of North Carolina Press, 1994), pp. 181–82; "Product Death-Dates—A Desirable Concept?" *Design News*, Nov. 24, 1958, p. 3; Ernest R. Cunningham, "Daggers to Death-Dates," *Design News*, Jan. 19, 1959, p. 3; Martin Mayer, "Planned Obsolescence: Rx for Tired Markets?" *Dun's Review and Modern Industry*, Feb. 1959, pp. 41, 74, 80.

19. Horowitz, *Vance Packard*, p. 103; "Selling the Consumer on Need for 'Seconds.' " *Business Week*, Sept. 5, 1959, pp. 46–48; Vance Packard, *The Waste Makers* (New York: David McKay, 1960), p. 41.

20. Packard, *Waste Makers*, pp. 55, 103.

21. Horowitz, *Vance Packard*, p. 181, 317n10; Du Pont ad reproduced on p. 184.

22. Seymour Martin Lipset, "The Conservatism of Vance Packard," *Commentary*, Jan. 1961, p. 83; Horowitz, *Vance Packard*, p. 18.

23. Franklin M. Fisher, Zvi Griliches, and Carl Kaysen, "The Costs of Automobile Model Changes since 1949," *Journal of Political Economy* 70 (Oct. 1962), p. 450; Harry A. Williams, "Better Cars? . . ." *Nation*, Feb. 17, 1962, p. 128; Bernard Nossiter, "Detroit's Annual Model Bill," *Nation*, Jan. 20, 1962, pp. 50–51.

24. Horowitz, *Vance Packard*, pp. 7–8.

25. Carol B. Stack, *All Our Kin: Strategies for Survival in a Black Community* (New York: Harper & Row, 1974), pp. 16–17; Carl Husemoller Nightingale, *On the Edge: A History of Poor Black Children and Their American Dreams* (New York: Basic, 1993), pp. 152, 160.

26. Mrs. John R. [Maie (Hewitt)] Williams, *The Thrift Shop Cook Book* (Washington: Junior League, 1932); Louise Teather, "Good New 'Ism' in California," *American Home,* Nov. 1954, pp. 17–18; American Hospital Association Committee on Hospital Auxiliaries, *Manual of Operation: Thrift Shops and Rummage Sales for Women's Hospital Auxiliaries* (Chicago: American Hospital Association, [1953]), pp. 28–31, 35 (quotation on p. 31).

27. American Hospital Association, *Manual of Operation,* pp. 42–43, 47; Harriet Hawes and Eleanor Edelman, *McCall's Complete Book of Bazaars* (New York: Simon & Schuster, 1955), pp. 39–40; Ann Seranne and Eileen Gaden, *The Church and Club Woman's Companion* (Garden City: Doubleday, 1964), pp. 170, 173; Carol Spicer, "Buyer, Seller, and Donor: All Win at the Rummage Sale!" *Saturday Evening Post,* July 1, 1961, p. 10.

28. American Hospital Association, *Manual of Operation,* pp. 21–22; "How to Set Up a Thrift Shop," *Good Housekeeping,* Aug. 1958, pp. 138–39; Spicer, "Buyer, Seller, and Donor;" Teather, "Good New 'Ism,' " pp. 17–18.

29. Geitel Winakor and Marcella Martin, "Used-Clothing Sales in a Small City," *Journal of Home Economics* 55 (1963), p. 358.

30. Gretchen M. Herrmann and Stephen M. Soiffer, "For Fun and Profit: An Analysis of the American Garage Sale," *Urban Life* 12 (Jan. 1984), p. 397; Lynn O'Reilly et al., "The Relationship of Psychological and Situational Variables to Usage of a Second-Order Marketing System," *Journal of the Academy of Marketing Science* 12 (Summer 1984), pp. 53–76; Denis F. Healy and Thomas D. Dovel, "The Garage Sale: A Growing Force in the Distribution of Used Household Goods," paper for the Southern Marketing Association, 1975.

31. "Selling the Consumer on Need for 'Seconds,' " pp. 46–48.

32. Herrmann and Soiffer, "For Fun and Profit," p. 402; Kevin Lynch, with contributions by Michael Southworth, *Wasting Away: An Exploration of Waste— What It Is, How It Happens, Why We Fear It, How to Do It Well* (San Francisco: Sierra Club, 1990), p. 60.

33. Stephen M. Soiffer and Gretchen M. Herrmann, "Visions of Power: Ideology and Practice in the American Garage Sale," *Sociological Review* 35 (Feb. 1987), pp. 48–83; Healy and Dovel, "The Garage Sale."

34. Gretchen M. Herrmann, "Women's Exchange in the American Garage Sale: Giving Gifts and Creating Community," Proceedings of the Conference on Gender and Consumer Behavior, University of Utah, June 19–23, 1991; Gretchen M. Herrmann, "Garage Sales as Practice: Ideologies of Women, Work, and Community in Daily Life," Ph.D. dissertation, State University of New York at Binghamton, 1990.

35. Soiffer and Herrmann, "Visions of Power," pp. 66, 80.

36. Louis A. Ferman et al., *The Informal Economy, Annals of the American*

Academy of Political and Social Science 493 (Sept. 1987); Soiffer and Herrmann, "Visions of Power," pp. 65–66, 80.

37. Charles Jencks and Nathan Silver, *Adhocism: The Case for Improvisation* (Garden City, NY: Doubleday, 1973), 65; Alicia Bay Laurel, *Living on the Earth* (New York: Vintage, 1970), pp. 39–41, 51, 71–72.

38. Louis Blumberg and Robert Gottlieb, *War on Waste: Can America Win Its Battle with Garbage?* (Washington: Island, 1989), p. 12; Busch, "Throwaway Ethic," p. 294.

39. "Meet the Kings of the Garbage Heap," *Business Week,* Sept. 12, 1988, pp. 112, 115–16; Harold Crooks, *Giants of Garbage: The Rise of the Global Waste Industry and the Politics of Pollution Control* (Toronto: James Lorimer, 1993), pp. 1–34.

40. Busch, "Throwaway Ethic," p. 348; Frank Ackerman, *Why Do We Recycle? Markets, Values, and Public Policy* (Washington: Island, 1997).

41. Blumberg and Gottlieb, *War on Waste,* p. 133; Robert Steuteville, "The State of Garbage in America," *BioCycle,* May 1995, p. 30; http://cbot-recycle.com; "Recyclables Commodity Market Project (1991–1996)," http://www.epa.gov/r10earth/offices/owcm/cbot.htm; Seth Schulman, "Trends: Curbside Commodities," *Technology Review Online,* Aug./Sept. 1996, http://web.mit.edu/techreview/www/articles/as96/trends.html; Barnaby J. Feder, "Market Place: Chicago Board Is Developing a System to Trade in Trash," *New York Times,* June 11, 1993.

42. John Tierney, "Recycling Is Garbage," *New York Times Magazine,* June 30, 1996, pp. 24–29, 44, 48, 51, 53; Blumberg and Gottlieb, *War on Waste,* pp. 125–26; U.S. Environmental Protection Agency, "Earth Day Facts," EPA 230-F-95-001, Apr. 1995.

43. See, for example, Jacqueline Killeen, *Ecology at Home* (San Francisco: 101 Productions, 1971); Julia Percivall, *Household Ecology* (Englewood Cliffs, NJ: Prentice-Hall, 1971); Gloria Naumann, *Homemaking Tips: Old and New Ways to Save, Stretch, and Substitute* (Salt Lake City: Hawkes, 1977).

44. "Bargain Buys from the Salvation Army?" *Good Housekeeping,* Jan. 1959, p. 95; Robert W. Houseman, "Going . . . Going . . . Gone . . . to a Country Auction," *American Home,* June 1961, pp. 30–33, 77; "How to Find Beauty in the Junkyard," *House Beautiful,* Mar. 1964, pp. 167–69.

45. Verni Greenfield, *Making Do or Making Art: A Study of American Recycling* (Ann Arbor: UMI, 1986), p. 10; Harold Rosenberg, "Collage: Philosophy of Put-Togethers," *Collage: Critical Views,* ed. Katherine Hoffman (Ann Arbor: UMI, 1989), pp. 61, 63, 64.

46. Miriam Schapiro, "Femmage," Hoffman, *Collage,* p. 296.

47. *Jac Leirner: Directions,* pamphlet from exhibition at Hirshhorn Museum and Sculpture Garden, Washington, D.C., Dec. 17, 1992–Mar. 14, 1993; "Recycling More Than Just Images," *High Performance,* Winter 1994, p. 16; Barbara C. Matilsky, "Mierle Laderman Ukeles: Reclaiming Waste," *Fragile Ecologies: Contemporary Artists' Interpretations and Solutions* (New York:

Rizzoli, 1992), pp. 74–79; Kimberly Ridley, "Trashing Convention," *Massachusetts Audubon Society Sanctuary,* Sept./Oct. 1994, pp. 10–12; Deborah Bright, "Paradise Recycled: Art, Ecology, and the End of Nature [Sic]," *Afterimage,* Sept. 1990, pp. 10–13.

48. Lucy R. Lippard, *Mixed Blessings: New Art in a Multicultural America* (New York: Pantheon, 1990); Greenfield, *Making Do or Making Art,* pp. 20, 22.

49. Robert Crease and Charles Mann, "Backyard Creators of Art That Says: 'I Did It, I'm Here,' " *Smithsonian,* Aug. 1983, p. 82; Greenfield, *Making Do or Making Art;* Guy Brett, *Through Our Own Eyes: Popular Art and Modern History,* quoted in Lippard, *Mixed Blessings,* p. 79.

50. Charlene Cerny and Suzanne Seriff, *Recycled, Re-Seen: Folk Art from the Global Scrap Heap* (New York: Harry N. Abrams, 1996).

51. "Trend Watch: Bowling Over," *Metropolitan Home,* May/June 1997, p. 80; Wendy Moonan, "Hooked Rugs Snag Buyers of Folk Art," *New York Times,* Feb. 20, 1998, p. B40.

52. Environmental Protection Agency, "Earth Day Facts."

53. Dana Canedy, "Where Nothing Lasts Forever," *New York Times,* Apr. 24, 1998, pp. C1, C3; Martin V. Melosi, "Down in the Dumps: Is There a Garbage Crisis in America?" *Urban Public Policy: Historical Modes and Methods,* ed. Melosi (University Park: Pennsylvania State University Press, 1993), pp. 102, 121; Carey Goldberg, "Where Do Computers Go When They Die?" *New York Times,* Mar. 12, 1998.

54. "The State of Garbage in America," *Biocycle,* Apr. 1998, p. 32; Patricia Poore, "Is Garbage an Environmental Problem?" *Garbage,* Nov./Dec. 1993, pp. 40–45.

55. Douglas Martin and Dan Barry, "Giuliani Stirs Up Border Tensions with Trash Plan," *New York Times,* Dec. 3, 1998; David M. Herszenhorn, "Reaction in New Jersey Runs from Skepticism to Fury," *New York Times,* Dec. 3, 1998; Bruce Lambert, "Mayor Tells Non–New Yorkers That City's Trash Is Price for What They Reap," *New York Times,* Jan. 14, 1999; "Garbage Is Gold, Mayor Says," *New York Times,* Jan. 19, 1999; Blaine Harden, "Trade Trash For Culture? Not Virginia," *New York Times,* Jan. 18, 1999. On protest in a Texas town where Waste Management built a huge landfill, see the film *Talking Trash,* by Leslie Schwerin and Jennifer Schwerin (Nomad Productions).

56. Gilles Lipovetsky, *The Empire of Fashion: Dressing Modern Democracy,* trans. Catherine Porter (Princeton: Princeton University Press, 1994), p. 146; James R. Chiles, "Casting a High-Tech Net for Space Trash," http://www.smithsonianmag.com/smithsonian/issues99/jan99/trash.html.

57. "The State of Garbage in America," p. 32.

58. Ackerman, *Why Do We Recycle?* p. 185.

Acknowledgments

I received financial support for this project from the John Simon Guggenheim Foundation and the German Historical Institute, and I had the privilege and pleasure of drafting one chapter at the Rockefeller Foundation's Bellagio Study Center. I am grateful to Jean-Christophe Agnew, Susan Porter Benson, Norbert Finzsch, Thomas K. McCraw, and Thomas Schlereth, whose letters made those grants possible.

My participation in the Ford Foundation Seminar on Representations and Meanings of Black Women's Work prompted me to do and present research that has enriched and strengthened the book. I introduced other pieces and stages of the work at the American Society for Environmental History, the German Historical Institute Annual Lecture and its Conference on American and European Consumption in the Twentieth Century, the Hagley Research Seminar, the Organization of American Historians, the Rutgers Center for Historical Analysis, the Southern Humanities Conference, the Washington Seminar on American History and Culture, the University of Delaware, Kenyon College, Pennsylvania State University, the University of Utah, the University of

Virginia, and the Yulee Lecture at George Washington University. Thanks to the people who arranged those talks, to the many who asked questions and spoke with me afterward, and especially to the ones who prepared formal remarks: Gunther Barth, Warren Belasco, Richard Butsch, Lizabeth Cohen, Wolfgang Erz, and Robert Friedel.

Many other friends and colleagues have expressed interest in this project over the years, by sending or suggesting materials for me to look at, responding to my questions, or tossing ideas my way. No doubt I've left out some names; I hope that those who are missing will forgive me. In addition to people thanked here for other reasons, I'd like to mention Rita Adrosko, Alok Bhalla, Anne Boylan, Daryl Braithwaite, Louis Cain, Melinda Chateauvert, Joe Corn, Mira Engler, Nancy Page Fernandez, Wendy Gamber, Bob Goldfarb, Kasey Grier, Barbara Henning, Suellen Hoy, David Landes, Jack Larkin, Mark Levensky, Reed Lifset, Steve Lubar, Elissa Marder, Rob Mayer, Judith McGaw, Clay McShane, Barney Mergen, Sidney Mintz, Maureen Ogle, Adam Rome, Rodris Roth, Margaret Rucker, Virginia Scharf, Phil Scranton, Laura Shapiro, Kitty Sklar, Christine Stansell, Alex Strasser, Joel Tarr, and Mary Helen Washington.

I owe thanks to many staff members at the Library of Congress, the Museum of the City of New York, the New York Public Library, the New York State Museum, and the Purdue University Library; to Fath Ruffins and others at the Archive Center, National Museum of American History; and to Darleen Flaherty at the Ford Archives, Phil Mooney at Coca-Cola, and Mary Jo Pouchnik at the Bemis Company. Reiner Gogolin, Iris Golumbeck, Gaby Muller-Oelrichs, and Luzie Nahr helped me at the German Historical Institute library. Florence Lathrop of the Baker Library, Harvard Business School, showed me the papers of Morillo Noyes. Ginger Marshall filled out an untold number of Library of Congress call slips.

I am especially indebted to those who helped me craft the book. Ann Romines and Phyllis Palmer were the initial readers for the first drafts. They set me deadlines, cut me slack, cheered me on, gave me ideas, and cooked me great dinners. Laura Anker, Maarten DeKadt, Jenna Weissman Joselit, Jim Sparrow, and Cristy Willer offered useful critiques of portions of those drafts, while Frank Ackerman read and commented on them in their entirety and shared his work in progress. Soon after I began to formulate the topic, Martin Melosi welcomed me into the small club of garbage historians, and toward the end, he commented on a complete manuscript. Donna Gabaccia, Nancy Koppelman, Jean Mandeberg, Kathy Peiss, and Judith Strasser also reviewed that version, and each provided numerous useful suggestions. So did Carolyn Goldstein, who had seen and helped with many of the pieces along the way.

Sara Bershtel's editing genius, generosity, and dedication have made me into a far better writer than I can be on my own. She accompanied me to the New York Public Library's "Garbage!" exhibit, sprinkled wet tea leaves on her floor in accord with nineteenth-century household advice, and, when the time came, helped untangle the parts of the manuscript that were still in knots, continually revealing my own thinking to me. Roslyn Schloss saved me from innumerable errors, lapses, and flaws. Thanks also to the staff at Metropolitan/Holt, especially Carly Berwick and Michelle McMillian, to Kathleen Babbitt, and to my agent, Mary Evans.

I had only vague ideas about this book when I met Bob Guldin, who soon thought up the title. Since then, he has performed numerous other title deeds, read early drafts of chapters, and offered countless ideas and editorial judgments. He has tolerated the demands of this book and much other work, shared my concerns and humored my obsessions about our own household wastes, made me smile pretty much every day—and, reader, he married me.

I only wish he didn't have to share the dedication. For nearly two decades, Susie Huston and I talked and laughed and worried about the underlying issues of this book and much else. I will always miss her.

Takoma Park, Maryland
February 1999

Index

Page numbers in italics refer to photographs.